GREEN CARD SOLDIER

Labor and Technology

Winifred Poster, series editor

Madison Van Oort, *Worn Out: How Retailers Surveil and Exploit Workers in the Digital Age and How Workers Are Fighting Back*

Sofya Aptekar, *Green Card Soldier: Between Model Immigrant and Security Threat*

GREEN CARD SOLDIER

BETWEEN MODEL IMMIGRANT AND
SECURITY THREAT

SOFYA APTEKAR

THE MIT PRESS
CAMBRIDGE, MASSACHUSETTS
LONDON, ENGLAND

The MIT Press would like to thank the anonymous peer reviewers who provided comments on drafts of this book. The generous work of academic experts is essential for establishing the authority and quality of our publications. We acknowledge with gratitude the contributions of these otherwise uncredited readers.

This book was set in Arnhem Pro and Frank New by New Best-set Typesetters Ltd. Printed and bound in the United States of America.

Library of Congress Cataloging-in-Publication Data

Names: Aptekar, Sofya, 1979- author.
Title: Green card soldier : between model immigrant and security threat / Sofya Aptekar.
Description: Cambridge, Massachusetts : The MIT Press, [2023] | Series: Labor and technology | Includes bibliographical references and index.
Identifiers: LCCN 2022022395 (print) | LCCN 2022022396 (ebook) | ISBN 9780262047890 (paperback) | ISBN 9780262373654 (epub) | ISBN 9780262373661 (pdf)
Subjects: LCSH: United States—Armed Forces—Noncitizens—Case studies. | Noncitizen soldiers—United States—Case studies. | Immigrant veterans—United States—Case studies. | Immigrants—United States—History—21st century.
Classification: LCC UB418.N66 A68 2023 (print) | LCC UB418.N66 (ebook) | DDC 355.2/2362—dc23/eng/20221028
LC record available at https://lccn.loc.gov/2022022395
LC ebook record available at https://lccn.loc.gov/2022022396

10 9 8 7 6 5 4 3 2 1

Dedicated to all who fight the empire

CONTENTS

1

INTRODUCTION

In the 2020s, the US government waged a war on migrants that had been ramping up across presidential administrations since the 1990s. The US border with Mexico was a site of inhuman disregard for life, occupied by the US Border Patrol and multiple militarized law enforcement agencies and their arsenals of military technology. Amid the suffering and death of migrants, politicians and pundits continued to claim that the borders were dangerously open. Not for the first time in US history, the US military patrolled the United States–Mexico border, even as its Coast Guard branch interdicted thousands of migrants at sea. In imagining US military facing off waves of purportedly dangerous migrants, it is unlikely that one would conjure immigrants on both sides. And yet, there are tens of thousands of immigrants working in every branch of the US military—deployed to the border, spread out across the hundreds of overseas military bases, and helping repress popular uprisings within the United States itself. There are hundreds of thousands of immigrant veterans. What do we make of the work of these so-called green card soldiers in the US military?

Many liberals argue that immigrants who work in the military are model immigrants who prove that immigrants are loyal to the United States and deserve full membership in society. In fact, immigrant rights advocates have demanded that undocumented youth be allowed to enlist in the military as a path to citizenship. Although supported by the US

Department of Defense (DOD), decades of advocacy have failed to create inroads for undocumented youth into the military. Not even arguments about being innocent children brought to the United States by parents can overcome the pervasive criminality attached to undocumented immigrants. The suspicion of immigrants is baked into the US culture. For hundreds of years, immigrants have been military workers,[1] voluntarily and against their will, and for hundreds of years, foreign-born soldiers have been suspected as a security threat. In addition, because the US government has long tied naturalization to military labor, immigrants face suspicion that they enlist only to get US citizenship.

The reality of the immigrant experience in the US military complicates the moral calculus of conservative and liberal tropes. There are multiple green card soldier stories, not least because immigrants without "green cards"—lawful permanent residency—also work in the US military. But even a single story can repudiate the myths and assumptions about immigrants in the military made across the political spectrum. Take Miguel, a Marine whose reasons for enlisting, lack of interest in US citizenship, and indigenous identity set up the complexities at the intersection of model immigrant and security threat that I analyze in this book.

In my interview with Miguel, he told me he was born in Peru and grew up in New York City. His family went through a spell of illegality, but they were able to secure lawful permanent residency, or "green cards," by the time he finished high school. A history of illegality is not unusual among immigrants who have lawful permanent residency or even US citizenship, contradicting facile dichotomies between documented and undocumented immigrants.[2] After a couple of lackluster years at a public college, Miguel left school to join the US Marine Corps. He connected his enlistment to the awe he felt toward one of his college classmates, a military veteran who appeared to have lived an exciting and glamorous life.

Feeling aimless, Miguel was drawn to the military for its promise of adventure and meaningful experience. Without access to resources or connections to wealthier social circles, alternative sources of adventure and meaning are often not obvious or available to youth like Miguel. He told me that he did not enlist to get US citizenship or solely for the steady pay and benefits, but neither was he driven by patriotism or desire to prove his loyalty to the United States. Miguel thought joining the Marine

Corps would help him toughen up into a real man, like his grandfather, who had been in the Peruvian military. Family legacies of military labor and masculinity play a compelling role in military enlistment, but Miguel's quest for unimpeachable masculinity traversed national borders. This small example of transnational militarist identity disrupts national categorizations even as the US military enforces imperial systems of extraction predicated on national borders.

Miguel had lawful permanent residency, not US citizenship. That meant that he was eligible to enlist and could have taken advantage of an expedited route to naturalization available to immigrants in the US military. Yet getting US citizenship was not a priority for Miguel, even as he worked in the US military. In fact, he said he was not always sure he wanted to become a US citizen. Immigrants are suspected of enlisting just to get citizenship, and they are suspect for not naturalizing. Was Miguel, a low-ranked "grunt," an agent of a foreign government infiltrating the Marine Corps? Hardly. But he failed to embody either a model immigrant or a security threat. His ambivalence about the meaning of US citizenship was layered onto significant obstacles to the supposedly expedited military naturalization process.

Miguel's time as a military worker predated the massive deployments to Iraq and Afghanistan that began in 2003. Instead, he was deployed to the US-Mexico border to assist Border Patrol agents and the local sheriff. Even before the buildup that followed 9/11, the southern border was already militarized through technology and deployment of US military. Immigrants have labored in the US military from its beginning, participating in the warfare against indigenous nations and the suppression of slave insurrections that marked the early history of US armed forces.[3] The massing of technologies of death at the border are continuous with the long span of US military history. Faced with his role on the border, Miguel recalled thinking, "How am I going to go do border patrol when I am an immigrant?" He remembered worrying that he would be unable to shoot at fellow immigrants attempting to cross the border. Although he was ultimately not faced with having to shoot directly at an immigrant, Miguel did his border work so well that he got an award. Miguel was an exemplary military worker, which many advocates would take as proof that immigrants deserve to be included and belong. Miguel remembered working alongside many other immigrants, mostly other Latinxs, doing the same work of patrolling the border. After his deployment had ended, another young Latinx Marine shot and killed Ezequiel Hernandez, a teenager herding goats on the Mexican side of the border.[4]

Exacerbating his internal conflict over the border work was Miguel's identification with Native Americans whose lands straddle the US-Mexico border—a border drawn across nations predating the US settler colonial state. Miguel felt kinship with fellow indigenous people of the continent. He grew close to the citizens of the tribal nation occupied by the Border Patrol. He said that they looked like his dad, and they looked like him. He found that he had more in common with them than what he called the average American. By "average American," Miguel likely meant white Americans, reflecting the white supremacy that shapes US nationalism and equates national membership with whiteness, leaving people of color to prove their belonging.

When we spoke, Miguel had been out of the military for over a decade. He completed a college degree and found a rewarding line of work. By all accounts, he was an immigrant success story, and military benefits helped pay for his college education. After some time, Miguel did end up becoming a US citizen as a civilian, alongside his parents, never having taken advantage of the expedited military naturalization provisions. Even as he kept up his critique of US imperialism, he said he felt happy to be an American. Miguel's account made it clear that it was not work in the military that made him feel happy to be an American. Rather, it happened years later, as he examined his life options, and worked on building a narrative that embraced the twists and turns of his transnational life. A story like Miguel's explodes many myths and assumptions. His claims of belonging seem rooted more in indigeneity and critique of settler colonialism than they are in his military labor. He did not enlist for citizenship, nor was in a rush to acquire it, yet judging from his awards, he was an exemplary Marine.

Looking back at his stint in the military, Miguel reflected on the racial hierarchies of the military that oppressed Latinx military workers and the psychological scars he sustained from the pervasive and normalized violence of military work. When advocates push for full inclusion of immigrants or women or LGBTQ people in institutions like the military, they fight for the Miguels of the world to assimilate to their position in the hierarchy, bearing the injuries inherent to being a racialized military worker. They fight for the chance for an immigrant to prove their worth by pointing a gun at another immigrant—or just another human being. Legitimating the US military with a veneer of diversity, they help whitewash the work that the US military does. That work is not integrating immigrants into the US society or providing opportunities for disadvantaged youth. It is the continual maintenance and expansion of empire.

This book focuses on the experience of immigrants, heeding critical ethnic scholar Eve Tuck's call for desire-centered research "concerned with understanding complexity, contradiction, and the self-determination of lived lives."[5] The complexity of these immigrant stories shows how the tensions between deservingness and suspicion shape their enlistment, military work, and identities, threaded through with colonial legacies, white supremacy, exploitation, and patriarchy. Their stories reveal the complex workings of the US empire, globalized militarism, and citizenship. They show the constant pull-and-tug experience of green card soldiers being held up as model immigrants while having their loyalty to the United States questioned. Even as we witness the damage they sustain, we see individual and collective strategies of making sense of, surviving, and resisting systems of oppression.

IMMIGRANTS IN THE US MILITARY

There is a long history of immigrants as military labor in the United States, from its founding through the ongoing Global War on Terror. Immigrants have participated in all US wars and campaigns against people within and beyond US national and colonial borders. Immigrants have been drafted into the US military, and they have voluntarily enlisted. Immigrants have resisted the draft, and they have organized against US militarism. Throughout US history, immigrants worked in the military without having US citizenship.[6] Citizenship, however, has been used a technology to manage the military labor force, all the way to the early twenty-first century when anti-immigrant policies combined with impoverishment to shape immigrant enlistment in the US military.

Early European immigrants to the United States—primarily German and Irish—played a key role in wars against indigenous people and the suppression of slave insurrections, with half of all military recruits by the 1840s born outside the United States. The US military recruited and employed noncitizens during the War of 1812, with its many battles on the western and northern frontiers against Native American nations. Immigrants also fought in the Mexican-American War (1846–1848), which occasioned the rise of manifest destiny as a US ideology and resulted in the US annexing a massive territory from Mexico.[7] In many of these wars, the United States was able to avoid a draft by attracting noncitizens and other impoverished and marginalized groups through cash bounties.[8]

Noncitizen immigrants were drafted and fought on both sides of the Civil War. It was after that war that the US government first reduced the requirements for naturalization for honorably discharged soldiers, creating a military path to citizenship.[9] This launched the era of using citizenship to recruit and manage the US military labor force. Considering citizenship as a tool of the military helps us see citizenship more generally as a tool of governance intended to maintain global inequities in access to rights and resources.[10] Hundreds of thousands of immigrants, primarily from Southern and Eastern Europe, gained citizenship as the result of their military labor in World War I and World War II. These mass naturalizations helped the US reinforce its military and ideological power globally and tamp down on dissent domestically. When the naturalized immigrants did not become compliant and complacent national subjects, they were denaturalized.[11] At the same time as European immigrants were made into US citizens, racist anti-Asian citizenship laws excluded most Asian immigrants from naturalization, regardless of their labor for the US military.[12] After World War II, white immigrants were able to use their veteran status to avail themselves of federal housing subsidies, gaining middle-class status even as these policies entrenched a system of racial segregation across the United States, and Black veterans were denied the benefits of the GI Bill.[13]

The United States employs immigrants as military labor throughout its global reach, often utilizing as troops the very same colonial populations it displaces.[14] One such case involved hundreds of thousands of Filipinos employed during World War II. Although President Roosevelt promised US citizenship and veteran benefits to Filipino soldiers, the promise was rescinded in 1946, and these veterans did not get citizenship until 1990. The survivors continue to fight for access to full veteran benefits.[15] The brutal colonial occupation of the Philippines by the United States explicitly drew on genocidal strategies developed in wars against Native American nations, as was later also the case for US war on Vietnam.[16] The continued US military presence in the Philippines for many decades after the 1946 independence and active recruitment of labor contributed to a flow of Filipino migrants to the United States. Between 1953 and 1992, the US Navy and US Coast Guard directly recruited 45,000 Filipinos, primarily into the lowest ranks.[17] Filipino immigrants, their children, and their grandchildren continue to work in the US military, disproportionately in the navy.[18] Filipinos are one example of how the US empire ravages and displaces communities, only to incorporate the displaced populations into its military workforce to further entrench globalized militarism. Even if we look only at current formal colonies of the United States, dozens of colonial soldiers hailing from Puerto Rico, the US Virgin Islands, Guam, the Northern Marianas, and American Samoa have been killed in the War on Terror.[19] Native Americans have the highest rates of any racial group of enlisting in the US military, which economist and activist Winona LaDuke attributes to "economic deprivation, domination and racism," and that historian Nick Estes traces to forced imprisonment of generations of Native children in militarized boarding schools that funneled these children into the US military.[20]

Beyond formal US colonies, there is the vast system of informal empire, with policies that include economic aid with strings attached, covert and overt manipulation of elections, and military training. These informal imperial policies fall short of direct political control of a colony, but are nevertheless implicated in disruption and displacement of communities around the world.[21] Thus, the United States provided military training to reactionary forces in order to violently suppress popular socialist movements in Central America, contributing to mass migrations of people who then became targets for recruitment by the US military.[22] Race and gender are central elements in understanding how US imperialism works. For instance, key actors in the US power structure portray Central American migrant men as violent gang members. Yet their characterization as hyper-masculine and violent also makes them well suited to work for the military, as can be seen in army advertising campaigns aimed at the Latinx communities.[23] Not only does the military draw on masculine stereotypes of Latinx migrants for the purposes of recruitment, but it also uses them to manage and control immigrant workers once they are enlisted, such as by channeling them to dangerous occupations.[24]

Today, noncitizens enlist in what since 1973 has been an all-volunteer force rather than being drafted. At the beginning of the third decade of the twenty-first century, the United States continues to fight what the US government refers to as the Global War on Terror, which began after the 9/11 attacks by al Qaeda. Al Qaeda, a fundamentalist Islamic organization based in Pakistan and Afghanistan, was headed by Osama bin Laden; its members were trained by the CIA in the Cold War conflict against the Soviet Union in the 1980s. Rather than engage in an international police investigation and action, the US government used 9/11 to justify an invasion of Afghanistan. In 2002, President Bush retroactively designated the period beginning September 11, 2001, as a period of official hostilities.[25] While the United States has been officially fighting the War on Terror since 2002, historian Roxanne Dunbar-Ortiz points out that the entire history of the United States has been a history of warfare against populations framed and dehumanized as terrorists, in North America and beyond.[26] As the *Afghanistan Papers* released in late 2019 indicate, the US military spent eighteen years in Afghanistan without clear strategies or goals, operating on racist assumptions about local society, all while the US government systematically and intentionally misled the public.[27]

Under the false pretext that the Iraqi government was hiding weapons of mass destruction, the United States invaded Iraq in 2003, peaking at 150,000 US troops.[28] Close to 7,000 US active duty military personnel have been killed in combat in Iraq and Afghanistan since 2001.[29] Some of the earliest US casualties were immigrant soldiers.[30] The toll of US invasion on the people of Afghanistan, Iraq, Pakistan, Syria, and other countries in the region has been devastating. Estimates of civilian casualties are uncertain, with conservative numbers around half a million in Iraq, Afghanistan, and Pakistan. The wars have produced millions of refugees and have wreaked profound destruction of physical and social infrastructures.[31] Today, there are US military bases in Iraq built to provide enduring US control of the mineral- and energy-rich region strategically located between Russia and China. Despite the official end of Operation Iraqi Freedom in 2011 and end of combat missions in 2021, 2,500 US troops remained in Iraq in 2022.[32] The withdrawal of US troops from Afghanistan in 2021 spelled not the end of US imperialism, but rather a shift of strategy toward an even heavier reliance on precision strikes, drone warfare, and private security contractors. The federal government expenditures on the wars in Afghanistan, Pakistan, and Iraq are estimated to be $6.4 trillion.[33] A war that has been so expensive to the US taxpayer has brought hundreds of percent returns in stocks to military contractors like Raytheon, with close ties to US political elites.[34]

The War on Terror continues within and across US borders, as surveillance technologies honed overseas are brought to bear on Black Lives Matter protests, pipeline occupations, and the US-Mexico borderlands.[35] The post-9/11 era is characterized by an intensification of militarism in all aspects of life, increased veneration of the military and veterans, bipartisan normalization of endless wars, and lack of a concerted antiwar movement.[36] With the troop drawdowns in Afghanistan and Iraq, the US military maintains its regional and global presence. In 2019, there were between 45,000 and 65,000 US troops in the Persian Gulf. Even more troops—almost 80,000—were deployed in South Korea and Japan, where the United States has had an extensive military presence since World War II. Roughly 30,000 US troops were in Europe. Overall, there were 1.4 million active-duty armed forces personnel with 200,000 troops overseas in 2019 and 800 overseas military bases in over seventy countries and territories.[37] At a time of peak economic inequality and difficulties faced by young adults in finding stable employment, enlistment in the military is a taken-for-granted alternative, buttressed by nationalist and militarist narratives. A multi-billion-dollar military marketing apparatus helps promote military labor, including campaigns targeting immigrants. After all, endless wars need a consistent supply of military workers.[38]

Immigrants join the military for all the same reasons as those born in the United States: lack of job and educational opportunities, patriotism, a sense of adventure, an image of powerful masculinity, and more. Some also join to get on an expedited path to citizenship at a time when the rights and security of immigrants are under attack. Although there is no formal draft, the United States essentially has a poverty draft, a term coined in the 1980s to problematize the purportedly voluntary nature of enlistment driven by lack of pathways to steady employment and benefits outside the military.[39] With student debt skyrocketing, many enlist to gain access to military educational benefits and pay for college.[40] As systems of education, health care, housing, and welfare are eviscerated, state resources have shifted to prisons, military, and the security apparatus. With steady pay, health and tuition benefits, and housing subsidies, the military is a system of welfare in a context where general social welfare is gutted and using public benefits is stigmatized.[41] The stark economic calculus that funnels youth into the military is elided by the powerful currents of nationalism and the celebration of the figure of the soldier-citizen. Immigrant youth are especially vulnerable to the poverty draft given their precarious claims to full rights. Immigrant children are more likely than US-born children to grow up below the poverty line.[42]

The Global War on Terror had a domestic component, changing the lives of immigrants in the United States for the worse. The punitive immigration laws passed in the mid-1990s set the stage for a further criminalization of immigrants—particularly young Black and Latino men.[43] The US government established registries of Muslim immigrants, with disappearances and deportations terrorizing entire communities.[44] International students faced new layers of visa restrictions and surveillance.[45] The acquisition of citizenship became an opportunity for immigration agents to identify immigrants they could strip of status entirely.[46] Others were pressured to become informants as they moved through the immigration system.[47] Even after getting citizenship, immigrants could not necessarily breathe a sigh of relief, as the US Department of Justice created a new office dedicated to denaturalization, echoing mass denaturalization of political dissidents in the early twentieth century.[48]

Mushrooming military budgets included funding of the US Department of Homeland Security (DHS), a new agency responsible for enforcing immigration law.[49] Homeland Security, and its agencies US Immigration and Customs Enforcement (ICE) and US Customs and Border Protection (CBP) administer a punitive and ruthless immigration regime of mass detention and deportation. The United States uses military-grade technology, including that previously used in Afghanistan and Iraq, combined with multiple local, state, and federal law enforcement agencies and the deployment of the military itself to profoundly militarize the US-Mexico border.[50] Increasingly, the equipment flows further south to militarize the border between Mexico and Guatemala.[51] These technologies are also directed to internal enforcement, with federal, state, and local agencies deploying armed vehicles, chemical weapons, and electronic surveillance on city streets and sites of indigenous resistance.[52] The connections and continuity between US military, internal policing, and immigration enforcement are endemic rather than new: similar flows of equipment and surveillance strategies took place after Vietnam War.[53]

The systematic attacks on immigrants' sense of security and livelihoods and the narrowing of pathways to citizenship help put an immigrant twist on the poverty draft. As I describe in chapter 2, the military uses the promise of citizenship in recruitment of immigrants, helping meet its labor force needs. The militarization of the border is thus accompanied by the militarization of naturalization and the immigration system itself. Citizenship is a technology used by the state to exploit immigrant labor, not just at the point of recruitment, but by disciplining workers through fear of violating conditions for naturalization, such as getting a dishonorable discharge. More broadly, citizenship in the sense of national belonging premises integration, social inclusion, and economic stability on condoning of the US empire. Many immigrant recruits come from communities around the world that have been violently disrupted by the US military. After being displaced by the US empire, they are recruited as foot soldiers of US armed forces. This labor force of immigrant soldiers is then used to further the global imperial project, sometimes directly in the communities from which they originated—after all, those are the places where their cultural and linguistic skills are most needed by the US military. Green card soldiers are positioned at a unique point of contact between the military and immigration systems, as labor force and objects of control of the US empire.

Some 80,000 noncitizens enlisted in the US Army, Navy, Marines, and Air Force between 1999 and 2010, at about 4 percent of all first-term military recruits. The army is the largest branch and has the highest number of enlisted noncitizens, while the navy has the highest share. Immigrants who enlist without US citizenship are more likely to be women, people of color, older, or to have dependents than enlisted citizens.[54] When we look at veterans, and not just those who are currently working in the military, we see even more immigrants. In 2018, there were 1.3 million people on active duty and over 18 million veterans. Around 3 percent of the veterans, or 530,000, are immigrants, with Mexican and Filipino immigrants together comprising roughly a third of this group. Almost 20 percent of immigrant veterans do not have US citizenship.[55] This matters because without citizenship, these veterans are vulnerable to deportation. In fact, it is estimated that thousands of veterans have been deported since legislative changes in 1996 criminalized immigrants and set the legal stage for mass deportations.[56]

All the branches of the military have rules requiring lawful permanent residency to enlist, but there is no federal law that stipulates an immigration status for enlistment. Between 2009 and 2017, the Department of Defense took advantage of this to institute a program for immigrants on temporary visas. Military Accessions Vital to the National Interest (MAVNI) targeted international students and other temporary migrants whose language and cultural skills were deemed vitally important to the military mission.[57] Over 10,000 immigrants enlisted through the MAVNI program, primarily in the army.[58] The precarious visa status of MAVNI recruits created additional incentives for enlistment of international students and some temporary workers who otherwise face a long and uncertain path to citizenship.[59] MAVNIs, as they came to be known, experienced a heightened version of the tension between model immigrants and security threat. Recruited explicitly for their skills and with much more formal education than the average enlistee, MAVNIs faced suspicion and thousands were trapped in a legal limbo when anxieties about their loyalty led to the suspension of the program. Having signed military contracts, they were waiting for months—and then years—to be shipped to basic training. During these extended waits, which were much longer than is normal for new recruits, some lost their immigration status. Others were ultimately discharged from the military and, with expired student and work visas, faced deportation to countries like Pakistan, where their connections to the US military placed them at risk.[60]

Since the Civil War, there has been an expedited track to citizenship available through labor in the military, which has historically meant a reduced residency requirement to be eligible for naturalization. There is also posthumous naturalization for those killed in line of duty, which most recently extends some immigration benefits to the family of the deceased.[61] Whereas civilian applicants must wait five years as lawful permanent residents to apply for citizenship—or three if they are married to a US citizen—immigrants have been eligible to apply after a day to a year after enlistment. Other components of the military fast track to citizenship have included the waiving of hefty application fees, facilitation of the process by the military, and access to naturalization overseas.[62] The acquisition of citizenship through the process of naturalization provides security from deportation, opens opportunities to sponsor the migration of family members, increases job options, facilitates international travel, and gives immigrants the right to vote. Citizenship protects immigrants from immigration detention and deportation.[63] Those who have not naturalized are vulnerable to deportation if they are charged with a broad category of offenses classified as aggravated felonies. Access to rights and protections that US citizenship provides is a feature of the global citizenship apartheid, where powerful states like the US police access to work, settlement, and opportunity, while positioning immigrants as supplicants having to prove their worth, humanity, and deservingness.[64]

From 2001 to 2017, almost 100,000 enlisted military workers became US citizens through the military naturalization pathway.[65] Over 80 percent of immigrants in the US military have citizenship, with some obtaining it prior to enlistment, some during, and some after.[66] In the past, the United States practiced blanket mass naturalization of immigrant military workers, but in the early twenty-first century, naturalization for enlisted military workers is not automatic.[67] Nor is naturalization always easily achievable for these immigrant workers. Immigrant enlistees and veterans have to go through the same process as civilian applicants, including passing the naturalization interview and submitting forms and biometrics. The fit between the military and immigration systems is poor. For active-duty military workers, especially, it is difficult to go through the naturalization process while working long hours, moving often, and being limited in the ability to leave the military base. In 2019, the US government rejected military naturalization applications at higher rates than it did for civilians, finding fault on the grounds of good moral character, fraud, and other failures to fulfill citizenship eligibility requirements.[68] While some call for more of an automatic naturalization process for the military, this would undermine the agency of immigrants like Miguel, who might not necessarily want to become citizens.[69]

The militarization of the US immigration system frames the experiences of immigrants with enlistment, naturalization, and military labor that I present in this book. The plight of immigrants in the US military is part of the larger struggle for immigrant rights. However, the questions around belonging and citizenship highlighted by the figure of the immigrant working in the US military extend beyond immigrants themselves. The military and the immigration system are key US institutions, and both do the work of defining the nation and its boundaries. Whose lives and property are to be defended? Who is the enemy and who the citizen? Who deserves to be included into the nation and who remains perpetually out of reach of belonging? The overlap between the military and the immigration system is a unique opportunity to understand the militarization of US citizenship and the reach of the US empire within and beyond national borders.

BETWEEN MODEL IMMIGRANT AND SECURITY THREAT

A cluster of popular ideas surrounds the figure of the immigrant soldier. These ideas shape institutions, communities, and individuals. Immigrants are said to be diverse, skilled workers whom the military needs. Their service and sacrifice prove immigrants' worth and exceptionality. American exceptionalism and foreign policy are reinforced through the spectacle of foreigners choosing to risk their lives for their adopted nation. On the other hand, immigrant workers in the military are suspected of holding multiple allegiances and spying, a suspicion that periodically erupts in policies that securitize and surveil them.

In the early 2020s, as the War on Terror continued apace, normalized and backgrounded in the US public sphere, the military, its workers, and veterans occupied a special place in the national imagination. In the post-9/11 context of what American studies scholar Irene Garza terms "mandated nationalism," the figure of the soldier embodies claims of citizenship and belonging. Members of groups that are treated as threats to the nation face the pressure to compensate for being cast as suspect through heightened performances of patriotism.[70] Military labor is a way for immigrants to demonstrate their willingness to assimilate and their deservingness of inclusion. Ethnic studies scholar Lisa Marie Cacho argues that the War on Terror provided an opportunity for Latinxs (who may or may not be immigrants) to integrate through joining the military as the focus of xenophobia temporary shifted away from Latinxs to racializing Muslims as terrorists.[71]

Across political divisions, Americans see enlistment in the military as a way for individual immigrants to integrate, to prove their fitness for citizenship, and to demonstrate loyalty. Some immigrant advocates use the figure of the immigrant soldier—extra poignant if injured or killed in combat—to argue for the deservingness of immigrants on a collective level. In other words, the immigrant soldier has become the new model minority.[72] To paraphrase sociologist Victor Ray, who questions "why blacks must buy this inclusion by bargaining with their lives,"[73] it is ironic that when immigrants buy their inclusion by bargaining with their lives, they are actually entering an institution where many of their rights as US persons are suspended. Active-duty military workers, as well as reservists, do not have full rights to free speech or assembly, or freedom from search or seizure, and are governed by a separate legal system, the Uniform Code of Military Justice.[74]

The fact that immigrants enlist in the US military is used to prove the deservingness of immigrants as a category, of some groups of immigrants over others, and of individual immigrants. For instance, immigrant rights advocates use military labor as evidence that immigrants deserve a less punitive and criminalizing immigration system. As Brett Hunt of Veterans for Immigration Reform put it: "Immigrants have always played a critical role in defending our nation, from our earliest days on Lexington Green to the mountains of Afghanistan. Immigrants make our military stronger, they make our country stronger. . . . Our immigrant soldiers and veterans deserve better than our broken immigration system."[75] The gesture of upholding the immigrant soldier as a model minority reveals the connection between military labor and citizenship. In other words, military labor is used to "up the ante" of deservingness beyond acculturation, civil engagement, heteronormativity, and tolerance for poor working conditions already required of immigrants to be considered worthy of citizenship and belonging.[76] In addition to all these, the apex of belonging is reserved for immigrants who are willing to risk life and health by signing a military contract. At the same time, the focus on immigrants in the US military, their deservingness and their contributions, helps us forget the reach of the US empire, its role in devastating communities and pushing people to migrate, and its use of immigrants as a labor force. It helps us gloss over the baseless assertion that immigrants were somehow defending the United States "in the mountains of Afghanistan."

When immigrants in the US military are held up as especially deserving of citizenship, they are differentiated from native-born Americans who do not enlist—particularly when advocates invoke the high quality of immigrant military workers compared to low physical fitness and criminal records of native-born recruits.[77] But this veneration also implies differentiation among immigrants, with military workers more deserving than other immigrants. As political scientist Cara Wong points out, immigrant soldiers "are admirable foils for the 'free-riding' immigrants, who are here only to take advantage of the economic opportunities, are not assimilating, and will not be patriotic Americans."[78] This hierarchy of deservingness is not particular to the immigrant rights movement, but is embedded in US culture, which positions oppressed communities as supplicants needing to prove their worth before accessing rights and opportunities. Successful assimilation into white supremacy means assuming one's place at the expense of others. Almost 200,000 immigrants were naturalized through their work for the US military in World War I, yet their contributions to the war effort did not necessarily result in an embrace of immigrants in US society. In fact, what followed World War I was heightened xenophobia, a spate of deportations, and a repressive new immigration policy that essentially closed off immigration from the very places where immigrant soldiers came.[79]

The promise of inclusion and citizenship through military labor is not unique to immigrants. African Americans have historically used their contributions to the US military to fight for full citizenship rights in the civilian world. However, integration gains by African Americans in the military too often have been followed by violent repression by whites, once these African American soldiers returned to their home communities.[80] After both World War I and World War II, African American veterans were a group most at risk of lynching.[81] The US elites and structures of white supremacy ensured that their claims to citizenship were violently rejected and suppressed, and excluded them from accessing veteran benefits such as housing and educational subsidies. Meanwhile, the US military took credit for reducing racial discrimination while helping maintain the larger stratification system. Today, in the era of an all-volunteer force, when African Americans are overrepresented among enlisted military workers, the military is held up as a paragon of integration.[82] But, as Victor Ray writes, "the illusion of Black progress . . . [is] hidden in the broader context of Black exploitation."[83] The overrepresentation of people of color in the military is driven by the discrimination they face in the labor market, but the valorization of the military works to suppress the claims of discrimination among civilians. W. E. B. Du Bois and Martin Luther King Jr. pointed out that another way to see the labor of African Americans in the US military is as foot soldiers in the global racial project built by the United States.[84] Rather than being a remedy to white supremacy, the military has been instrumental in constructing and maintaining the racial hierarchy within and beyond the United States.

Many in the United States across the political spectrum continue to uphold the military as an institution that can instill dominant cultural values in populations deemed to deviate from the mainstream and to be in need of assimilating, particularly when the military faces personnel shortages. The primary target tends to be racialized urban youth and their purportedly deviant social values and lack of discipline. The citizen soldier is a model for the deserving poor.[85] It has also been true for immigrants. In fact, the Junior Reserve Officers' Training Corps (JROTC), a high school program, began specifically to inspire a sense of duty and loyalty in new immigrants in the early twentieth century, whom US political and military leaders saw as untrustworthy and deviant in their masculinities. Today, JROTC is disproportionately found in schools serving poor students and students of color.[86]

The promise of military labor to overcome marginalization for immigrants has not lost its currency. Like employers more generally, the military is framed as a job creator, and enlistment in the military as an opportunity, not exploitative labor. The military is supposedly providing an opportunity for immigrants not only to integrate into the US society and experience social mobility but to repay the United States. In this common framing, immigrants are forever indebted for being allowed within the US borders.[87] US representative Ruben Gallego articulated it when advocating for a 2015 defense bill amendment that would have allowed undocumented youth to enlist: "they should have the opportunity to serve and repay their country."[88] Radical critics point out that the liberal quest for inclusion in institutions like the military—whether for people of color, women, LGBTQ people, or immigrants—does little to root out the structures of oppression. Instead, it legitimates the US military with a veneer of diversity. The exchange of military labor for citizenship and welfare reproduces militarism and militarizes the immigration system.[89]

Like other similar measures, the amendment to allow undocumented youth to enlist failed amid concerns about the threat to national security that these youth ostensibly posed and desire to protect military jobs for the native-born. Yet the Department of Defense has been a supporter of the DREAM Act, seeking to expand the pool of potential recruits by tying a path to citizenship for childhood arrivals to college or military.[90] Undocumented childhood arrivals are especially attractive as military workers, their status putting them into a more vulnerable and exploitable position than green card holders. Margaret Stock, an army lieutenant colonel and a longtime advocate for inclusion of immigrants into the military, referred to them as "recruiter's dream candidates for enlistment."[91] The idea is that the so-called Dreamers would get a chance at legalization in exchange for enlistment, and thus they would be more motivated to enlist than immigrants who already have lawful permanent residency—which, of course, means that it is their legal vulnerability as undocumented people that makes them better recruits and military workers. Stock pronounced the DREAM Act a "win-win" for the DOD and the United States.[92]

In reflecting on who serves in the military, we must also think of whom the military serves. This moves the focus from the assimilationist lens of how the military helps immigrants integrate into the US society to who benefits from immigrant labor in the military.[93] The military considers immigrant youth to be "higher quality" recruits: less likely to have criminal records or to drop out before the end of their contracts.

Immigrants often have language and cultural skills the US military needs in its many projects across the globe.[94] Racialized minority populations and their cultural and linguistic skills are valuable to the US military as it carries out its military objectives against people who look and speak like them.[95] It is not so different from the recruitment of native intermediaries by colonizing forces in India or South Africa, or the use of Native American scouts in the United States. Military leadership considers diversity to be a "combat multiplier."[96] The immigrant soldier is too often a product of US interventions abroad, only to contribute to the US empire's reproduction as its foot soldier.

The US military actively supports federal policies that would channel more immigrant workers into its ranks. It also consistently advocates for affirmative action policies, such as when top military leaders submitted an influential amicus brief in the 2016 *Fisher v. University of Texas at Austin* case in support of affirmative action in higher education.[97] As with the DREAM Act, the argument was based on the need of the military for workers whose cultural and linguistic skills—and their embodied existence as people of color in the military—enhance national security and military readiness. Colleges are training grounds for future military officers, and ensuring the diversity of the college student body diversifies the officer pipeline.[98]

Aside from the material labor performed by the immigrant soldier, immigrant workers in the military function as a tool of legitimation for the American nation and its foreign policies. While they may comprise a relatively small portion of the military labor force, what is characterized as their choice to enlist makes US military operations seem approved and justified even by those not born in the United States—to the extent that they are willing to put their lives on the line to participate in the work of the military. This is a crucial political tool at a time when polls show that a rising number of people in the world see US power and influence as a major threat, and most Americans say that the wars in Iraq and Afghanistan were not worth fighting. What's more, US veterans, whether or not they participated in these wars, say that the costs outweighed the benefits.[99] In this context, US political leaders can point to immigrant soldiers to try to legitimate themselves, the endless wars, and the military itself. We can see this in the following excerpt from congressional testimony given by Senator Harry Reid in 2003 to argue for expedited naturalization for immigrants:

In Iraq, the brave men and women of our Armed Forces and the coalition forces fought against those who hate our Nation's values. They hate us because we believe that all men are created equal regardless of their nation of birth, regardless of their religious faith. They hate us because we believe in the God-given rights to life, liberty, and the pursuit of happiness, rights that extend to all mankind. They hate us because we still say: Give me your tired, your poor, your huddled masses yearning to breathe free. These brave immigrant soldiers are taking on the uniform of our Nation, serving under the flag of our Nation, and fighting the enemies of our Nation and our values.[100]

The immigrant soldier helps the United States portray itself as an inclusive democracy and to justify its wars and occupations of other lands and nations under the premise of spreading freedom and rights—as embodied in the free choice made by immigrants to fight for their adopted nation. In this way, young Japanese Americans who grew up in US concentration camps were used by the US military specifically to interrogate prisoners of war during the Korean War because their inclusion "into the national project of US warfare would serve as persuasive evidence to the 'Oriental' prisoners of war that they should embrace the benevolence of the United States."[101] The immigration system, regulating US borders and disciplining migrant populations, is an integral part of the US imperial project. The immigrant soldier is a figure that helps legitimate that system by demonstrating that with patriotism and sacrifice, deserving immigrants successfully integrate and contribute to the US society.

While immigrants in the military are held up as the exemplary immigrants, they are simultaneously treated with suspicion as potential spies or infiltrators. Their willingness to risk life and limb in the service of the US military before they become US citizens is seen as setting the ultimate example of loyalty and patriotism for other immigrants, as well as for US citizens who take their citizenship for granted. But time and again, their very foreignness leads to harsh scrutiny: Where do green card soldiers' loyalties *really* reside? The immigrant soldier may be a model minority, but just as with Asian Americans who are constructed as model minorities, the flip side of this coin is evergreen suspicion and othering. The loyalty of immigrant soldiers is forever suspect, particularly when these soldiers are excluded from citizenship as racialized others.[102]

Immigrant soldiers are still immigrants. As such, their affiliation with the military—even when exemplary—does not always outweigh the stigma of foreignness. Case in point is Lieutenant Colonel Alexander Vindman, a senior member of the National Security Council who testified in the Trump impeachment hearings in 2019. A Jewish refugee from what was then Soviet Union and is now Ukraine, Vindman grew up in New York and is a naturalized US citizen. He has had a successful career as a military officer and was awarded a Purple Heart for being wounded in Iraq. Neither his Purple Heart nor his impeccable credentials as a functionary of the US empire protected Vindman from a wave of vitriol and threats that tie his foreign birth to allegations of secretly working for Ukraine.[103] Vindman's case highlights how the figure of the immigrant soldier embodies the close relationship between military labor and citizenship: the boundaries around who can be in the military are also the boundaries around who belongs and has access to rights. A pall of suspicion hangs over Vindman's military work, identity, and his very claims to being an American.

Vindman's experience attracted media attention, but it is neither new nor exceptional. After all, the United States produced a whole movement questioning the birthplace and US citizenship of Barack Obama, a child of an immigrant. Immigrants—as well as the internally colonized and formerly enslaved groups—have to prove their loyalty in a way that most white US citizens never do. As early as the 1820s, state militias and national guards excluded immigrant soldiers from Ireland and Germany, whose Catholicism tainted their loyalties. These restrictions were dropped when the military needed soldiers to fight in the Civil War.[104] During the Red Scare of the 1950s, US government officials spoke out against having immigrants work in the military, lest they be communist infiltrators. After the 9/11 attacks, some military leaders expressed concerns about immigrants once again, suspecting them of conveying sensitive military information to enemies.[105] In the late 2010s, the anxiety about the foreign-born in the US military focused especially on the possibility of ISIS infiltration.[106] Concerns within the Department of Defense about "security, counterintelligence, and insider threat" posed by noncitizens in the US military led to an imposition of an unprecedented level of security screenings of noncitizen recruits and increased requirements for naturalization eligibility.[107]

The narratives surrounding immigrants in the US military are an uneasy and unstable balance of suspicion and glorification. When the balance tips toward suspicion, the military and immigration systems discipline the immigrant, withdrawing the promise of citizenship. But even when the undercurrent of suspicion runs lower, the glorification comes with the strictures of deservingness politics and the use of immigrant soldiers to legitimize empire.

METHODS AND ROAD MAP

Much of this book analyzes the perspectives of the immigrants who enlisted in the US military, the eponymous *green card soldiers*—although, of course, some are green card Marines, like Miguel, whose story opens the book, as well as green card sailors and green card airmen.[108] Although the card issued to lawful permanent residents is no longer green, the status continues to be commonly known as having a green card. A green card is marked by restrictions in access to public benefits, voting, and international travel, and it does not protect against deportation. However, the immigration status it represents denotes the possibility of acquiring US citizenship. And a green card opens the doors to military recruitment.

This book is based on interviews with seventy-two noncitizen immigrants from twenty-eight countries who enlisted in the US military. Participants lived all over the United States and in northern Mexico. I conducted interviews between 2015 and 2019 in person, over video conferencing, and on the phone, recruiting through veteran-serving agencies and organizations such as community college veteran offices and legal clinics, referrals through personal networks, and posts on social media. I told participants that I was a first-generation immigrant interested in immigrants in the US military, but one who was not intimately familiar with the institution. Twenty-eight participants had left the military by the time I spoke to them; thirty were still working in the military; and fourteen had enlisted and were waiting to go to basic training. Forty-four had become US citizens and the rest had not, including five interviewees who were deported. To better understand the way immigrants fit into the US military, and the friction between the US immigration and military systems, I reviewed media stories, military and immigration agency documents and reports, and research and policy documents created by military researchers and immigrant and veteran advocates. (For more details on methodology, see the appendix.)

Green Card Soldier is concerned with noncitizen immigrants who enlist in the US military and live at the intersection of the military and immigration systems. At the same time, immigrants' lives must be understood intersectionally, as they are positioned in multiple hierarchies of race and ethnicity, gender identity, social class, and other dimensions. Some of the findings here will resonate for military workers and veterans who are not immigrants.

In chapter 2, I investigate why noncitizen immigrants sign up for the US military and how the enlistment process unfolds for them. Many immigrants enlist for the same reasons as their nonimmigrant counterparts. The military seems like the best career option in marginalized and impoverished communities, especially for those growing up in the United States and targeted by recruiters in school. Like US-born enlistees, some immigrants see the military as glamorous and exciting, a way to gain status and societal recognition, or a way to show patriotism. But immigrants also have unique reasons for joining the military, such as getting citizenship quickly and pushing back against anti-immigrant prejudice. Some whose immigration status derives from marriage use enlistment to escape abusive relationships. I also show how militaristic constructions of masculinity can transcend borders. Enlistment occurs in the context of families, friends, and communities, and shapes subsequent military careers and civilian life.

Chapter 3 tackles a process unique to the green card soldier: naturalization. Expedited military naturalization policies meet reality in this chapter. I explain how military workers are supposed to get US citizenship, as well as the stakes involved—not least of which is protection from deportation. I outline the swings in policy that have occurred since 9/11. Then, I analyze how race, accent, military branch, age, age at migration, and other factors shape the naturalization process, which ranges from smooth to impossible. I also show what naturalization means for immigrants in the military, including how lack of citizenship limits career opportunities in the military and exposes immigrants to higher risk of injury on the job. Citizenship is used to recruit immigrants, and it is also a form of workforce management, or a technology of labor.

The enlistment and naturalization processes are key sites for understanding the intersection of the military and immigration systems. Military labor itself is hailed by many immigrant advocates and military leaders as instrumental in immigrant assimilation. In chapter 4, I show the injuries that immigrants sustain by assimilating to and through the US military. As a racialized institution that continues to reproduce heteropatriarchy, the military assimilates immigrants into racial and gender hierarchies. Its culture of warrior masculinity normalizes extensive physical and psychological harms, especially affecting vulnerable noncitizens. Upon leaving the military for civilian lives, immigrants experience the same troubles as do veterans more generally, but with the added threat of deportation. These troubles reveal the exploitation of military labor that belies the celebration of the military as a paragon of immigrant integration.

The vast majority of immigrants working in the US military enlisted as green card holders. This was not the case for immigrants who enlisted through the Military Accessions Vital to the National Interest (MAVNI) program. Chapter 5 investigates the unique MAVNI experience, including of those stuck in the "MAVNI limbo" between enlistment and basic training and those discharged and facing difficult immigration situations. Many MAVNIs had a very quick transition from temporary visitor to naturalized citizen bearing arms on behalf of the United States. Predominantly Asian, MAVNIs were affected by the dominant racialization of Asians in the United States as model minorities and forever foreigners, sharpening the contrast between model immigrant and security threat in their experience. The plight of MAVNI soldiers highlights the difficult fit between the mammoth immigration and military systems. Their enlistment illustrates the way both systems are grounded in the US empire and reproduce it.

Noncitizen immigrants live under threat of detention and deportation. Thousands of US military veterans have been deported after they encountered the criminal justice system without the protection of US citizenship. In chapter 6, I explain how racism and economic exploitation contribute to these deportations, and I examine survival strategies and collective coping of deported veterans. Like veterans in general, immigrant veterans face difficulties reentering civilian life, exacerbated by the physical and psychological injuries sustained in fulfilling the terms of their military contracts. When charged with crimes, they may not realize that taking a guilty plea will result in being transferred to immigration detention after their sentences. I address the struggles of veterans fighting in immigration detention and those who have been deported.

I conclude the book by considering the place of immigrants in the US military. I present a vision of border and population movements that connects the role of the US empire to migration flows and recruitment of migrants into the military. I critique the liberal push for inclusion through the military, arguing for an expansion of migrant justice work to encompass anti-imperialism and antimilitarism. By considering past, current, and future acts of resistance, I hope to share the inspiration and courage we all need to imagine a world after the empire and bring it into being.

THE IMMIGRANT TWIST ON THE POVERTY DRAFT

"I thought this is a much better opportunity than working my way through McDonald's and community college," Ranil told me in a phone interview. At the time that he enlisted, Ranil was a teenager clocking long shifts at a McDonald's in New York City. Recently arrived in the United States, he wanted to go to college but was not sure how to pay for it. Above all else, he faced financial stress: "I was actually looking for a job initially before even thinking about college . . . because my parents were unable to get any form of employment." Ranil and his brothers paid frequent visits to the local library, where they studied military recruitment flyers. Ranil figured out that as a green card holder, he could join the navy and pursue his interest in physics.

A member of the Tamil ethnic minority, Ranil grew up in a Sri Lanka embroiled in a decades-old civil war. As a child, he had an avid interest in the military, poring over the Sunday paper that serialized Sri Lankan battlefield history. Ranil could not sign up for the Sri Lankan military as a Tamil, nor did he want to, but neither was he up to joining the Tamil rebels. As his family was preparing to leave for the United States and reunite with the relatives who sponsored their green cards, Ranil read about a decorated US Marine Corps veteran in the local paper. The veteran was a Sri Lankan immigrant, and Ranil told himself that he would see about enlistment once in the United States: "when I came here, that became an option; I didn't hesitate to jump on it." The Sri Lankan paper translated the Marine Corps as the navy, helping plant a special interest in that branch in Ranil's mind.

Once in the United States, Ranil studied the US Navy website and braved an unfamiliar train system to visit a local recruitment office. He started practicing for the Armed Services Vocational Aptitude Battery (ASVAB) exam, focusing especially on improving his English. The higher he scored, the more occupations opened to him from a short list available to noncitizens. Initially interested in the reserves, Ranil was quickly persuaded by the recruiters to be active duty in order to get better benefits. He signed a six-year active duty contract and learned about educational benefits and health insurance, although he could not recall if the recruiters said anything about the expedited military route to US citizenship. As a green card holder, he knew he would be eligible to apply for citizenship eventually anyway.

Ranil's family did not understand his decision to enlist. Recounting the family conflict that ensued, he said he would hear: "If you want to die, you could have died in Sri Lanka! Why did you have to come to the United States and die in Afghanistan?" A freshly minted adult, Ranil told them that it was his decision: "if something was going to happen, it might have happened anywhere" and "if that's the choice then I would rather die in Afghanistan than in New Jersey." At the same time, Ranil understood his family's fear. In the bloody Sri Lankan conflict, being in the military meant being part of the infantry and facing high casualty rates. Although Ranil admitted that he understood little about the US military at that point, being so young and new to the country, he said he knew it would "pay me enough that I could settle down and you know, start your own business or something like that. That's the only reason I started viewing military as an opportunity, I think not a fantasy, something out of my league."

There is no typical or average experience of immigrant enlistment in the US military, yet my research uncovered a set of patterns. I find that reasons for enlistment among immigrants who grew up in the United States—referred to by immigration scholars as the 1.5 generation—is similar to those of their US-born peers. But for immigrants like Ranil, who arrive in the United States as older teenagers or young adults, there are immigrant twists on each of the four components of enlistment that I identify: poverty draft, militarism and masculinity, citizenship, and patriotism. First, both US citizens and immigrants enlist due to poverty and a lack of viable job options in the civilian sector. Immigrants like Ranil face difficult economic circumstances, in part, due to the struggles of immigrant families. Second, while plenty of US-born enlistees grew up interested in the military and glorifying war, Ranil's interest was specific to his home country, Sri Lanka. Like other first-generation immigrants I spoke to, Ranil transferred his militaristic inclinations from one country to another. Third, we might assume that as an immigrant, Ranil would be keenly aware of the fast road to citizenship military enlistment would provide, yet citizenship benefits were peripheral for him—which is not unique. Others, particularly if they grew up in the United States, are not even aware of the fast track to citizenship through the military. I also found that enlisting in the military did not mean that one necessarily wanted to become a US citizen. Finally, some immigrants view enlistment as a patriotic act reflecting their attachment to the United States. Others also understand enlistment to be strengthening their case for belonging as immigrants who may be viewed as foreigners no matter how long they live in the United States. This pattern of using military labor and identity to bolster claims of deservingness reproduces militarism.

Decisions to enlist are made within the context of families, friends, and recruiters. Here, too, I identify a pattern of differences between those who grew up in the United States and those who immigrated at older ages. The latter are more likely to have family members who live in sending countries or to have strong ties to home communities—and to grapple with competing national loyalties. Their friends, if they are fellow adult immigrants, have been less exposed to United States militarism and can be less supportive of their choice to enlist. Those who grow up in the US interact with recruiters and absorb marketing information about the military in their schools and communities. They are both advantaged in communicating with recruiters in English, yet may be less aware of citizenship benefits and immigration-related obstacles in military careers. The enlistment process is important to consider because it often shapes subsequent military career and civilian life. The information that recruiters share or withhold during enlistment affects not only the choice to enlist but expectations about citizenship acquisition, careers, benefits, and harm. The eventual repercussions range from disappointment about occupational fit all the way to deportation: some deported veterans say that the way recruiters explained—or did not explain—military naturalization to them influenced their decisions within the criminal justice system and eventually led to deportation.

In this chapter, I investigate why immigrants volunteer for the US military and the role of family, friends, and recruiters. When asking people to share reasons for enlisting in the US military, the answers are stories they decide to share with the researcher, but the shape of these stories reveals meaningful patterns and larger shared narratives, which I examine in light of immigration policies, economic and social inequality, and the organization of the US military. When resources increasingly flow to securitization, war, and surveillance, while social problems are individualized and privatized, enlistment is more than a choice of individual immigrants to join the US military. Enlistment takes place amid a lack of other opportunities to earn a living wage, impoverishment, and marginalization. In the case of immigrants, these conditions combine with the evisceration of immigrant rights and a sense of insecurity to provide workers for the US war machine.

THE POVERTY DRAFT

The United States moved from a military draft to an all-volunteer force in 1973, at a time of widespread criticism of the war in Vietnam and the US military's corruption and racialized conflict. Many in the United States considered the draft to unfairly target the most disadvantaged young men, since college students could get a deferment. Free market economists of the time successfully advocated for an all-volunteer force, which they said would harness the power of the market to fix the inequalities by having rational players acting to maximize their utility.[1] Part of the argument for eliminating the draft was that market dynamics in recruitment would lead to a superior performance by young people choosing to enlist, rather than being forced to through a draft.[2] To attract volunteers, the military began to market itself, relying on consumer research and advertising campaigns to paint a picture of individual opportunity, education and job training, exciting foreign travel, and even equal pay for women.[3] It also increased pay substantially for enlistees and relaxed grooming standards.[4] Yet, as historian Jennifer Mittelstadt shows, the military ultimately discarded the free market economics and created a massive social welfare system for military workers and their families to assure sufficient labor force absent the draft.[5] Some commentators have noted that the US military is, in many ways, the most socialist of US institutions, as it provides housing, health care, child care, and education for its workers, albeit increasingly privatized through contracts with for-profit companies.[6]

Even more so than during the draft, volunteer enlistees were more likely to be African American or have low socioeconomic status.[7] The military continued to reproduce race and class inequities endemic in US society. In fact, counter-recruitment organizers often refer to the current system of recruitment as the poverty draft, meaning that "the decision to join the military is coerced, given economic circumstances and objective life chances."[8] Empirical evidence supports a negative relationship between socioeconomic status and propensity to enlist in the military: youth from wealthier families are less likely to enlist. In a 2006 study, sociologist Meredith Kleykamp found that enlistment was associated with aspiring to attend college, lower socioeconomic status, and military presence in the area. Others have found that larger family size and lower education levels of the parents are connected to enlistment.[9] The poverty draft would be severely undermined by raising the minimum wage, and is already affecting recruitment in municipalities like Seattle that have passed local minimum wage increases.[10] The DOD's own polling indicates that in 2017, 49 percent of sixteen- to twenty-one-year-old respondents reported that paying for college would be their main reason for enlistment were they to consider joining—the top reason cited.[11] Not surprisingly, proposals to make college free are also seen as a threat to military recruitment.[12] At the same time, the most disadvantaged youth are not eligible to enlist due to requirements for a high school degree, minimal ASVAB scores, physical fitness, and limits on debt.[13]

That immigrants, too, are part of the poverty draft is not surprising given that earnings of immigrants are lower than those of the US-born on average—with immigrants from Latin America, Africa, and some Asian countries experiencing the largest gaps—particularly closer to the time of immigration.[14] Immigrant children are more likely to grow up below the poverty line.[15] Many immigrant youth, even if they have lawful permanent residency, face obstacles in finding employment that pays a living wage and struggle to pay for college. Since 80 percent of US immigrants are people of color, they confront pervasive structural obstacles in employment, housing, education, and other realms of social life faced by people of color in the United States.[16] At times, the criminalization of immigrants directly pushes youth into the military. For example, one of the veterans I interviewed enlisted in the army and chose artillery as her specialty because it came with a $10,000 bonus. Her family urgently needed the money after a legal fight to stop her brother's deportation led to their financial ruin.

Critics of US militarism "situate military recruitment in a context of structural inequalities and suggest that the issue is not one of misplaced priorities, but of a deliberate elimination of opportunities for some communities so as to ensure that the military continues to meet its manpower needs in the absence of a (*de jure*) draft."[17] After 9/11, the US military had intermittently struggled to meet recruiting targets, and resorted to issuing waivers for recruits who failed to qualify based on physical fitness, education, or criminal convictions, raising maximum enlistment age, and instituting cash bonuses for enlistment. There have been multiple reports of recruiters providing misinformation and assisting in fraud in order to meet their quotas.[18] All the while, the military had ramped up recruitment of youth of color in poor communities, not only because they were the mostly likely to enlist but because, as anthropologist Roberto Gonzalez points out, they were needed by the US empire to "monitor and infiltrate people that look and speak like them" in military actions abroad and on US territory, where the US military continues to play an active role in repressing indigenous, Black, Latinx, and Asian liberation movements.[19] The military hires public relations companies to market itself to Latinx and Black youth and promotes the more than 3,000 JROTC programs in high schools serving poor and minority neighborhoods. Recruiters convince immigrant youth of color to enlist by holding up the military as an institution that will repair their marginalization.[20]

The US immigration system helps the military meet its labor needs by narrowing and eliminating pathways to legalization, criminalizing immigration, and eroding the rights of lawful permanent residents and naturalized citizens.[21] This makes it more likely that immigrants turn to selling their labor to the military to secure some semblance of rights and security for themselves and their loved ones. With the passage of the Affordable Care Act in 2010, recently arrived immigrants have reduced access to health care benefits, which may make military employment further attractive, as it provides health care benefits for military workers and their families.[22]

One example of how the structure of the economy, the lack of affordable educational opportunities, and the dearth of a social safety net all work to push immigrant youth into the military comes from a study participant I call Manuel. Manuel was born in Mexico and came to the United States as a baby. When he was a senior in high school, he joined the Marines. As graduation ticked closer, the military seemed like the only option to Manuel. His immigrant parents worked long hours preparing and distributing home-cooked food to support five children. Manuel said that as worried as they might have been about their teenage son enlisting, "it also made them a little happy that I wasn't going to follow in those types of footsteps working real tough, tough jobs. You know, like, minimum wage kind of thing." For Manuel, the military meant steady employment in a context with few comparable alternatives, an enlistment experience he shared with US citizens. Beyond Manuel's individual options in life, however, we see how structural forces work to provide a supply of workers for the US military. Immigrants are a part of that supply. Lacking US citizenship, their job opportunities are narrower. Moreover, they lack intergenerational roots and connections and face the threat of deportation.

Manuel's father first migrated to the United States as a teenager and traveled back and forth from Mexico for a few years. Neither of Manuel's parents finished high school. The family obtained legal immigration status as part of the 1986 amnesty,[23] which gave Manuel a green card and made him eligible to enlist. One way to understand Manuel's story is to hold him up as an example of a hard-working Mexican immigrant who overcame his tough environment to vindicate the choice of his humble parents to migrate. That is the story often told by immigrant advocates, as well as by the military itself when it highlights immigrants working in the United States military. Yet this story is incomplete. Manuel's parents were part of a long-term migration system from Mexico to the United States, which relied on recruitment by US businesses who sought cheap workers with few rights. Their economic precariousness in Mexico is a result of US dominance in the region, its penetration and disruption of the local economies to extract wealth for US companies and global elites. Manuel grew up in a racially segregated neighborhood in a Midwestern city deprived of public services and plagued with violence. Were he to be criminalized along with many of the other local men of color, his green card would not have protected him from deportation to Mexico. As sociologists Tanya Golash-Boza and Pierrette Hondagneu-Sotelo note, the disproportionate incarceration of Black and Latinx men connects with US immigration law to create a gendered racial removal program.[24] As Latinx immigrants, Manuel's family had few social mobility options. Manuel attended a segregated school—a military academy—that imbued young people of color with the culture of militarism and prepared them to become military workers. Manuel's pathway into the military took place within this larger structural context, exemplifying the immigrant variety of the poverty draft.

When he enlisted, Manuel was a high school graduate who had no plans to go to college. For youth who are not college-bound, the military is one of the few options for a steady and nonstigmatized job. In fact, some of the veterans I spoke to described enlisting as an alternative to going to jail. Rodrigo, a Mexican immigrant army veteran, put it this way: "I looked for something positive for me to turn to other than gangbang, or ending up in jail, or doing who knows what for survival." Gangbanging could mean being involved in organized crime or being criminalized as a youth of color who is labeled as a gang member by schools and police regardless of criminal activity.[25]

However, college-bound youth are also pushed into the military, because the military subsidizes college education for its workers and even for some of their family members. A combination of several programs covers educational expenses for military personnel on active duty, veterans, reservists, and dependents. For instance, someone who worked on active duty for thirty-six or more months after 9/11 could receive around $24,000 per year for up to four years of payments to cover tuition, a housing stipend, books, and supplies.[26] A larger share of Americans are in college than ever before, and college costs and debt are at record highs.[27] Not surprisingly, then, many enlist to pay for college, immigrants included.

This was the case for Danilo, who migrated to the United States from the Philippines as a child. Danilo grew up in a one-bedroom apartment with four siblings and his mom. He says he rarely saw his mom, a single parent who worked multiple jobs. After graduating from high school, Danilo tried to go to community college, but could not afford it: "I didn't have any money, so I decided I wanted to join the army for school." Others enlisted to try to avoid crippling student loans. Juan, an immigrant from the Dominican Republic said that his family was not "poor by any means" but "having college debt was a huge concern for all of us. And it came down to one day, my mom kind of [said], 'Listen, you're running out of options, and I don't know what to do for you if you want to go to school.'" In fact, when the military exceeded its 2019 recruitment goals, it was attributed to the student debt crisis.[28]

Even after graduating from college, the military remains a draw for economic reasons. For US citizens, a college degree can mean being commissioned as an officer in the military, a management position with better pay and prestige. But noncitizens cannot be commissioned as officers. They can only enlist, regardless of their college degrees.[29] Yet they might still decide to do so because even college graduates are increasingly struggling in the labor market. When James, an immigrant from Jamaica, graduated from college during the Great Recession, he could not find a job. His degree in information technology got him only so far, in a position at a friend's auto body shop, which went out of business a few years later. At that point, now in his mid-twenties, James was worse off than when he graduated. He had no experience related to his IT degree: "So, I made a conscious decision. I sat down with my family. I was like, 'Look, the military is probably the best option to go right now. One, because it's going to offer me the opportunity to get my, to fast-track my citizenship. . . . And it's a steady paycheck.'" In fact, James did not learn about the fast-tracking of naturalization until he went to talk with a recruiter. It became a compelling argument with his family, although it was his economic situation that initially motivated him. At first, James attempted to join the navy so he could stay close to family. But after nine months of back and forth, navy recruiters told him that he was too old, and they would have to pay him too much money because of his education. He had better luck with the army, although he was not able to sign up for an occupation related to IT because he was not a US citizen. James's experience demonstrates the difficulties some immigrants face in the military, which is structured to enlist younger people who are US citizens and high school graduates.

The high rates of poverty, lack of access to affordable education, and difficulties faced even by college graduates ensure a supply of workers for the military. Military welfare in the form of educational benefits, health care, and housing subsidies has been expanding in recent decades, even as neoliberal austerity policies shrink welfare provisions for the general population.[30] Politicians across the political spectrum cite the lack of money available to fund education, housing, and health care, while they rubber-stamp the massive and growing budgets for defense and security, shifting ever more of the state capacity into those sectors.[31] Given their vulnerabilities due to immigration status, immigrants are a robust source of labor for the military, which actively recruits them.

PURSUING WARRIOR MASCULINITY AMID THE GLORIFICATION OF WAR

Militarism pervades US society. Sociologist Emily Brissette notes that US militarism leads Americans to "accept war as a reasonable or inevitable solution to conflicts."[32] The legitimation of war that is emblematic of a militarized culture may not have always had such a stronghold in the United States, but it holds supreme after two decades of the War on Terror. Military values extend beyond military affairs, infusing civilian life and shaping civilian institutions.[33] US entertainment media, from movies to sporting events, as well as school textbooks are full of messages celebrating the military and war. This not only increases the number of young people who join the military, but shapes how all Americans understand the military and its role, strengthening the associations between the military and honor, service, and sacrifice. Vaclav, who immigrated from Slovakia as a young teenager, recalled being influenced by military commercials on television, and thinking that he "really wanted to be part of the team and do something honorable, do something more than work at a Walmart nine to five type of stuff . . . fighting for the United States. That's just badass as hell."

Youth growing up in the United States, especially those in poor and marginalized communities, are exposed to militarism from an early age. The militarization of public schools naturalizes militarism and military identities and is framed as a solution to poor academic performance and youth gangs.[34] The turn of the twenty-first century has seen a tremendous growth of JROTC programs in high schools, as well as an increasing number of military-themed charter schools.[35] JROTC was first established in the early twentieth century as a response to class and racial uprisings and as an attempt to instill proper masculinity and loyalty in immigrant youth.[36] There was a surge in JROTC funding again in the early 1990s as a reaction to the Los Angeles riots, with the familiar framing of instilling discipline in minority youth.[37] Some students are placed into JROTC programs without their consent.[38] The leadership of JROTC reports that about 20 percent of JROTC participant go on to enlist.[39]

The No Child Left Behind educational policies of the early 2000s gave the military access to high school student contact information, which the military supplements by buying data from private corporations and by marketing the ASVAB exam as a career exploration test. In some schools, military recruiters have extensive access to students, even teaching classes and pulling them out of class for recruitment activities.[40] Militarism and its brand of violent masculinity is spread through popular video games: the army has a flourishing video game recruitment program, which includes popular army-developed first-person shooter games, army teams competing in video game tournaments, and recruiters virtually chatting with young gamers.[41]

Immigrants who grew up in the United States are affected by the pervasive images of the US military as an honorable service and viable career path. Gilberto migrated from Mexico with his parents at a young age and grew up in California. Even as a child, Gilberto knew he wanted to be in the military: "I've always wanted . . . to be in the military, since I was a young kid. I think, I, I've been wearing dog tags since I was in eighth grade. I used to go to the surplus store, and I had my own custom tags made, and . . . You know, watched all the war movies, read all the books, you know. I knew almost everything there was to know about the Marine Corps already when I went into boot camp. . . . I researched the history and all that stuff. . . . It was just always a dream for me." Throughout his childhood, Gilberto imbibed cultural products like books, movies, and consumer goods that shaped his idea of his future as a Marine. He planned to enlist as soon as he graduated from high school but had to wait until he obtained lawful permanent residency first, because it was required for enlistment. While he waited for his green card, Gilberto said he went to the recruiting station every day, trying to convince the recruiters to let him enlist.

Militarism undermines critical consideration of foreign and domestic policies carried out by the US military, sweeping it under the carpet of undifferentiated patriotism and "fighting for freedom." When militarism dominates public discourse, media, and culture, the emphasis on winning wars and defending the homeland dehumanizes people at the receiving end of US military might. Their suffering and deaths are framed as just, as unfortunate collateral damage, or are not spoken of at all.[42] This was striking in the interviews I conducted: almost none of the immigrants I spoke to mentioned killing or hurting people as something they considered or worried about when enlisting. Yet many were concerned with themselves being injured or dying. Of course, when someone uses enlistment to build a case for deserving inclusion into US society, discussion of harm and violence likely detracts from such a case.

Part of the culture of militarism is the idea that military labor is a way to set youth on a straight, disciplined path, and to do so through a particular vision of militarized masculinity. Militarized forms of hegemonic masculinities are part and parcel of recruitment efforts.[43] Working for the US military is presented as a way to become a man, to acquire an undisputed and superior brand of masculinity based in violence, stoicism, and stiff hierarchies of obedience to power. As one of my participants' mothers told him about the Marines: "They're going to make a man out of you." Enlisting, then, is connected to a hegemonic masculinity that posits military labor as a physically demanding way to prove one's worth.

Tadeo, a Marine born in Mexico, told me that he had wanted to do something challenging as a youth. When he graduated from high school, Tadeo went to the recruiters' office, and a few weeks later, he was in boot camp: "School buddies, from high school, a whole bunch of them were joining the military . . . they were all the time the hardest, the toughest. Yeah, that's for me! That's what I wanted. I played football since I was twelve years old. All the way through high school and I was kind of like . . . I wanted the action." Here we see Tadeo's understanding of the military as a place for the toughest, and it was a natural transition for children already socialized in a culture of high school football.

Tadeo was interested specifically in the Marines, not another military branch. The US Marines have the highest percentage of Hispanic-identified people among all military branches. In recent years, over a third of new marines are Hispanic-identified.[44] The association between Latinxs, Latinx masculinities, and the Marines is something my study participants themselves articulated. Miguel, a Peruvian immigrant and a Marine, listed all the different Latin American countries from which his fellow Marines came:

For whatever reason, there is a disproportionate amount of Latino Marines than there are other races. For some reason, especially from Queens. From what I can see now, there is a certain machismo that is important to Latin culture, where you become a soldier, especially a Marine because, as you know, there is . . . Air Force is the cushiest one, because, you know, it's kind of like a desk job. Navy, Army, and the Marines are supposed to be the most hardcore. Outside of Navy Seals. So Latin dudes in Queens, they are, like, yeah, I want to be a Marine, I want to be in the Marine Corps. So I think that brings a lot of us there for that reason. Just want to be tough, you know?

As Lisa Marie Cacho points out, the overrepresentation of Latinos is framed as a natural cultural trait associated with Latino masculinity. Cultural stereotypes about Latino masculinity have not only become a part of multicultural brand of US militarism, but these ideas about machismo are used to explain the overrepresentation of Latinos in military ranks exposed to the worst risks of injury and death. This use of machismo naturalizes the disproportionate employment of Latinos in dangerous military occupations.[45]

Feminist scholar Cynthia Enloe argues that the enlistment of women in the US military has not disturbed its masculinized culture. Rather, women soldiers are expected to fit into this existing culture.[46] Some of the women I interviewed were worried about how they would cope with military environments dominated by men. Others anticipated lack of accommodation for women as a special challenge to overcome. For instance, Anita, an immigrant from Poland who was a competitive triathlon athlete, emphasized that she wanted to meet the physical challenges of military labor alongside men. Immigrant women are of particular interest to the US military because their gender, ethnicity, and language skills can make them more effective at such tasks as body-searching women in places under US occupation. I explore the experience of immigrant women in the military further in chapter 4.

Even immigrants who grew up in other countries and were not exposed to a barrage of images and products of the US military were affected by the US brand of militarism once they migrated. For example, Rabindra did not think of the military as an option while growing up in Nepal, but was drawn to it after he came to the United States for college:

Whenever I watched the NFL games a lot, like football and stuff, whenever the game starts, how they always thank the military for the service. . . . Even before I thought about this, that always fascinated me. I never thought about it back home because I don't think we have that concept, appreciating military during the times like that. But when I came to the US, how always the military service is being appreciated here, that kind of fascinated me. And everybody is quite appreciative of their service and it's quite recognized everywhere. Even now, whenever I'm in uniform somewhere, people thank me for the service and all that. That kind of makes me feel very good about what I'm doing. That, in addition to the citizenship, I think that also attracted me a lot.

Rabindra was influenced by the militaristic displays that are part of the multi-million-dollar military marketing strategy. International students can also be influenced by the militarism they see on their campuses. For example, Daniel, a student from China, admired the ROTC cadets he would see on his campus. He even started following their Facebook page: "At least from the pictures they posted were awesome and I thought that I want to try it outside the university." Truda, an adult immigrant from Poland, mentioned the role of Hollywood movies in her decision to enlist:

"You know how you watch movies, and it looks so nice and prestige [*sic*]? It's like you are the future of the country. You go and fight for it." Although they grew up outside the United States and rarely had direct contact with veterans in their social networks, these young adult immigrants were nonetheless influenced by the militarism saturating cultural products and institutions in the United States, contributing to the push to enlist.

Immigrant youth growing up in the United States are clearly influenced by the US brand of militarism that surrounds them. But US militarism is a powerful force that transcends US borders, influencing even those immigrants who come to the United States as older teens or adults through exposure to US cultural products and the 800 US military bases located in seventy countries abroad.[47] Some immigrants' path to enlistment starts before immigration because they admire the image of the US military that they see in US movies. For example, Anildo, who grew up in Cape Verde, recalled always liking the US military because he grew up watching US movies. Anildo immigrated in his mid-twenties and joined the army.

Another adult immigrant, George, was impressed by the US military base he visited in Korea. George was born and grew up in Korea, where he also performed his mandatory military duty. The transformative visit to the US military base occurred during a demoralizing stretch of his required Korean military service, setting him on a future path of enlistment in the US Army Reserves as an international student: "I was in Korea, I was having so much miserable time, and my office captain [in the Korean military] brought me to the US base when he was visiting. . . . I was really impressed with all of the facilities, really top-notch. This is what the military is supposed to be. I had a lot of respect for the US military and if given the opportunity, I would like to be part of it or work for it or whatever. That experience really transformed the way I viewed the US military." Like a few other immigrants I spoke to, George admired the power and technology of the US military. Of course, US military bases do not always provoke admiration. People across the world have engaged in resisting the presence of US military, whether as part of anti-imperial struggles or as focused on specific abuses perpetrated by US military workers on these bases.[48] However, as sociologist Victoria Reyes showed in the case of the former US Navy base in the Philippines, Subic Bay, military bases can become wrapped up in narratives of modernity and aspirations of progress for some people living around them.[49] For George, suffering from poor living conditions and a loss of class status in the Korean military, the US military base became a symbol of military superiority. The heavy US military presence in Korea and connections between the US and Korean militaries were reflected in the experience of another Korean immigrant, Jae-in, who heard about the MAVNI program while completing his mandatory military duty in Korea, subsequently coming to the United States and enlisting. Similarly, David, who grew up in the Philippines, saw enlistment in the US Navy in Subic Bay as his ticket out of the Philippines.

The US military exerts a pull on youth across the globe. However, some first-generation immigrants were shaped by militarism in different national contexts than that of the United States and then transferred the values and beliefs of those militarisms to the US context. This is an example of transnational militarist identities, which deemphasize the objectives of specific conflicts or identification of specific enemies in favor of shared or overlapping valorization of military technologies and disciplines. Through transnational militarist identities, the normalization of warfare and the valorization of the military life that developed in another country, in relation to another country's military, shapes how immigrants approach military labor in the United States.

Some immigrants, especially those who migrate as teenagers or young adults, are attracted to the US military because of values of militarism developed in other contexts. Some had family or ethnic legacies of militarism in the countries from which they migrated, complete with beliefs that the military instills discipline and makes boys into men. Others have actually tried to join the military elsewhere, usually unsuccessfully, and then tried to enlist in the US military when they came to the United States. One immigrant might have fought for the Indian Army in Kashmir if not for a missed application deadline. Another was in the Ecuadoran Army, liked it, and enlisted in the US Army once he immigrated. These immigrants wanted to be in the military first and foremost, and the nation of the military force was negotiable. Just as it is common for youth from nonimmigrant backgrounds to be influenced by family legacies of military labor, this was true of some immigrants whose parents worked in other militaries.[50]

Nikolai's enlistment is one example of transnational militarist identity. He came to the United States from Russia's Far East as a college student and enlisted through the MAVNI program. He told me: "I wanted to be in the military all my life. Even probably would not have left Russia and live all my life in Russia. I most likely would have joined the Russian armed forces to some extent, or any kind of Russian paramilitary organizations. Because I really enjoy that since I was a kid. . . . Why I wanted to [is] kind of like this heroic narrative which existed in Russia. . . . In my perspective, I grew up with an idea that military service is the best. It's an honorable job. It's a hard job." Nikolai explained that it is because he associated military work with honor and nationalism that he wanted to obtain US citizenship "the most honorable way," through the US military.[51] Once he migrated to the United States and decided to settle there, he brought his notions of military honor to bear on his new context.

The US culture of militarism is a powerful force that shapes immigrant participation in the US military, and it even extends beyond the US borders. Militarism is laced with ideas about masculinity and becoming a real man that shapes youths' decisions to enlist. However, immigrants who come to the United States as older teenagers or adults sometimes also draw on militarism from the countries where they grew up, constructing transnational militarist identities. These militarist identities draw on US and other militarisms, with different constructions of enemy or social values attached to military jobs. I explore the latter in more detail when I consider how immigrant youth negotiate enlistment decisions in the context of their families and communities because it is in that context that competing meanings of war and the military come into relief.

THE VARIABLE MEANINGS AND SIGNIFICANCE OF CITIZENSHIP

Although naturalization through the military is not automatic and immigrants have to apply for it, the military pathway to citizenship has been, at least theoretically, faster than the civilian one. The US military uses the promise of citizenship to recruit immigrants in an effort to meet its personnel needs, diversify the military labor force, and get access to immigrant-specific skills, such as languages and cultural knowledge.[52]

Naturalization serves as a technology of labor recruitment and management for the US military. In the official period of hostilities post-9/11, military workers had been immediately eligible for naturalization and were exempt from the hefty application fees, although since 2017, new security check requirements have considerably slowed what was for a while a quick naturalization process.[53]

It is common in the US-based immigrant rights movement to use the figure of the immigrant soldier to argue for moral deservingness of immigrants. Immigrants prove that they deserve to be included because they are willing to join the military even without access to a full set of rights. But modern-day deservingness narratives resting on military labor are met with suspicion that immigrants are enlisting only to get citizenship. In fact, for some immigrants, citizenship is the primary or only reason for enlisting. They want to acquire US citizenship as soon as possible, and enlisting in the military allows them a better chance of doing so. For many other immigrants, however, US citizenship is far from being a central reason for enlistment. They may not think much about it much or know how the military path to citizenship works. Sometimes they do not even want to pursue citizenship at the time they enlist. Reaching beyond the narrower definition of citizenship as a legal status, I consider citizenship as belonging and inclusion: some immigrants view military labor and identities as a more promising pathway to full membership and acceptance in a militarized society than available to them in the civilian world.

SPEEDING UP THE LONG ROAD TO CITIZENSHIP

US citizenship is, in fact, a significant reason that some enlist in the US military. Among the immigrants whom I interviewed, the mostly likely to report that citizenship drove their enlistment were those who were not lawful permanent residents: Deferred Action for Childhood Arrivals (DACA) recipients and immigrants on temporary student and work visas. During the brief existence of the MAVNI program between 2009 and 2017, some people in these categories could enlist in the military. A small number of recipients of the temporary DACA—those who spoke languages deemed to be of vital national interest—enlisted through the MAVNI program and were able to become naturalized. If not for the military option, these DACA recipients would have most likely continued to live with the uncertainty of renewing their temporary work authorization every few years and fear that the program would be discontinued. The chances of obtaining lawful permanent residency are better for immigrants on temporary student and employment visas than they are for DACA recipients. At best, they find an employer who sponsors them or they marry a US citizen. More likely, they live for many years from one visa renewal to the next, falling out of status in between, and a substantial number never gain lawful permanent residency.[54] Those DACA recipients and temporary visa holders who were successful in being processed into the military through the MAVNI program had a shortcut to naturalization otherwise not available to them (see chapter 5).

Minzhe, a graduate student from China, exemplifies the options open to immigrants who are in the United States on student visas. He knew he wanted to stay in the United States and discussed the choices open to him:

For me, I have always been looking for opportunity to stay here. I know many ways to stay here. But, that's pretty long and time consuming and not easy looking for employment. For marriage, for family, for investment. So there's this other way. I think that it's not easy. I mean, it's depending. Okay, but I don't want to spend that money to investment so my original plan was for looking for job. And later, actually I . . . always heard about this MAVNI program long time ago. When I came to US I think or after a year I came to the US, I heard about this program. But at that time, [it] only offered active duty. So . . . you have to have a four-year commitment, full-time as a soldier in the military, so that's not for me. I mean, I mean, that's too much time, too much time commitment for me. But later when in 2015, I think, they started to open the reserve also to the people . . . I said, why not?, because [in] the reserve you can still finish out school, and you still have your civilian life, and you just [serve] once per month and two weeks per summer, for the reserve. That's okay for me.

First, there is an employer-sponsored green card, which Minzhe points out is time consuming and not easy to find. He could marry a US citizen or lawful permanent resident and hope that their sponsorship of him would be approved. He could become eligible for permanent residency through the EB-5 Immigrant Investor program by "investing in a new commercial enterprise that will benefit the US economy and create at least 10 full-time positions for qualifying employees."[55] Weighing these routes to citizenship, Minzhe held out for the employment option until MAVNI added the army reserve to the program. His commitment would still be four years in active reserve, then four more years in inactive reserve, after which time the military might keep him past the end of his contract through the Stop Loss program if his labor was needed.[56]

Those on temporary student and work visas from China and India face especially steep obstacles to gaining lawful permanent resident status because the yearly ceilings on adjustment of status are the same across countries. US immigration law mandates a cap of 7 percent of the total number of green cards allocated (or about 25,000) for each country, allotted in a first-come, first-served manner. Migrants from China and India—which together comprise about 85 percent of all highly skilled temporary work visa petitions (H-1B) and about half of all international students—wait in line until a spot opens up. Depending on the category through which they are adjusting, this could be well over a decade, not including the additional time it takes to process the application.[57] Ravi, who came to the United States from India to study information technology in graduate school and to join a part of his extended family already in the United States, noted this feature of the immigration system explicitly:

So, in the United States the immigration system is broken, regardless of how qualified you are, especially if you are from India or China. If you have a master's degree and your employer sponsors the green card, assuming that you're lucky enough that you secure an H-1B, it would take at least twenty-five years if not more to get a green card. So I just felt like I don't want to be in a modern-day slavery and stuck with an employer, so I thought that this [enlisting through MAVNI] would be a nice way of me, you know, actually being part of the country where I want to live.

In essence, there is an immigration bottleneck for Indian and Chinese immigrants on temporary visas. By making military enlistment open to those with temporary visas between 2009 and 2017, the US military tapped into this pressured bottleneck, channeling highly educated, mostly Asian immigrants into its ranks with the promise of quick naturalization.

Most noncitizens who enlist in the US military have lawful permanent residency, not DACA or temporary visas. As lawful permanent residents, they have a civilian pathway to citizenship after a waiting period and upon satisfying naturalization requirements. In most cases, the fast track to citizenship through the military is not as momentous for them when enlisting, yet there are some exceptions. Truda, who grew up in Poland, was married to a US citizen and had a green card through that marriage. Yet she feared losing her green card and enlisted in part to secure citizenship for herself: "My marriage was kind of falling apart. My husband was abusing prescription medication. And I was really afraid that he's going to do something that will jeopardize my stay in the United States. That they could deport me because he's abusing narcotics and doing things like that." Given that immigration courts operate without due process and legal representation is costly, it is not without basis that Truda was worried her husband's substance use disorder could somehow result in her losing immigration status. Joining the military was a way for Truda to escape her relationship and the uncertainty of the immigration status that she derived from her spouse. Thus, even for those with lawful permanent residency status, the military can attract recruits by promising citizenship, which provides more security and permanence. Quicker naturalization may also be something immigrants need to sponsor the migration of a family member who is sick or otherwise needs to join family in the United States.

The reality that some immigrants enlist in the military for the path to US citizenship provides an opening to critique an immigration system that makes other pathways to citizenship so onerous or impossible that immigrants choose to give multiple years to military labor. After all, most US-born Americans do not join the military. Admitting that some immigrants do enlist to obtain citizenship encourages a critique of the poverty draft, pointing as it does to systemically constrained choices faced by so many military workers.

INCIDENTAL OR UNWANTED CITIZENSHIP

Immigrants who grew up in the United States with green cards tend to be less focused on or aware of immigration processes. They may not even realize that enlistment in the military qualifies them for naturalization, particularly in periods when citizenship benefits are less emphasized in recruitment promotion. Some are informed of the fast path to citizenship by their recruiters, and others are not. Observers might see immigrants not centering citizenship as a reason to join the military as evidence that they are enlisting for the "right" reasons, such as out of patriotism or to defend their adopted country. I see this, rather, as an indicator of a double vulnerability of immigrants in the military. Veterans in general contend with the mental and physical consequences of their military labor, high rates of substance use disorders, and housing insecurity, all of which make them more likely to come into contact with the system of mass incarceration.[58] When that happens for noncitizen veterans, it can lead to deportation. The deported veterans I spoke with were, in fact, those who did not know about the military pathway to citizenship, were misinformed about how it worked (some thought it happened automatically), or did not understand the implications of being a noncitizen veteran. All had grown up in the United States.

Here is Hector, recounting enlisting as a seventeen-year-old:

SOFYA: So at the time [of enlistment] you were aware that, like, "Hey, I only have a green card, I kind of want citizenship."

HECTOR: I know I had a green card, but my mom is the one that remembers, and my dad, they recall the recruiter saying, I don't know if it was automatic citizen or we'll take care of him, either of the two, but I don't remember.

SOFYA: Ah, so the recruiter was saying that to your parents. About the citizenship.

HECTOR: And then the other thing is like anytime I sign a contract I don't even read half the crap that's in it. So you know, twenty pages, sign, sign, sign.

Years later, Hector pled guilty to a crime he said he did not commit when threatened with fifteen years in prison. He says that he did not realize that as a noncitizen, he would be deported. Jose, who also got deported as a veteran, told me he did not think about citizenship when he enlisted because he felt American: "It was just like, always do something for my country, the country I grew up in, you know?" In effect, being so "assimilated" as to forget his immigrant status actually ended up hurting Jose.

That is the double jeopardy I refer to: the jeopardy of military labor is compounded by the criminalization of immigrants.

Most of the immigrants I spoke to knew that they could get citizenship quicker than in the civilian world, but it was just one of many considerations for them. It is likely that this is true of most noncitizens in the US military, just as US citizens who enlist have multiple reasons for doing so. We must not assume, however, that joining the US military means that a person wants to be a US citizen. Jack told me that he did not care about getting citizenship when he enlisted. A Mexican American growing up in a white community, he was subjected to so much bullying that he refused to be naturalized: "I don't want to be one of these people! They keep messing with me! I don't want to be an American!" Miguel, whose story opens this book, learned that he could naturalize once he was already in the Marines. But he was not interested in citizenship for a long time.

The presumption that Miguel and Jack would, as a matter of course, want US citizenship feeds into US exceptionalism and obscures the realities of why many immigrant and nonimmigrant Americans join the military. Empirical evidence helps dispel such presumptions and more accurately and critically situates immigrant military workers within the machinery of the US empire while highlighting their agency as political and human actors. This becomes poignantly important when immigrant soldiers are killed in the line of duty and the state has better control over inserting them into the dominant narratives of militarism and US exceptionalism by granting them posthumous citizenship.[59]

The issue of citizenship acquisition through the military is complex and is explored in detail in chapter 3. But the promise of naturalization at the point of enlistment means different things to immigrants. To those who migrated as young adults, it can be the primary driver for joining the military. For those who grew up in the United States, it may be far less important, or they may not be aware of it at all.[60] Joining the US military does not mean that one wants to be a US citizen.

LOOKING FOR BELONGING AND ACCEPTANCE

Citizenship is a legal status that the US grants to those born within its national borders or to citizen parents abroad. Immigrants obtain citizenship through the process of naturalization. But citizenship can also mean rights, participation, and belonging.[61] In this broader sense, the military has been said to provide a pathway to citizenship for racialized minorities in the United States, especially for African Americans, whose labor in the US military has been tied to expanded access to citizenship rights.[62] As anthropologists Leslie Bartlett and Catherine Lutz wrote in their analysis of JROTC textbooks: "soldiering is the route to cultural citizenship, especially for minorities whose status within American political culture remains marginal. Through the military . . . minorities can prove their loyalty to the nation."[63] Although meant for the Canadian armed forces, geographer Deborah Cowen's characterization of the military applies to the United States: "a form of work and citizenship for the deserving poor."[64]

For immigrants, the military can provide a fast track to naturalization and the legal status of citizenship, but it can also influence other aspects of citizenship, such as a sense of belonging and acceptance. More precisely, it can help them make a stronger claim to rights in a way specific to their experience as the foreign-born. For instance, enlistment in the military is a way to immerse oneself into US culture and the English language, as well as a trump card to wield in response to xenophobia. For instance, Sergei, who migrated from Russia to join his American wife, explained: "It is a very good opportunity to assimilate faster in the country because you are immediately immersed in a native environment. That is, you are going to have to speak English. You will understand American mentality faster."[65] Sergei saw the military as a place to acquire the skills and knowledge he needed to claim belonging in a small Midwestern community with few other immigrants. Sergei also explained that when people inevitably saw him as a foreigner because of his accent, he wanted to be able to respond with the shield of military identity:

Another reason that I have to share, really, really important reason for why precisely service, why I wanted to serve in the Marine Corps, is because I wanted to earn my place here. That is also a very important reason. So when people ask me—because my accent, obviously, is not going anywhere—when people ask me where am I from, I am not ashamed to say where I am from and that I am an immigrant. But if they laugh at me a little, I can tell them what I have done, for this country. Because most Americans did not do that. And for me, that is a very, very important reason why I went to serve, why I join the Marine Corps. So write that down too, that reason for service—to earn my place here. For me, that is one of the reasons.

Sergei wanted to make sure I noted how important veteran status was for resisting exclusion as an immigrant. Interestingly, he mentioned earning his place in the United States as a way to combat xenophobia by proving his worth. He then went on to recount a painful experience that occurred soon after he moved to the United States. An acquaintance of his father-in-law asked him where he was from and made a joke that implied that his migration was connected to a mail-order catalog. This is a common trope that Eastern European women migrants contend with, but here it was wielded against Sergei, who married a white US-born woman. He did not fully understand the slight at the time, but "now, if someone made a joke like that, I would have full moral authority to punch that person or at least to put him in his place. So I would feel full moral right to do that. Because I know what I have done for this country. That is one of the reasons why I decided to serve." So in addition to earning his place in the United States, enlisting also empowered Sergei to respond to xenophobic insults.

Research on immigrants in the military has often approached military labor as a mechanism of integration and assimilation.[66] Immigrants themselves sometimes view the military in that way, especially if they arrived in the United States as older teenagers or young adults and feel their differences more acutely. Ravi, whom I quoted above on the difficulties of Indian and Chinese temporary visa holders, ended up enlisting through the MAVNI program to get citizenship and be able to stay in the United States. However, he also thought that the military would help him be treated as less of an outsider:

I was born an Indian . . . I'm Indian by birth and American by choice. So that was one of the pros, citizenship. And then [the] second pro was that, you know, I feel like I will be more assimilated in the society. . . . From my opinion people see you as an outsider when you're an immigrant; when you look like this and you talk with an accent, you get boxed into various stereotypes. And I felt like if you have more representation in the armed forces, which the majority of the people have very favorable views about, I think, that would help me be part of the country and its story better.

Ravi suggests that being a military veteran would help him overcome stereotypes and belong on an individual level. In addition, representation of immigrants and/or South Asians like Ravi in the military may change stereotypes on a group level. This clearly reflects a perception of the US military as embodying legitimate Americanness, one that is difficult to access for Asian immigrants. Another Indian international student, Guarav, considered military labor as a way to build a claim to belonging that would help not only him but his future children, whom he implied would be racialized as foreigners:

The pro was not just the citizenship, that's one thing. Also, what I figured was it would be a good option for me to establish myself in this nation because if I were to settle down in the US, and if I were to have kids in the future and all that, it's probably going to be a good thing even for them because they would feel they belong here if their family member has actually served in the army and all that. And especially for people that are minorities here. I feel like that's something they want to feel. That would be a big part of their heritage, of their sense of belonging and all that.

Both Ravi and Guarav came to the United States as young adults. Their thinking around joining the military was framed by their experience being treated as foreigners due to the way South Asians are racialized in the United States, as well as their accents. Enlistment would give Ravi and Guarav a path to the legal status of citizenship, but they thought it would also help them and their future children grasp more firmly onto rights and a sense of belonging. Military labor can be a way for immigrants to demonstrate deservingness at a time when their claims to rights, belonging, and even humanity are predicated on distancing themselves from the dehumanized and devalued categories of Other.[67] It also serves to further militarize the immigration system, to tie citizenship more closely to military labor, and to help entrench the values of militarism in US society.

Using enlistment in the military to stake a claim for belonging was also something that some immigrants wanted to do within their own immigrant community, not only around those US-born people whose belonging was not questioned. Nikolai encountered assumptions about his intentions when dating in the United States. As a struggling student with uncertain immigration status, Nikolai was infuriated when a girlfriend's father accused him of trying to get a green card through marriage:

I can join the Army, I can give my time to this country. Because I don't want to hear after. Because I have heard it here a million times. I used to date this Russian-speaking girl [who had US citizenship] and her parents were like, "Oh he is dating you just because of the passport." And I have heard it here on multiple occasions. And I hate it by all the fibers in my body. I hate when people say it to me. Specifically when Russian immigrants, I have heard it so many times [say], "So he is dating you just because essentially he has nothing back in Russia." I had more than enough back in Russia. My life was all set back in Russia. I could have been an MD in Russia. And I am listening to this construction worker [his girlfriend's father] who is earning like 50K and he barely speaks English even though he has been here for ten years, he barely speaks English. And he tells me, "Oh, you are dating this girl just because of the citizenship. Man, you won in a damn [Diversity Visa] lottery!"

In fact, out of the limited options available to him to adjust status in the United States, Nikolai was adamantly opposed to getting a green card through marriage. Given his experiences with dating within his own immigrant community in the United States, it is clear why enlistment in the military seemed like a more honorable way of getting citizenship—one that was earned. Nikolai's dilemma was also one of class: a highly educated middle-class migrant, he felt superior to working-class co-ethnics, who, nevertheless, had more secure immigration status than he did. He contrasted enlistment in the military to "unearned" or "less-earned" citizenship, such as that of his ex-girlfriend's father.

Other adult immigrants stressed the military route to naturalization as the most honorable because citizenship would be earned, the way it presumably would not be if one got it through marriage or a job. Paresh, a highly skilled immigrant from India, saw himself as different from other Indian immigrants: "Once you get the citizenship through the MAVNI program, you're not one of those people who applied for it through a job, you know? Like other Indians who kind of pay their dues and stuff to acquire this. So there's a little bit of that as well. I don't know how [*laughs*] practical that thinking is, but I still feel that way. I mean, if my daughter grows up here and we end up living in this country, we will not be, we kind of earned it." For Paresh, too, the belonging he earns through military labor will extend to his daughter.

These immigrants are living in a context where their loyalty to the United States is questioned regardless of how long they have lived in the United States or their ties to it through work, community, and faith—and the suspicion may even extend to future generations. They hope that military labor will provide compelling evidence of their loyalty, compared to other immigrants who get green cards and citizenship through other routes. This politics of deservingness is understandable and widespread in the US immigrant rights movement. Immigrant veterans are perhaps the most extreme manifestation of the deservingness narratives, since they risk life and health for a country that has not yet even given them citizenship. As I explore in chapter 6 on deported veterans, these narratives and claims are so powerful that they continue to be used by immigrants and their advocates even when their experiences in the military and as veterans clearly indicate that not even military identities can overcome their exclusion and marginalization as racialized subjects of the US empire.

Overall, if we consider citizenship as a legal status, then citizenship is a reason that some immigrants enlist in the military, particularly among those who arrived as young adults and did not grow up in the United States. Immigrants who came to the United States as children and spent most of their childhoods there are more often only weakly motivated by the fast track to citizenship available through the military. Some may not even be particularly aware of citizenship benefits of enlisting, or do not prioritize them in deciding to join the military. Beyond a legal status, citizenship as rights and belonging is also part of the enlistment process. Some immigrants enlist in order to demonstrate and earn their belonging, pushing back against racialized narratives that exclude them from membership in the nation. As Lisa Marie Cacho points out, "for those living with little or no rights, the possibility of dying on the front lines is transformed into an 'opportunity' for legal recognition."[68]

Americans tend to associate military labor with patriotism.[69] Undoubtedly, devotion to the United States plays a role in pushing young people to enlist. It would be difficult to imagine otherwise, given the hegemonic discourses of US exceptionalism and the pervasive valorization of the US military. Immigrants, too, sometimes feel love for country, even if they are not born within its borders. Those who grow up in the US may adopt cultural narratives of patriotism not very different from those who are US-born. Manuel told me that he was "fervently patriotic" and driven to enlist as a response to 9/11: "I consider myself a patriotic person, but at the time, it was just like, it was so fresh, 9/11 was just so fresh to me. Any decision, every doubt that came to mind about joining the military—I just kept coming back to that." Another Mexican immigrant who grew up in the United States, Jose, said: "I want to serve my country, something to do for my country, give back to my country, you know? And that's what motivated me to go to the military. . . . I felt American when I joined the army, and it was always something for the country I grew up in." In an anti-immigrant environment focused in part specifically on Latinxs, expressions of patriotism can be a response to racial exclusion and an attempt to subvert stereotypes that paint Latinxs as inherently excluded from belonging in the United States.[70]

Claims to patriotism can be more complicated for immigrants who arrived in the United States at older ages, since they are socialized in different national contexts and may be more likely to have social, cultural, affective, and political ties to other countries—and to be suspected of a lack of American patriotism. It was common among the adult arrivals whom I interviewed to express love for the United States, combined with a desire to give back. The latter was couched in specifically immigrant terms. For example, John saw enlistment as a way to pay back for the social mobility he experienced in the United States and that he said would be unattainable for him in his country of origin: "I appreciate the life that the United States has [given me], the opportunity to study computer science. And I think I live a lot freer here compared to Malaysia. I have a lot more freedom here than in Malaysia. I just want to give something back. . . . I had nothing and now I have something, and I just want to show my appreciation. So that's why I just join. I know it's kind of like, somebody could say like on TV, but that's the truth."

For other adult arrivals, enlistment was a way to make a claim that the United States was their country too. They might feel like the United States is now home, or becoming home, but the way others see them does not reflect that, particularly if they are racialized as foreigners or have an accent that identifies them as foreign-born. Enlistment in the military is a way to demonstrate their attachment to the United States. That this pattern is more common among those who immigrated as adults, particularly on temporary visas, is reinforced by the case of Lee, who actually grew up in the United States. Although he spent most of his childhood in New Jersey, Lee was still living in the United States on a temporary student visa, ever since he came from Korea as a child. This uncertainty of status made him more similar to adult arrivals than to childhood arrivals who had green cards. Lee told me, "If I'm going to call this place home, I just felt that I wanted to at least show the fact that I support it. And the fact that when I was growing up here in the States, I thought about the reasons why I so fell in love with this country. Yes, I had problems. There were challenges, but it's what made me who I am. I was like, you know what? What can I contribute to protect our livelihood here? So that was my main motivation." Lee felt the need to show his support for the place he calls home. His statement about contributing to protecting livelihood is ambiguous. He can be framing military labor as protecting the American way of life—a well-entrenched trope—and he may be referring to the way his military service would protect the livelihood of his family in the United States, by giving him a pathway to citizenship otherwise blocked. For immigrants like Lee, enlistment in the military can be a way to prove their loyalty in a context where they are excluded as outsiders and face increasingly punitive and criminalizing immigration policies.[71]

Perhaps more than others, immigrants—particularly those who did not grow up in the United States—may feel pressured to express gratitude and patriotism with respect to the United States, and to draw on these to explain why they joined the military. Even as they hope that military labor secures their claims on belonging, immigrants need to actively work to create and support these claims. This is not necessarily to call into question their patriotism, which they may very well genuinely experience, but to point to the complicated ways in which "volunteering" for the military actually operates for marginalized and excluded people. As cultural scholar Jocelyn Pacleb points out, immigrant enlistees are forced to "prove their loyalty and Americanness in the face of rejection of their own ethnic communities by the very same state that employs them."[72] Some immigrants, such as Arabs and South Asians, bear the additional burden of being associated with terrorism, raising the stakes and hopes of being able to prove patriotism through military service.[73] The appeals of adult immigrants to honor and arguments about earning citizenship are a response to their past and present experiences as immigrants, and extend to worries about the future of their children. When they say that enlistment in the military is a way to give back to their adopted country or to earn citizenship, it is a reflection of a realistic assessment of how the status at least symbolically conferred on US veterans may help counteract their vulnerabilities as immigrants.

Moreover, when immigrants like Jose, above, emphasize that they enlisted to serve their country, it can be in response to suspicion and scrutiny that they face regarding their motives. Jose was sharing his story of enlistment with me from Mexico, where he lives post-deportation. He emphasized patriotism to underscore his claim that he did not enlist for US citizenship. Thus, expressions of patriotic sentiment can be used by immigrants to support their claims to rights and even humanity—to be recognized as worthy people. Jose wanted me to know that he was not the kind of immigrant who would join the military just for immigration benefits. Similarly, a nonimmigrant veteran might support their claim to honor by proving that they did not enlist only for the benefits.

But not all immigrants express patriotism in relationship to their enlistment in the US military. For many, it is not a factor that they mention at all, focusing instead on pay, benefits, or fast track to citizenship. A few explicitly explained that patriotism is complicated for immigrants. Sergei did not think people born outside the United States could really feel full patriotism. He contrasted patriotism to the feeling of brotherhood with his fellow Marines. Loyalty and patriotism are topics that can come up in the context of families and communities that immigrants are part of and have to negotiate when enlisting. I now turn to contextualizing enlistment in the immigrant's family and social milieu.

ARGUING WITH PARENTS, IMPRESSING FRIENDS, LOOKING UP TO RECRUITERS

When immigrants enlist in the military, their decisions are embedded in social networks made up of family members, friends, and communities. Many also negotiate the enlistment process through building relationships with military recruiters. The military recognizes the role of parents in enlistment decisions, and targets them with marketing.[74] Like any family members, immigrant family members may worry about their young person getting injured or dying, or they might feel proud that they are joining a socially valorized institution. But they can also have concerns that are specific to them as people with uncertain legal status or as immigrants socialized in contexts where military labor has different meanings. Friends and communities affect enlistment of individuals as well, by providing role models, peer effects, and cultural scripts around enlistment and the military. Immigrants who grow up in the United States have greater exposure to recruiters and marketing information about the military in their schools and communities than immigrants who come to the United States as young adults.

FAMILY WORRIES AND PRIDE

So far in this chapter, I have discussed the role of the poverty draft, militarism, masculinities, citizenship, and patriotism in influencing immigrant enlistment in the military. But green card soldiers also grapple with considerations of combat, injury, and death when enlisting—and this plays out primarily in the context of the family. The topic of deployment and its risks is one that study participants brought up when explaining how they negotiated their families' reactions to their enlistment. Some of the immigrants I interviewed hoped they would get deployed, for adventure, experience, honor, or, in one case, for the higher pay that comes with deployment. A few were worried or scared about deployment, because someone they knew came back with injuries, and they thought about risks to themselves. Those who enlisted before the War on Terror did not really think they would be involved in a war. For those who did enlist after the War on Terror began, the most common thoughts about deployment revolved around dismissing the risks to self—and this was central to many negotiations with family members. Many parents are concerned about injury and death when their children enlist. These children, in turn, reported arguing that the military jobs they chose would not expose them to much risk or that there were risks in civilian life, such as being killed in a car accident. Others kept the details of their contracts vague to reduce familial anxiety. Vaclav, an immigrant from Slovakia, told his parents that the chance of dying was worth "doing something":

They [his parents] tried to talk me out of it, of course. My dad was telling me like, "You know, this ain't going to be a video game, it's going to be real bullets flying." Because obviously my dad has real experience because he was in the Slovakian Army back during Communism and everybody was drafted, so he knew what he was talking about. He told me, "Look, people going to pick on you, people going to mess with you, it's going to be rough, you're going to be completely changed person, and right now United States is waging two wars, so you're going to probably see some shit." And I'm like, "Well, you know, I guess we all going to die one day so I might as well do something."

Vaclav's father drew on his own experience of military labor in Slovakia to caution his child about the costs of war to the soldier. Yet Vaclav recounts dismissing these concerns in a way that minimized the risks and pointed to the universal experience of mortality.

While most commonly, family members oppose their young person's interest in the military because of the risks associated with deployment, some were critical because of their understanding of the role of the US military in the world or opinions about the United States as a whole. Adult immigrants, especially, might have to negotiate family opposition to their enlistment across national borders, since they are more likely to have come to the United States without their parents. Relations between the United States and China are tense, and a few Chinese immigrants I spoke to revealed the disappointment their family members expressed over their enlistment in the US armed forces. Russell's grandfather was a regiment commander in the Chinese People's Liberation Army and fought in the Korean War against the United States. Russell juxtaposed his grandfather's "patriotism kind of style" with his own "globalism."[75] Li Wei's father in China was also a "patriotic type": "So he thinks, you know, that if you join the US Army, does that mean that you're going to be a natural rivalry with your own hometown?" Like Russell, Li Wei said that he had a globalist orientation, and critiqued the system of attachment to one nation.

Malik and Muhammed were both young men who argued with their Pakistani families about enlistment. Malik characterized his family's reaction as confusion due to "false information going around about the role of the United States in the world politics." When it became known in his small hometown that he joined the US military, Malik's family faced threats of violence. Muhammed considered his Pakistani's family security when he decided to enlist, and he kept it from them for a while. He knew that they would never approve: "I am a Pakistani who's joining an army for a foreign country. Worldwide, the connotation for the US military is not good." One of Muhammed's sisters opposed his enlistment because "she doesn't really like what the US military does as an institution. . . . The negative perception and the negative acts that the military has done in pursuing the US foreign policy." A brother opposed it from "a very ethical, moral, or even I'd say a political and religious point of view." Both Malik and Muhammed enlisted in large part as a way to stay in the US, despite their families' objections to this way of securing citizenship. Muhammed successfully naturalized, but Malik became mired in security clearances emblematic of the last years of the MAVNI program. Malik's keen proclamations of attachment to the US in the interview are likely connected to the danger he faced were he to return to Pakistan—danger that he highlighted in his petition for asylum.

Although enlistment in the US military can clearly be a pathway to social mobility and status in working-class communities, it is associated with working and lower middle classes, in contrast to being commissioned as an officer, which carries more prestige. Immigrants often bring their own class-based understandings of the military rooted in different national contexts. For example, Asian migrants on student and work visas tend to come from wealthier families, which might balk at the idea that one of their own enlists into the lower ranks of the US military—ranks that are stigmatized in India, China, Nepal, and Korea as unsuitable for those from their social class. Andrew, an immigrant from Malaysia, had this argument with his parents:

They [parents] don't even understand how the country works. And in Malaysia, the military is not a respectable, positive thing. Only people who are poor and people who don't have an . . . education join the military. It's a means to survive. Right, so it's completely different than the US where here, the military is treated very respectably, you know. Officers have bachelor's degrees, master's degrees, so like . . . they really didn't understand why I would want to do that. Like, be a private especially. Because being a private is just like, you know, according them, a very, a small, tiny soldier who is part of, like, a big unit. And, like, they're just, like, expendable really. If you're gone, you're just a number. So they were kind of like concerned about that. But I convinced them.

Note that Andrew recognizes the class structure within the US military as well, and his own placement within it as a private, not an officer. Other college students may become officers, but Andrew's lack of US citizenship channels him into lower ranks. Immigrants who came to the United States as young adults to attend college and then enlisted in the military must juggle contrasting social status hierarchies. In a way, they are taking a downward step by enlisting as privates despite their college education to take the upward step in securing permanent immigration status. The latter can seem worth the social demotion but requires negotiations within families and communities.

Families of immigrants, just as nonimmigrant families, supported enlistment of their youth passively or actively. Among people that I interviewed, this usually happened either because of limited alternative paths to social mobility or because of a militarist orientation of the parents themselves, particularly in regard to desirable masculinity.[76] Some immigrants in the military have parents who worked in militaries of countries other than the United States and thought of it as a positive experience, or who hold up military labor as honorable and character-building. For example, Xijin, an international student from China, explained that enlistment through the MAVNI program was a decision made by him and his family together: "My parents want me, both think that the military training is good for a man because it makes you stronger and [you gain] perseverance, and some skills. You learn like how to combat, how to survive in the world. It's also a good skill for a man." Minzhe's parents approved of his enlistment in the US military because of their political stance as dissidents in China.

INFORMATION AND PRESSURE FROM COMMUNITY AND PEERS

Outside the family, co-ethnic communities, peers, and social networks more generally play a role in the enlistment decisions of immigrants. Working-class immigrants of color are often embedded in social networks and communities that are targeted by recruiters and where many enlist due to the dearth of other employment or education options. Co-ethnic communities can discourage participation in the US military and can serve as a source of information through other immigrants who enlisted. Emmanuel, who came to the United States from Haiti at fourteen, told me that "Haitians generally do not have a good opinion about the military life, or military personnel, based on their experience. Because they always think military means war, killing, and all that." He thought this too, but persistently courted by a military recruiter in high school, he ended up changing his mind and becoming a career sailor. Mary's Kenyan immigrant community—as well as her mother—discouraged her from joining the military. Mary herself had doubts, afraid to be a woman in the masculine military environment. Yet she also got information about the military, and first began to think of it as a real option, because of her mother's Kenyan immigrant friend, whose sons enlisted. Mary's desperation to escape her miserable job and living situation pushed her to overcome her fear and she joined the army. Of course, immigrants, like nonimmigrants, are also influenced by their friends, neighbors, employers, classmates, roommates, and others in their lives. In fact, immigrants I spoke to often told me about such social connections with those who were veterans, and the way these connections could tip them toward enlistment. Peers are particularly important for immigrants who grow up in the United States or go to college as international students. Friends and classmates navigate recruitment together, or even go through enlistment together.

RECRUITERS: THE NICEST GUYS OR CAR SALESMEN IN UNIFORM?

It is the job of military recruiters to ensure a flow of workers into the military. Certainly, recruiters play a significant role for immigrants, whether these immigrants say they provided inaccurate information, tricked, or pressured them, or were honest and supportive mentors and role models. Recruiters operate within extensive marketing campaigns meant to entice youth to enlist and to convince "influencers" like family members to support that choice. The army alone spends around $400 million each year on advertising.[77] Some of the marketing campaigns have focused on specific racial groups, such as the army's Yo Soy El Army campaign, which targets Latinx immigrants and their families, as well as those who are US-born.[78] Especially early in the War on Terror, recruiters faced tremendous pressure to fulfill their quotas, leading to many instances of unethical behavior, such as false promises made in order to get youths to enlist.[79] There is evidence that recruiters promise recruits US citizenship and immigration-related assistance for the recruit's family members, even though these are both outside the purview of the military.[80] There are recruiters with specific ethnic and immigrant backgrounds and language skills that are dispatched to target immigrant communities.[81]

Immigrant youth don't just come across military marketing in their everyday lives; they are groomed for recruitment in school. Recruiters target low-income neighborhood schools, where students have limited career and college options, which helps feed the poverty draft.[82] They develop relationships with youth, painting military labor as an exciting adventure and a unique pathway to honor and heroism. When emphasizing skill development, recruiters often leave out the fact that there are no civilian versions of many military jobs and that veterans have higher unemployment rates than the general population.[83] There are a growing number of public schools that are military academies, which instill militarism and channel students into the military.[84]

Emmanuel had a scholarship to attend a local college in Florida, but a Marine recruiter came knocking on his door: "It was part of the whole recruiting strategy, you know, come and pick you up in nice car. The military does that. They drive you around, take you out to eat, and things like that, spend time with you. It's all part of mentoring. And I signed the paper, and I think it was right after high school, a month later, I was on the bus going to boot camp." Emmanuel said he went to one of the toughest high schools in Miami but stayed out of trouble due to his peer group. He recalled that the recruiters quizzed him about drugs and crime, and acted pleased with how clean his record was despite being in his stigmatized environment. Emmanuel explained further how he went from being a college-bound high school senior to joining the military instead:

Somehow, I didn't know all this, all the seniors that are going to graduate, they get their addresses, and he [recruiter] came in and, I don't know, I was like, "You look sharp, dude!" You know, I'm talking . . . he's like, "Yeah, you can look just like me if you want" [*laughs*]. So, he would come in and visit, we talk, but the whole time, I'm just like, "Man, that's . . . that sounds kind of like attractive, doing the military." I had a big old poster of a Marine in uniform, I had one of those up in my room, you know. And, then the closer I came to graduation, and I was like, that might be a good idea, to join the military. . . . So, the day I had the appointment to go [to the recruiting office], I just forgot about college, the whole thing, so the whole military just took over.

Emmanuel was interested in pursuing a medical career, and he ended up enlisting in the navy because the Marine Corps did not have a medical program. He retired after twenty years.

Like Emmanuel, other immigrants who grew up in the United States and enlisted out of high school were sometimes heavily courted by recruiters, who drove them around, fed them meals, and visited their homes. Even so, these immigrants' relationship to the recruiters was one of trying to convince the recruiter of their fitness for enlistment, particularly around not getting in trouble with the law and being open to deployment. In many cases, recruiters did not broach the subject of citizenship, and the immigrants may not have known to ask. For instance, when I asked whether her recruiter mentioned a faster path to citizenship, Mary, an immigrant from Kenya, said, "He didn't talk about citizenship. Because all I knew, I came with a green card so I have to stay, like, five years, to apply for citizenship. So, I didn't even ask about that." Mary did become a citizen through the military. Had she not, she would have been vulnerable to deportation, even as a veteran.

Immigrants who grew up in the United States tended to have more positive views of their recruiters. For example, Joaquim, who immigrated as a child, said his recruiter was one of the nicest guys he had ever met. Joaquim described a situation where he was trying to prove he was good enough to be recruited, and he appreciated the recruiter's forthrightness, including his insistence on getting Joaquim to commit to the risks of deployment. The recruiter went to the gym with Joaquim and other recruits to help them lose weight and get in shape. Joaquim summarized his experience with the recruiter as being akin to having an older brother. In fact, he thought the recruitment system itself was like a Big Brother program.

Joachim grew up in the United States. Those who arrived as adult immigrants could be far more cynical of recruiters, criticizing their recruiters' lack of understanding of the immigration system and their misrepresentation of the ramification of being an immigrant in the military, either purposefully or out of ignorance. Their relationship to the recruiters was one of recruiters trying to sell them enlistment, rather than convincing recruiters of their fitness. Particularly embittered were MAVNI recruits who signed their contracts but were not then shipped to basic training, stranding them in legal limbo. One explained that recruiters were like used car salesmen in uniform. Another said they were like taxi drivers at a foreign airport. Certainly, immigration issues subsequent to enlistment could shape how immigrants saw their recruiters in hindsight. Deported veterans may have had a positive view of their recruiters at the time of enlistment, only to realize years later that they were misled about naturalization, with dire consequences.

At the point of enlistment, noncitizens face issues that are specific to them. Because they lack citizenship, most military occupations are closed to them. Some recruiters are better at realistic explanations of military careers for immigrants than others. Miguel scored high on the ASVAB exam and was set to go into military intelligence, only to be told at the last moment that as a noncitizen he did not qualify:

So I took the ASVAB, the exam, and my recruiter said, "You did great! You can go in intelligence, whatever." But then the last day, right before I was supposed to, like the last week before I was supposed to ship out, I had ten days off, that's the other thing. I signed the paperwork and other people have like a year, they train for a year. I did nothing. I didn't even watch any war movies, I knew nothing. I just knew it was like a challenge and I wanted a challenge. And at the last minute he was like, "Yeah, there is no more intelligence, you will have to be in infantry." And

I said, "But I thought you said I was going to join intelligence?" And he is like, "But you want to be a Marine, right?" And again, I am twenty, I don't know anything. I am like, sure. Years later, I realize the severe difference between infantry Marine and a regular Marine.

This difference includes the nature of everyday work in the military and transferability of skills to post-military careers. Most importantly, it is a difference in risks that are faced in military work. Immigrants like Miguel joined the ranks most vulnerable to injury and death because these were the ranks open to him as a noncitizen. Here, again, we see how the immigration system helps channel immigrants into the ranks of military workers; their deportability is converted to expendability as military workers. Recruiters play an important role in enacting the bait and switch, dangling the carrot of careers and skills only to pressure immigrants to enlist into the lowest ranks.

When recruiters fail to inform and advocate, immigrants may not only lose career pathways but also suffer financial penalties by forgoing signing bonuses. Anildo, an adult immigrant with a college education he completed in Cape Verde, recounted losing a chance to enlist at a higher rank and missing out on a signing bonus:

Actually, there was a few more information that I found out later on after I join[ed] that he [recruiter] didn't mention to me then. Because when I came in, I already had my [bachelor's] degree from back home. I didn't know that I could transfer, get some credits. . . . So, that's one thing he missed. He didn't tell me that I could join, instead of joining at a lower rank; I would've got some rank already. . . . That was frustrating because I could get up some type of rank, could have made more money right away. And, I could've [gotten] a bonus for enlisting too. So, I didn't get no bonus to enlist for four years.

Recruiters may not know or share adequate information about citizenship acquisition with prospective recruits. This especially affects immigrants who grew up in the United States and have a lawful permanent residency. Unlike adult immigrants, they are less likely to be focused on immigration benefits and thus less actively promote their needs as immigrants in the immigration system in interactions with recruiters.

Enlistment in the military takes place in the context of family, friends, and communities. Immigrant youth negotiate their pathways to adulthood in relation to loved ones, pushing away some and building new connections with others. Young immigrant adults contend with desires for belonging and security amid complex and conflicting cultural expectations. Whatever immigrant enlistees' views on military recruiters at the time of enlistment or in retrospect, the interactions with recruiters can have weighty consequences for many years after the military enlistment contract is signed.

CONCLUSION

Immigrants enlist in the US military for all the same reasons that non-immigrants do, plus a few more that are specific to them as people born and sometimes raised elsewhere and living with the insecurities of their immigration status. They get pushed into the military by the dearth of viable job options, astronomically high college costs, and relentless recruitment and marketing. Some embrace militarism and seek to prove their masculinity. As immigrants, this sometimes means that their ideas about the military and war are shaped also by other national and cultural contexts, transcend borders, and complicate stories of patriotism.

Some green card soldiers are drawn to the promise of fast-track citizenship acquisition, but others, especially those who grew up in the United States, are not particularly attuned to this benefit as much as hoping for a steady wage, social status, or assistance with college costs. Immigrants may not even want to get US citizenship, even as they enlist in the US military. In addition to legal status, citizenship means belonging and rights. As for US-born racialized minorities, the military is seen by some immigrants as a tool for gaining access to belonging and rights for themselves and future generations. This immigrant strategy is situated in a hostile anti-immigrant context where immigrant rights are continually under attack and people of color bear the brunt of a white supremacist system regardless of immigration status. Is the strategy of performing military labor for the United States in exchange for access to citizenship in its broad and legal sense successful? Veterans who sustained life-altering moral, mental, and physical injuries and deported veterans provide cautionary individual tales. Collectively, however, we must ask, as anthropologist Roberto Gonzalez does: "What kind of society is it whose citizens define 'serving your country' in terms of employment with the military or intelligence agencies, as if other institutions didn't matter?"[85]

The process of enlistment itself is worth considering in detail, as initial promises and decisions about enlistment contracts shape subsequent working conditions, career paths, and even criminal and immigration outcomes. Too many of these enlistment stories point to the profound power imbalance between the military employer and the vulnerable youth it targets for exploitation. The next four chapters unravel the ways enlistment continues to haunt the naturalization process, military labor, separation from the military, and, finally, even ejection from the country.

3

THE MILITARY ROAD TO CITIZENSHIP

"It was funny because at the time I'm wearing this military uniform, and I got a bunch of awards for my service, one of which was a Purple Heart at that time. And I still kind of felt like, well, I'm finally, I'm finally an American!" Manuel laughed as he recounted his naturalization ceremony, which took place after his second deployment to Iraq. The Purple Heart was for being wounded during his first Iraq deployment, and Manuel told me it was kind of weird to still feel that naturalization was making him American.

Born in Mexico and brought to the United States as a baby by his parents, Manuel was a lawful permanent resident when he joined the Marines at age seventeen. He wanted to go into intelligence, but non-citizens are not able to work in that field, so he went with his second choice, infantry. Had Manuel gone into intelligence, he likely would not be as exposed as he was to injury in Iraq. So Manuel knew US citizenship meant something in the US military. There was just no time to make naturalization happen. After his first deployment and the injury, he was busy with physical therapy and trying to avoid being medically separated from the Marines.

A phone call with his mom during his second tour of Iraq prompted Manuel to go to the judge advocate general (JAG) office and ask for help with naturalization. Wasn't it supposed to be easier to be naturalized if you are in the military? JAG told Manuel that they could try to make it happen in Iraq, but it would be easier if he waited until he got back. Manuel chose to wait and went to the JAG office stateside. JAG officers asked him why he wanted to naturalize, and he said it was so he could reenlist and get a new job that required a security clearance and, hence, US citizenship.

Things moved quickly, if stressfully, from there. Manuel got the naturalization forms from JAG but little help in filling them out. Although he should have qualified for a fee waiver as active duty military, Manuel told me he took out a $500 or $600 loan to pay for his naturalization fee. Still in the military, Manuel spent his post-deployment summer juggling an intense training tempo and repeated trips to a US Citizenship and Immigration Services (USCIS) office to submit paperwork, get fingerprinted, sit for the naturalization interview, and attend the swearing-in ceremony. He recalled that it was difficult to ask for any time off, even using his own three yearly vacation days, because his command was prioritizing training.

Manuel studied for the civics test and passed his naturalization interview. USCIS asked him to attend the naturalization ceremony in uniform, and sat him in the front row of a massive auditorium filled with thousands of immigrants. He was nervous and excited, even as he thought of the weirdness of the occasion for someone who completed multiple tours of combat and had a Purple Heart. Recalling the oath of allegiance, Manuel said: "That was kind of cool because anybody that has joined the military has already done an oath of service that is essentially the same thing that you do when you do the citizenship ceremony, but it was kind of like a double swear-in. I think that was it in terms of recognition."

US citizenship is acquired by foreign-born lawful permanent residents of the United States through the process of naturalization. This process is lengthy, costly, and risky, but the outcome is an expanded set of legal rights and a measure of security and stability. Manuel's story illustrates how military labor can pose unique challenges as well as provide unique benefits for naturalization. Citizenship facilitates military careers, which was Manuel's goal, and by doing so, it can lower the risks of injury and death on the job. It also opens job opportunities in the civilian world, helps family members get naturalized, makes travel easier, and enables voting. Especially important at a time of increased criminalization of immigrants, citizenship protects from deportation.

In this chapter, I show the stakes of citizenship acquisition for military workers and the stakes for the military of having its immigrant workforce acquire citizenship. Aside from using it as a tool of recruitment, the military's facilitation (or lack of facilitation) of naturalization is a form of workforce management. Yet it also benefits from naturalizing its labor force because of more efficient allocation of human resources. In fact, Manuel's naturalization resulted not in him getting the job he wanted but in being reassigned to recruiting duty, capitalizing on his fluent Spanish. Below, I explain how the military naturalization process unfolded in four time periods (pre-2004, 2004–2009, 2009–2016, and post-2016), tracing the evolution of policies that provided support for citizenship acquisition only to be walked back a few years after implementation. Finally, I explore the complex meanings of posthumous naturalization of military workers who died in combat, diving into one poignant example. But first, I begin with the history of the military route to citizenship, and its differences and similarities to civilian naturalization.

EXPEDITED BUT NOT ALWAYS EASY: HOW TO GET US CITIZENSHIP THROUGH THE MILITARY

Military naturalization shares much of its process with civilian naturalization. Although rates of citizenship acquisition in the United States have been increasing since 2005, they remain low compared to similar settler colonial nations with mass immigration inflows, such as Canada and Australia. In 2015, only 67 percent of immigrants in the United States who were eligible for citizenship were naturalized.[1] In addition to relatively low uptake of citizenship among those who are eligible to apply, many immigrants, such as those without state authorization to live in the United States or those on work or student visas, do not have access to citizenship at all. In order to apply for US citizenship, immigrants have to have lawful permanent residency status, colloquially known as a green card. Access to this status is regulated by an immigration system that privileges family ties and professional skills, with numerical ceilings that make migration from countries with close migration ties to the United States, such as Mexico and the Philippines, very difficult. Those who do manage to become lawful permanent residents are eligible to apply for citizenship after five years of living in the United States (three years for spouses of US citizens) and are required to pass a civics and history exam, and demonstrate proficiency in English and good moral character. Filing fees for naturalization applications were $725 in 2022, not including any attorney fees that immigrants might incur.

Given the criminalization of immigrants and convergence of criminal justice and immigration systems, naturalization applications can result in deportations, with USCIS treating the process as the final chance to catch deportable immigrants.[2] With attacks on voting rights and moral panics about voter fraud, applicants for citizenship have been denied citizenship and even lost immigration status altogether because of ostensible voter fraud, sometimes because many motor vehicle departments merge driver's license applications with voter registration. Told by government workers to register to vote when applying for a license, these immigrants were later denied naturalization on the grounds of voter fraud, which is also grounds for removal from the United States.[3]

The process of naturalization for immigrants working in the US military differs slightly from civilian naturalization, primarily in how long one waits to be eligible. There are two military-specific naturalization provisions in the Immigration and Naturalization Act. Section 328—the peacetime provision—covers lawful permanent residents who "served honorably at any time in the US armed forces for a period or periods totaling at least 1 year." Section 329—the wartime provision—applies to those with or without lawful permanent residency who "served honorably in the US armed forces during a designated period of hostility."[4] They can even be eligible if they have an outstanding order of deportation or removal.[5] In 2002, then-president George W. Bush retroactively designated the period since the attacks of September 11, 2001, as one of official hostilities, and it was ongoing as of 2022. Until the imposition of the new requirement of 180 days of active duty or one year in reserves and new security screenings in 2017, immigrant workers in the US military were eligible for naturalization after just one day. There are two notable facts around military naturalization: it is in no way automatic, requiring the same application process as for civilians; and under wartime provisions, citizenship can be revoked if the immigrant leaves the military with a less-than-honorable discharge before five years.[6] Around 4 percent of all first-term military recruits are noncitizens.[7] Between 2001 and 2018, about 130,000 immigrants acquired US citizenship through the military.[8] In 2008, as much as a third of immigrants in the military were not citizens, as well as 18 percent of all veterans.[9] Like other noncitizens, these immigrants had limited—and continuously eroding—rights.

Although the focus of this book is on the early twenty-first-century military workers and military veterans, immigrants have worked in the US military since the beginning of the United States. Throughout US history, citizenship has been used to recruit, manage, and incorporate immigrants in the military. For instance, state militias in the Revolutionary War used citizenship as an enlistment incentive. Immigrants comprised a quarter of the Union Army, and, starting during the Civil War in 1862, immigrant soldiers qualified for naturalization after one year of waiting, rather than the usual five.[10] Nearly 200,000 immigrants naturalized through the military during World War I.[11]

At the same time, some groups of immigrant soldiers have historically been excluded from naturalization, such as Asian immigrants at the turn of the twentieth century. Although a small number of Asian veterans were able to successfully argue for their individual naturalization, for most, race trumped claims for deservingness based on military labor.[12] Moreover, people colonized by the US empire who participated in US armed conflicts, such as Filipinos in World War II, had limited, delayed, or no access to US citizenship, even as over 100,000 mostly European immigrants became citizens.[13] Contemporaneously, the US government deprived Japanese American soldiers of citizenship. This was not reversed until 1944, when interned Japanese Americans were offered the opportunity to fight for the United States in a segregated unit.[14]

Since the United States started the War on Terror, several policy developments have influenced the accessibility of citizenship to US military workers. In 2004, the National Defense Reauthorization Act made it possible to conduct citizenship interviews and ceremonies on military bases abroad, ushering in an era of all-military citizenship ceremonies in places like Kandahar, Afghanistan.[15] The ability to go through the naturalization process abroad made it easier for active duty military personnel to become citizens. Between 2001 and 2018, more than 11,000 immigrants

FIGURE 3.1

Naturalization ceremony held at the Joint US
Military Advisory Group Thailand in Bangkok,
August 8, 2011. U.S. Navy photo by Mass
Communication Specialist 1st Class Jennifer
A. Villalovos, © Commander, U.S. 7th Fleet.

naturalized overseas, predominantly in Iraq, Japan, South Korea, Afghanistan, and Germany (see figure 3.1).[16] Starting in 2004, naturalization fees were waived for those naturalized through the military. In 2008, USCIS streamlined the biometrics collection, allowing the use of fingerprints collected at enlistment. This occurred after a high-profile case of an immigrant soldier killed in Iraq on his way to get a new set of fingerprints for his naturalization application.[17] Under the guise of troop readiness and following publicized cases of family members of military workers facing deportation, USCIS instituted policies to temporarily suspend deportations of individual immigrant family members of military workers.

Thus, under parole-in-place, which became an official policy in 2013, USCIS could consider individual cases of undocumented family members, allowing some of them to adjust their status.[18]

Starting in 2009, USCIS piloted a program called Naturalization at Basic Training, first in the army, then in the navy, air force, and finally the Marine Corps, in 2013. The program was developed by Margaret Stock, an army lieutenant colonel, former West Point instructor, immigration attorney, and the architect of the MAVNI program, which is the subject of chapter 5, who would go on to receive the MacArthur Fellowship for her work on national security and immigration. Stock proposed Naturalization at Basic Training as a solution to address the criticisms the Department of Homeland Security was facing for delaying military naturalizations. She argued that building naturalization into basic training would be more efficient, elevate morale, and minimize legal problems.[19] Once the program was rolled out, many immigrants applied for citizenship during basic training and received it soon after successfully completing boot camp a few months later.[20] Despite the provisions meant to facilitate naturalization and avoid the need for posthumous naturalization, some military workers did not get US citizenship, and many others worked in the military before policies facilitating naturalization were implemented. Less obviously, there are also those who do not want to be US citizens, as well as those who face barriers in acquiring citizenship.[21]

The period of facilitated naturalization turned out to be brief. In 2016, the Obama administration introduced enhanced security screening requirements, which were subsequently ramped up further by the Trump administration and remain in place under the Biden administration in 2022. The new background checks were in addition to the already extensive and onerous checks conducted by the Department of Homeland Security. Naturalization at Basic Training was ended in 2018.[22] For many new immigrant recruits, it was now faster to apply for US citizenship as civilians.[23] Data from 2019 indicates a 70 percent decline in military naturalization applications.[24] In 2019, USCIS had drastically reduced the availability of naturalization services outside the United States, making fewer personnel available to conduct interviews and swearing-in ceremonies and limiting the locations to just four overseas sites.[25]

Just as naturalization in general has increasingly become criminalized, with the process used to identify deportable immigrants, so has military naturalization. USCIS uses the naturalization process to look closely at the applicant's file, including applications for previous visas and permanent residency, in order to detect what it considers fraud not caught during those earlier processes. This is reflected in the high denial rates and stories of military applicants for naturalization like that of Yea Ji Sea, whose plight garnered media attention. When Sea applied for naturalization through wartime provisions, USCIS uncovered what it characterized as fraud earlier in her immigration trajectory. Korean-born Sea moved to the United States as a nine-year-old dependent on her parents' temporary visas. When she aged out of that status, Sea got an international student visa, which USCIS alleged was fraudulent. The language school that had certified Sea's documents had been shut down for a scheme to create false immigration forms—a scheme that was run by a Customs and Border Protection agent.[26] Sea's naturalization application was delayed for years while she feared detention and deportation, until, with the help of the American Civil Liberties Union (ACLU), she was naturalized.[27]

Access to naturalization in the United States is limited, and the process can present hurdles and risks to eligible immigrants. Peacetime and wartime provisions for naturalization through the military speed up the wait for eligibility while imposing the same screening process as for civilians. There is a long history of connecting military labor to citizenship status in the United States, as well as exclusion of some immigrant military workers from citizenship. The War on Terror saw policies that facilitated naturalization through the military—until 2016, when securitization made military naturalization more fraught than civilian naturalization.

THE STAKES OF CITIZENSHIP

The literature on naturalization in the United States points to the significance of citizenship for increasing chances of building a secure life in the United States, through protection from deportation and having access to better job opportunities and family reunification.[28] As I discuss below, these benefits of naturalization extend to military workers. In addition,

US citizenship has a unique implication for immigrant military workers because it affects career opportunities to a larger extent than in the civilian sector. Not having citizenship not only stops or slows down promotion, but it can also make it more likely that an immigrant works in a military occupation that exposes them to a higher risk of injury or death. Unlike civilians, those who acquired citizenship through the military during wartime may have their naturalization revoked if they are "separated from the US armed forces under other than honorable conditions" before five years.[29]

Military naturalization is often framed as a reward for military labor, a transaction of paying back an immigrant for sacrifice and patriotism. While some immigrants themselves see it that way, they are also in a unique situation where they have already pledged an oath to the United States and promised to bear arms for it—when they enlisted. Thus, when they get naturalized, some immigrants feel that they are "double citizens" and assign a variety of meanings to getting citizenship compared to being sworn into the military. Working in the US military does not necessarily mean you want to be a US citizen; the naturalization process can elicit feelings of loss, serious doubts, and even resistance.

Pursuant to the 1996 immigration legislation, lawful permanent residents face detention and deportation if convicted of a wide variety of crimes classified as aggravated felonies. This is retroactive, so even those who were convicted of crimes years before could nevertheless lose their status in the United States and be deported.[30] Military workers who have not become naturalized also face detention and deportation. The consequences of not having US citizenship are exacerbated for veterans, who have higher rates of homelessness and PTSD-related issues than the general population.[31] When these veterans come into contact with the criminal justice system, they can be deported as there are no special provisions in immigration courts for US military veterans.[32] Hundreds and maybe thousands of noncitizen veterans have been deported to their countries of birth, where most cannot access their veteran benefits[33] (see chapter 6 on deported veterans).

My interviews with immigrant veterans revealed that some of them seek naturalization defensively, to protect themselves from deportation.[34] When I asked Angel, who was born in Mexico and grew up in the United

States, how he felt at his naturalization ceremony, he said: "It felt good because knowing that, hey, you don't have to worry about being deported back, or you don't have to worry about having to reapply for your green card." Angel worried about applying to renew his green card because if he were to be denied, he would become undocumented. And he had frequent reminders of what the undocumented life was like from several undocumented members of his family.

Like Angel, Gilberto was from Mexico and had immigrant relatives to remind him of the protection US citizenship afforded. In his case, two of his cousins who had lawful permanent residency were deported. In reflecting on naturalization, Gilberto said:

Mostly it was relief that I wouldn't have to deal with immigration anymore. . . . And, then again, feeling secure that for whatever reason, I can't be deported anymore. If you mess up. I mean, some people they get in car accidents . . . you know? DUIs [driving under the influence], they can get deported too. You know, for making mistakes and . . . so that was always a fear of mine, what am I going to do in Mexico? Yeah, I have a lot of family there, but I'm not from there anymore. I don't identify with that culture anymore. So that was always a fear in the back of my mind. Not that I'm a criminal. Not that . . . I'm out committing felonies, but it was always one of those worst-case scenarios for me. . . . In fact, to this day, I, I still fear going to prison. . . . Even though I don't do anything wrong. . . . This is America, innocent people go to prison, you know? So, that's always been one of my biggest fears, is going to jail and getting deported. So, for me it was a huge relief, knowing that no matter what, I will never have to leave this country.

As Gilberto points out, immigration enforcement priorities are such that a drunk driving conviction could get someone deported. Moreover, Latino and Black immigrant men, like their citizen counterparts, face widespread criminalization, which puts them at risk of deportation.[35] Many immigrants in the military do not think US citizenship is a big deal or that different from having a green card. Why were Gilberto and Angel so attuned to the protection citizenship gives from deportation? Because both had intimate experience with illegality from close family members who were undocumented.[36]

In a gendered twist, a few women that I interviewed viewed citizenship as emancipatory. Truda, who immigrated to the United States from Poland, feared losing her green card as her marriage was falling apart. Her immigration status derived from her husband. She shared a similar sentiment about her naturalization ceremony as Gilberto and Angel: "I was so proud when I received my certificate. It was just . . . It felt so much different. I'm like, 'They finally can't do anything to me. . . . They can't deport me anymore.'" Similarly, Amy was not escaping a bad marriage, but citizenship acquisition for her meant independence from her traditional Chinese immigrant parents. I asked Amy how things might be different for her without US citizenship. She said: "Probably going to be like a traditional Chinese woman, just like my mom, very submissive, not really adventurous, doesn't really have a lot of skills and taking shit from her husband. And probably two or three kids and trying to struggle." Truda and Amy saw naturalization as a way to establish stability independent of male partners.

Research on the civilian population reveals that many immigrants view naturalization as a natural part of the immigration process, one that follows from settling in the United States, establishing families, careers, and social ties to place. In researching my first book, *The Road to Citizenship*, I was surprised by how many naturalizing immigrants said, "Why not?" when I asked them why they applied for naturalization. At the same time as they saw naturalization as a normal pathway to follow, many immigrants were variously interested in specific benefits of naturalization, including sponsoring family members' migration and access to jobs.[37] These motivations found in the civilian population came up in my conversations with military workers as well. Several immigrants connected getting citizenship to sponsoring the status of their parents. Emmanuel's mother fell ill and—after many years of equivocating—he rushed to file for naturalization so he could sponsor her migration from Haiti. Tragically, she died before he was able to do so. The primary benefit that James, an immigrant from Jamaica, saw with US citizenship was: "If I didn't become a citizen, I know my mom wouldn't be here right now." Joe's parents were already living in the United States, but they were undocumented. Himself a DACA recipient, Joe enlisted through the MAVNI program on the basis of his Chinese-language skills. After he became a citizen at the end of basic training in 2016, he successfully petitioned for his parents' lawful permanent residency. Thus, naturalization can be a way to reunite with or assist family members.

Whereas many civilians appreciate that having a US passport can facilitate international travel, travel benefits of US citizenship were not as prominent for military workers. I learned that especially for those who worked in the military before the latest securitization measures, their military ID served as a passport to much of the world and facilitated travel across borders. Emmanuel explained that "a lot of military members that I've worked with didn't even have passports. But they've been everywhere. You see what I'm saying? They use the military ID and of course, that became their passport."

Some jobs, particularly in government and in firms contracting with the government, require US citizenship. Immigrants who had been in the United States on temporary student and employment visas, especially, associated US citizenship with expanded job opportunities. Heena, who supported herself and her family with a below-minimum-wage job before enlisting, said: "This can give me so many opportunities than just working at a gas station. I felt like it opened many doors for me." For temporary visa holders, employment opportunities are drastically limited. Immigrants with green cards usually did not see that much of a difference in civilian employment opportunities between the immigration status they already had and US citizenship. Nevertheless, certain civilian jobs do require US citizenship, including much of law enforcement, which is not an uncommon career pathway after military work. Anildo, who immigrated from Cape Verde with a green card, became a police officer after leaving the military, which he could not have done without US citizenship. He had not been aware of this at the time, nor was yet planning to be a police officer, but rather saw naturalization as one of the benefits to collect from the army: "Why not? And try to become a US citizen and maybe, you know, that would help me out in the long run. . . . At that time, I didn't think about it. Just, some opportunity came up. I was trying to use every benefit you can get in the army back then." As we can see from Anildo's explanation of how he thought about citizenship, some immigrant military workers did not see a significant difference between having a green card and being a citizen.

While few civilian jobs, such as police officer, are reserved for US citizens, many military occupational specialties require US citizenship. This is often because of the required security clearances. In addition, officer ranks are reserved for US citizens. As I described in chapter 2, many immigrants I interviewed were not particularly interested or aware of the fast track to citizenship when enlisting. However, naturalization became more salient once they realized the limited job options available to them as noncitizens. When the army started to turn into a career for Filip, an immigrant from the Netherlands, he wanted to reenlist and was offered an instructor position that required a security clearance. Filip saw few career alternatives: "I'm trying to put myself back in those shoes, but I'm twenty-seven, twenty-eight years old. I don't have a college degree. My only marketable skills are infantryman in Iraq. I don't really have any savings. I don't want to go back to college. I like what I'm doing. So in order to keep doing what I'm doing, I need to change passports." Filip naturalized after eight years as a noncitizen in the military, and he did so reluctantly. Although he came to the United States as a child, he felt a strong attachment to his country of birth. On the day of his naturalization, he recalled bittersweet feelings: "I think I had more emotion about the fact that I knew my Dutch passport date was, the expiration date was coming up pretty quickly, and I wasn't going to be renewing it. So I think that was more of a sense of loss, the idea that I had never lived in the Netherlands but I've always been a Dutch national and I was allowing that to go away."

The United States has a de facto dual citizenship regime. Unless another country has rules prohibiting multiple citizenship, naturalized citizens can continue to have their other citizenships. In Filip's case, Dutch rules taking away citizenship from people living abroad long term and acquiring another citizenship did not make dual citizenship a possibility. This was also true for Fan, who was from China. Fan told me that there was "no real push for me to get it [US citizenship]." Until she became interested in becoming an officer in the army, she did not want to give up her Chinese citizenship: "Because in China, they never accept anything from a different country if you are [a] citizen." However, even when dual citizenship is possible for civilians, it is more difficult to maintain for military workers because it interferes with security clearances. For that reason, naturalization for immigrants in the military is more likely to result in loss of other citizenships than it is for the civilian population.

While some immigrants may be reluctant about naturalization because of a sense of loss in reference to their other citizenships, others may actively not want to be US citizens. Emmanuel, who did not naturalize in time to bring his dying mother to the United States, chose not to become a US citizen as a teenager. His father naturalized, which could have made Emmanuel a citizen as a dependent child, but he refused: "I didn't know any better. I've always been patriotic. So, it's like, I don't want to renounce my Haitian citizenship. I love my Haitian citizenship." A few years later, Emmanuel enlisted in the navy.

Some advocate for automatic naturalization for military workers, who, after all, already swear an oath to the United States. Automatic naturalization would eliminate posthumous naturalizations and deportations of veterans. However, as the stories of immigrants in this book indicate, enlistment in the US military does not always equal desire to naturalize.[38] Although I did not interview anyone who did not eventually develop an interest in US citizenship, a number of immigrants spent years undecided—while wearing US military uniforms. The interests of these immigrants would not be served by making naturalization automatic. In many cases, however, people do want US citizenship and face obstacles.

The pattern that I observed in my interviews with immigrants in the military is bifurcated when it comes to attitudes toward US citizenship. On the one hand, we have those who really want citizenship and even enlist in order to fast track it. These are often immigrants for whom a lot is at stake: they do not have a green card and/or they have an urgent situation that citizenship would repair. Or they do have a green card but experience vulnerability as racialized subjects of state violence or through proximity to precarious immigrants. On the other hand, we have immigrants who do not see a big change with naturalization. They are usually already lawful permanent residents. For instance, a Kenyan immigrant with a green card, Mary, did not understand the citizenship benefits of enlistment, nor was she told about them by the recruiter. She became a citizen, nonetheless, because of the Naturalization at Basic Training program, which was in place between 2009 and 2016, and realized that her naturalization process had been cheaper and easier than in the civilian world. Mary struggled to identify any benefits of citizenship. She said she did not know and had to think, eventually coming up with voting and jury duty. Five years after getting her US citizenship, Mary had not registered to vote, nor was she sure how to go about it.

Mary's experience of Naturalization at Basic Training was common in that immigrants were ushered through the process in the midst of grueling and intense weeks of boot camp. Sleep-deprived and physically and psychologically on edge, these immigrants often did not have much of a chance to reflect on citizenship. When they were sworn in as citizens, their feelings of euphoria and excitement were wrapped up with successfully completing basic training. For example, Kiran, an immigrant from Nepal, described being naturalized during basic training graduation this way: "My mom and my uncle was there, and I felt very proud, not just because I was naturalized. Because I completed that hurdle of my life, I would say. That was a big achievement for me to finish that training, because I didn't think I would be able to make it." Kiran then told me that nothing much changed with citizenship except that he can say he is a citizen now.

Whether or not naturalization felt like a big deal for them, some immigrants felt that they were already Americans.[39] Angel, who connected naturalization to protection from deportation, felt that he became more American when he signed his military contract. Between that signature and "going to combat, you do feel more American because you know what you're fighting for, you know the country that you're fighting for. . . . Because once you go out into combat, you're not fighting for Mexico or from whatever country you're coming from. . . . The United States sent you there, so it's like hey, that's my country. I'm an American ambassador on a different soil, fighting for my country. And the citizenship is just a piece of paper." Muhammed, from Pakistan, said he already felt like an American, not even from his work in the military: "I don't know who it was, either Ronald Regan or somebody else. I think it was FDR [Franklin Delano Roosevelt] who said that being an American is a feeling. If you are an American, you just know. It's in your heart. And I feel that. It's a feeling. In your heart, you know? If I always felt like an American, a piece of paper's not going to change me. It's going to protect me from the system that is vicious and unforgiving. But in my head, I always felt like an . . . well, not always, but I've felt like an American for a long time."

Even though immigrants in the military might already feel American, naturalization can bring a sense of belonging and empowerment to claim full rights. Some also see it as transactional: citizenship in exchange for military labor. Thus, Fajing, who came from China on a student visa, said that getting US citizenship after a tough time in boot camp made him feel that he earned and deserved it. A few juxtaposed military naturalization to other ways of getting citizenship in a way that valorized the former. For instance, Anna, a Ukrainian immigrant who enlisted through MAVNI, explained her pride this way: "To me, it meant so much more. Some people, they just wait because they know they are going to get it. They have wives, family members, or something like this. They just know it's coming because they have a green card for five years and now it's time to get citizenship. . . . It's better to give people a chance to earn citizenship instead of doing all these things that are less than honorable. I'm really happy to have a chance to say that I earned my citizenship." Thus, some immigrants use military naturalization as a chip in the deservingness politics. This makes sense because, like Anna, these are immigrants who did not come with a green card and are seen to fall short of the often-impossible standard to "stand in line" and immigrate legally. Anna came on a visitor's visa instead. Given the suspicion she faces as an Eastern European woman of cheating the system by marrying for immigration status, her ability to point to her military uniform as a source of citizenship is likely a relief, even as it allows her to stay in the United States, obtain US citizenship for her daughter, and reunite with her mother.

So far, I have considered naturalization from the perspective of immigrant workers. However, the military itself has stakes in the naturalization of its immigrant workforce. The military uses citizenship to recruit immigrants in times of pressure to meet enlistment goals during the ongoing War on Terror. Once the immigrants have enlisted, the military has a lot of control over immigrants' access to naturalization, either to hinder or facilitate it. Citizenship serves as a technology of labor. Active-duty military life makes it difficult for immigrants to file for citizenship. As I describe in more detail below, without a program like Naturalization at Basic Training, immigrants are at the mercy of their superior officers to release them to travel to their immigration appointments or to gather necessary documents and biometrics. It is not difficult to imagine a situation where an immigrants' desire to naturalize is used by their managers as an exploitative tool in the workplace, or where these managers simply prioritize work tasks over days off needed to complete naturalization applications.

The promise of citizenship can shape the way immigrants perform as military workers. For instance, those to whom naturalization is important will worry about being separated from the military before they get naturalized, or even after, lest they lose the citizenship they obtained through the military. Ravi, an immigrant from India, was worried about getting injured during training: "My constant fear was that even if I . . . if my foot hurt or my head hurt, I never went to see the doctor because I knew that if something is more wrong than it's supposed to, it may cause me disqualification. A medical discharge. And if you have a medical discharge then you're not eligible to be a citizen." At the same time, granting citizenship to immigrant soldiers benefits the US military as an organization, as citizens can fill officer positions and obtain security clearances.[40] Without citizenship, some military personnel cannot be shifted to occupational specialties or promoted to ranks that are needed.

Noncitizens can present public relations problems for US military marketing, not only because their presence raises suspicions of disloyalty and spying, but because it undermines the image of the military as a successful assimilationist and diverse institution to have noncitizens be killed in action. When noncitizen soldiers were among the first Iraq War casualties on the US side, it raised uncomfortable questions for the military and threw a public spotlight on the recruitment and enlistment of immigrants.[41] Overall, the military, as an institution, likely benefits from having all of its immigrant workers gain citizenship. On the micro level between management and workers, however, access to citizenship becomes another factor that can be used in disciplining immigrant labor. The effects of the latter should not be underestimated, especially as military naturalization becomes increasingly more difficult, as I describe next. We must also keep in mind that the complexity of what US citizenship means to different immigrants cannot be flattened into patriotic narratives. They may or may not want to naturalize or see much reason to do so. And their reasons vary widely from protection from deportation to facilitation of military careers to sponsoring family members.

Even when immigrants are eager to become US citizens, the military naturalization process may not be easy to navigate. Legal scholar Ming Hsu Chen notes a gap between military naturalization policies and their implementation in the general enforcement context of the early twenty-first century. Chen found that military officers did not understand immigration processes and recruiters misrepresented how easy it would be to become naturalized. Immigration officials, on the other hand, did not sufficiently account for the conditions of military labor that made already onerous immigration applications more difficult.[42] Applying for naturalization is an involved and lengthy process that can be stressful and difficult to manage for civilians. Many immigrants engage the services of immigration attorneys to get through the application process, and many others are deterred from applying by the hurdles or lack of funds. Getting the necessary forms, biometrics, fees, and keeping appointments with immigration officials is made that much more difficult for military workers, particularly those who are on active duty.

Immigrant military workers have different experiences with naturalization, from extreme obstacles to applying for citizenship to a quick and streamlined process with proactive assistance by the military. Much of the variation is due to the changes in policies over time, particularly the recent era of naturalization facilitation, and what matters is the period in which one enlisted. Thus, immigrants who enlisted before 2004 rarely got any help or information when applying for naturalization and experienced multiple military-related obstacles. Things improved somewhat between 2004 and 2009, and a more dramatic improvement took place for those who enlisted after 2009. Given the most recent changes in 2017 and 2018, the pre-2004 period provides a sense of how naturalization may unfold for those enlisting in the 2020s. Below, I explain the differences in naturalization processes for immigrants by era of enlistment, as well as additional factors that affected naturalization, such as age, race, contextual factors such as recruiters' and superior officers' knowledge and willingness to help, and mode of enlistment. Even as the policies changed over time, citizenship remained a way for the military to attract and manage the immigrant labor force.

DOING LITTLE OR WORSE, PRE-2004

Immigrants who enlisted in the military prior to 2004 tended to get little or no assistance in applying for citizenship. Many recruiters were not familiar with relevant immigration processes and did not inform immigrants about the military naturalization process upon enlistment. The military played at best a neutral role in their naturalization, and active duty working conditions often presented obstacles to obtaining US citizenship. Soldiers deployed overseas had to be physically present in the United States to be naturalized. Frequent moves common in the military did not align well with mail-based communications between the USCIS and immigrant applicants, leading to miscommunication and missed deadlines. Earlier in the chapter, I quoted Angel, a Mexican immigrant who associated naturalization with protection from deportation. Angel enlisted in 2002 as a teen and wanted to become a US citizen but ended up going through the process entirely outside the military years later:

ANGEL: So the whole immigration thing isn't that bad. The only time that it's hard is when you're trying to apply for your citizenship. You know, because I tried doing it through the military and I got frustrated with it, I just said hell with it. And I did it through the outside, through a regular person. And I was able to get it done a lot faster.

SOFYA: Really? Okay, tell me about that.

ANGEL: Well, see . . . as a military vet, while you are active duty, you have to go through certain processes: you have to go get your own records, you have to go obtain all the information that you need yourself. So it's like you have to take the time out of your schedule to obtain all the information that they need. You know they don't do anything for you. So, in other words, it makes it a lot harder because now you got to take time off of work to go get what you need. So it's a chance that either you can do it or you can't, because if they really have you occupied then you're not really going to be able to take that time to go down to the DMV [Department of Motor Vehicles], or down to the courthouse or wherever it is that you have to go. You know, so for me I tell everybody it's easier to save up some cash and do it outside.

SOFYA: So . . . you waited until you were out?

ANGEL: No, I was still active duty but I was married during the time and my ex-wife's aunt had known of an immigration lawyer not too far from where we lived at and when I went out there, I was talking to the immigration lawyer. I paid $500 to get all my documents done and through that I was able to go through the whole process, and I was able to get my citizenship.

By the time Angel obtained US citizenship, he had been a Marine for four years, even though he was immediately eligible for citizenship after enlisting.

There was no assistance for naturalization for most of these immigrants while they were in the military. In fact, the realities of military labor presented considerable obstacles to the logistics of the naturalization process in some cases. When he enlisted, the recruiter mentioned to Juan that if he wanted to advance in the military, he would eventually need US citizenship. Juan, an immigrant from the Dominican Republic, was vaguely planning to deal with naturalization after his first contract expired, but once deployed to Iraq, he suddenly needed US citizenship in order to do his job. Despite his overall positive evaluation of the help he received, his description of naturalizing while deployed includes multiple snags in the process:

To be fair, it was during the beginning stages of the war. We went during the last part of the ground war. They called it the last surge of the ground war. . . . We got in country [Iraq] in January of 2005. So, they were backed up with a lot of different things. It was constant emails back and forth. At one point, my [naturalization application] packet was lost in Rome somewhere. . . . They couldn't find it and they didn't know what was going on. So, I was on standstill for a long time, and then it was found. And, then, they were trying to process it here because of, you know, somebody misplacing the file, and . . . It ended up working itself out, but it was frustrating because there were times where I'm just like, "I did my part and I just want it done now."

It took Juan about ten months to become naturalized. After his application was found, he learned that it could not be processed while he was in Iraq. Juan's fingerprints and photo expired, and he had to redo them when he returned from his deployment. As Juan put it, "I was basically with a bunch of other people that had other things to worry about."

Juan and Angel were at least to some degree knowledgeable about the naturalization process. Through interviews, I confirmed what the 2016 ACLU report found for deported veterans: some thought they had gained US citizenship through completing their military contracts, or even had been told by superiors that naturalization was automatic.[43] Rodrigo had not been deported. A Mexican immigrant who enlisted in the army in the 1970s, Rodrigo did, however, think that he became a US citizen automatically:

RODRIGO: Like I said, I assumed that because I had been accepted into service and I swore to defend this country and the oath that I took that that would automatically make me consider me to be a naturalized citizen.

SOFYA: So you thought that when you took the oath to enlist, to join the military, that would make you a citizen?

RODRIGO: No.

SOFYA: No?

RODRIGO: No, I didn't, it didn't come to mind. I just assumed that because of the oath that we took that would make me—not that I was looking for that, that's not what I was trying to do. But just because I did swore to this country and to defend this country then I would be considered as a citizen of this country.

SOFYA: Yes, because that oath, in that oath you swear allegiance, right?

RODRIGO: That's what it states!

In fact, Rodrigo traveled back and forth across the US-Mexico border for years, telling Customs and Border Protection agents that he was a US citizen and showing his military ID. It was not until further securitization of the border that he realized that he did not actually have any proof of his citizenship. Had Rodrigo been convicted of a felony, he would have suffered the same fate as the deported veterans I write about in chapter 6.

While many of my study participants who enlisted prior to 2004 had difficulties obtaining US citizenship while in the military, there were a few for whom the process went relatively smoothly. For some, this happened because they did not want to naturalize until years after enlistment, when some structures were in place to support naturalization in the military. Had they applied sooner, they would have likely experienced problems. But others had smooth naturalization experiences prior to 2004. For instance, Emmanuel reported his naturalization process as being uneventful, taking seven months total. Maude, an Irish immigrant, enlisted in the 1970s, a year before Rodrigo, the army veteran who thought he became a citizen automatically. Unlike teenage Rodrigo, Maude was a mother of two in her thirties and had wanted to apply for citizenship for a while. She was able to naturalize once in the military. Almost thirty years later, Anildo, an immigrant from Cape Verde, had a similar story as an older enlistee who was motivated to obtain US citizenship and was able to do so relatively painlessly. What Emmanuel, Maude, and Anildo have in common is that in the context of few special provisions for immigrants in the military seeking naturalization, they not only were motivated to seek citizenship but also were older (in their late twenties and thirties). Their years of experience likely helped them figure out the naturalization process, in contrast to those who, like Rodrigo, Juan, Angel, and others, enlisted as teenagers. Overall, the pre-2004 period is marked by lack of help for immigrant military workers to get US citizenship.

GRADUAL IMPROVEMENT, 2004–2009

Acquiring citizenship through the military became somewhat easier for those enlisting between 2004 and 2009. Some got assistance through the naturalization process, while others continued to experience difficulties. Truda got a call from the navy legal office asking her whether she would like to get US citizenship while she was still undergoing training for her specialty. They sent her to get fingerprinted and helped with the immigration paperwork. Another sailor and immigrant, Albert, likened the help he got from navy legal department to having a lawyer. Within a couple of months, Truda successfully completed the citizenship interview. However, the letter from USCIS informing Truda of her naturalization ceremony got to her after the fact: "Since I was living in the barracks, I received the letter of the swear-in after the date. . . . So, I called the number that was provided in the letter and I was like, 'Hey, I'm on the military base and all the mail is filtered through our command. . . . So, the letters go to our command and then they get distributed to us. So, I didn't get that letter after the date that I supposed to go and swear in.' They're like: 'Oh, that's not a problem. I'm going to set up a new date for you.' And they asked me if this new date is good for me." Truda went on to explain that the immigration officials were accommodating, offering to send an email rather than a letter. She contrasted her experience to that of civilians, who she thought would not receive such nice treatment. This opinion was informed by her own experiences with USCIS prior to enlisting.

The US Army veterans I interviewed had more of a mixed experience. Some experienced difficulties in obtaining US citizenship, while others did not. Joaquim, a Brazilian immigrant who enlisted in the army in 2008, was unable to naturalize until he came back from his deployment in Afghanistan. For the first two years, while he was working in the United States, he had difficulty finding time to apply for citizenship: "When you're a soldier, you get up at five thirty in the morning. You don't come home until six, seven o'clock. You know, half the time, I was trying to . . . My first two years in the army, I was trying to go to sleep at eight, nine o'clock at night." In Joaquim's case, a senior officer, himself an immigrant, encouraged Joaquim to apply for naturalization, and provided help in negotiating military bureaucracies. Joaquim submitted his application, then was deployed to Afghanistan, and had to wait until he came back to become a US citizen. Vaclav, an immigrant from Slovakia, on the other hand, naturalized while deployed in Afghanistan. He needed a security clearance to work on certain missions and his superiors encouraged him to get citizenship. Here again, we see how citizenship is used by the military to manage its labor force. Vaclav was sent from his base to the large base in Kandahar in what he characterized as a two-week vacation of sorts, easily completing the naturalization process and taking the oath of citizenship.

John, a Malaysian immigrant in the army, was naturalized while stationed in Korea. His story shows both some support and continuing difficulties of being a naturalization applicant and a military worker at the same time. He was encouraged to apply for US citizenship by his superior officers, who wanted him to advance in rank. The legal department helped John fill out his naturalization paperwork a year into his enlistment, which he appreciated because it was very difficult to find the time to deal with the process while on active duty:

When in the service, it's kind of different when you are out on the field or working or doing something on a mission. You can't, you don't even have the time to deal with all this legal paperwork. . . . That's the reason why they make it easier for you. You don't want to get interrupted: "Oh, you know what? You have to go and do all this legal paperwork. Yeah, you can take off, you can go." No! There is no such thing. You have to be there 24/7. You are a soldier. You are 24/7 . . . . People can call you anytime to get up to, you know, do your work or something like that. So we just don't have time to deal with all this legal paperwork.

Unfortunately, John's paperwork was lost, and for seven months, he repeatedly called USCIS offices, only to be told to keep waiting. By the time he got his citizenship, he had suffered a career-ending injury. Had he gotten his citizenship sooner, he may have avoided this fate by advancing in rank. More generally, not having US citizenship can expose immigrants to increased risk of injury and even death because it keeps them out of many of the less risky occupations in the military. Even when their superiors pushed US citizenship because the military itself benefited from the naturalization of these immigrant workers, the process could be full of pitfalls, with serious consequences for the immigrants.

Joaquim, Vaclav, and John were naturalized after the change in immigration law allowed naturalization ceremonies to take place abroad. Yet Joaquim had to wait until he returned from Iraq, which indicates that this change did not translate uniformly into practice. Unlike John and Vaclav, who had immigrated as teenagers and spoke English with non-US accents, Joaquim immigrated as a child. He said that people in the army tended to assume that he was already a citizen: "Nobody, nobody ever questioned my citizenship. They just assumed. You know? Like, I'm a white, I'm white, so . . . they just assumed."

It is possible that the pressure to naturalize experienced by Vaclav during his deployment in order to meet the needs of his unit was not the same for Joaquim because his superiors were not reminded of his lack of citizenship. Albert, who said he had an easy naturalization process, nevertheless reported that a superior officer "looked at me like I'm joking" when he mentioned wanting to get his immigration paperwork done because this European immigrant spoke with a US accent. Thus, it seems that race and accent can play a role in how immigrants experience naturalization in the military: being racialized as white and nonforeign can actually slow down citizenship acquisition. With these caveats in mind, the policies of 2004–2009 provided increasing support for naturalization in the military, with a decisive leap forward with the institutionalization of the Naturalization at Basic Training program in 2009.

NATURALIZATION AT BASIC TRAINING ERA, 2009–2016

Immigrants who enlisted between 2009 and 2016 had a much easier time with the naturalization process, especially in the army, which was the first to adopt Naturalization at Basic Training. As part of this program, most got naturalized at the end of combat basic training, also known as boot camp, or soon after. Preparation for the citizenship exam and the filing of paperwork took place during basic training, with assistance from the military, as well as support from fellow immigrants going through the process. By all accounts, the juxtaposition of basic training and the naturalization process was intense. James, an immigrant from Jamaica who enlisted in the army, recounts:

In between the drill sergeants yelling at you and just berating you with, with physical and strenuous stuff, they would gather all the immigrants, or they said everybody who is a resident, we need you all to meet in this room and, we're going to take you down to this building. . . . They carted us in a bus, they took us down to Atlanta. . . . Immigration officers from down in Atlanta come up and they sat us down in a room, they give us all the paperwork. They said, "This is what you need to fill out, we need, you know, birth certificate, your residency cards, all the information that we need from you, we're going to walk you through step-by-step how to fill this process out." Did all the paperwork right there. . . . They took it with them, they went back, and it was like, probably . . . I was in the beginning of basic training, I say, by week four? Like, they came back, they did a ceremony, they lined us all up. I, we walked up there, they give us the naturalization paper. They took pictures and that was it.

The new program that instituted naturalization assistance within the framework of basic training no doubt increased the likelihood of naturalization for many immigrants in the military. However, even with these improvements in place, there were ways for immigrants to slip through the cracks. Ranil, who enlisted soon after migrating as a teenager from Sri Lanka, broke his leg during basic training, delaying his naturalization:

RANIL: I was actually afraid to ask, like, how come some people got their citizenship in boot camp and why I didn't get my citizenship, you know, because I think, like, on the day of the graduation from boot camp, actually I think three or four people had naturalization ceremony as part of that and they actually even mentioned them during the graduation, like, so-and-so became a citizen on this day as well, so I was wondering, like, what is the process and, like, why I didn't get to do that.

SOFYA: So did you ever find out why?

RANIL: I didn't actually find out why but I think the reason was that since I broke my leg and I had to be sent to another division, like, my paperwork nobody ever followed through my status and all that stuff. That might be the reason, I think . . . I think maybe I had transferred from the first division and then by the time that I went to the second division it was probably already late. I'm assuming that's why I was, I fell through the cracks. But I think, I know that when I went to the A School, it was not only me, there was about five or six people who actually got the citizenship the same day as I was, who also [were] in the second phase of training with me. So, I don't know exactly how that works. I think, like, it all depends on their, what we called RDCs [Recruit Division Commanders, equivalent to drill sergeants], like the instructors in the boot camp, they take initiative to actually ask the recruits and make it happen, otherwise I don't think, like, it will happen. It's no automatic process. You know, in the boot camp, if you want to get it, I think it is at the mercy and kindness of the instructor who had to take the initiative and let you know because it was a very controlling environment. But I think after that, I think, like, once you finished all your training and you still don't have citizenship, I think you could actually do it, you could initiate it yourself and go to the legal and ask them how to do this. But usually, I think, in the boot camp, it's completely in the control of the instructor.

Ranil's emphasis on the role of drill sergeants in controlling access to naturalization for new recruits highlights the way citizenship is used in the military as a tool of labor management. In this case, it takes place during an especially grueling period of military labor, when immigrants are purposefully forced through physical and mental violence into conformity with their role as military workers.

Brian, a white immigrant from Canada, did not naturalize in basic training, but not for the lack of trying. Brian's experience, like that of Joaquim, Filip, and Albert in the previous section, is an example of how being seen as already a citizen because of race and accent can hamper efforts to naturalize. Brian was mocked when he responded to the drill sergeant who asked, "Who's got immigration issues?" in basic training, which turned out to be the gateway to naturalization. Brian felt that his superiors suspected him of trying to get out of something, and he watched from the sidelines as his classmates got naturalized at boot camp graduation. Later, in Advanced Individual Training, Brian had to "pester" superiors to allow him time necessary to apply for naturalization, some of whom did not believe that he was an immigrant. After multiple two-hour drives to the nearest USCIS office, he finally succeeded in obtaining US citizenship. Brian's racialization as a white US man made it more difficult for him to naturalize. At the same time, his experience points to the entrenched racial hierarchies within the military, which integrates immigrants like Brian into a different social position, closer to belonging than his immigrant peers racialized as foreigners.

Immigrants enlisting in the US military between 2009 and 2016 were able to take advantage of a naturalization process that was better tailored to their needs as military workers than the situation presented to immigrant enlistees only a few years earlier. Although their situation was improved, there were still ways for vulnerable immigrants to stumble on the path to citizenship through the military. Interestingly, some of the immigrants who enlisted before Naturalization at Basic Training and were not particularly interested in citizenship probably would have naturalized through this program, were it available. When I explained how naturalization was then built into boot camps, Miguel, who had taken a while to naturalize, told me: "If I had had that option, I totally would have done it." The facilitation of the process, the collective nature of the experience, and the way naturalization was built into boot camp and promoted by the management could sway those uncertain about citizenship. For many, there was more support through the process, but also less breathing room to consider the complexities of their desires.

The new security screening requirements imposed on noncitizens in the military made the path to naturalization for those recruited after 2016 difficult, likely more so than prior to 2004. USCIS statistics indicate a decline of 23 percent in military naturalizations between 2016 and 2017.[44] Between 2017 and 2018, military naturalization applications declined by 72 percent, and the number approved declined a further 59 percent.[45] At only 2,588, military naturalizations in 2020 were 71 percent lower than they were in 2016.[46] The Biden administration failed to reverse or make less onerous the policies imposed on immigrants in the military by the Trump administration—even after the US District Court for the District of Columbia vacated these policies and directed the DOD to comply. In 2022, the DOD instead continued to implement the policies while the Biden administration appealed the court decision, despite Biden's own 2021 executive order calling for a plan to facilitate military naturalization.[47] The bipartisan push to exclude immigrant military workers from citizenship means that most noncitizen enlistees will have to wait until separating from the military to file for naturalization as civilians. Those who enlisted in 2017 started to leave active duty in 2021. Without facilitated naturalization, it appears likely that the pool of deportable veterans will grow.

Even during the years that naturalization was facilitated for military workers, it was not automatic. Nor are all military naturalization applications approved. Between 2003 and 2015, USCIS approved over 88,000 military naturalization applications. But an *Al Jazeera* investigation found that 7,255 naturalization applications were denied in that time period. An unknown number were administratively closed, which adds to the number of immigrants who do not obtain citizenship through the military.[48] Most were denied over poor moral character, which has long been among the criteria for US citizenship and can mean committing crimes, committing fraud earlier on in the immigration process, being what USCIS refers to as a "habitual drunkard," being part of the Communist Party, or some other, unspecified trait that the USCIS officer decides disqualifies an applicant from being considered a person of good moral character. Interestingly, poor moral character does not play as important a role in the denials of civilian naturalization applications.[49] Other reasons for denial of naturalization applications through the military include not responding to requests for more information—easy to imagine for immigrants deployed and moving from place to place. By 2019, denial rates for military naturalization applications had surpassed the civilian rate: 17 percent of military naturalization applications were denied compared to 11 percent of civilian applications.[50] Deemed good enough to enlist in the US military, some immigrants are subsequently deemed not good enough to receive citizenship by the US immigration authorities. In fact, in her work with deportees, legal scholar Beth Caldwell encountered veterans who had been deported for convictions that predated their military service, meaning that these convictions did not disqualify them for military service but made them deportable once they were retroactively reclassified as aggravated felonies years later.[51]

POSTHUMOUS NATURALIZATION

No account of immigrants in the military in the twenty-first century would be complete without posthumous naturalization. Although it is overshadowed by the devastation the US military has inflicted on Iraq and Afghanistan, military labor during the War on Terror came with considerable risk of injury and death for the military worker. By November 2019, there had been 7,028 military casualties in the five operations constituting the War on Terror.[52] When noncitizen military workers die in combat, they can be granted posthumous citizenship, which USCIS defines as an "honorary status commemorating the bravery and sacrifices" of an "alien or noncitizen national whose death resulted from injury or disease incurred on active duty with the US armed services during specified periods of military hostilities."[53] Over a hundred have been naturalized in this way.[54] Moreover, since 2004, surviving spouses, children, and parents can receive some relief from deportation and limited opportunities to adjust their immigration status.[55] Posthumous naturalization has to be initiated by surviving family members within two years of death.[56] Once posthumously naturalized, the immigrant is considered to have been a citizen when they died.[57]

When immigrant soldiers die while on active duty, making them citizens posthumously confirms that they died for a country that was theirs.

Posthumous naturalization allows a particular set of meanings to attach to their death, one that benefits the US military and does not disrupt dominant narratives of the War on Terror. The alternative is imagining the military as being staffed by foreigners—whether private contractors or exploited immigrants—because few "real" Americans are willing to fight for their country. Military labor is reframed as the American Dream worth dying for.[58]

In the fall of 2007, I attended a naturalization ceremony at City College in New York. Some 250 immigrants took the oath of citizenship in an airy hall of the college, presided over by immigration officials and university administrators. Unlike most naturalization ceremonies, this one had a somber note. One of those being granted US citizenship was Juan Alcantara, a young Dominican immigrant who had been killed in Iraq a month earlier. Representative Charles Rangel had the job of addressing the new citizens on that day. After speaking generally about the benefits that immigrants bring to the United States, as is typical of ceremony speeches of that era, Rangel turned to address Alcantara's family, seated in the front row.[59] Rangel remarked on Alcantara's dreams to join the police department and be a good father and husband, but then he spoke of his own story. Like Alcantara, Rangel had been part of the second infantry division of the army, albeit sixty years earlier. He said that when he thought about Alcantara not coming home, he thought of himself not coming home from the Korean War:

Would people be saying that I had been fighting the wrong war? Would they have condemned President Truman for sending me there? Would they have condemned the United Nations because I was there? I would hope not. I would hope that they would say that the late Sergeant Charles B. Rangel was a proud member of the Second Infantry Division. He was not a politician, he could not decide where my division was stationed on the border of North Korea or these days, Iraq. Because he took an oath to defend the flag, an oath to defend the flag, the flag, the flag. He took an oath that said when his Commander in Chief ordered him to defend the flag, he was to defend it for you, and for you, and for me, and for generations that follow. He took an oath that he was not going to challenge the political wisdom of where he was but that we could depend on him to defend this country as I would hope they would have said about me, if I didn't come home.

In his speech, Rangel had the tough job of making posthumous citizenship legible in the context of an unpopular war with mounting US casualties. He juxtaposed his own story of being attacked by Chinese soldiers in North Korea in 1950 and being one of the few survivors in his unit with Alcantara's death by explosives while searching a house in Iraq. Throughout his speech, Rangel struggled to separate the honor he wanted to associate with Alcantara from criticism of the war. He painted both the younger version of himself and Alcantara as loyal people "that don't have the political opportunity to determine whether certain wars are right or wrong," and thus to be spared criticism as tools of empire. The comparison between Iraq and Korea was apt. Both were imperial wars that inflicted devastating damage on the land, infrastructure, and people they targeted, with long-term political, economic, and environmental effects. In both, the US military relied on workers who struggled in a deeply inequitable society stratified by race. Although Rangel did not mention it, some African American soldiers alongside him in Korea defected to the side of Communist China, convinced that their lives there would be better than in the United States and in the US military, where they faced racism.[60]

As one news story noted, Rangel, a critic of the Iraq invasion, "left politics at the door," insisting that what soldiers like Alcantara were doing was defending the flag, the country, and Americans, present and future.[61] In fact, he told the new citizens that it is because of soldiers like Alcantara that they could become citizens "in the land of freedom." Rather than commenting on the goals or tactics of the war on Iraq, Rangel sketched the distinguished genealogy of the Second Infantry Division. He spoke of the uniform that he shared with Alcantara, and described the division shield: a white star on black, with an "Indianhead." In fact, the Second Infantry Division's shield does feature a stereotypical image of a Native American, with red skin and blue feather headdress. This shield is just one of numerous ways that the US military uses Native American languages and images: think Apache helicopters and Tomahawk missiles. The US military uses "Indian Country" for Iraq and Afghanistan, just as it had for Vietnam. It used the code name Geronimo for Osama Bin Laden, drawing a parallel to the Apache warrior who fought colonizer aggression.[62] The evocation of the Second Infantry shield in Rangel's speech betrays the fallacy of separating the US military from the wars it fights simply as a collection of loyal individuals following politicians' orders. As an institution, the US military has its foundation in indigenous genocide and enforcement of slavery, yet baked into US culture are stories of aggression presented as self-defense, whether of settlers fighting off indigenous attacks or US soldiers besieged in North Korea and Iraq.[63] Every Indianhead decorating the soldiers of the Second Infantry Division is a reminder that the United States continues to be a settler colonial nation with imperial strategies long honed on violent oppression of indigenous people.

Meanwhile, Alcantara's family members accepting posthumous citizenship on his behalf were angry. Alcantara was supposed to come home to New York after a year in Iraq, but his tour was extended. The military denied his request for leave so he could be there for the birth of his daughter, who would now never meet him. In interviews with the press, Alcantara's fiancée said that his posthumous naturalization "didn't make any sense." Alcantara's mother was blunter: "Bush killed him. . . . He'd already done a year. He deserved to be home." With Bush's presidential address to new citizens playing on a large screen, she lowered her head.[64] Alcantara enlisted to pay for college. He worked service jobs through high school and then used his military pay to help support his mother and sisters. In other words, Alcantara was part of the poverty draft. As Hector Amaya notes, giving posthumous citizenship to dead soldiers like Alcantara "failed to acknowledge that the Armed Forces is structured to attract mostly the poor and the non-white."[65] As we can hear in Rangel's speech, posthumous citizenship upholds the liberal myth of the US military as a patriotic institution manned by honorable volunteers defending the nation and American freedom. But, to paraphrase the refrain of antiwar veterans, what were American freedoms doing in the Iraqi house where Alcantara and his fellow soldiers met their deaths by a homemade bomb?

What's more, Alcantara was from the Dominican Republic, which was occupied by the US military for eight years in the early twentieth century, an occupation that set the stage for what Latinx studies scholar Lorgia García Peña calls "the permanence of the 100-year marriage between Dominican politicians and US-backed corporate exploitation of the Dominican poor."[66] The US military played a central role in disrupting and displacing Dominicans, who then became another source of labor for it, sent as military workers to places like Iraq. The granting of posthumous citizenship without consent to deceased military workers evokes the history of the imposition of US citizenship on Mexican, Puerto Rican, and indigenous people as a way to bring them under imperial control, defeat their own national formations, and draft them into the military.[67] The historical cycles of empire alternately displace and absorb racialized populations. In this sense, citizenship may indeed be a tool of integration, as is often pronounced by scholars and policy makers, but it is integration into one's place in the global empire, not integration into full membership and rights afforded to the white and native-born.

CITIZENSHIP AS PROTECTION AND LABOR TECHNOLOGY

Hundreds of thousands of immigrants have acquired US citizenship through the military—and many tens of thousands have not. Although as people of color many immigrant veterans will continue to suffer in a white supremacist society in multiple realms of their lives, from access to health care and education to encounters with police, US citizenship protects them from deportation, opens up additional job opportunities, and facilitates family reunification. The stakes in accessing citizenship are higher for veterans because too often their time in the military results in mental and physical disabilities, substance use issues, and homelessness, exposing them to risk of deportation. Patterns in how immigrants in the military experience naturalization, such as differences by race and gender, articulate with existing modes of stratification, exacerbating inequality.

The military route to citizenship has been alternately more or less onerous for immigrants who live and work at the intersection of immigration and military systems. A line that runs through the various policy changes is the use of citizenship as a technology of labor by the military. Used to attract immigrant workers to the military, not always with accurate information, citizenship is involved in allocation of labor to different work tasks and occupations and as an additional disciplining tool to control those trying to naturalize and those who fear losing citizenship by not getting an honorable discharge. Even at the height of naturalization facilitation, the process of naturalization could be challenging, and as the facilitation itself put pressure on immigrants who may not be sure about naturalization. Naturalization trajectories of variously racialized military workers reveal the tenacity of racial hierarchies in the military. The immigrants who were racialized as white and nonforeign experienced delays in naturalization because they were seen as already belonging.

The uneven edges where the immigration and military systems come together become apparent in the experience of immigrants in the military. Some naturalized because they were encouraged or pressured to do so by their superiors. The military itself benefited from these workers having security clearances and access to higher ranks. Yet, even in these situations, naturalization was not always smooth because of the disjuncture between the way the military and the immigration systems work, evidenced in the lost communications, forms, fingerprints, and the general difficulty of combining military life with applying for citizenship. And when immigrants wanted to naturalize and were eligible to do so, they were sometimes discouraged until a more convenient moment— convenient for their employers.

Immigrant soldiers, airmen, Marines, and sailors are workers. Like other immigrant workers, particularly those without citizenship, they are vulnerable to exploitation. The US military has long operated on a poverty draft, meaning that although there is no draft, many enlistees are poor and people of color who are heavily recruited into the military in the context of few alternatives, placing themselves at risk of harm or even death. Like their citizen counterparts, immigrants signing up for the military are enticed by educational and career benefits, as well as by patriotism, sense of adventure, glorification of military culture, and all the other reasons people enlist. Unlike their citizen counterparts, many immigrants enlist because of the fast track to US citizenship. Aside from facing risks as individuals, they work for a military force that has too often destabilized the very countries from which immigrants to the United States come. Thus, they enlist to participate in the US empire, forced to trade personal safety for the security of US citizenship and in the process bolstering an imperial military. Military naturalizations pose thorny ethical questions—not least the posthumous ones—and continue to exist in a political climate and a set of institutional systems that are ill fit to benefit the immigrant worker.

4

INJURIES OF ASSIMILATION

There are two mostly disconnected stories when it comes to military labor and life after leaving the military. According to one story, a patriotic youth gains valuable skills while keeping America safe, and serves as a model citizen afterward, enjoying the honor of being a veteran, as well as educational, health care, and housing benefits. The other story evokes different images altogether. A disheveled veteran sitting on a sidewalk behind a cardboard sign or panhandling on a highway ramp. Debilitating physical and mental injuries. Women soldiers raped and murdered. This second story focuses on the damage that military workers sustain in the service of the US empire, and the current of stigma that runs under the honor heaped on veterans.

The narrative of damage and stigma is almost never told about immigrant veterans. The liberal framework in which much of immigrant advocacy operates insists on foregrounding the success stories, bypassing critiques of the US military in favor of advocating for inclusion into it. The story of skills, honor, and social mobility dominates the scholarship and advocacy fields, framing military labor as a way for immigrants not only to gain skills and social mobility but to acculturate and integrate into US society.[1] It draws on the deeply entrenched narratives of immigrant assimilation, a process whereby immigrants and their children are supposed to become less and less different from the mainstream. Although not always explicitly defined in those terms, the mainstream in the assimilation framework is native-born, white, heteronormative, and able-bodied.[2] As ethnic studies scholar Catherine Ramirez points out, the history of assimilation as a cultural paradigm in the United States reaches back to the idea of civilizing African Americans and Native Americans.[3]

The reality of immigrant labor in the military and the transition to civilian life contain elements of both stories: mobility and despair, belonging and exclusion. Some immigrants move through their time in the military relatively unscathed, then build civilian lives that work for them and check off boxes for conventional success, including going to college and owning a home. Others struggle mightily. Rather than explain the causes behind different trajectories, I examine the military as an assimilative institution. What are the consequences of treating military labor as a mechanism of integration into US society? What happens to immigrant workers in the military, an institution that ostensibly concentrates and models Americanness? I show the workings and pitfalls of a version of assimilation that takes place through the military, what it requires of immigrants, the injuries they sustain, and their modes of survival and resistance.

Lisa Marie Cacho argues that racialized and marginalized groups, such as noncitizen Latinxs, "are recruited to participate in their own and others' devaluation."[4] The price of incorporation into US society is participation in the oppression and exclusion of others. More specifically, immigrant incorporation in the United States has long meant distancing from and denigration of African Americans while being fitted into a racial system marked by proximity to whiteness.[5] It can also mean denigrating and distancing oneself from stigmatized people within one's own group and internalizing racial frames.[6] And as historian Roxanne Dunbar-Ortiz points out, immigrants too often passively contribute to normalizing and perpetuating settler colonialism by embracing their place in the multicultural notion of the nation of immigrants.[7] Assimilation is always about inequality and domination. Although it promotes itself as a racially inclusive institution, the US military is deeply structured by race, gender, sexuality, and disability. An institution of entrenched hierarchies, the military practices decoupling between public-facing multicultural images and backstage practices.[8] Assimilation through the military means immigrants learning their own place in the hierarchies while distancing and denigrating excluded groups. It also, of course, means participation in violent devaluing of the people outside the United States—or even those within the United States who, like urban protestors or oil pipeline resistors, are targets of the military. Even when immigrants see military labor as a way to belong and become successful in the United States, they incur the costs of assuming their place in the hierarchy. These are the injuries of assimilation.

By spotlighting the injuries of assimilation among immigrants in the military, I seek to disrupt assimilationist rubrics and dominant military narratives alike. These injuries range from the toll military labor takes on the bodies and minds of military workers to the specific oppressions and violence faced by women in the military; from the bodily harm of having to prove one's fitness and loyalty as an immigrant to the psychic injuries of normalizing having to do so; from bearing the burden of racialized hierarchy to internalizing and reproducing oppression at the cost of solidarity.

I examine military labor from several related angles, highlighting what immigrant military workers have in common with non-immigrant military workers, as well as factors that are unique to being an immigrant. As the people I interviewed themselves pointed out, their experiences have been shaped by intersections of power structures and social hierarchies. In the interest of clarity, I artificially lift different layers of these intersections one by one to gain insight into how race and foreignness, then gender and sexuality, and finally injury and disability converge in the lives of green card soldiers. I consider both military labor and the transition to civilian life after active duty.

LABORING IN A RACIALIZED IMMIGRANT BODY

The military is often hailed as an institution that has overcome racial bias and which operates as a meritocracy regardless of race—even as reports of white supremacist organizations in the military ranks multiply.[9] While there is strong evidence that the military is, in fact, a racialized institution, the meritocratic image of the military is quite powerful, attracts enlistees of color, and shapes how workers understand their experiences in the military. Among the diverse group of immigrants interviewed for this book, some military workers of color insisted that racism was not a problem, while others recounted racism and discrimination. Some of the white immigrants reflected on the privileges that came from their position in the racial hierarchy. Speaking another language, speaking English with an accent deemed foreign, and not being familiar with American popular culture all carried negative repercussions in the military workplace.

While the military is in some ways more racially integrated than many civilian institutions, sociologists James Burk and Evelyn Espinosa challenge the claim that it is a model of race relations. Following a review of research on race and the military, Burk and Espinosa note evidence of racial bias in officer promotions and military justice. They further point to the effects of discrimination during deployment on increased risk of PTSD among military workers of color.[10] Exacerbating these injuries is the fact that the US Department of Veterans Affairs (VA, formerly the Veterans Administration) is not a haven from the racism pervasive in the US health care system more generally, with racial minorities facing barriers to quality care.[11] Victor Ray argues that the US military is a racialized institution: "the assumption is that minorities must integrate into the military, revealing the unmarked white background on which this assumption rests."[12] African Americans are overrepresented but are disproportionately in the lower ranks and experience barriers to promotion. In his study of veterans, Ray identified incentives to not report racist harassment, including having to prove intent, usually operationalized as explicit racial slurs. Yet Ray also found that white military workers did use racial slurs casually and with little consequence. Those who filed harassment claims experienced retribution and got labeled as troublemakers and poor workers. Ray concludes that racial inequality shapes the everyday labor of military workers, and this is covered up with a discourse of colorblind ideology.[13]

When I interviewed immigrants in the military and immigrant veterans, some insisted that there was no racism in the military, that they worked harmoniously among diverse troops. The internalization of dominant narratives by the oppressed is part and parcel of how racial regimes operate, and it is also possible that these immigrants were reluctant to voice critiques of the military in the interviews. However, a number of study participants did mention the use of racial slurs in the military, as well as their trivialization. We can see this in the story shared by Juan, a Dominican immigrant who grew up in a Latinx community in the Northeast:

Him [a Dominican friend from the same community] and I were on shift and someone was just being really loud and part of our job was to keep things quiet. And, he [the friend] walked up and told him that, "Hey, it's lights out. You have to be quiet. People are trying to sleep. Don't be an ass." And they got into a verbal altercation, back and forth, and he turned around and he looked at the both of us. He was like, "Why don't you two spics go back to where you come from." And I had never been. Again, I came from a really Hispanic community, Hispanic high school, Hispanic middle school, like, I've always been surrounded by my people so, I never . . . I never even heard . . . I know the word, but I've never heard anyone actually use it. Especially a white man. And the minute he said that, the two of us got obviously really, really upset. And an altercation happened.

The late-night screaming attracted the attention of their drill sergeant, an African American man: "When we told them what happened, the drill sergeant was a Black man and he just kind of looked at him and he looked at us, and he had said something really, really smart. He was like, 'In here, people always call you names. Like, that's because they're ignorant. They're kind of stupid, and they don't know any better.' He was like, 'They just don't.' He was like, 'Instead of being mad at him, why don't you ed-ucate him?'" The drill sergeant shared a coping strategy that Juan took to heart, and that reflected an explanation of racism as individualized ignorance that was on the recipient of the slur to remedy without getting mad. There was no consequence for the white man who uttered the slur, and definitely no filing of harassment claims. Juan and his friend learned that in order to become incorporated into the military as Latinxs, they were required to accept the ubiquity of racial slurs, their responsibility for defusing racist attacks, and the need to conform to their inferior place in the white supremacist hierarchy in order to belong.

The drill sergeant's invocation of ignorance evokes a colorblind expla-nation of racism focused on the way the military brings together groups of people who had previously had little contact with each other: this en-counter with the unfamiliar was assumed to naturally bring to the surface racial slurs and abuse.[14] The ideology of colorblindness is powerful within the military and beyond it. Not surprisingly, many immigrants themselves embraced this ideology and tried to see their experiences with racism through that lens, insisting that race did not matter in the military even when they recounted racial slurs and discrimination. For example, Jose, who described being called a "beaner" in the military on many occasions, as well as witnessing racially motivated fights, explained it by saying that there were white people who "have never seen Mexicans before." Fan, who was from China, explained the racism she encountered in the army also as a result of white people who had little prior exposure to Asians: "It wasn't a lot of people from city. So they always been in the same neighborhood. A lot of people had, like, first time shock attack because all the things going on. Some of them have never met an Asian before, so they think I am odd. Once they know me, oh, oh, that's where Chinese at. So it was just a lot of things you have to put on yourself. I feel like, imprisoned in your race, as well." Fan was burdened by having to represent Asians to these soldiers, yet she also prided herself on her tolerance and acceptance of all races, which she saw as breaking down stereotypes about the Chinese being intolerant. Getting along in a white supremacist society and institution means preforming one's racial identity for the consumption of others. It's a survival strategy that can feel like a prison. However, the focus on the encounter of previously segregated groups as generative of racism not only ignores the racism built into the way the military itself functions but supports the narrative of military as an institution that repairs the racism of the US society, rather than reproduces and benefits from it. Individuals reacting to a novel racial encounter exist within a societal context where they have undoubtedly spent many years absorbing the cultural material of white supremacy, whether or not they were racially segregated. They have learned to see the world and their place in it through a racial lens.

The quote from Fan about the "shock attack" of interracial contact reveals the narrative arc of this military diversity narrative as it moves through tolerance, acceptance, and even brotherhood "once they know me." As Andrew, an immigrant from Malaysia, characterized it in arguing that the military is more accepting of racial diversity than the civilian world: "At the end of the day, in combat, I still trust the person to my left and my right to have my back. And I'd do the same." Certainly, the military actively promotes an ideology of racial colorblindness, complete with its own lingo, such as references to seeing "not white, brown, or black, but 'green.'"[15]

Military workers may all be "green," but there certainly seemed to be a culture of race-based slurs, insults, and jokes in the military workplace. Jose, an immigrant from Mexico who enlisted in the late 1990s, recounted racial slurs and fights: "It wasn't more about your citizenship or anything like that. It was more about the color of your skin. That was basically the biggest issue in there. They would just call you beaner, the Black guys niggers, you know what I mean? They called them niggers. They even called me nigger a couple of times. I was, like, 'What the hell?'" Jose said that not only did the commanding officers do nothing about the slurs, but the drill sergeants in basic training themselves used racial slurs: "So it was just a normal thing, you know. But they didn't mean it as racial. . . . Come on, beaner, you know? Or, you know, like. It wasn't like another person calls you a beaner because they meant ill, you know. And the drill sergeants were there to motivate you and pump you up." Political scientist Sandra Whitworth explains the pervasive use of "gendered, raced and homophobic insults" during military training as a way of constructing and reinforcing "exaggerated ideals of manhood and masculinity demanded by national militaries."[16] Whitworth points out that through such insults, dismissed as harmless jokes, recruits are working on themselves to expel and deny everything that is denigrated by the military as deviating from ideal masculinity, from women to sexual minorities to people of color. Note that Jose bristled specifically at being called the N-word—being placed in the wrong racial category—but otherwise described the use of racial slurs as normal, and as an acceptable motivational tool. Assimilation into the military required soldiers like Jose to accept the normalization of racialized hierarchies and his place in it as a Mexican American in order to survive as a military worker.

Even though many of the immigrants I spoke to did not bring up having racial slurs hurled at them, some experienced their work environment as racist in other ways, revealing the range of racial injuries. This was the case for Bernard, a Canadian-raised Taiwanese immigrant who pointed out the narrow avenues for recourse that were available to victims of racist abuse:

Since a new president [Trump] took office, the situation got even worse. Our work environment, like, other soldiers, let's say, I'm going to use that as an example. So soldier A is a native-born American, born and raised in America, made gestures and comments to soldier B who is maybe a MAVNI soldier, an immigrant. And soldier A shows hostility towards immigrants, get[s] away with it. So this is kind of struggle that we're facing right now that. Why it's so difficult for us to stay here? Because you have people now, Joe Shmoe over here can do things because they're higher ranking than you are, and make you feel extremely uncomfortable and then in the process coerced in many different ways. But as according to the law, you can't really use the Equal Opportunity rights to get back with them, or try to set the situations right, unless certain keywords are being said; I'm not saying make a racial term, slur, or degradation comments, unless you have something solid. But how do you describe a climate and a culture? You feel it, you see it, but you don't really know how to say it. You know? That's the kind of situation we're facing.

As Bernard points out, the military process for reporting racist abuse requires a proof of intent even beyond the use of slurs.[17] As we saw, slurs can too often be dismissed as harmless jokes. Yet Bernard is a target of what sociologist Philip Kretsedemas argues is territorial racism directed at immigrants as outsiders to the US national community.[18] Racialization of foreignness occurs within a hierarchical structure where Bernard is made to feel not only uncomfortable but also coerced. Bernard's references to "a climate and a culture" point to the pervasiveness of the experience that nevertheless falls short of officially censored behavior. Having to push through in this hierarchical environment of racist hostility and microaggressions is the price Bernard pays for assimilation through the military.

Asian migrants like Bernard occupy a complicated position in the US racial hierarchy. As Kretsedemas points out, "nonblackness can bestow a privilege on migrants that allows them to occupy a racialized status position that is a step above black, but it can also be viewed as an undesirable 'alien' difference."[19] There is a long history in the United States of violent oppression and exclusion of Asian immigrants as figures used to define the borders of belonging.[20] Territorial racism that racializes immigrants and anti-Black racism operate in distinct and related ways in the US military, as can be seen in the comments of military workers and veterans racialized as foreigners. In this way, Asian immigrants told me stories of their coworkers and supervisors treating them as categorically different bodies, whether by drastically misjudging their age or assuming an intrinsic aptitude with technology.

Like Bernard, Fan described a discriminatory environment in basic training that fell short of racial slurs and felt that her drill sergeants hated her because she was Asian. She had no "really harsh words" to report as racial discrimination, yet Fan felt hostility constantly. The white people that Fan encountered acted "like they are the Americans." They did not need to call her names to make her feel like a foreigner. Fan felt a reprieve when she started as a reservist back home in New York, where her racially diverse military coworkers were more accepting of her claims on belonging. Even in this more accepting context, Fan recounted racial humor among fellow soldiers—"like how you are Asian Chinese eating dogs, or Black people hate whatever"—but dismissed it as jokes rather than "real" racism. Such dismissal signals the internalization of racial frames, but rather than condemning Fan's complicity or naivete, I see her story as evidence of immigrant survival and hidden injuries of assimilation in the imperial military that evokes the classic work of Franz Fanon on oppressive colonial relationships.[21] Fan enlisted just a few years after another Chinese American New Yorker, nineteen-year-old Danny Chen, committed suicide after brutal and explicitly racist hazing by fellow soldiers in Afghanistan. The hazing began in basic training with jokes about Chen's name and questions about his origin. In his journal, Chen wrote "that he was running out of jokes to respond with."[22]

Asians were not the only immigrant military workers to experience racialization as foreigners. The names of immigrants born in Latin America were used to identify them as outsiders. Several Latinx participants explained that inclusion of their full last name (father's and mother's last names) on their name tags drew ire from their commanding officers and singled them out for abuse. For example, Miguel was targeted by drill sergeants in basic training:

Another thing that immigrants face from Latin American countries is that, you have to use the name from your passport, and in Latin America, there are two last names. . . . And if you are a drill instructor and you are strong tempered, the fact that your name is that long. I ended up doing a lot more pushups than a lot of people. Because he [drill instructor] would look at my name and blah blah. You would just get crap. You could tell who was from Latin American countries because they would have two names. And they would be squished together. So it would just be a long list of letters. And, yeah, I've seen a lot of that. But it builds character, right?

Note that Miguel naturalized the abuse meted out to soldiers with Latinx names by referring to the strong temper of the drill instructor and by connecting the abuse to the ostensible purpose of basic training to build character. Regardless of what this did to recruits' characters, they were learning that incorporation into the military came with denigration of their family names. Miguel also explained that being a Latinx recruit from New York was especially bad: "They see you are from New York, and you have that name, and it's just not good. Tough times." Miguel spoke of a "racial disparity" he experienced as a person of color training in the US South. He continued to be picked on because of his last name, which was purposefully mispronounced. In this way, the military reinforced the outsider position of its Latinx migrant workers.

Dismissing racist incidents as harmless humor was one common way of coping, as we saw when Fan dismissed comments about Asians eating dogs as jokes. Similarly, Jaehoon, an immigrant from Korea, insisted that there was no racism in the army, that what might sound racist was only a joke: "Things like, 'Man if you don't shut up I'm going to slap you so hard you go back to where you came from.' Things like that. It's just movie lines. The old *Rush Hour* movie lines." In the exhortation to "go back where you came from," we see the specific construction of immigrant soldiers as foreigners who do not belong. Muhammad, an immigrant from Pakistan, likewise insisted that there was no discrimination against him as a Muslim, immigrant, or South Asian. In fact, he said that he expected discrimination, but it did not materialize. Yet Muhammad readily recounted instances that singled him out for differential and abusive treatment, only to dismiss them as humor:

There were one or two small incidents. . . . It's a joke and I don't mind sharing. This one time, I was in advanced training, where we do our job training. One thing about me is, like, I'm a really funny person. I do a lot of, make jokes and shit. People appreciate it a lot, too. So, when I was in the advanced training this one time—and this is completely a joke. I love this guy. He was our platoon sergeant. He was our leader. One time he got mail, how we get, like, boxes. What's it called? Care packages. They usually distribute it in front of the formation. Sometimes they make them check it for contraband. So we were in formation. Everybody was there. He called me: "Muhammad, come here, check your package and make sure there's no bomb in it!" For me, I took it as a joke because I knew that was his kind of humor. I knew his intent. Some people are, like, when you know where the joke is coming from, it's not coming from an ignorant perspective, you appreciate it. I laughed. Everybody laughed. I enjoyed it.

Muhammad went out of his way to insist that his commanding officer's evocation of Muslims as terrorists when he called out his name in front of a large group was just a joke. It is an understandable way to cope with such an experience, particularly given the pressure that Muslims in the military face during a multi-decade war that is explicitly against Muslims. Muhammad cultivated an image of himself as a funny person, which eased his strategy of trying to turn being laughed *at* into laughing *with*. Muhammad also had to deal with another drill sergeant antagonizing him about Islam during training. In this case, Muhammad insisted that it had "nothing to with me being a Muslim" but rather was generally inappropriate behavior by this drill sergeant. In a situation of an extreme power imbalance between a new recruit and an abusive drill sergeant, Muhammad chose "not to play his game." If the military is an institution that is supposed to help immigrants assimilate, it is clear that soldiers like Muhammad were not merging with the white mainstream, but rather forcefully thrust into their place in the racial hierarchy as embodying the enemy, their loyalty forever suspect.[23] Their experience echoes that of Asian American veterans of the Vietnam War, many of whom suffered race-related forms of PTSD due to being identified with the enemy by their fellow US soldiers.[24]

In the early twenty-first century, antagonism against Russia and anything associated with it was normalized as the United States positioned Russia as a geopolitical enemy in a way that framed Russians as inherently susceptible to authoritarianism.[25] Not surprisingly, then, Russian—or even just Russian-seeming—immigrants in the US military experienced their share of Russophobia, even before Russia invaded Ukraine in 2022. Sergei treated the abuse he was getting in the military as a Russian immigrant as "a game that I have to pass through and not pay attention [to] because it's just three months and you have many plans for the future." From the first day in boot camp, Sergei was referred to as a Russian spy. A drill sergeant heard his accent, found out that he was Russian, and made Sergei yell thirteen times across a packed mess hall that he was not a spy. Sergei did not stay in the Marine Corps after his first contract because he knew that his clearly Russian name and accent would continue to be met with Russophobia, hampering his career. Sergei leveraged his military identity in the civilian world to strengthen his claims to belonging in the United States. At the same time as Sergei emphasized that "most Americans, even those serving, they don't care, they don't have negative feelings towards Russians," he defended Americans who suspect immigrants in the military of being disloyal. To make his case as a loyal immigrant and US Marine, Sergei distanced himself from Asian and African coworkers in the US military by pointing to his common Christian heritage with Europeans, which made it easier for him "to adopt to the US in terms of white American," and which made Russian soldiers willing to defend the United States even though they were immigrants. He cast doubt on the motivations of other immigrant military workers, who he thought were in the military for instrumental reasons. In contrast, Sergei argued that Russians enlisted in the Marine Corps—which he pointed out was the whitest branch—and volunteered for combat roles. Here, again, we see how the military as an assimilating institution positions immigrant soldiers within racial hierarchies, and how they both internalize and utilize these hierarchies to reproduce oppressive mechanisms.

Sergei's accent and recent arrival in the United States kept him from blending into US whiteness. Other white immigrants fit in with US-born whites better, and their experiences illustrate the dynamics and costs of successful assimilation. Joachim, who was from Brazil but identified as European because of the ancestry of his grandparents, told me that he was "the whitest guy you'll ever know." In the army, people not only assumed he was a white US citizen but felt free to express racist and anti-immigrant sentiments in front of him. Joachim recounted one instance when a white friend was saying that it was wrong for the United States to let immigrants enlist in the military. This did not necessarily bother Joachim, who said that he loved this friend and could not change his stupidity. Rather, he used this as a proof of how convincing his whiteness was—and hence how protected he was from racism in the military that darker-skinned Brazilians might have experienced. Joaquim evoked a fellowship and trust with peers regardless of race:

Soldiers. It's a brotherhood. Even if you're a white guy and you hate Black people, you're still going to love the Black guy that's in your platoon. He's going to be your brother. You're going to hate every other Black guy, but for some reason you're going love that guy. You know, and it changes people. Yeah. It's just like, it's a brotherhood, you know? . . . When you or some guy from Arizona used to hate Mexicans when he joined the army, and you [are] going to make Mexican friends, just like you do a complete 180. It's a 180 change. And it's incredible. It brings people together so fast. Like it changes your whole mind.

Notably, Joaquim painted a vision of the military as a space that brackets the racism of the larger society but on the individual level. According to this vision, individual soldiers—presumably Joachim is speaking of white soldiers like himself—are able to maintain their hatred for racial others while loving individual members of these groups. They might also change their mind and overcome their prejudice. Again, this is a racial ideology that embeds racism within individuals, eschewing structural analysis, and reducing racism to horizontal hatreds across different racial groups. Note also the gendered emphasis on brotherhood, which positions women soldiers as outsiders.

Other white immigrants I interviewed may not have reveled in their whiteness quite as much as Joachim, but revealed other aspects of their racialization as military workers. Albert, a white immigrant from Germany, noted the distinct advantage of being white and speaking with a US accent: "Quite honestly, I mean, if you're white Caucasian-looking and you speak fairly without an accent, nobody really knows. Nobody really cares." Filip, a white man from the Netherlands, passed so successfully as a US citizen based on his whiteness and US accent that he was assigned to a task that was restricted to citizens:[26]

I'm a white Anglo male without an accent. And I think that the majority of my leaders didn't even realize I wasn't a US citizen. In fact, in Iraq at one point, I was issued a piece of sensitive equipment and I looked at the platoon sergeant and I said, "I can't carry this. I'm not allowed to. I'm a foreign national." And I had to prove to him that I was in fact not a US citizen and therefore could not touch this item that he gave me. So I think a lot of it, . . . the prejudice against foreign citizens in the US military, I didn't encounter for that reason.

Filip concluded that he did not look or sound "like the stereotype" of an immigrant. Unlike Joachim, this bothered Filip. When he made a point to mention his immigrant experience to other immigrant soldiers, Filip tended to get rejected as not understanding what immigrants go through, and he felt it as a lack of connection precipitated by the privilege of passing as a US citizen. Sergei rued his inability to assimilate, Joachim reveled in his whiteness, and Filip experienced his taken-for-granted whiteness as an erasure of his immigrant identity.

Racial inequities in the military workplace must be considered in intersection with class. The military is a highly hierarchical institution, with personnel arranged by rank and a divide between the enlisted—who are the focus of this book—and commissioned officers. Economic resources and authority are unequally distributed by rank. Rank, in turn, is unequally distributed by race.[27] Assimilation into a system that is celebrated as colorblind and meritocratic but is structured by race and class in this way means experiencing one's social position within the system in everyday work. Despite the ideology of colorblindness prevalent in the military, the racial hierarchy was noticed and felt by my study participants. For example, Juan was repeatedly censured by white supervisors for using Spanish with other Latinx coworkers: "My peers predominantly were Hispanic. The senior staff were predominantly white. So, it's difficult when your peers are the same rank as you and they, they don't, I mean, obviously, they're not going to care [about speaking Spanish]. But when your supervisors and your officers in charge, and your sergeants, when they're all white and they don't understand, it's very difficult." Jack was Mexican American, and saw that people like him were in the service sector of the military, as they were in the civilian world:

You know, there's little things that you see here and there. I remember this, specifically. I remember where I was at, there was a supply admin[istrator]. And one of my friends that was in the buddy program was right around the corner in the airway [aircraft route]. And I was all like, "How come all the . . ." And it sounds stupid, but I was like, "How come all of the, like, if you look at the two parts of the unit, all the airways was majority white boys, and all the supply, admin, cooks, were, like, Mexican dudes and Black dudes?" It was like [a] clear difference. That was one of the moments. And everybody from, like recon[naissance] and stuff. . . . Well, recon[naissance] is different because [there were] not a lot of them. It was mainly just a white unit. But that was because, the way it was explained to me, Black dudes couldn't pass the swim qual[ification]. So it was mainly just Mexicans and whites. Which is, you know, little bits like that, and I was like, "Weird."

Jack said he was not sure whether the racial segregation in the military workplace that delegated Latinx and Black Marines to service roles was intentional. Although he felt that his experience in the military was great, segregation was one of the things he did not like. Jack's observations are borne out in statistics that show racial inequities in US military ranks.[28]

Military coworkers sometimes tokenized and stereotyped immigrants who were recent arrivals and could not blend in as US citizens. When he first enlisted, Ranil was asked a lot of questions about his origins and race. While there were other immigrants, they were Latinx or Black and had grown up in the United States. Ranil was the only South Asian and recent immigrant in his group when he first joined the navy, and he got a lot of scrutiny and attention. Having grown up in Sri Lanka, Ranil did not yet fully understand the US racial order, and his self-identification as Asian was rejected by fellow sailors who understood Asian to be East Asian. Other sailors could not wrap their heads around Ranil being a lawful permanent resident who would enlist in the US military and asked why he did not join the Indian military instead. Constantly made to feel like a foreigner, Ranil at first went along but then gained a more critical perspective:

At the time, it was kind of entertaining because people would come to me and ask about my culture, my language, and actually, I think everybody in my division—eighty-one people—asked me to write their names in my language. At the time, it felt entertaining but like, right now, once I'm out reminiscing on all these experience, I think I was pretty much like an exotic zoo animal, like seeing a panda bear or something, but at the time it felt, you know, like, "Whatever, it's entertaining and I'm not in trouble so it's good to go," but, thinking back, how ignorant the United States was, or like how the society is, was. I mean, I didn't make of it much because, at the time, it was not my main concern but, like, thinking back, how ignorant and how disenfranchised I was viewed as.

Ranil felt put on the spot as "a representative of everything that is South Asian." It made him feel lonely too. It wasn't until years into his employment in the military that he started working in a context with many other South Asian military workers and did not "have to be the standard bearer for the whole of South Asia which sometimes I think it becomes like exhaustion and a burden." The exhaustion and burden that Ranil felt is part of the injury of assimilation to the United States for immigrants who are racialized as forever foreign. It was expressed by other Asian immigrants, including Danilo, a Filipino immigrant who grew up in the United States and insisted that there was no racism or anti-immigrant sentiment in the military. Yet Danilo noted that Asian immigrants worked harder in the Trump era to prove their worth in the military: "If you're not part of the other color, like, if you're not white or Black, they, they think that you should get out of their country." Danilo's racialization as neither white nor Black made him feel that he needed to prove his worth through hard work.

Asian immigrants, in particular, were treated as foreigners regardless of whether they grew up in the United States, as Danilo had, or were recent arrivals, like Ranil. However, part of Ranil's difficulties in the military did stem from being a relatively recent immigrant. On a basic level, several immigrants recounted that difficulties understanding US English made performing military work difficult, from understanding commands and instructions to being themselves understood. This was the case for those who were learning English, as well as for those who spoke English but were not used to or could not reproduce the US accent. Immigrants who did not grow up in the United States faced more discrimination and exclusion because of their lack of cultural knowledge and their accented English. For instance, Jim, who came to the United States from Trinidad as a young adult and enlisted shortly thereafter, identified his accent as a major issue: "Basic training was the most difficult because I had just migrated to America, and, of course, my accent became an issue. The unit that I was in dealt a lot with communication, so it really made it kind of complicated. And so, I was punished a lot because of my accent." Immigrants who spoke English with a US accent and could pass for citizens noted the advantage of passing.

Shortfalls in US cultural knowledge made recent immigrants vulnerable in the military. Heena, an immigrant from Nepal, said that her lack of cultural knowledge made her feel particularly isolated in her mostly white unit: "Back then, you make an American joke and I'm like, 'What's that from? What movie is that from? What reference are you talking about?' We don't watch the same things. We don't make the same jokes. So yeah. That was the biggest thing too because there was so many white people in the army." At the same time, a presentation of self as a military worker might work to counteract their foreignness outside the military. Michael, an immigrant from Kenya who came to the United States as a young adult, noted the effects of his uniform in public: "If I go to a store in uniform, people don't see that I'm a Black man or whatever, I'm from Africa. Or I have an accent. Or people see a US Army soldier and then you get treated differently. People just see you as a human being. And my thing is like, 'Why don't people just see me as that without the uniform?' With the uniform I feel like, 'Wow. I belong.' Or something. You feel like that's the most American you can be, with the uniform." Whatever the actual realities of racial hierarchies within the military, the uniform had the effect of temporarily overshadowing Michael's identity as a Black man and as an African immigrant. This speaks to the power of militarization of the US society and the symbolic status associated with the military.

The immigrants I interviewed generally did not speak of the military as an institution that helped them integrate or assimilate into the US culture and society, despite this being a common frame in the scholarly literature on immigrants in the military. One exception was Anildo, who enlisted shortly after immigrating from Cape Verde as a young adult. Although Anildo struggled mightily with English fluency when he enlisted, he felt that his military work helped him make effective claims on his entitlements as a citizen, which he said he learned from interacting with a much wider range of Americans in the military than he would have in his Cape Verdean immigrant community in New England. As an example, Anildo listed understanding his rights and getting confidence when claiming these rights in interactions with police. Given the racialization of many Cape Verdeans as Black in the US context, this example of how the military helped one immigrant acquire and embody cultural knowledge suggests that Anildo learned about being a Black American in the military.[29]

Although other immigrants I interviewed did not explicitly describe how the military helped them assimilate the way that Anildo did, their stories did reveal how the military assimilated them into a racial hierarchy characterized by anti-Blackness and territorial racism. Performing military labor in racialized immigrant bodies could mean replicating colorblind narratives, coping with racial slurs and jokes through individualized contact frameworks, and being used to demarcate the boundaries of belonging and foreignness. In seeking acceptance and meaning, immigrant military workers grappled with their desires and constraints imposed on them, which sometimes meant internalizing and reproducing oppressive mechanisms and at other times pushing back and negotiating more resistive ways of being.

MASCULINITIES, GENDER, AND SEXUALITY

Although this book foregrounds immigration status, immigrant workers in the military are situated within intersecting grids of power and oppression. We saw that race, for instance, shapes how foreignness is met by the military and lived by the military workers themselves. Gender and sexuality are additional dimensions that must be attended, although, of course, there are many others. Not only is the US military a racialized institution, but it is also a profoundly gendered one.[30] I take up race and foreignness and sex and sexuality separately, with a caveat that pulling them out for analysis belies the way they are intertwined in life. Or, as Juan described his experience in the military as a gay Latinx immigrant: "It's like an equal opportunity nightmare. Because on top of being Hispanic or being minority, I'm also gay. So I had both things playing against me for one reason or another while I was there." Fan characterized her experience as a queer Asian immigrant woman in the military as being akin to that of a unicorn. Experiences of multiply oppressed military workers like Juan and Fan demonstrate that being an immigrant did not have to be the most salient identity. Rather, how they lived and worked in the military was shaped by immigration and other dimensions of intersecting power structures simultaneously. This was the case even when their foreignness felt like the identity that set them apart the most in the military.

As I described in chapter 2, militarized masculinities played an important role in the enlistment of immigrants into the US military, with many youth—and sometimes their parents—drawn to the promise of the military to turn them into tough, adult men. Latinx study participants referred to the significance of machismo in enlisting specifically in the Marines, where Latinx people are overrepresented.[31] Racial hierarchies shape masculinities in US society and in the military. Hundreds of years of white supremacist US policies against Asian Americans, Asian colonized subjects, and Asian migrants have reinforced the stigma around Asian masculinities as deficient and inferior—yet threatening—to white masculinities and the white supremacist gender order.[32] This stigma can push Asian youth to enlist in the military to try to counteract it, and to push themselves to perform hegemonic masculinity once in the military. This is how George, a Korean immigrant, explained it: "Part of it was, like, me trying to prove that, you know, I hated this bias against Asians. They look at Asians as non-masculine, like in America? And I really didn't like it, so I wanted to kind of prove that I wasn't that kind of stereotypical Asian. And so it's something I wanted to overcome and it was my way of doing it." To be fair, George was not joining the military to overcome the bias; he had already structured his life in the United States to do so, even before joining the military. Most notably, he became involved and distinguished himself in a heavily masculinized extreme sport. George said he did not necessarily want to do this sport, but he "kind of had to" in order to counteract the stereotypes.

That George was not exaggerating the stigmatization of Asian masculinity in the United States is even apparent in the comments non-Asian study participants made to situate their own masculinities favorably in relation to it. Nikolai, who was white and migrated from Russia, disparaged the attempts of Asians to assume the traits of militarist masculinity:

You can see this Korean guy, you can see this actually, it's very funny to see this change. There used to be this Korean guy, I saw him before he joined. Typical Korean guy, cap, glasses, all that. After he joins, he is like the Terminator. You know, "I am defending America now." And you look at him and you are, like, man, you are twice as small as everyone. You've just never been beaten up in your life. You think you pass through all the basic training and change much? I don't like [it]. Asians specifically. It's like them specifically. But you look at them, and you look at them, and you are, like, "What the fuck is wrong with you?" They really think that they did this great thing and it's very disturbing.

It is striking how disturbed Nikolai is by the image of an Asian soldier in the US military. Note his emphasis on the diminutive statue of the Asian soldier and his hat and glasses as being incompatible with Arnold Schwarzenegger's white Terminator figure. It seems that there is nothing this Asian soldier can do to prove the authenticity of his warrior masculinity to Nikolai. Notably, Nikolai appeared to be venting his frustrations with his own difficulties in enlisting in the army, which were due to the vicissitudes of the MAVNI program. His critique was based on the images and text posted by successful—and predominantly Asian—MAVNI soldiers on Facebook. Nikolai seemed to feel that his own warrior masculinity as a white Russian man was inherently more authentic and deserving of entry into the US military than that of a man from Korea. Nikolai's skepticism of Asian warrior masculinity is wrapped up in doubting the authenticity of Asian American patriotism. As army reservists, these Asian soldiers' deficient masculinity exacerbated their forever-foreigner status.

The warrior masculinity and masculinized culture of the US military has not been significantly disturbed by the enlistment of women, nor even by the inclusion of women in combat occupations starting in 2016.[33] Rather, women are expected to conform to the existing culture of the military. In 2017, 16 percent of active duty enlisted military personnel were women, up from 5 percent in 1975. Black women comprise 30 percent of women in the military and are the most overrepresented racial group among men or women.[34] Given the low numbers of women, being identified as a woman can feel more salient and pervasive in the experience of military labor than being an immigrant. This is not only because women are a minority who are expected to fit into the masculinized culture, but also because this culture breeds rampant sexual harassment and abuse.

A 2016 study based on a representative survey of veterans of military operations Enduring Freedom and Iraqi Freedom found that 41 percent of women reported military sexual trauma, which the VA defines as sexual assault or sexual harassment experienced during military service.[35] The Department of Defense's own surveys show that in just the year prior to the survey, 6 percent of women on active duty experienced sexual assault, younger and low-ranked women were most vulnerable, and the rates have increased from previous years.[36] Given the stigma in self-reporting of sexual violence, we can expect these estimates to be conservative.[37] A steady stream of media stories and high-profile documentaries about rape and murder of women has made the public aware of the pervasiveness of violence against women workers in the US military.[38] Fewer observers connect this violence to the gendered violence that the US military has perpetrated and continues to perpetrate across the world, or see it as inherent to the institution of the military and unlikely to be remedied by sexual harassment training.[39]

Among the eleven women whom I interviewed for this book, it was those who had been in the military the longest and had been deployed who volunteered their experiences with harassment. Heena explained what it was like to be the only woman in a special forces training unit: "There were a few guys hitting on me. A few guys thinking I'm not good enough to be in their team, that they have to babysit for me and I cannot take care of myself. So I just made my ways in, like, you know, things that I had to do, and get to their level. And I had people making sexist jokes." Heena went on to recount bearing the brunt of her coworker's annoyance at her presence when they were stuck in close quarters and had to change clothing. Fielding unwanted romantic advances, sexist jokes, and negative assumptions about her performance, Heena also had to be representing all women in the military, singlehandedly changing perceptions of women soldiers. She went out of her way to prove that she could do the same physical tasks:

I was carrying a forty-pound weapon and walking around all day. Not complaining even once because I was like, "You know what? You're going to think I'm weak but I'm not weak. I can do this." That's when they were like, "Okay. I guess she can do the things that we do." And that's why at the end of the training selection, this guy came and told me, "You know, you changed the perception of female for me. I've always thought they were little whiny people who always complain about everything but you never complained."

The resolve to prove one's worth as a woman soldier resonates with the way many immigrants felt that they were representing their whole racial group while in the military, as when Ranil said he was the standard bearer for the whole of South Asia. Heena considered herself lucky that some of her coworkers accepted her ability to perform her job. Rather than relying on the culture of male comradeship that structures military units—the brotherhood exalted by Joachim—Heena was at best a conditional member, having to prove herself. Being an outsider not only made Heena vulnerable to being treated with contempt and violence by her coworkers, but also left her less defended by her "battle buddies" in situations of combat. Rape culture and racialized misogyny structure civilian workplaces as well, particularly in industries even more male-dominated than the military, such as construction.[40] However, abuses in the military are exacerbated by rigid hierarchies, difficult-to-leave work contracts, and victims' isolation from supportive social networks.[41] The few victims who dare to come forward are likely to be blamed and punished for doing so, setting a precedent for others who consider reporting.[42] Those who became naturalized through wartime provisions risk losing their US citizenship.

Leila, too, worked in a special forces unit dominated by men, and keenly felt that male coworkers resented her presence as a woman. She experienced harassment on deployment, and she also referenced her young age as making her a target. Thirty at the time I spoke to her, Leila said she no longer felt that type of unrelenting sexual harassment. However, she said that her experiences as a woman in the military had changed her personality. She became more cautious, less trusting of people, and relied on a "really big dog" to feel safe. For Leila and some other women, enlistment is an attempt to escape gendered expectations of their families.

Leila did not want to get married to a US citizen to solve her immigration problems, and had to convince her parents that it was acceptable for her to "step out," which went against expectations for girls in her Pakistani immigrant community. Despite—or maybe because of—its terrible reputation for violence against women workers, the US military markets itself as building strength and independence among women enlistees, even as many of its wars are fought ostensibly to liberate women and girls under enemy regimes such as in Afghanistan.[43]

One of my study participants trained with a unit that had only recently started to include women. Amy was a MAVNI recruit who trained only on the weekends, while fruitlessly waiting to get shipped to basic training. However, even with this quite limited exposure to military labor, Amy experienced dynamics similar to those experienced by Heena and Leila, in that she was positioned to prove herself in a male-dominated environment. To do so, she carried out demanding physical tasks alongside her more experienced and physically larger coworkers. When her supervisors offered her a way out, pointing out that the others had been to Afghanistan and she hadn't even been to basic training, Amy refused. Notably, had Amy been injured while carrying forty-five pounds for miles in the middle of the summer, she would have ruined her chances of going to basic training and getting US citizenship. She also technically did not have to attend these drills, nor perform all the tasks in them, since she was yet to complete basic training. The gendered institution of the military pushed her to prove herself as a woman soldier, even as the risk of injury threatened her life in the US as an immigrant. At the same time, Amy's unit had not set up separate quarters nor bathrooms for women while she trained.

Overall, Amy said she liked the unit she trained with while waiting for basic training. Her male coworkers were nervous around her as they tried "to watch for their words because they get used to talking to each other because they are guys." Her commanding officers told Amy that they were getting used to the presence of women, and apologized in advance for the "jokes" she would hear: "They [the men in the unit] like to do gay jokes or some kind of bad jokes [*laughs*]. If anything make you ladies feel uncomfortable just let me know." Just as immigrants in the military reported humor that used race, ethnicity, religious identity, and foreignness as content—sometimes dismissing racial animus as just jokes—so they recounted jokes about women and queer people.

The military is a heteronormative institution, treating heterosexuality and concomitant gender roles as normal. When after decades of exclusion of gay men, bisexuals, and lesbians from the US military the Clinton administration implemented the "Don't Ask, Don't Tell" policy (DADT) in 1994, the scrutiny and surveillance of military workers led to thousands of expulsions.[44] Women and people of color were disproportionately among those discharged under the policy. As former Marine Corps Captain Anuradha Bhagwati explained, the military used DADT to expel unwanted workers: "In this way, racist and misogynistic attitudes get combined with or subsumed by homophobic policy."[45] Women working in the military experienced lesbian-baiting, meaning male coworkers pressured them to date and have sex lest they be labeled a lesbian, in addition to scrutinizing them for conforming to feminine norms—even as these women had to prove their physical toughness to be accepted. The ban on transgender people in the US military was lifted in 2016, reinstituted in 2019, and lifted again in 2021.[46] Transgender people are twice as likely to work in the military than the general population.[47] The prevalence of LGBTQ people in the military should not be surprising because LGBTQ youth face considerable economic obstacles in their transition to adulthood, often exacerbated by rejection from their families and discrimination in the workplace.

Only three of the people I interviewed volunteered their queer identities. All were cisgender. Two were gay men who enlisted under DADT, and another identified as a bisexual woman who enlisted after its repeal. Juan felt that both his race and his sexual identity made his time in the military difficult. Filip foregrounded being gay rather than a noncitizen immigrant in his decision to enlist: "I was openly gay to my friends at the time. So, I was basically agreeing to go back into the closet for the military and obviously lying under 'Don't Ask, Don't Tell.' That was a consideration. Although I didn't, at the time I was pretty immature, I didn't think too big about the repercussions. If I was found out or if I got kicked out, [it] wasn't something I was, you know, for lack of a better expression, I was a dumb twenty-year-old private in the army." When I interviewed him, Filip was sixteen years into active duty and planned to retire after twenty years. For the first part of his term in the military, he had to hide being gay, living with anxieties and concerns until DADT was repealed. Despite this experience, Filip bristled at being identified as a gay soldier. He did not want the identity qualifying the label of soldier, and he pointed out the intersectionality of his experience: "I cross into a whole bunch of categories: balding, white, immigrant, college educated."

Enlisting in 2017, Fan did not have to hide her queer identity, but her descriptions of service illuminates some of the conundrums of post-DADT military life. For example, Fan explained that just because they technically could be open about their sexual identities, many queer people were not out in the military. Yet she described how queer women recruits eventually found each other during training, and the awe and joy of being in a sizable community:

FAN: People kept up their appearances but there is a definitely a lot of gay people there. And in my basic training, there was not a lot of straight people. Straight people in my dorm it was like [*laughs*] [a] minority.

SOFYA: Really?

FAN: Ten girls are straight, then thirty of us are all gay. They thought I am straight because my hair used to be longer and I was quiet. But I was dating a girl during that time. So I kept receiving like photos and letters. And they later find out, "Oh what? You are gay too? I'm like, yeah" [*laughs*]. But it was a whole group of gay people there.

Fan went on to say that she had never seen as many lesbians in her life as she did during basic training. It was relief because she had been worried that she would be the only queer woman. Laughing, she recounted the growing realization in her unit that the small number of vocally out lesbians belied a much greater number of those like Fan, who were passing as straight. Fan's pleasure at this experience of bonding and community contrasted with her descriptions of long and tedious training sessions on sexual harassment policies in the military: "It was part of the training for three hours, like just PowerPoint slides, but no one really giving it attention. . . . 'Oh you guys just have to be there with this auto on.'" Being among other queer women, Fan felt relatively safe, and dismissed racist and homophobic comments by framing them as jokes. She also said that homophobic jokes were primarily focused on men, not women.

The fight for full inclusion of women and LGBTQ people into the US military and for the repeal of DADT conforms to a familiar narrative of US citizenship, whereby oppressed groups campaign to be included in the military, valorizing and legitimating it as the highest form of belonging, and emphasizing their utility to the US empire.[48] Although DADT was finally repealed by the Obama administration in 2010, more radical LGBTQ activists were critical of benchmarking inclusion through the military, pointing to the close connections between queer organizing and anti-military and antinuclear struggles of the twentieth century.[49] The inclusion of gay, bisexual, and lesbian military workers reinforces, rather than challenges, hegemonic masculinities dominating the military. In fact, the price of their inclusion is the preservation of the dominant social order of the military, with its ingrained misogyny, homophobia, and transphobia.

The claims to citizenship through the military made by LGBTQ people are important to consider in a book on immigrant soldiers, not only because immigrants can be queer themselves, but because there are strong parallels to the struggle for citizenship among undocumented immigrants. Advocates of inclusion of immigrants and of queer people in the military put forth similar arguments about the value of diversity in the military, the skills and patriotism of these military workers, and the way their inclusion helps buttress the US military's and the US empire's reputation as a supposed beacon of equality fighting terrorist, misogynist, homophobic regimes. Sociologist Tamara Nopper made this connection explicit in an essay opposing both the repeal of DADT and the DREAM Act, which would offer a path to citizenship to undocumented youth who enlist in the US military:

The inclusion of more gays and lesbians and/or undocumented immigrant youth in the US military is not an ethical project given that both gestures are willing to have our communities serve as mercenaries in exchange for certain rights, some of which are never fully guaranteed in a homophobic and white supremacist country. Nor is it pragmatic. By supporting the diversification of the US military we undermine radical democratic possibilities by giving the military state more people, many of whom will ultimately die in combat or develop PTSD and health issues and/or continue nurturing long-term relationships with the US military, including a political affinity with its culture and goals.[50]

Inclusion through the military comes at a high price for too many, and in all cases, it furthers what Nopper characterizes as "one of the main vehicles in the expansion and enforcement of US imperialism, heterosexuality, white supremacy, capitalism, patriarchy, and repression against political dissent and people's movements in the United States and abroad."[51]

The gendered nature of the US military is evident in how military workers experience their workplaces. When thinking through gender, we often turn directly to consider women. In fact, women military workers walk a tightrope of masculinized military culture, expectations of empowerment, and realities of sexual violence. Immigrant women carry the burden of having to prove themselves to their male coworkers, even as they face stereotypes and discrimination as immigrants and women of color. But gender is an organizing structure for men, too. The stories of immigrant men show them seeking—and failing—to achieve hegemonic warrior masculinity with not a small dose of white supremacy shot through it. The fraught history of queer workers in the US military highlights the limitations of strategies that channel struggles of rights through the military, as well as possibilities of solidarity.

THE MENTAL AND PHYSICAL TOLL OF MILITARY LABOR

When the US military is touted as a tool for integrating immigrants, the images conjure up clean-cut, capable youth in uniform rather than the aftermath of war-making labor on those workers, their minds, and their bodies. What is labeled service in the US military is physically and mentally harmful work. Military workers who are deployed to war zones like Iraq and Afghanistan suffer from physical injuries to the body and brain, exposure to harmful substances, and deep psychological wounds.[52] Veterans who have been deployed exhibit high rates of substance and alcohol use disorders and mental health issues, often connected to PTSD.[53]

But even those who are not deployed to war zones are often working in conditions harmful to their health. Veterans, in general, report declines in emotional and mental health.[54] And even adjusting for age and sex distribution, the veteran suicide rate has been 50 percent higher than in the general population between 2013 and 2018.[55] In 2019, 25 percent of veterans who were not institutionalized had a disability connected to their work in the military. Forty-one percent of post-2001 veterans had a military work-related disability; out of those who had disabilities, more than half were rated by the military as 60 percent disabled or higher, indicating the severity of the disabilities.[56] It is important to note that statistics underestimate the prevalence of injury and disability among military workers and veterans due to underreporting—particularly for mental health issues—which is related to both stigma attached to seeking treatment and difficulty in accessing services.[57]

Immigrants who work in the US military are exposed to the risks of injury and harm, and they work in a context where injury and harm are expected, normalized, and even valorized. They experience the same pressure to push through physical and mental pain as non-immigrant military workers. However, some immigrants whose access to US citizenship hinges on their job in the military experience extra pressure to downplay their injuries and not seek help, lest they be deemed unqualified. At the same time, immigrants face suspicion that they are faking injuries in order to get a medical discharge from the military once they get citizenship and are pressured by their coworkers and commanding officers to prove otherwise. The military consumes immigrant bodies, facilitated through the linkage of citizenship to stoicism and denial of health concerns.

Many of the immigrants I interviewed for this book mentioned serious injuries and harmful consequences to their physical and mental health stemming from their military work. Out of fifty participants who progressed past basic training in the military, twenty-two spoke about the damage they sustained.[58] This is remarkably high, considering I did not directly ask about health issues, some had not been in the military for very long at the time of interview, and many were in the reserves, where part-time work reduces the risk of injury. Those who talked about their injuries brought up serious issues without which it would be difficult to understand their military careers and life stories.

Some physical injuries occurred in basic training, mere weeks into enlistment. Mary, from Kenya, fractured her hip in basic training. Ranil broke his tibia in basic training. Both stayed on, recovered, and completed their contracts. Other injuries occurred after boot camp, during training, or during deployment. Truda described a serious knee injury sustained during army training, which required multiple surgeries, resulted in a medical discharge from the military, and caused her to spiral into years of depression and addiction. Gilberto injured his shoulder while training in the Marines. He was medically discharged after four surgeries to repair it proved unsuccessful. John's career plans in the army were cut short by a knee injured while training, which left him unable to walk for the better part of a year. He left the military and struggled with depression. Jack had three knee surgeries to try to repair an injury he sustained while working in the military and had to leave at the end of his contract. Heena fractured her hip, both ankles, and a wrist while parachute jumping.

The military exposes its workers to harmful chemicals, drugs, and other substances, particularly during deployment.[59] The Department of Veterans Affairs lists multiple categories for exposure to hazardous chemicals and materials that could qualify veterans for disability compensation, including being used as subjects for medical research; exposure to unspecified toxic chemicals during the Gulf War, in Afghanistan, and in Iraq; being around "warfare testing" of chemicals for various projects; exposure to radiation; and more.[60] Many military bases in the United States are polluted with toxic chemicals that can affect the health of military workers and the communities in which they are located.[61] Vaclav experienced mental health problems when he returned from a deployment in Afghanistan:

I was stressed out, I was taking anti-depressants, I couldn't sleep at night. You know, it just really ruined my health, left and right, all the chemicals that they had us use over there, you know, throughout the army. And another thing was, in the army, when something had to be done, you had to use like hydraulic fluids or epoxy or what-have-yous and there's no protective gear, you know, well they wouldn't be like, "Well, okay, we'll just wait for the shipment of protective gear to come in and you know, do it next week." No! Hell no, you go out there and you do it now!

Vaclav left the military and found a job, but he was struggling. The VA classified him as 50 percent disabled. He continued to take medications and receive psychological counseling.

Jim described his exposure to drugs during the first Gulf War in Iraq and the effect it had on his health:

Training in the desert, we suffered a lot. We were induced [sic] drugs. We were physically trained, mentally trained, and we were drug induced to be able to kill. Because my unit is what is called a do or die unit, whereby what we do is we go in, we don't take prisoners, we just take out airports, take out cities, we just go through, that's what we do. Even before the war, a lot of soldiers in my unit had to go back because the training was extreme. They weren't able to handle it. And therefore, a lot of them were kicked out of the military. I had even one officer who actually was kicked out because of depression. He ended up shooting his gun at someone. Yeah. And there was a lot of fights because the drugs we were given which made us want to fight.

Jim damaged his back in Iraq while operating ammunition. Feeling a sense of obligation to his unit, Jim pushed through the pain and kept working. He started to drink, smoke cigarettes, and became addicted to crack cocaine. For many years after leaving the military, Jim struggled with addiction and depression. He attempted suicide multiple times and was hospitalized. Jim said that when he first left the military, he went to a VA hospital but was ignored when he shared his PTSD symptoms: "They gave me medications for physical issues, but not for mental issues." A 2011 study found that 20 percent of veterans with mental health disorders in New York State did not access mental health services.[62] Research shows pervasive delays in needs assessments for veterans, with concomitant lengthy delays in military benefits and pensions.[63] More than twenty years passed before Jim went to the VA again. This time, he was classified as 100 percent disabled, but was not given any retroactive compensation for all the years that passed between the harms he sustained in the military and his second VA visit.

Jim connected not being able to access retroactive benefits to the cost-cutting imperatives of the military when it comes to the health care of veterans who sustained injuries from their military labor. He noted that deportations of immigrant soldiers also saved the government money, since the deportees could not access their benefits. These comments about military cost savings are striking when we consider defense budgets, running in the $700 billion per year range by 2021.[64] Yet research by anthropologist Ken MacLeish demonstrates the way military workers' bodies and lives are used up to fulfill the needs of their employer, ignoring their injuries and destructive behavior when their labor is needed, and spitting them out when downsizing.[65] When I spoke to him, Jim, in his early fifties, lived in unremitting pain. He took over twenty medications and went to the VA hospital four days a week for appointments addressing his many medical problems. As Leish writes, "War can become too much in the people who make it."[66]

Mental health issues afflicted many immigrants whom I interviewed. Researchers note that many veterans report feeling stigma and are discouraged from asking for help for their mental health symptoms. Military culture not only stigmatizes workers with mental health illnesses as weak, but also puts up barriers to their promotion within the military. In the stigmatization of mental fallout from military labor, we glimpse barriers put up against examining the substance of what the US military is doing and how it does it. Workers' mental health is a symptom and judgment of empire in itself, one that proponents of the military as an integrative institution must downplay. When framing the military as an avenue for inclusion of marginalized populations, it becomes necessary to bracket the widespread damage of military labor on those who perform it, even when they are not deployed to a conflict zone.[67]

There is an additional stigma to experiencing mental health problems for those who have not been deployed. Brian described difficulty being in crowds, trouble concentrating, and obsessive checking for threats. Although these symptoms pointed to possible PTSD, Brian did not feel comfortable seeking help: "I don't want even to think that I have it because I don't want to have a crutch to lean on. I want to just be able to be normal. . . . You know, there's so many other people that have lost limbs, there's those who've had concussions, or have lost a best friend, or whatever it might be that have more than enough reason to have post-traumatic stress. I don't believe that I have ever experienced anything to warrant it." Brian did not experience deployment, and hence did not feel justified in claiming injury from his military work. In fact, military workers and veterans whom I interviewed moved in a culture of militarism that both valorized wounded soldiers and scrutinized and stigmatized them, all while routinizing harm and injury in military labor.

The valorization of the wounded soldier is readily apparent in the public sphere through honors bestowed on selected disabled veterans during public events, usually on those with physical disabilities. A memorial dedicated to disabled veterans was erected in Washington, DC, in 2014. This valorization does not consistently embrace veterans suffering from traumatic brain injuries, PTSD, and other mental health issues stemming from their military labor, not least because veterans experience high levels of criminalization and incarceration tied to their mental illness.[68] Anthropologist Zoë Wool characterizes media coverage of soldiers' struggles with mental health as evoking "the pathologizing monster-out-of-place soldier figure."[69] President Trump's minimization of traumatic brain injury as headaches after an explosion in Iraq in 2019 injured US military workers demonstrates both the skepticism around less visible injuries and the fact that military valor is firmly associated with toughness.[70] Nothing short of a missing limb or two seems to be real enough as a disability. There is also the suspicion that veterans might be faking it to receive disability benefits.[71]

Like other military workers, immigrants experience the normalization of harm and injury, and the pressure to push through the pain. Miguel described a commanding officer forcing him to hold onto a part of a machine that gave him an electric shock: "Hold onto this thing and crank it up, electricity go through it and I flew to the wall [*gestures being knocked down*]. Which didn't bother me that much because all you are doing is painful training." Fajing described the extent to which injury was normalized: "All the soldiers in the service have some kind of broken bodies, to an extent. Even my mentor, he's a pretty good shaped man, he got back problems. And he got anxiety problems. I have a lot of health issues as well. I have lower back pain. I have a chronic sprained ankle. And then, I have some anxiety issues going on as well. But I don't try to get out of the army, try to get away [from] what I'm obligated to do with those excuses and issues." Fajing had been working in the military for five years at the time that I spoke to him. Despite his injuries, he strove to differentiate himself as a good soldier against those who supposedly claim injuries to get out of their military contracts. As a MAVNI recruit and an Asian soldier racialized as a forever foreigner, it is likely that Fajing had to go extra lengths to prove his worthiness as a soldier.

Fajing was not alone in describing the normalization of injury. In 2019, when I traveled to Ciudad Juarez to meet with deported veterans living there, I was struck by the way they spoke about their injuries. Over breakfast in a large restaurant, the four men recounted injuries they sustained as soldiers. The common threads that emerged from these accounts were how routine these injuries were and the expectation that no medical care would be provided by one's superiors. Laughing at the memories of their wild youth, the veterans recounted falling from great heights during training and being unconscious for many minutes, and trekking miles with broken ankles or ribs. They told me it was not cool to report injuries during training, and during deployment, it was not really a situation where you could report it. Anyway, they said, their superiors would just tell them to take a painkiller.[72] Although several were only in their early forties, their grave bodily injuries made them seem much older. They jokingly brushed off the callousness with which their injuries had been ignored and dismissed, yet it was clear how their then-young bodies had been used up by the military, which extracted their labor and treated them as disposable even before they were deported. The lack of medical attention at the time of the injury meant no record of it—and, thus, difficulty in proving disability that resulted from work in the military (see figure 4.1).

When I interviewed one of these veterans, Hector, one on one, he told me that he sustained multiple head injuries while jumping from planes in the army, which meant difficulties concentrating and memory lapses: "I don't know when it happened, but, basically like every fall that you have, the way you land, your body impacts the ground really hard. I remember on one occasion I was unconscious. I don't even know for how long. But like, you know, you're young, you're eighteen years old and you don't want to be a wuss, you don't want to go on sick call, and have a profile. When you get a profile you can't do anything, so you suck it up. You suck it up, dust it off." These repeated head injuries were not noted in his army medical record, although his broken back and ankle were. Hector had been eager to jump from planes to escape the stigma of being a "leg," or

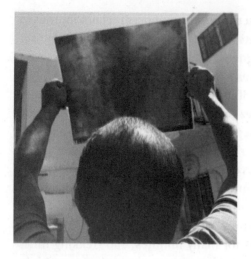

FIGURE 4.1

A deported veteran examining his X-ray film.
© Joseph Silva.

someone in an airborne unit who has not yet jumped. The stories of harm
and injury told by these immigrant veterans and military workers bring
home the reality that although they tend to view the military as a vehicle
of social mobility, in some ways, their experience is the same as that of
their parents who are farmworkers and factory workers. Just as the bodies of Hector's parents were prematurely aged through the repeated and
untreated strain of working in factories, mowing grass, and picking up
cans, so is Hector's body worn down by military work, self-medication,
and chronic disease.

These are the literal injuries of assimilation, reinforced by the culture
of warrior masculinity that requires military workers to push themselves
through life-changing injuries and not show pain. As Hector put it, "you
don't want to be a wuss" or be known as drawing attention to your injuries. In fact, some scholars argue that the epidemic of military suicides

is connected to military masculinities that force military workers and veterans to internalize their distress.[73] Fan was yet another person to be injured during basic training, and felt she had to demonstrate her recovery to her commanding officers. Fan missed some training sessions because of her injury but still graduated from basic training on time. She pushed through the pain to pass all the tests she needed to pass. By performing a fast recovery from injury, she demonstrated her fitness for the military. As noted earlier, Fan and many other immigrants felt extra pressure to demonstrate their excellence in military work because they faced scrutiny as foreigners, people of color, women, sexual minorities, or a combination of these.

Manuel told me that he did not pursue naturalization because his time between deployments was consumed by trying to recover from the injuries he sustained while deployed: "After the first deployment . . . I was too busy with physical therapy, and I was actually trying to stay in the Marine Corps. Because of my injuries the talk initially was that they were going to medically separate me, but I was very focused on doing PT [physical therapy] and getting back into really, really good shape and improving my health in that state." Manuel, like Fan, was working on his injured body to be able to hang onto the pay and benefits of a job that caused his injuries in the first place.

When Heena broke her hip jumping from an airplane and had to take a break from intense physical training while it healed, she remembered being pushed to recover faster and told that the military could not keep her while injured. As someone who enlisted through the MAVNI program, she faced suspicion as well. In fact, despite the MRI that clearly showed her fractured hip, Heena's commanding officer accused her of faking it:

The first sergeant came and he was like, "You MAVNIs are just trying to get med boarded."[74] And he pointed at me and he was like, "You were supposed to go to civil affairs qualifications course and you're just here faking an injury." That's how he put it. And that was when I was just so frustrated that I went to his office and I was like, "You know I'm not faking an injury. And I want to get out of this unit and I'm going to qualifications course next week, just send me." And he did. He was like, "Okay. You have to jump before you go." And I hadn't jumped in a year and a half after the injury. And I was like, "Okay, I'll jump." And I just jumped

[the] next week, and a week after that, I was in training. So it wasn't an obstacle. It was just to prove them wrong [*laughs*] and then, the frustration of how some MAVNIs are being treated. I think I was treated bad too but every time they said something, I took it in a way like, "Hey. I need to prove this person wrong and do something better."

To be sure, Heena was still in pain when she decided to start jumping again, and she went on to sustain multiple additional injuries. She wanted to prove that she was fit for military work but she had her doubts as well: "I really wanted to do this and I was also thinking, 'I broke my hip. Why am I doing this? I'm going to have to go jump again.'" After many more jumps and multiple additional bone fractures, Heena finally decided to stop jumping. As a woman of color, Heena sustained physical and mental injuries of assimilating to a violent masculinist institution under the pressure to withstand pain and not show it.

The injuries of assimilation through the military are most obviously apparent in the mental and physical toll incurred by military workers. The normalization of injury and harm in the military is part and parcel of the dominant warrior masculinity norms and has long-term consequences. For immigrants, linking citizenship to using up one's body and mind exerts an additional pressure to downplay the damage and push through the pain. For the military to be seen as a mechanism of immigrant inclusion, it becomes necessary to ignore the costs of military labor to the immigrant workers.

TRANSITION TO CIVILIAN LIFE

Physical and mental injuries sustained during military labor compound the transition from military to civilian life. Scholars have long debated the effects of military work on people's life trajectories. Many factors appear to play a role, including social class, race, and gender, as well as type and era of military work. Whether or not one experiences combat is also key, particularly when it comes to disabilities and their effects on post-military life.[75] In a 2021 study of different generations of veterans, Alair MacLean and Meredith Kleykamp concluded that those who worked in the military in the 1970s through 2000s were less privileged in terms of earnings than nonveterans their age, and the earnings gap grew as they aged. MacLean and Kleykamp attribute this pattern to the initial position of disadvantage among those who enlist in the military compared to those who do not, and to differences in educational attainment.[76] Researchers have also examined veterans' barriers to employment, difficulties with housing (including homelessness), low uptake of services and benefits, and social and cultural issues in transitioning from military life.

Twenty-nine of the enlisted immigrants I interviewed had left active-duty military when I spoke to them and were able to share their experiences of transitioning from military to civilian life.[77] Only two were retiring after twenty-year-long military careers. The rest had been on active duty between three and nine years, which is consistent with the average for enlisted personnel.[78] All new military enlistments carry a total of eight years of obligation of service, but as much as half of that time can be spent in the reserve forces or the National Guard. Military workers can be discharged earlier for medical or disciplinary reasons, but they are otherwise contractually obligated to complete their terms of employment.[79] Although many of the study participants found stable work or pursued a college education after leaving active duty, a number faced obstacles in transitioning to civilian life, even if they were only in the military for a short period of time. Their experiences were in line with those of non-immigrant veterans, yet there were several ways in which being an immigrant could complicate the transition out of active-duty military, such as fewer connections with and knowledge of civilian society for those who did not grow up in the United States.

Danilo's transition out of the military was not particularly complicated by being an immigrant. After four years on active duty in the army, Danilo was in the army reserve and working on an undergraduate nursing degree. He was born in the Philippines and grew up there and in the United States, experiencing a spell of illegality before adjusting to lawful permanent residency right before his enlistment. Danilo started planning for leaving the military two years before separation: "I had like a five-year plan, like what I am going to do, where am I going to live, what school am I going to, so I already had everything planned out even before I got out. And as soon as I got out, I was ready. I followed through and did everything that I planned: getting a house, getting situated, and going to school." Danilo did not feel that his transition out of the military was difficult. He participated in the Army Soldier for Life program and found it helpful for understanding how to use his educational and health benefits, prepare a resume, be successful in a job interview, and compare the cost of living across different geographic areas.[80]

Anildo, an immigrant from Cape Verde, also remembered going to sessions that prepared him for leaving active duty. Anildo's transition out of the military was complicated by the fact that he was deployed as a reservist after leaving active duty. This meant that he essentially had to transition to civilian life twice. In fact, MacLeish notes that the way the military manages its labor force belies analytical distinctions between service and demobilization.[81] Being in reserves or the National Guard can make career building difficult because some employers—although they legally cannot discriminate—do not want to risk having an employee called up for duty. In fact, National Guardsmen and reservists were reported to experience high levels of food insecurity during the COVID-19 pandemic in 2020 and 2021, as they lost their civilian jobs and struggled to support themselves and their families.[82]

While both Danilo and Anildo found the military to be supportive in providing information that would help them move from military life to the civilian world, Emmanuel pointed out that for some military workers, the classes and information provided prior to separation could be overwhelming: "The military put all these classes right before you get out. They teach you all this training. They got all these professionals coming in. But it's a lot of information to digest. A lot, a lot. But you really don't go in knowing anything until you actually get to that point." Emmanuel enlisted as an eighteen-year-old Haitian immigrant who had been in the United States for only a few years, then spent twenty years in the navy. He did not have much of a frame of reference for civilian life, and had difficulty assimilating the information presented to him upon his retirement. When immigrants enlisted soon after they came to the United States, then spent several years on active duty in the US military, they could face additional difficulties in adjusting to civilian life. As Jim put it, "I didn't know how to function being that I just came from Trinidad, joined the military. I didn't know where to go." Jim had been in the military for nine years, after enlisting as a new immigrant. When he left the military, he recalled not knowing how to navigate the city to which he was returning, nor how "the system" worked. Of course, US-born people who enlisted at young ages also do not have much experience with civilian life as adults. Yet most are probably in a better position given deeper understanding of US culture and more established social networks.

Some scholars, as well as advocates, view the military as an institution that helps immigrants integrate into the US society, focusing on acculturation, purported meritocracy, and racial integration, which are measured as upward job mobility in the military or earnings post-military.[83] This framing of the military is usually disconnected from the research on the difficulties of reentering civilian life more generally, and it does not seriously grapple with how different life in the military is from civilian life. Immigrants like Jim are not helped in their "integration" through military labor but rather are removed from everyday civilian life and immersed in an overwhelming military culture and system. Particularly when coupled with physical and mental injuries and lack of experience with civilian life before enlistment, this could result in profound disconnection and pain.

The economics of transitioning to civilian life can trip up veterans, even though veterans are entitled to services and benefits meant to support them after separation from the military. While on active duty, the military takes care of housing and bills and provides a steady paycheck. When Ranil was getting ready to leave the navy, he became anxious: "The loss of financial, you know, what would I do without . . . Because I was an E5 [sergeant], I was making pretty decent money for a high school graduate. So the last month I was really anxious, and I was kind of afraid of what's going to be in the future." Ranil eventually succeeded in getting a part-time job and using his educational benefits to pursue a college education. But he explained that moving out of military life where "you kind of live in a safe bubble, your medical is taken care of, your dental is taken care of" into civilian life where "I had to find information, I had to do it myself, personally, I had to figure it out" was stressful. Other immigrant veterans had a more difficult time than Ranil, particularly those who were not college bound. Some even ended up working in the same informal day laborer jobs as their immigrant parents, although the military was supposed to liberate them from such exploitation. Luis worked for a while alongside his father as a dairy farm laborer—the same work that pushed him to enlist as a way out of that difficult life. Angel also had a hard time after eight years as a Marine, and he shared incisive analysis of the difference between more and less successful transitions out of the military:

ANGEL: It's kind of scary, though, you know. The military . . . It can go both ways, depending on what you do. You know, if you're pretty much, you the person who has, you know, the time to sit, to put yourself in the position where you have gone to school, where you have saved up enough money, or you know to put yourself in a position to where when you get out, you're financially stable and you already have a job to go into. Then you're fine. Now, when you're constantly gone and, you know, and you didn't have enough chance to really save up, when you get out it's a little bit harder because now you got to try to look for a job to replace the income that you had. You know, but you don't know where to look or how to start.

SOFYA: Was that your experience?

ANGEL: Yeah, it was a little bit difficult because I didn't know where to go. I didn't know who to turn to or where to start or any of that. You know, because the military is good. But once you talk to all these other companies, well, we need a resume. Or well, you have the time but you don't have the training or you don't have a degree, you know. You have the experience but you don't have the degree. Or you have the degree but you don't have the experience. That's what makes it difficult to do things out in the real world. I went and applied for my disability benefits and I got denied, and so that made it a little bit harder, and then I pretty much had to take any job that came around.

Angel pointed out that it was difficult to prepare and save up for civilian life while in the military. His years in the military meant lack of work experience in the civilian sphere, and he struggled with finding a stable, well-paid job.

Despite the veneration directed toward veterans in the political and cultural spheres, from NFL games to remarks of politicians across the political aisle, research points to veterans experiencing stigma from employers. This stigma is hinged on stereotypes of veterans as suffering mental illness and/or being ill suited for civilian jobs due to lack of skills. Angel's experience is borne out in studies that show lack of access to employment support that the VA provides, and a mismatch in skills between the military and the civilian sector. The difficulties are exacerbated for African American and Latinx veterans, who have a harder time finding work after separation. In some areas of the United States, studies indicate high rates of poverty among veterans who had been enlisted personnel, especially among women and people of color.[84] Difficulties getting decently paid jobs are connected to difficulties finding housing. VA assistance with home loans is not adequate in the many areas of the United States where housing prices are high. Young African American women veterans are the most likely of all groups of veterans to be homeless, although older white men compose the largest portion of homeless veteran population.[85] Some of the study participants ended up moving from communities to which they were connected through family and social ties to cheaper locales where they were more socially isolated.

Given the obstacles to civilian jobs, it is not surprising that many veterans aspire to work in military-related sectors after they leave the military. These jobs can draw on military skills and provide a similar work culture and a more veteran-friendly space. This is the type of job that Vaclav was able to obtain after six years in the army: "And, there's this contracting company, pretty much same place where I worked for the army but like a hundred yards down the road. Civilians work there and they do pretty much the same job, but they get paid ten times more than the soldiers get paid, so I'm like, 'Eh, you know, this doesn't sound half-way bad.' I mean, [in the] civilian world I can wear shorts or whatever this is. I mean, just being civilian, I mean, this is like, wow, I felt like I just got out of prison or something." Vaclav worked for the military contractor for $30 per hour for two years. When their contract with the army expired, Vaclav got laid off. For a while, he lived off his savings, trying to decompress from military life and cope with physical and mental injuries. Eventually, Vaclav and another veteran drew on another military skill—weapons expertise—to open a gun store.

Aside from jobs with military contractors, government jobs at the federal, state, and local levels all have veteran preferences. In 2010, a quarter of federal employees were veterans, and around 8 percent of state and local government employees were veterans.[86] Some of the veterans I interviewed were aware of these preferences and tried successfully or unsuccessfully to obtain these jobs. A further complication for immigrants trying to get jobs in government or for military contractors is that many of these jobs are restricted to US citizens.[87] Thus, lack of citizenship among immigrant veterans can preclude their employment in these sectors. It is often the more disadvantaged immigrants who are unable to obtain citizenship, thus entrenching inequities for immigrant veterans.

As immigrants, the veterans I interviewed had experienced the vicissitudes of the US immigration system, with its bureaucracy and delays. Some remarked that this prepared them for the delays endemic to the VA's handling of veteran benefits. As Gilberto put it: "You go from dealing with immigration to dealing with the Veterans Department. You know, the Veterans Department, they are exactly the same. They take forever." Disability determinations and benefits can take a long time to process. Not all veterans use their benefits, even when they were attracted to these benefits as aspiring enlistees. For instance, subsidized college attendance may no longer be a viable option for veterans trying to support families and/or grappling with injuries. Moreover, research shows that many veterans have problems figuring out how to access VA and GI Bill resources or may not even be aware of resources available to them.[88]

Traditional masculinity is associated with more difficult transitions to civilian life, and researchers have found that some veterans, particularly men, do not use veteran's services because they say they do not need them.[89] A few of the veterans in my study did not want to use their benefits. Thus, Tadeo said: "I had no need for the benefits. Buy a house, put a dollar down, get my GI Bill, I didn't use them. What do I bother for? It's a big hassle. I didn't want to deal with it. I didn't want to go to the VA office. I got a job, I was living a nice life, had a girlfriend, a nice house, rented a nice house, good paycheck. And I would party. At the time, I was in my twenties. That was all that mattered at the time." For Tadeo, applying for benefits was a hassle to be avoided, and we can also see in his words that he did not feel he had a need for these benefits. In fact, looking back to the time when he left the military decades before we spoke, Tadeo said he was fine without them and lived a good life, a young man partying, not collecting benefits. Few of the immigrants I interviewed were as explicit about rejecting veterans' benefits as Tadeo. It was more common that veterans did not know about benefits or had trouble accessing them. For those veterans, the transition to civilian life could feel akin to being forsaken. Rodrigo remembers receiving his separation forms and not much else, not a thank you nor "any kind of direction of where I should go to Veterans Affairs." He said he felt exiled and abandoned. Hector felt that leaving the military was like the military "pulling the rug from under" him.

The transition out of the military is difficult not only because of loss of regular pay and having to navigate a bureaucracy, but because it is often a profound social and cultural transition as well. We glimpse it in the difficulties that veterans have working in the civilian workplaces, where they must adjust to nonmilitary expectations of interpersonal interactions and work ethic. The military, along with prisons and mental hospitals, are what sociologist Erving Goffman called a total institution, with groups of people socially controlled and isolated from the rest of society.[90] We see this reflected in Vaclav's characterization of transition out of the military as being akin to leaving prison, illustrating what it can feel like to transition to a job that is just a job and not a total way of life. Researchers have found that the transition to the civilian world can result in feeling isolated and estranged from civilian communities, a loss of identity and a sense of purpose, and struggles to adjust.[91]

These struggles highlight the differences between military and civilian life. As Albert pointed out, the military has its own subculture: "The military is really a subculture. And well, a culture by itself. And your entire lifestyle, your entire environment changes dramatically once you get out, just because certain values, certain goals that are standard no matter where you go in the military, they do not apply in the civilian world anymore. So, it's a huge change of pace to get adjusted to being surrounded all of a sudden from all military to all civilians." Albert recounted that he felt plunged into a civilian work environment where he was "surrounded by tons of females all of a sudden" and had to adjust to meet civilian norms on appropriate workplace behavior, including use of profanity, talking "rough" to coworkers, and keeping some comments to himself. (We can also draw on his comments to reflect on the kind of experience that his women coworkers might have had in the military.) It was certainly a cultural change. Research on the military bears out Albert's assessment of shared values among military workers and the role of socialization in military institutions.[92] John said that he had to change the way he talked in order to reintegrate into the civilian world. Even when they were happy to leave the military, veterans sometimes found themselves wishing to be back, even back in deployment. Leaving the military meant leaving a regimented life and a subculture and could feel like a loss of identity. For some, it also meant replacing a tight social network with lack of structure in personal as well as work life.

When Angel left the military, his struggle was exacerbated by the lack of social networks in the civilian world, especially when he had to reestablish himself in a new state in pursuit of a lower cost of living. Researchers have found significant problems in work life, conflict between work and home, loss of resources, and lower self-evaluations of health among post-9/11 veterans.[93] Immigrants are not exempt from experiencing these problems, alongside their US-born counterparts. But especially when more recent immigrants lack experience of civilian life in the United States, immersion in a total institution with its own culture can make for a rough transition when they leave the military. Integration into the military as an institution is not necessarily a means of integration into the civilian society.

CONCLUSION

The US military as an assimilative institution disciplines immigrant workers to fit into their places within hegemonic hierarchies. Immigrant workers survive amid normalized and violent white supremacy and heteropatriarchy within the US military, which reflects and reinforces structures of inequality in the larger society. Many seem to internalize dominant narratives that dismiss and individualize racist, homophobic, and misogynist abuse and naturalize workplace injury. Living and working at the intersection between model immigrant and security threat creates obstacles to solidarity among immigrant military workers who try to prove their deservingness and loyalty as individuals. The numerous problems faced by all veterans separating from the military—and exacerbated by some aspects of being a foreign-born noncitizen—belie the insistence of migration scholars, immigrant rights organizers, and military recruiters that military labor enables assimilation and mobility. Instead, we see the harm that this assimilation inflicts.

The US military touts its diversity and racial integration, but the experiences of military workers described in this chapter reveal the fallacy of assuming that the opposite of segregation is always a good thing. The workers who perform difference within this institution do so to shore up its racist, masculinist culture rather than transform it. To become battle-ready and cohere as a military unit, they are forced to conform to the white cisgender straight male norm. As they are absorbed into the military apparatus, they sustain the injuries of assimilation. The military gets a lot of mileage out of its diverse image, and its reputation, in turn, reinforces the framing of the United States as a multicultural meritocratic nation. When the military is treated as a mechanism of integration into US society, it further entrenches the militaristic culture of the United States and normalizes its imperial reach across the globe.

Of course, individual immigrants continue to be drawn to the military for all the reasons enumerated in chapter 2, even when they are realistic about and aware of all that possibly awaits them, including injury, violent misogyny, racism, and homophobia. If reading of the more egregious examples raises the question of why people would put themselves through such harm, we must keep in mind that workplace injury, exploitation, abuse, bullying, and discrimination organized through racial, gender, disability, and other hierarchies structure the civilian world as well. These are constrained choices in a deeply unequal society. In fact, soldiers who volunteer for repeated and grueling combat tours that place them at heightened risk in order to collect untaxed combat pay have much in common with migrants who work long days and live a dozen to an apartment in order to save enough to build a house, pay off debt, or start a business back home. Both are wringing the utmost out of their bodies—with long-term damage—and postponing the business of living. Both are held up as examples of work ethic and sacrifice. When we tout the military as an integrative institution, we must be honest about the violent nature of this integration on the immigrants but also the oppressive continuities with the civilian world in the United States and the globe at large.

THE RISE AND FALL OF MAVNI

The US military generally limits the enlistment of immigrants to lawful permanent residents and naturalized citizens, but between 2009 and 2017, it recruited around 10,000 "non-immigrants" through the Military Accessions Vital to the National Interest, or MAVNI, program. Most MAVNIs, as they came to be known, were international students or workers on temporary visas, whom the US government does not consider to be immigrants.[1] They qualified for naturalization upon enlistment, and thousands became US citizens a few months after they joined the military, drastically reducing the normally long path from temporary status to citizenship. Toward the end of the program, however, MAVNI enlistees became stuck in a legal limbo triggered by newly imposed security clearances. Not only unable to get US citizenship as they had hoped, some lost their temporary visa status and suffered profound disruption to their lives and plans for the future. MAVNIs experienced a heightened version of the green card soldier tension between model immigrant and security threat. Praised as highly skilled even as they filled military positions that did not use those skills, MAVNIs were also under additional scrutiny as noncitizen foreigners who were mostly recent arrivals in the United States.

I include the story of MAVNI soldiers not only to highlight the unique experiences of these immigrants but also to show how this program fits into the management of temporary migration in the United States. The proliferation of temporary migration regimes characterizes many wealthy countries. For temporary migrants in the United States, like those recruited by MAVNI, it is difficult to translate temporary visas for study or employment into a more secure immigration status like lawful permanent residency. In fact, it can take decades of uncertainty and being tied to an employer, even for those who are successful in acquiring permanent status. The vulnerability of temporary migrants makes them into a more pliable and exploitable labor force for US companies, fueling the enrichment of the technology sector, among others. When MAVNI was established, migrants on temporary visas flooded the limited spots available. MAVNI offered a drastically abridged route to US citizenship to migrants otherwise facing a long wait with an uncertain outcome if they wanted to settle in the United States.[2] The vagaries of the immigration system channeled these workers into the US military.

In this chapter, I discuss what drove the enlistment of immigrants through the MAVNI program, why citizenship and naturalization held a special significance for them, and what it was like to perform military labor while facing suspicion and resentment. In many ways, this chapter continues to examine injuries of assimilation, especially when describing the experience of bearing the brunt of the MAVNI program's securitization and collective and individual responses of affected immigrant workers. I begin by providing a timeline of the MAVNI program from its launch to subsequent waves of suspicion and securitization, which culminated in its suspension a scarce decade later.

A BRIEF HISTORY OF A BRIEF PROGRAM

The Department of Defense launched the MAVNI program in 2009. Over 10,000 immigrants enlisted through the MAVNI program by the time it was ended in 2017, primarily in the army.[3] Under MAVNI, the Secretary of Defense authorized the military to recruit "certain legal aliens whose skills are considered to be vital to the national interest." Those holding critical skills—physicians, nurses, and certain experts in language with associated cultural backgrounds—would be eligible.[4] The vast majority of MAVNIs were in the United States on student visas. But immigrants on temporary employment visas, asylees, refugees, and immigrants with temporary protected status (TPS) were also eligible.[5] All but a couple of hundred each year were recruited for their critical foreign language skills, with a four-year active-duty contract.[6] The most common languages among MAVNI recruits were Korean, followed by Mandarin, Hindi, Nepalese, Swahili, French, and Tagalog. Seventy-two percent of MAVNIs through the end of 2015 were Asian, 20 percent were Black, 7 percent were white, and only 1 percent were Hispanic.[7] Spanish was never on the list of critical languages, not because the US military has no presence in Latin America, but because there are Spanish-speaking military workers with green cards or US citizenship who can fill that need for language and cultural skills. The history of the MAVNI program is one of fits and starts. Suspended soon after it began, MAVNI reopened, expanded for a few years, only to be halted again.

MAVNI LAUNCH

Instrumental to the development and implementation of MAVNI was Lieutenant Colonel Margaret Stock, who served as a project officer at the time. Stock proposed the program in a military conference presentation when brainstorming ways to address the recruitment crisis of mid-2000s. She argued that the legal authority to recruit immigrants without green cards already existed; the military had only to make a policy decision. Skilled immigrants on temporary visas would be attracted by a path to citizenship that would save them as much as fifteen years of uncertainty and legal fees.

By the end of 2008, Stock had convinced the Secretary of the Army and the Secretary of Defense to approve a trial program that would recruit a maximum of 1,000 in one year. Over 15,000 applied for these slots.[8] Stock received a medal for her work with MAVNI, which was supported by the leaders of US Special Operations Command.[9] Special Operations focuses on working with foreign militaries and militias and was heavily involved in the creation of MAVNI, with a third of recruits assigned to it. As a former army ranger, Paul Scharre, explained in an interview with the *Washington Post*, the military found it invaluable to have interpreters who lived in the United States and had "American insight": "They can bridge cultural divides and explain why locals are behaving a certain way that US troops can understand." Soldiers with linguistic skills also cut the costs of paying contractors for local interpreters.[10]

SUSPICION PLACES MAVNI ON HOLD

Despite support from within the military, MAVNI attracted suspicion as an enlistment program because it enlisted foreigners. As immigration reporter Julia Preston noted in a 2017 investigative piece: "From its earliest days in 2008, the MAVNI program has been caught in a tug-of-war between supportive recruitment commanders, who saw the exceptionally high education and skill levels of the immigrants, and doubting Pentagon brass who thought it could be an entry point for foreign spies or terrorists."[11] Here we see how the tension between a model immigrant and security threat was intensified in the figure of the MAVNI soldier.

Soon after it was implemented, MAVNI was halted, partly in reaction to the mass shooting at Fort Hood, which raised concerns about internal threats. It took two years to restart the program, this time with a new set of security screenings. Notably, the Fort Hood shooter, Major Nidal Malik Hasan, was born in the United States and was not associated with the MAVNI program.[12] Proponents advocated to reopen MAVNI, relying on claims of superior quality of the first class of recruits: they had higher-than-average ASVAB scores, extremely high levels of education, lower rates of attrition, and many went into the selective Special Forces. Unlike citizens and lawful permanent residents, who can receive conduct waivers for criminal records, a criminal record was a disqualification for MAVNI.[13] In 2012, a Nepali MAVNI even won the army's Soldier of the Year award.[14] Thus, MAVNI offered a high-quality workforce at a time of personnel shortages.[15] The imperative for more military workers temporarily trumped the suspicion of foreigners.

Although these arguments for superior quality were made in support of MAVNI, Pentagon reviews also revealed that language-based recruits were often placed in military occupations unrelated to the skills for which they were recruited or to their levels of education. Many were working in military occupations with low entry bars, such as supply and logistics. It appeared that the army used MAVNI solders as "interchangeable cogs" in its operations.[16] A RAND report commissioned by the military reported that 79 percent of MAVNI soldiers it surveyed expressed dissatisfaction with the program because their skills were not utilized.[17] MAVNIs were channeled into military occupations with low test score requirements because they lacked security clearances needed to enter more critical occupations—including the occupation of linguist. This also meant that they did not get enlistment bonuses, which go to those filling these occupations that the military deems essential.[18]

MAVNI REOPENING AND DEMISE BY SECURITIZATION

MAVNI reopened in 2012 and recruitment expanded from a few metropolitan areas to across the country. In 2014, MAVNI grew to include the US Army Reserve. By 2016, more than half of MAVNI recruits entered the reserves rather than the active army.[19] This meant that they would go through the same training as active-duty personnel, then return to their studies or work, with an obligation to train one weekend per month and an additional two weeks each year. Reservists can be activated and deployed, as happened extensively in the 2000s.[20] In the same year, the program started to allow applicants with Deferred Action for Childhood Arrivals (DACA) status. In the next few years, over 800 DACA recipients enlisted through MAVNI and obtained citizenship.[21] The yearly cap on MAVNI recruits was raised from 1,500 to 3,200 in 2015 and 5,200 in 2016.[22]

The DACA expansion exacerbated the tensions within the military between proponents of MAVNI and those who viewed immigrants with suspicion. The MAVNI cap for fiscal year 2017 was lowered to 1,400, with a new focus on meeting the specific critical skills requirement rather than recruiting "high-quality" workers more generally.[23] In the fall of 2016, Acting Undersecretary of Defense Peter Levine issued a memorandum that began the year-long winding-down of MAVNI. Levine halted enlistments through MAVNI. Those who already signed their enlistment paperwork and were awaiting basic training were not allowed to begin their training. This meant around 1,800 immigrants were now stuck in MAVNI limbo. Those who were already in basic training were not allowed to proceed to their advanced training or assignments, remaining in boot camp for months or even years. Those who were past basic training were barred from having security clearances regardless of their citizenship status, hampering the military careers promised to them.[24]

A leaked 2017 Department of Defense memo called for enhanced screening of MAVNIs already working in the US military for years, even the US citizens among them.[25] In fact, naturalized citizens who enlisted through MAVNI were now under continual monitoring through recurrent security checks, something not required of any other citizens, naturalized or not. If, after separating from the military, a MAVNI soldier worked as a civilian for the government or for a Department of Defense contractor, they would have to undergo these security checks as well.[26] Why this extreme scrutiny of MAVNI soldiers? The reasons that the Department of Defense gave pointed to a flare-up of security concerns of infiltration, which began to tip the fragile balance away from seeing MAVNIs as high-quality personnel. In the fall of 2017, the *Washington Post* reported: "Some anti-immigration sentiment has swirled in the Pentagon for years, former staffers have said, with personnel and security officials from the Obama administration larding the immigrant recruiting process with additional security checks for visa holders already vetted by the Departments of State and Homeland Security."[27]

Concerns ranged from MAVNIs ostensibly entering the program without proper background checks and having access to information they should not have to criminal activity by some recruits. The criminal activity accusation focused on fraudulent visas. The Department of Homeland Security ran entrapment operations, setting up fake colleges as a sting to catch student visa fraud. As mentioned in chapter 3, some MAVNIs had apparently listed enrollment in these colleges.[28] More practically, the military had trouble coping financially and logistically with the extensive and expensive security checks it implemented for MAVNI recruits. But since these security checks were designed to show that foreign enlistees had foreign ties and were thus disqualified, it seems that they were a way to end the increasingly controversial program.[29] The naturalization process for MAVNI recruits was also derailed. The Department of Defense instructed the Department of Homeland Security to suspend the processing of MAVNI enlistees' naturalization applications, pending the successful completion of security investigations.[30] The media spotlight resulted in the reinstatement of some discharged MAVNI soldiers.[31] The plight of MAVNI soldiers whose visa status expired while waiting for security clearance, who faced deportation, or who were discharged from the military altogether received repeated sympathetic coverage in major publications. This, said a senior Obama administration official, was "a potential propaganda victory attacking not just the United States but its most revered institution—the military." After all, treating MAVNI soldiers so poorly could play into the hands of American enemies, like Russia, "to convince people that America is amoral."[32] The figure of the green card soldier is useful for legitimating US foreign policy and exceptionality; treating the green card soldier unfairly poses a threat to this narrative. This is similar to the fears in the mid-twentieth century that racism against Black soldiers would help the communist enemy to discredit US claims to freedom and democracy.[33]

The Department of Defense lost some of the lawsuits MAVNIs filed against it, including a class-action lawsuit by MAVNI reservists, a number of whom were able to obtain citizenship without ever being shipped to basic training. Ironically, active-duty MAVNI enlistees ended up in worse

TABLE 5.1

Military Accessions Vital to the National Interest (MAVNI) timeline

2009	MAVNI starts recruiting, cap of 1,000
2010	MAVNI suspended after Fort Hood shooting
2011	No new MAVNI recruits
2012	MAVNI reopens, cap of 1,500 New security checks: Single Scope Background Investigation (SSBI) and counterintelligence (CI) security review
2013	Recruitment continues, cap of 1,500
2014	Expanded to include DACA, cap of 1,500 MAVNIs can now enlist in the US Army Reserve
2015	Cap increased to 3,200
2016	Cap increased to 5,200 New rules for security clearances MAVNI recruitment halted, followed by year-long extension to clear backlog Beginning of MAVNI limbo
2017	Cap reduced to 1,400 MAVNI lawsuits MAVNI officially halted New naturalization policy for MAVNI troops and green card enlistees: honorable service of 180 days and full security screening must be completed before applying for citizenship.

situation than the reservists, despite making a heavier commitment.[34] The program officially closed in the fall of 2017. Around the same time, a new naturalization policy for all noncitizens enlisting in the military required "honorable service" of 180 days before applying for citizenship, up from immediate eligibility.[35] The new security checks have made naturalization through the military a more risky and lengthy process than naturalization for civilians.[36]

In the following sections, I draw on my interviews with thirty-nine MAVNI recruits to analyze the particularities of their enlistment process, naturalization, and military labor. Among the participants were fourteen who enlisted without serious problems, eight who enlisted and experienced long waits and uncertain legal status that were in the end resolved favorably, and another fourteen who were still waiting for their situations to be resolved when I spoke to them or had had an unfavorable outcome. Interviews with the latter group allow me to reflect on the experiences of MAVNI recruits who were trapped between the immigration and military systems when the program was securitized and ground to a halt. I show the absurdities of the security screening processes that MAVNIs were subjected to by the US government, and the way that the securitization upended many of their lives—albeit unequally, with heavier impact on those already more vulnerable. While MAVNIs have often been painted as victims by the media, there is more to their story: they are complex people whose agency and desires result in different ways of making sense of and surviving their circumstances, individually and collectively.

ENLISTMENT: COMPETING FOR A SHORTCUT TO CITIZENSHIP

Two factors stand out in the enlistment of immigrants into the MAVNI program: limited spots available and the outsized role of a path to citizenship compared to regular immigrant enlistees. MAVNIs were in a unique situation compared to most other enlisted workers: they competed for limited slots. This competitive situation was in contrast with the rest of the military, which does have minimal requirements for enlistees (although some can be waived) but in general does not turn away qualified candidates. The competition for MAVNI spots was in keeping with the general experience of temporary migrants, who vie for a limited number of employment visas. At the same time, the MAVNI program was not familiar to many recruiters. At times, immigrants had to work with their recruiters to figure out how the MAVNI recruitment process was supposed to unfold. Recruiters' lack of knowledge of the MAVNI program could jeopardize immigrants' chances of getting US citizenship, getting to basic training, or getting a military job they wanted. Anna, an immigrant from Ukraine, recounted that her recruiter "put a lot of nonsense on my form. I guess some things he just made up because he thought it's not important." As a result, Anna had discrepancies between the forms filled out by recruiters and the documentation she herself provided during the security clearance process. She had signed a contract yet was unable to start her training or get citizenship. Another respondent told me his recruiter mixed up Indonesia and India on his form.

In this competitive process where the recruiters themselves may not have known how MAVNI worked, some immigrants traveled across the country to recruitment offices that were equipped to deal with MAVNI, and others took language skill tests in languages that they did not know well. Why did international students and other temporary migrants want to join the military and go to such lengths to do so? Immigration status played a prominent role in accounting for MAVNI enlistment. Like other noncitizen recruits, MAVNIs were eligible to apply for naturalization upon enlistment. But while lawful permanent residents could become eligible for US citizenship regardless of the length of time they worked in the military and already had a relatively secure status, MAVNI offered a tremendous shortcut from a temporary status to citizenship. The international students and temporary highly skilled workers who filled the ranks of the program shortened their very uncertain path to US citizenship by decades. Of course, many other factors played a role in MAVNI enlistment, from financial difficulties to transnational militarist identities. Heena, for example, was looking for a job better than her gig at a gas station and had a family military legacy in Nepal. Yet immigration status played an outsized role for MAVNIs, because it provided a path to citizenship not otherwise easily obtainable.

The US immigration system is characterized by draconian enforcement combined with robust pathways for temporary migration, particularly for highly skilled workers beneficial to US firms. As Philip Kretsedemas argues, the state treats temporary migrant flows "as if they were a form of capital" or a resource, reflecting a "utilitarian orientation that is characteristic of neo-liberal economic priorities."[37] The United States benefits economically from these flexible workers with tenuous status in what sociologist Payal Banerjee describes as an "immensely convenient and profitable system of flexible hiring critical for maintaining the viability of late capital."[38] Due to immigration regulations that restrict and surveil temporary migrants, they are precarious and vulnerable to exploitation.[39] International students are under special scrutiny by the US government under the Student and Exchange Visitor Information System (SEVIS), which tracks them, their dependents, and the programs they participate in, down to class attendance.[40]

Despite this surveillance, increasingly harsh visa policies, and rising costs of higher education, the United States continues to attract hundreds of thousands of international students at undergraduate and graduate levels. From the perspective of US colleges and universities, international students are an important source of revenue and a remedy for declining enrollments. International students bring much needed tuition dollars to public education systems whose state funding has precipitously declined in the past twenty to thirty years, and they prop up the margins of private institutions. International students also bring racial and ethnic diversity, which institutions of higher education use to brand and promote themselves.[41] Thirty-five percent of international students come from China and 18 percent from India, also significant sources for MAVNI recruits. For 56 percent of international students, their families or personal funds pay for tuition and fees. The rest rely on scholarships, employment, and other sources.[42] Notably, international students are severely restricted in access to legal employment.

Although officially designated as non-immigrant, many temporary migrants seek to settle in the United States, yet have limited pathways to do so. In fact, some temporary migrants become undocumented, particularly at junctures where they move or attempt to move between legal statuses.[43] George was an international student from Korea, and he accumulated degrees in the United States—extending his student visa—to avoid returning to Korea, which he grew to resent deeply after his mandatory service in the Korean military. Scrambling for a way to stay on in the United States, George enrolled in a STEM master's program. The company that hired him for Optional Practical Training (OPT), which is part of the student visa provision, announced that it would not hire any temporary workers through the temporary work visa (H-1B) program or sponsor any worker's application for permanent residency because of the newly onerous requirements imposed by the Trump administration. George then applied to PhD programs to further extend his stay. At the point when he was not accepted to any of these programs, George had been living in the US for fifteen years. He feared deportation and contemplated ending his life. It was then that he learned about MAVNI: "After the Korean military I just wanted to get the hell out of there [South Korea], whatever the cost. MAVNI was like my way out. It was like literally my way to the heaven. It's like, that's the path to the promised land. I need an exodus from Korea." When George heard about the program—"a non-immigrant F-1 visa already becoming a citizen in one shot"—he thought it was too good to be true but signed up immediately. Ironically, George signed up for the US military as a negative reaction to military labor elsewhere. Despite his STEM degrees at prestigious institutions and work experience in the United States, the temporary migration system did not provide a pathway for George to settle in the United States.

After OPT, international students must obtain an employment-based visa, like H-1B, to remain in the United States. Starting in 2005, 20,000 H-1B visa slots were designated for MA or higher graduates of US universities.[44] A 2014 study found that fewer than half of international graduates were able to find employment in their metropolitan area.[45] Some international students end up working in academic settings outside their field of study because academic settings are exempt from yearly caps.[46] International students comprise a large pool of potential employees for US employers, but qualified candidates far outstrip employment visa supply, even as employers pay temporary migrant workers less than US citizens.[47] Employers are aware of the hurdles to obtaining temporary employment visas, making it that much more difficult for international students to find jobs and settle in the United States. Many temporary migrants never succeed in gaining permanent residency, despite living and working in the United States for decades. As students, they are an important source of revenue for US colleges and universities. As workers, they are a boon to the industry as a cheap and vulnerable labor force.

Temporary migrants with STEM degrees had an additional reason to seek US citizenship through MAVNI besides the drastically shorter waits. Guarav, a STEM worker from India, pointed out that enlisting in the military would open career opportunities for him in national laboratories that required security clearance. Clearance would not be obtainable for someone waiting for permanent residency and citizenship. Similarly, Li Wei, a PhD student from China, explained that US citizenship would allow him to apply for federal grants. Amy, a Chinese international student, pointed out that the more attractive medical residency programs would not bother with sponsorship visas, giving US citizens an advantage: "That's one of the main reasons I joined MAVNI because I can become a citizen faster then, so I can ... be more competitive in residency programs when I apply for those."

Due to the considerable obstacles faced by international students who want to remain in the United States, it is not surprising that applying for lawful permanent residency through an employer has been less common than applying for it through marriage to a US citizen.[48] Those who marry US citizens do not have to wait as long as those sponsored by employers. Few of the MAVNI enlistees whom I interviewed mentioned considering the marriage route to citizenship other than to distinguish their choices from what other migrants might do. Malik, an international student from Pakistan, said that his family wanted him to marry as a way to get citizenship. But to the twenty-two-year-old Malik, the marriage route to US citizenship seemed daunting. Nikolai, a graduate student from Russia, was also aware of the marriage route to US citizenship but adamantly rejected it in favor of enlistment. Dating had been a trial for him given constant suspicion by romantic partners and their parents that he was only interested in getting US citizenship, and he was also worried about the scrutiny such a marriage would face from the government. It is likely that those who are more amendable to the marriage route to citizenship— and face lower levels of scrutiny by the immigration authorities looking to catch fraudulent marriages—were less likely to enlist through MAVNI.

In all, we see how legal vulnerability and limited avenues toward settlement of temporary migrants made MAVNI, with its promise of US citizenship, a desirable option. Unlike regular enlistees, MAVNIs competed for limited slots in the military, mirroring the competitive context they faced in the civilian job market. Earlier cohorts of MAVNIs went on to get US citizenship, bypassing what they had expected to be years, if not decades, of uncertain waiting while tied to employers. In the next section, I describe their experiences with naturalization, before turning to those MAVNIs whose expectations of getting US citizenship were shattered.

HIGH STAKES OF NATURALIZATION

A shortcut to citizenship was a strong motivator for many MAVNI recruits, who otherwise faced many years of status uncertainty. Naturalization was a bigger deal for these immigrants than for regular immigrant recruits, and more was at stake. Transition to citizenship means being able to stay in the United States legally and apply for jobs without restrictions. Rohit, an international student from India, had worked for a year on an OPT extension of his student visa and was able to get an H-1B visa to work for private company. That step alone is one that many international students never surmount. Yet Rohit enlisted in the military and described his naturalization as a dream come true: "If I have my green card here, once I work on H-1, it takes me twenty-five years to get my United States citizenship, right? Which I got in like six months. Can you call it a dream come true? Yes, you can. So, why not? I can't explain you that happiness." Less fortunate MAVNIs, who had not been able to secure anything as their student visas neared expiration, not only breathed a sigh of relief at being able to get a job but also could stop worrying about falling out of status.

For a few, getting citizenship threw them into a crisis: after years of organizing their lives along the uncertain pathway from student visa to work visa to lawful permanent residency to citizenship, they were suddenly at their destination. George likened the feeling to that of elite athletes surpassing a goal. George had made major life decisions, from degrees he acquired to anglicizing his Korean name, in a single-minded pursuit of a way to stay in the United States. Becoming a US citizen felt surreal:

It's very hard to describe. Because I spent literally twenty years trying to become an American, right? And I really struggled hard in the last eight or nine years, like some serious failures and literally setting my academic and career pursuits, just to maximize the chances of becoming an American. So, on that day, it was just all surreal, to be honest with you, and I still cannot come to terms with it fully. . . . And in the last ten years or so, I have made decisions so that I can do something to reach a certain goal. It didn't matter I wanted to do something A or B or C, it's a . . . I did what I could do. So now I have to kind of like sit back and think about, okay, what is it that I want to do with my life? And all the important decisions in my life have been driven by not my desires and wants, but literally what can I do to get there, to become a green card holder or a citizen.

Sebastian, who came to the United States from Brazil on a student visa, also felt relief to have his status successfully resolved. Now that the uncertainty and the waiting were over, he could "focus on the things that I want to do for my future. . . . So now I can commit to it one hundred percent."

The way MAVNIs experienced becoming naturalized as an ability to stay in the United States and find jobs contrasts with the meaning of citizenship for most immigrants in the US military, who already have the right to stay and work in most fields as lawful permanent residents. Yet the naturalization of MAVNIs through the wartime military provisions was less secure because it could be revoked if they did not complete five years of honorable service.[49] Until 2022, when a US district court ruled that an "uncharacterized" discharge from the army based on medical reasons was to be considered honorable, such a discharge was a barrier to naturalization.[50] With more at stake if they were to separate from the military, especially before getting naturalized, immigrant workers experienced anxiety about injuries. As new security requirements were imposed on the program, and MAVNIs waited longer and longer to get naturalized, the threat of injury grew as they went through physically trying work for months or even years without the protection of citizenship, particularly when these MAVNIs became "stuck" while in the training phase. In one tragic case, a MAVNI soldier from Serbia was in training for an additional eleven months while waiting for his security checks to clear, only to die during a physical fitness session.[51]

Naturalization processes are meant for lawful permanent residents, not immigrants on temporary visas. This was a problem for some MAVNIs, as they tried to fill out forms that attempted to verify that they complied with the obligations of residency—which they were skipping entirely. Thus, Sebastian was puzzled when faced with a question about filing tax returns, required of lawful permanent residents applying for citizenship: "I've never been a legal resident. I went straight from being an international student here on a normal visa to becoming a citizen." Sebastian sought the help of his family's immigration attorney. Many MAVNIs turned to each other, creating communities that exchanged information. Hope credited the MAVNI community with how smoothly her naturalization process during basic training went: "They informed me of the things that I needed to bring, and I made sure that I brought that." Michael trained with a large MAVNI cohort and described mutual support: "We also had these soldiers who were US citizens who didn't care. So you are just going to stick with the other MAVNIs. You're going to be friends with the MAVNIs. All your friends are going to be MAVNIs because you all have a common goal and you all feel each other. If you have a crappy day, you can tell the other, 'Hey remember we're doing this for the paper [naturalization certificate], okay?' So . . . for us MAVNIs, it's like a thing, our thing. We kept each other going." Citizenship meant having the ability to stay and to get jobs, but it fell short of making Michael belong: "Even with the citizenship, you think, 'Oh, now I'm an American and I can do all these things.' They still remind you you're a foreigner." Despite their US citizenship, MAVNIs stood out in the military.

"NOBODY CALLED US SOLDIERS"

As immigrants, MAVNIs shared military labor experiences with other immigrant workers. However, there are several aspects of their work experiences that were unique or accentuated. Most MAVNIs were recent immigrants who arrived as young adults, not always knowing and understanding everything expected of a young person who grew up in the United States. At the same time, MAVNIs tended to be older and more educated than other enlisted personnel. Their experiences in the military and civilian spheres were shaped by this class mismatch. More so than immigrants who enlisted through standard pathways, MAVNIs experienced stigma and differential treatment because of their association with the program. Recruited ostensibly for their language and cultural skills of vital national interest, few MAVNIs used these in their military positions. In coping with the suspicion, stigma, and resentment that many of them faced in the military, MAVNIs bore the costs of militarized inclusion and grappled with the injuries of assimilation.

Many MAVNIs were international students who had been in the United States for only a few years. Although they were attending US colleges and had to pass an English proficiency exam to enroll, some still felt that their language and cultural fluency came up short. Struggles with English and US cultural knowledge could be thrown into relief during stressful military training. For instance, Heena recounted beginning basic training after having been in the US for two years: "I had these drill sergeants yelling at me and sometimes I didn't understand them, so the whole basic training is a blur for me because I was so scared at the time." Heena had been a radio announcer in Nepal and prided herself on her communication skills and outgoing personality. The language barrier silenced her: "I think language was a big thing. I was like, 'Are they going to understand what I say? Are they going to judge me?'" One evening in basic training, Heena's drill sergeant discovered her lack of cultural knowledge:

Everybody was getting yelled at and the drill sergeant was like, "Okay. Sing the national anthem." I was like, "Okay. I don't know the national anthem" [laughs]. I didn't know how to salute, so I saluted like that, because that's how they salute in Nepal. And the drill sergeant came and yelled: "What the fuck are you doing?!" And I looked around and everybody was saluting like this, so I corrected that. The lyrics I didn't know so I started moving my lips. Just moving my lips and the drill sergeant was passing and one of the drill sergeants, he caught me, he came to my face and he's like, "What are you saying?" I was like, "National anthem" [laughs]. And then he said, "I don't think you are." I was like, "No. I'm not." And he was like, "Why don't you know the national anthem?" I was like, "Because I'm not American." That was it [laughs]. I say, "I'm not an American." And then [with] everybody waiting, I got smoked for hours. [The drill sergeant said:] "I don't care what planet

you come from. I don't care what country you came from. You better know the national anthem because you're going to serve this country." And I was like, "Okay.
You could have told me in nicer voice but . . ." [*laughs*]. They smoked me for like
three to four hours and it was like, "By tomorrow, have it memorized." I went up-
stairs, asked my friends and they just helped me, it took all night. Around one or
twelve they would put it in my head. Then, I still remember the national anthem.

It's possible that being a South Asian woman attracted additional scrutiny from Heena's drill sergeants. Heena's story of punishment for not
knowing the national anthem is not a uniquely MAVNI story. It is rather
a story of military hierarchy that oppresses and humiliates recruits using
anything that sets them apart. Yet another, similar story points to the way
immigrants' association with MAVNI could be stigmatizing. Leila was
made to do pushups after failing to answer a series of US civics questions
to her sergeant's satisfaction. Leila recounted the sergeant saying: "What
is wrong with America for people like you [to be allowed to enlist]?" The
incident stayed with her years later because she actually was not a recent
immigrant like Heena and many MAVNIs but had attended high school
in the United States. Her gaps in civic knowledge could be blamed on the
US educational system, not Leila's foreignness. Yet it was being racialized
as a foreigner and being a MAVNI that attracted scorn and scrutiny.

Although the military could be a place where MAVNIs faced disdain,
and even humiliation, due to their perceived foreignness, some saw the
military as a way to overcome foreignness and gain belonging in the wider
society. For Kiran, an international student from Nepal, the uniform
erased the stigma of immigration outside the military: "I came in with
my uniform on and people didn't see me as an immigrant. They saw me
as an army soldier who is back from their training and they would come
and hug you, for no reason." Anna, from Ukraine, pointed out not only
the respect immigrant soldiers received, but a psychological boost and
social connection:

I really feel that being in the military, first of all, when you are in the uniform, any
kind of accent you speak with, people would look at you with respect. I guess that
for a lot of people that means a lot who just come here and feel, like, uncertain.
They have some type of problems with this. I guess it helps self-esteem. It helps,

on the side of other things that military gives us like discipline, other nice things that are not the same for everyone but for immigrants specifically, it's a way to get involved and to feel like you really belong to this society and you really belong here. It's also a way to make really good friends and [be] in a safe environment. You know, you can always use new friends when you come to a new country.

Anna acknowledged that some MAVNIs were discriminated against in the military, but also pointed out that some people are just awkward and blame discrimination for their awkwardness. I suspect that Anna's white femininity may help explain the way she dismissed other MAVNIs' experiences with discrimination, not least because awkwardness itself can be racialized. Strikingly, Anna referred to military labor as bringing safety to immigrants.

These MAVNI soldiers' experiences show that even as some MAVNIs are made to feel excluded within the military, a military identity can help racialized immigrants get treated as though they belong in the United States. In other words, their incorporation into the US society is militarized and requires a multi-year contract tying them to a job that can send them to participate in any of the many imperial aggressions going on at a given time. As we saw in chapter 4, the injuries of assimilation in a climate hostile to immigrants are normalized even by immigrants themselves. In the end, some MAVNIs are never fully accepted as members of the military, with the MAVNI label continuing to signal their suspect difference.

The military targets high school graduates when recruiting into the enlisted ranks. By contrast, the MAVNI program recruited older people who were already in college, in postgraduate studies, or even working as professionals. MAVNIs were, thus, far more similar to the officer corps than to fellow enlisted in terms of both age and education.[52] These characteristics are why the military referred to MAVNIs as "high-quality" recruits.[53] What was it like to be older and more educated in the military, as well as an immigrant?

Many of my respondents remarked on the age and class differences between MAVNIs and other enlistees when I asked them to describe their military experience, particularly while training. Military training is harder on older bodies. Jae-in, a Korean immigrant who enlisted in his early thirties, mentioned that boot camp was tough on him, even though his time in the South Korean military had prepared him for it. He said his fellow recruits were so young they could have been his children. During training, some MAVNIs were recognized for their age and maturity. For instance, Raj, an immigrant from India, recounted that his sergeants gave him additional responsibilities as an older and more experienced enlistee. Rohit, also from India, had been the oldest trainee in his unit and saw it as a special responsibility. Rohit told me that his captain appreciated that Rohit was willing to engage with fellow recruits despite the gap in age and experience: "He [the captain] said that's awesome that you were mingling with all these people and all that. So they're a young bunch of people. That's good you were understanding them, you were talking to them. You were acknowledging them because I've seen different country now, so that's because these young people, they never left the country."

Like several other MAVNIs I interviewed, Rohit reveled a bit in being a "high-quality" soldier: "The sergeant major was like wow, you guys [MAVNIs] are, like, so talented. You have master's and all that. You prove, you are kind of the face of the army and all that so. It made me so happy." Others noted their extraordinary high scores on the ASVAB. Some MAVNIs juxtaposed their educational credentials with stereotypes of regular enlistees as coming from broken families, having little life experience, or joining the military to avoid prison. A few explained that they chose to be reservists rather than on active duty—once that option became available to MAVNIs—because active duty would be a waste of their intelligence. As Shuang, an international student from China, put it: "They [non-MAVNI people in unit] are not the most successful people in their life. . . . But I do see wonderful MAVNIs. Get their PhD, getting their MBA. They're working hard in their life. So, you see different people. And unfortunately, most people in the military are not really planned out with their life. And you feel desperate. It's, like, am I, this is the people I'm dealing with in the future? [laughs] I think thank God it's only reserve, so it's not a big deal." Having high levels of education compared to other enlistees was not always comfortable for MAVNI soldiers, who had to explain to fellow soldiers over and over why someone with a college degree would enlist in the military. George said that enlisted people made him uncomfortable because he was overeducated. Gaurav, who enlisted with a master's, even said that he would not talk about his advanced degree: "I typically don't tell people that I have a master's just because a lot of them are . . . I wouldn't say spooked out, but they're very surprised to know that I have a master's in engineering and all that, and I'm an enlistee." Instead, he just said that he "went to school." Of course, MAVNIs are straddling a well-defined class divide within the military, with enlisted ranks on one side and officers on the other.

Interestingly, a few reservist MAVNIs I interviewed also described coping with a class mismatch in their civilian circles by selectively disclosing their military service. Raj said most people in his social and work networks did not know that he was in the reserves. He observed that many people he knew had negative opinions about the military. Guarav noted that he did not "tell people straight away that I'm in the army. Once I gain their confidence, that's when I tell them. Most of them are shocked. They're very surprised." Guarav would then explain to them that he was in the reserves, not on active duty. Some thought this was great, most were neutral, and a few fellow Indian immigrants considered him a traitor to India. George recounted his friends' negative reactions to his enlistment by pointing to the class mismatch: "A lot of my friends come from upper-class backgrounds, socioeconomic backgrounds because they all went to private schools and whatnot, and they look at the military as sort of like [a] middle-class or mid-low-class kind of thing to do."

In the military, MAVNI recruits' high levels of education helped them pass tests and training needed for promotion. When they did so, however, they could become targets for resentment by those who struggled to advance. As Heena explained:

There [were] already people talking about how MAVNIs are privileged because in order to be promoted from an E-4 to a sergeant, you need college education, which gives you lots of points. If you have different, extra language, you get points for that. And you get points for doing online trainings, and MAVNIs are some educated, smart people. They went online and did the training. Lots of people in my unit, they were still stuck with E-4 ranks for years because they could not finish those trainings and did not have college education. So there was this hatred towards lots of MAVNIs because they were being promoted quick. They were getting in all the posts they [other enlisted] wanted. And there was jealousy, I think.

While their high levels of education allowed many MAVNIs to advance in the enlisted ranks to some extent, there remained a major mismatch between their skills and military occupations, particularly when they struggled to clear security checks. Michael got trained to be a vocational nurse, which he described as "one of the best jobs as an enlisted soldier if you don't want blow up things." But because Michael did not get a security clearance, his was unable to use his nursing license, which is critical to maintaining it. Michael felt that his "area [of expertise] and skill is just all going to the waste. So this master's degree, I'm not using it. I could be using it." Michael said that he could have been using his skills in laboratories that the military runs if not for his problems with security clearance. Raj had a master's degree and worked in IT. While in the Army Reserve, he was informally asked to help with computers, but was not able to use those skills in his military occupation: "The problem is that the commander and everybody know that I'm an IT master and they want me to go to the IT. But because of MAVNI I can't go." Like many of my respondents, Li Wei explained that very few options were given to him when he enlisted: "There's not a lot of choice for us [in military occupations]. Even if they enlist us, they don't really fully trust us."

Bernard contrasted the lauding of MAVNIs as high-quality soldiers with the barriers they faced to career advancement in the military. Coming in as enlisted personnel rather than officers, MAVNIs expected that once naturalized, they would be like any other US citizen working in the military: "You go through this hoop, you get there on the other side of door; once you swear your oath, you receive your US citizenship; you are treated as everybody else." As the crackdown on security clearances for MAVNIs took effect, Bernard listed all the careers that were now cut off for him and his peers: "For people who wanted to go do bigger and greater things, who let's say go and become a commissioned officer, want to go to the OCS [officer candidate school], want to go become a military JAG [judge advocate general] advocate, which is like a military lawyer, or even go [to] some really, really high levels of different research job, you all need security clearance. So now, that opportunity . . . that prospect is cut off." Other immigrants can also have social mobility issues within the military because of security clearances, but MAVNI's mismatch of skills and military occupation is particularly acute.

By definition, MAVNIs were recruited for their skills of vital national interest. For the vast majority, these skills were operationalized as the ability to communicate in one of the languages designated as of vital interest. Yet almost every MAVNI recruit I interviewed admitted that they did not, in fact, use their language skills while working in the military. As George put it, "The MAVNI program screwed it up. They put us in MOS [military occupational specialty] positions that have absolutely nothing to do with the skills that are vital to national interests!" George himself—a fluent speaker of Korean with two master's degrees—was an automated logistical specialist, which the army career website describes as "similar to a laborer or freight mover."[54] Michael, who was not able to use his medical skills because of security restrictions, never used his language skills either: "I thought . . . they're going to deploy me to areas where people speak Swahili at least. That's Africa, I'm going to get trained for that. So they say we're these soldiers with these special skills to join but they are not using any of those special skills. . . . I would think they would put me in a unit that deploys in regions like that. That's what I would think. . . . My MOS has nothing to do with language." Language and cultural skills are useful in specific military occupations, many foreclosed to MAVNIs because of their status as foreigners. But these skills are also particularly useful in contexts of overseas deployment, where MAVNIs might draw on them while performing many kinds of military labor. Yet some of the MAVNIs I interviewed were deployed to overseas bases where their language and cultural skills were not needed, such as when Kiran, a Nepali who qualified for MAVNI based on speaking his native language, was deployed to South Korea.

MAVNIs were not only older and more educated than the average military recruit. Even after becoming US citizens, some reported being treated with suspicion as foreigners. As Andrew put it, "a MAVNI who has been through the system already or who's already a citizen, like at least they should treat us like citizens. Like, not like second-class citizens. You know, because we're American and we should be treated like Americans." Andrew and others were frustrated by what they saw as a broken promise from the military. The equal treatment they expected once getting US citizenship did not materialize. Rather, recruited for their foreignness, they were not allowed to blend into the general military workforce. Bernard explained:

You're saying that we're not eligible for security clearance, now you're saying we're not trustworthy. We're like insider threats. We're all fucking bad piece of shits, excuse my language. So, if that's the condition that you want us to work under, and then not trusting us, then my question is why the hell are we wearing this uniform for? I mean, there's no point anymore. And then when a lot of people, a lot of MAVNI soldiers started trying to look for ways to get out, the army turns around and bite us in the ass and say, "Well, look at all of you. You all joined because of the citizenship. As soon as you got your citizenship, you all quit." Okay, that's fine, that's cool. But then when we start dropping like flies, when we start quitting, don't you come back and say we did it because of citizenship.

Bernard was livid about experiencing this treatment and being suspected as an inside threat within the military. It bothered him that MAVNIs who did not renew their contracts or otherwise left the military as a response to being treated as foreign spies were then further accused of only enlisting to get US citizenship.

Part of the frustration stemmed from the way security clearances imposed on MAVNIs thwarted careers, yet MAVNIs reported experiencing prejudice as foreigners more broadly. For instance, Heena recounted that "nobody called us soldiers": Heena and other MAVNIs in her special operations unit were referred to as MAVNIs. Heena said she would have to explain that MAVNI was not her title or her military job, but just the program through which she came into the army. Yet MAVNIs in Heena's unit were understood by fellow soldiers not to be military personnel in a variety of occupations who came in through a recruitment program, but as an othered and suspect group. While Bernard discussed the suspicion MAVNIs faced as potential spies, Heena's experience was that MAVNIs were resented for their language skills—because they got extra pay—and for ostensibly faking injuries. This treatment drove Heena to prove everyone wrong:

We are soldiers. Despite that, people considered us like MAVNIs, we were not soldiers. That's why I wanted to prove these people wrong and say, like "Hey, I can do the same thing that you can do and be better at it and do better things in the army." That's why I wanted to stay in and go to this course and stay in and show all these people, because they thought MAVNIs are just MAVNIs. And they are educated people, very educated, a lot more educated than the colonels and generals and the sergeant majors. So there was a lot of discrimination.

There is a high cost to this fight to prove oneself, harkening to the litany of injuries of assimilation discussed in the last chapter. The military labor of MAVNIs was characterized by experiences of othering as foreigners and a mismatch in social class and skill sets. Yet we also see the complex desires of MAVNI enlistees to belong, drawing on the power of the uniform in the civilian world even as they both experienced rejection within the military and attempted to distance themselves from the pool of younger, less educated recruits.

MAVNI LIMBO: FROM GOLDEN SHORTCUT TO A CRISIS

Living in such a limbo, it's a torture. Not just physically but also mentally. This is not an easy process, this is not an easy life to live under these circumstances.[55]

Like many others, this young man [an anonymous young Pakistani student] was kept in limbo with little or no information until finally being told he was being rejected. Now, the student not only won't be able to enlist, but his path to citizenship is blocked as well, with a visa expiring in six months and potential deportation looming.[56]

By 2018, "limbo" became a common way to describe the situation of about 4,000 MAVNIs who signed military contracts but were waiting interminably for their security checks to clear so they could begin their training.[57] The MAVNI limbo was an extension of the uncertainty experienced by temporary migrants in the United States, and it exacerbated precarity among the most vulnerable of these migrants.

The Delayed Entry Program was extended to 730 days to accommodate the wait for security checks imposed on MAVNI enlistees, yet some reached this deadline with no resolution and were discharged from the army.[58] MAVNIs were subjected to screenings by the FBI and CIA normally reserved for top-secret clearance, which included day-long interviews with questions about every aspect of life, travel, relationships, habits, and financial history.[59] The high cost of these screenings, the lack of personnel to carry them out, and the fact that information had to be verified in foreign countries all contributed to the delays.[60] Rather than a source of highly skilled labor, temporary migrants who enlisted through MAVNI became a liability. There were instances of MAVNI recruits receiving texts from their recruiters giving them ten minutes to respond to confirm that they still wanted to enlist, then canceling their contracts if they failed to respond in time.[61]

For many who enlisted in 2015 and 2016, multi-year waits between enlistment and basic training had become the norm. The army did give these recruits shipping dates initially, only to reschedule them repeatedly and eventually eliminate the shipping date altogether. This meant that people prepared to pause their lives time and time again to undertake a multi-month training. They took leaves from studies and jobs, canceled their leases, and sold their cars. Ravi moved seven times in three years because he would sign only temporary apartment leases, expecting to be shipped. Sebastian transferred from a community college to a four-year college, counting on getting citizenship shortly and qualifying for in-state tuition. When his ship date was delayed, he had to drop out and return to the community college.

Amitabh, an international student from India, postponed graduation at the request of his recruiter. Postponing graduation meant that he could keep his student status while waiting to be shipped to basic training. The military did not provide these temporary workers with work authorization while they waited to begin their training. And it expected them to maintain their immigration status through strategies like postponing graduation or signing up for more education. In this way, the MAVNI experience became an augmentation of the temporary migrant life in the United States more generally, characterized by visa renewals, uncertainty, waits, and the threat of falling out of status. Expecting to start training at the beginning of the fall semester, Amitabh told his supervisors that he could not accept his graduate assistantship, "because I don't want to just leave in September and then they have to find someone else. They thanked me and took away my assistantship." A few weeks before he should have shipped, Amitabh learned that he would now ship in January, leaving him stranded, without income. In the end, he was glad that he decided not to postpone his graduation again, "not to rely on the Army further": his new January ship date was canceled in the end. Living in a MAVNI limbo continued to affect Amitabh's life after graduation:

When I was applying for jobs, I suffered a lot, because people would ask me about any constraints or anything, and I never lied. So, I told them, "Hey, I'm here in this program called MAVNI. I'm part of the military, but I don't know when I will ship." So they would ask me, "When you would ship?" Maybe in three months? Then the response would be, "Okay. We will let you know." Then I have to lose those jobs. It would have been my dream job in California at a biotech company. I have to just see my jobs slipping out of my hands. Because I understand. Any employer would not like [that the] person who he or she is recently hiring would leave within three months.

Robert, an international student from Indonesia, was all set to go to basic training after college graduation. Trusting his recruiter and the contract he signed, he did not apply for OPT, which would have given him a work authorization for a year. His shipping date to basic training was pushed off twice. The onus to keep his temporary visa status and remain qualified for MAVNI had been on Robert himself. When I interviewed him, Robert had been discharged from the military without ever starting his training and lived as an undocumented immigrant. Xijin's recruiter told him that the military would give him employment authorization until he was naturalized. This, of course, is not true, and cost Xijin a job offer. When Xijin went back to the recruiting office, he said that he was told that "it would be more helpful if you can keep your status legal [on] your own."

Amitabh, Robert, Xijin, and other MAVNIs bore the brunt of the lack of legal status provisions for immigrants on temporary visas whom the military targeted with the program. Amy voiced this critique when she highlighted the difficulties specifically of those with temporary status during long MAVNI delays: "Especially for immigrants, they need working visa, some kind of temporary documents for them to stay and work

[and] live normally here. But [the] army didn't think of anything like that. They could offer us some kind of temporary document. If I could renew my driver's license, at least I could work, then that won't be like it [would] damage people's lives that much."

The MAVNI limbo exacerbated the precarity of temporary migrants. International students and temporary workers became stuck between the institution of the military and the immigration system, which operated on different clocks. Researchers have explored the role of time and temporality in the experience of migrants.[62] Temporary migrants, in particular, can get stuck in what scholars Jean-Baptiste Farcy and Sarah Smit call "time traps" when their lives depend on contingencies of visa renewals and employer whims and it is difficult to plan for the future.[63] In this case, the schedule of clearances imposed by the Department of Defense, riddled with lack of information, uncertainty, and frequent rescheduling, met the immigration system, with its own exacting timeline.

The systemic vulnerability of temporary workers and international students, who commonly fall out of legal status, was an unfortunate combination with the long waits faced by the last cohorts of MAVNI enlistees. Daler, an international student from India, was waiting for resolution for many months by the time I talked to him, living on financial support from friends and family. He felt that the immigration authorities should be responsible for extending legal status to MAVNI recruits who were waiting to be shipped to basic training, particularly those on expiring student visas. The military had extended Daler's contract to three years to accommodate the long wait to start his training, but there was no coordination between the military and the immigration agencies to extend his immigration status. Facing expiring visas, migrants enrolled in additional educational programs when they could find the funds to do so. Daler pointed out not only that there did not seem to be respect for people's lives affected by MAVNI limbo, but that the system was set up to keep temporary migrants forever unsettled and anxious: "It seems as if their [immigration agencies'] intentions [are] they don't want to let you relax, they want to keep you on your toes . . . don't want people to relax, they don't want people to breathe even." The cycle of visa applications and reapplications, waiting periods, extensions, and other obstacles kept temporary migrants like Daler "on their toes." If anything, signing a contract with the military exacerbated the typical experience of the temporary migrant in the United States, with the golden shortcut to US citizenship morphing into a crisis for many MAVNIs.

Another alarming disconnect between the military and the immigration system for MAVNIs in limbo pertained to the requirements for student visas. For international students on F-1 visas, enlistment in the military meant that they could have difficulty renewing their visas or getting new ones because they had demonstrated an intent to settle in the United States.[64] The condition for these temporary visas is being able to show that one will not, indeed, settle. The need to remain in the United States during what became several years of waiting weighed heavily on many MAVNIs in limbo. Sebastian said he felt like he was in a jail, particularly when the grandmother who raised him became ill and died, and he could not return to Brazil to be with her. Minzhe explained how waiting for years to begin his military training post-enlistment affected him as a temporary migrant:

So a very heavy thing, a very difficult situation is that I cannot go back to China. The reason why is that for [an] F-1 student, it's a non-immigrant visa. If we show our immigrant intent, we will not be able to enter back to the US. . . . We sign a contract to show our immigrant intent. If we want to go back, and leave, come back—no way. . . . I miss my family. I miss my home country's food and I really miss a lot of things. But I haven't met my family for two years. Two and a half years. So that's also a pressure. I cannot work.

Minzhe would not be able to reenter the United States if he left, and so he stopped going home to China. His student visa also severely limited his ability to work and support himself.

Minzhe worried about going back to China for another reason: he feared that enlistment in the US military would be viewed unfavorably by the Chinese government, which, he noted, could prosecute him for treason. My Chinese study participants differed in their concern over possible prosecution in China, although US media coverage tended to highlight those who said that they feared returning to China and filed asylum applications.[65] Margaret Stock, the creator of MAVNI, was now helping these MAVNIs with their asylum applications, and using anti-MAVNI posts on the Chinese social media app, Sina Weibo, as evidence. Ironically, Sina Weibo was where some of these Chinese MAVNIs first learned about the program from recruiter posts.[66] MAVNIs from other countries who got stuck in legal limbo also feared retribution if they were to be deported. For example, Malik's family in Pakistan was harassed and threatened with violence over his enlistment in the US military. Eventually, Malik applied for asylum. Different countries have different laws about service in foreign militaries. Anna, a Ukrainian participant, lost her Ukrainian citizenship entirely when she signed up for MAVNI. Instead of a fast track to citizenship, Anna remained precarious in the United States and was stateless when I spoke to her.

Many MAVNIs who had signed up for the Army Reserve, which became an option in 2014, continued to attend monthly drills with their reserve units, as they waited to be cleared for basic training. These experiences could be uncomfortable, as fellow reservists did not always understand why these recruits had not gone to basic training for much longer than normal. Robert described being perpetually treated as the "new guy" for two years, the only one without a uniform. Without the training, MAVNIs could engage only in some activities and tasks during these drills, doing cleaning while everyone handled weapons, for instance. They also had to cover the costs of traveling to the drills and the accommodations, which for some meant sleeping in cars. Ravi drove two hundred miles for monthly weekend drills. Guarav flew from North Carolina to California to attend his drills after leaving California for a job while waiting for basic training. He was not given permission to change his unit to something more local—because he had not gone to basic training—but he was able to go every few months, rather than monthly.

Temporary migrants who got stuck in the MAVNI legal limbo were made more precarious, but there was a variation in the effects that was not always apparent in the media coverage, focused as it was on MAVNIs whose losses fit into the narrative of deservingness and vulnerability. Some became undocumented, eked out a precarious living, or feared violence if they were to return to their home countries. Mental health suffering was widespread. Robert said that his "anxiety nerves [are] already broken," after months of frustration, anxiety, sleeplessness, and the difficulty of explaining his situation. Others, however, suffered from uncertainty and botched plans, but generally returned to the longer pathway to residency of international students and temporary professional workers. Some planned to move elsewhere, like Canada or Europe, or did not mind returning to the country of their birth. A few participants were able to implement backup plans. For instance, Shuang, who had been a master's student from China when he enlisted, was now going for a PhD and hopeful about future employment in STEM.

Not everyone had the options that Shuang had, however, and the most extreme cases of MAVNI suffering came from temporary migrants who were already precariously positioned by attending non-elite colleges, or who had come as international high school students. Stories like that of Jung-soo, who did not quite fit the highly skilled image of MAVNIs, were less publicized. Jung-soo was a Korean immigrant who came to the United States for high school and was recruited into MAVNI while still in high school when recruiters visited his JROTC program. To satisfy MAVNI requirements, Jung-soo enrolled in a community college. He failed his security investigation after three years of waiting to be shipped to basic training. When I interviewed him over video chat, Jung-soo's student visa was set to expire, and his only plan seemed to be to try to renew it for more community college classes. Jung-soo appeared even younger than his twenty years and sounded every bit depressed as he said: "I'm right here in the limbo." Given the increasing obstacles and extreme competition for international students to get lawful permanent residency or even temporary work visas in the United States, it seemed unlikely that Jung-soo would find a pathway to US citizenship through his community college education. From the opposite side of the spectrum, George reflected on the unequal class effects of the MAVNI limbo:

And it looks like they were picking on people, they are discharging people who are more vulnerable. . . . When they look at my file, my file is much more solid than others because I come from [Ivy League university], I come from upper-class background. I come from top boarding school. . . . So it's not in their interest, I don't think, to fuck with me for my file. Whereas they pick on some random third-tier school guy, then they feel safer. I'm sure they're doing all sorts of calculation about it. Lawyers do that all the time. If they are trying to fuck with somebody else, they're going to calculate, "Okay, does this guy have resources to come back to me?," right? They pick on some random, vulnerable Chinese or Indian guys I suppose. They pick on whatever reasons to kick them out.

MAVNIs like George had enough resources to hire attorneys, improving their chances of getting redress to their situations. By contrast, after getting discharged from MAVNI, Amy worked fifteen-hour days in fast food, slept on a friend's couch, and had no money for legal assistance. While there was variation in the effects of MAVNI limbo on immigrants who enlisted through the program, even those who could pursue alternative plans and did not worry about becoming stateless or being charged with treason experienced the stress of being between the military and immigration systems with two different and unforgiving sets of clocks and requirements. They had to repeatedly place their lives on hold and devise ways to maintain their immigration status.

RECRUITED FOR BEING FOREIGN, REJECTED FOR BEING FOREIGN

When new security checks were implemented toward the end of the MAVNI program, their very structure made it difficult for immigrants with ties to other countries to pass. Moreover, the security investigations could threaten the employment of already precarious workers. As Jadhav, from India, put it:

The way I kind of see it, by its very definition . . . [I cannot have security clearance] because I am a foreigner in the US dominant sense. I'm flabbergasted but what's the logic in there, actually? By the very definition of MAVNI, all of us should have a foreign passport, all of us have some sort of visa. All of us should have, like, relatives and, like, family back in our home country. So I'm kind of, like, very curious, like, what exactly everyone will find out this so-called derogatory information. That's, like, the very definition of MAVNI is all of us should be non-immigrants, and we are foreigners who the US let in.

The investigation meant that government agents interviewed Jadhav's office coworkers and supervisors, putting him in what he termed a "tricky" situation in a new workplace where he was already precarious by the dint of his temporary employment visa. By the time I spoke to him in 2018, Jadhav had been waiting for three years to find out what would happen with his MAVNI enlistment.

Amitabh, another Indian immigrant, used a Freedom of Information Act (FOIA) request to find out what exactly got him unfavorable judgments in two investigations. The first investigation listed only one concern, having a foreign family, and deemed him to pose a major security risk. The second report determined that he provided faulty information and, thus, posed a minor security risk. The faulty information was an Indian bank account containing several hundred dollars, which Amitabh did declare, and a father-in-law who the investigators said was a low-level government employee, even though he had never worked for any government in India. Amitabh was ready to provide copious proof of his father-in-law's employment history, but there was no outlet to do so. He agonized about closing the bank account, because closing it would be seen as a suspicious foreign money transfer. If he gave the money to his mother, it would be "like I asked some foreigner to keep my money." The security requirements placed MAVNIs into impossible situations. Ravi explained how they worked: "Basically it's a comprehensive interview to check whether you are terrorist or not [*chuckles*]. Basically the program was set up to detect any espionage, but because of xenophobia and everything they use that apparatus to vet [MAVNI enlistees] nowadays. Wasting thousands of taxpayers' money."

The securitization of the MAVNI program disqualified temporary migrants due to their foreignness, the very characteristic on which the program was based. International students faced a particularly absurd situation. Required to demonstrate that their families had enough to pay for their college education in the United States, that very support caused them to fail security checks. Daniel recounted that when he applied for his student visa at a US embassy in China, his parents had to show that they had enough money to support him: "It's actually a requirement when I went to the US Embassy in China for my formal visa interview. They asked me for the financial . . . asked me for the bank statement from my parents. I needed to show that my family has enough funds for me to go. But right now, it's become a burden, it's become a problem. It's really strange for me." A requirement for getting a visa to come to the United States was now a disqualification for Daniel and other international students. Notably, international students are severely limited in the amount and type of employment they are able to legally access while studying, making family support necessary. The counterintelligence interview requirements that were imposed on MAVNIs at the end of the program viewed financial support by parents as accepting funds from foreigners, an inherently suspicious activity in the eyes of the security apparatus in the United States. MAVNIs failed the security screening for sending money to parents abroad, for calling family abroad, for socializing with noncitizens, and even for failing to laugh at jokes. People failed for having wealthy families and for having poor families—both might influence the soldier's loyalty. Although it was the opening of MAVNI to DACA recipients that may have precipitated the end of the program through securitization, DACA recipients had an easier time passing through security screenings because they had arrived in the United States as children, usually with their parents, and had few ties to other countries by the time they enlisted.

Aside from the obstacles to passing security checks for any immigrant with ties to countries outside the United States, some of the MAVNIs I interviewed were hampered by the way their military recruiters filled out paperwork. I already mentioned Anna, who said her recruiter wrote down "nonsense" in her forms due to unfamiliarity with international context and MAVNI. For one of the required security processes, Anna sat for an eight-hour interview. The investigator noticed multiple discrepancies between what she was saying and the information entered into the system by the recruiter:

Let's say that he put I am talking to my father on the phone every month and I didn't see my father since I was eleven, so I mean [*laughs*]. Or that I am talking to my grandfather on the phone and my grandfather passed away in 2008, so it's impossible. A lot of things, yeah, a lot of things that were there that didn't make sense at all. When I got my SSBI [Single Scope Background Investigation] interview, this lady [the investigator], she didn't understand what was going on because what I was saying and my form were two separate things.

The unfavorable judgment was not reversed even after Anna submitted a request for an amendment, painstakingly documenting every discrepancy with documents like her grandfather's translated death certificate. Amy failed her security screening and had her MAVNI contract terminated. She told me that her recruiter submitted a list of references meant for another person, who were then contacted by the investigator to describe a literal stranger. When Amy got a hold of her file, she saw multiple mistakes throughout, such as misspellings of family members' names.

The screening process itself appeared inconsistent, capricious, and opaque, and some investigators unqualified or even unscrupulous. There were flagrant mistakes in the reports, attributed to the lack of training and experience by the personnel hired by the Department of Defense to carry out the screenings.[67] Zhang Wei, an immigrant from China, got an unfavorable recommendation for "lack of candor, dishonesty, and not following rules" due to an unpaid traffic ticket. He had actually paid this ticket before the investigation, and it was no longer in the system. The investigators knew about it only because he had listed that ticket on his form: "They used my honesty against me. That makes me feel somehow very sick." Not all MAVNI recruits even knew what garnered unfavorable recommendations because they did not pursue the FOIA requests necessary to see their own reports. In all, the security screenings imposed on MAVNIs made it impossible for many of them to pass, highlight the tensions with the requirements of the immigration system, and brought to light unscrupulous and inconsistent work of recruiters and screeners.

INDIVIDUAL AND COLLECTIVE RESPONSES TO MAVNI LIMBO

The media focus on individual stories of suffering fails to capture the collective experience of MAVNIs, who are a relatively small group connected to each other densely through social media and social networks. Although the experiences of MAVNI limbo differed, MAVNIs did develop an impressive network and community, providing each other with information, support, and solidarity, as well as managing and containing MAVNI narratives. The MAVNIs whom I interviewed explained the important role played in their lives by the MAVNI-related Facebook groups. Of course, this was to be expected since I recruited participants through one of these groups. However, this group had 15,000 members and multiple posts per day, clearly acting as a clearinghouse of information and community-building tool. The Facebook groups served as sources of information to help MAVNIs understand repeatedly delayed shipping dates and the workings of security investigations. For the most part, the people whose job it was to provide this information to MAVNIs—their recruiters—did not know it themselves. As a Chinese MAVNI, Daniel, explained: "Most of the time I got information from the MAVNI Facebook, or I don't think the recruiters are aware, they are not very updated with this stuff. I need to find out everything on my own."

For a few participants, the Facebook pages were a source of support and connection. Guarav, an immigrant from India, had used a MAVNI Facebook group to build supportive relationships: "So I try to help people in the same situation who are trying to find answers as much as I can, and also to learn about the latest developments. I've made some MAVNI friends whom I've never met in life, but I just spoke to them over the phone and we became friends on Facebook, quite a few of us, so you know, just to keep up with what they're doing and all that." Likewise, Malik coped with mental health effects of the long, indeterminate waiting by talking with other stuck MAVNIs he met online, sometimes crying together. Although the online community provided crucial information and meaningful connections for some, for others, it became an emotionally trying experience. For instance, Xijin said: "I try to avoid, like, to review the Facebook. I may just seldom check it, but not repeatedly because I feel like if I check it too frequently, it makes me more nervous."

While MAVNIs shared their personal travails navigating the military and immigration systems on social media, comparing their situations, and sharing advice and rumors, I observed a pattern of speech policing. If posts were too despondent or critical in tone, commentors would tell the original poster to trust that the system would work. Often, these commentors were MAVNIs whose individual cases had been favorably resolved or whose enlistment and naturalization went smoothly because they enlisted earlier on in the program. A few study participants also noticed this pattern online, which conformed to their experience with successful MAVNIs in real life. Zhang Wei, an immigrant from China, said that some MAVNIs insisted that "you're MAVNIs, you have to stand for the MAVNI program," but he was different because he acknowledged that the program was not thought-out. Nikolai explained the dynamic in this way: "MAVNIs [who] passed through, you can even see it on the MAVNI page, they really believe that it's right [the way the program works]. . . . 'We made it, we don't care anymore.'" Nikolai, who was in MAVNI limbo, expressed skepticism at the effusive performance of patriotism on the MAVNI Facebook page. Similarly, Zhang Wei, who was in MAVNI limbo for years, looked askance at the performativity that characterized the Facebook posts:

I would say, I have seen the posts, like, people say, "I love America. I want to become American soldier. I want to protect this country." Yes, maybe some of them do or maybe some of them just write them up to try to make them look like this way. But from inside, I'm a very realistic person. So, from what I see, I will say 95 percent of those soldiers don't mean that. They don't mean that. Yeah, of course we want to protect America. We don't want the US to come like being invaded. Of course, we want to keep the systems going up, yeah, but using the extra languages, writing those very clear statements, I don't think those are very true.

This collective policing of how MAVNIs talked about the program and their experience of being in MAVNI limbo is not surprising considering the high stakes and the relative powerlessness of a small group of temporary migrants. As is true in immigrant rights advocacy more generally in the United States, the fight to have the United States honor the MAVNI contracts was premised on their deservingness. Media coverage of MAVNI recruits' travails emphasized their high quality as military labor, their patriotism, as well as the pathos of their situation. Defenders of MAVNI leaned heavily on the moral superiority of MAVNI recruits compared to US-born soldiers. They pointed out that US-born troops were not subjected to nearly the same vetting, despite multiple examples of non-immigrants in the military perpetrating various acts the US government considers to be terrorism.[68] Moreover, while the army routinely granted waivers to enlist US citizens with drug and criminal histories, even felons with prison records, MAVNIs were entirely ineligible for these. One news story of a Ukrainian immigrant, Alina Kaliuzhna, stressed her bachelor's degree, her work ethic, and her exemplary performance in medic training.[69] News stories covering Yea Ji Sea, a Korean immigrant who was discharged from the army after four years, emphasized her A average in the premed program and potential as a future army doctor.[70] The images of highly educated and patriotic MAVNIs and the evidence of their innocence as security threats contrasted with media stories' mention of formerly incarcerated US citizens receiving waivers to enlist.

MAVNI advocates argued that the attack on MAVNI was an attack on immigrants, as Margaret Stock told CNN: "It's a fear of foreigners. It's a couple of bureaucrats at the Pentagon who don't want foreigners in their ranks."[71] The Department of Defense insisted that it was not about immigrants, but about a risk of "insider threats such as espionage, terrorism, and other criminal activity."[72] After instituting the new policies, it bolstered its claim by pointing to a new case of a MAVNI reservist from China who allegedly provided secret information to a Chinese intelligence officer.[73]

Given public narratives that framed them as a security threat, MAVNIs faced a difficult balancing act of pointing to the obvious failure in the system that they experienced without being too critical. A few even justified what happened to them as understandable and reasonable. Sebastian said that he "wouldn't want it any other way. Especially because you don't want anybody that has some sort of bad intention going into the military and having access to all that stuff." Several of my respondents even declined to criticize the recruiters who ruined their chances of passing security screenings through incompetent actions. MAVNIs also had to be careful not to overemphasize the path to citizenship they had been promised, lest it appear that they enlisted only for that. Some focused on insisting that the contract they signed with the US military simply be honored. This is how Lee explained why he engaged in public advocacy with fellow MAVNIs: "I just wanted to at least let everyone know that we're not asking for money. We're not asking for any special treatment. All we're asking is the honor of the contract from the government side."

In explaining the MAVNI limbo, MAVNIs themselves used multiple variants of deservingness. Some pointed out that while MAVNIs faced extreme vetting, it was US-born Americans who perpetrated mass shootings, joined anti-American groups, and committed treason. Others listed all the ways in which MAVNIs were superior to regular soldiers. Paresh juxtaposed MAVNI doctors and scientists with "these young kids [US-born enlistees]: most of them come from broken homes. Army is the way out for them." This argument positioned MAVNIs as deserving of access to the military and its benefits because they were better, and because their labor would benefit the United States more than the labor of US-born enlistees. Ravi argued that MAVNIs saved the US military money because they come already equipped with vital skills and don't need costly training. Ravi extended his cost analysis to calling out the waste of taxpayers' money represented by the extreme security screenings of MAVNIs.

Part of the deservingness narrative was internal differentiation of MAVNIs from other immigrants. Some said that they were earning their citizenship in a morally superior way to those who got their citizenship through marrying an American. As Malik put it, "I'm going to give something to this country and take something back from it." Others argued that MAVNIs deserved remedy because they followed all the rules and arrived in the United States legally, implicitly or explicitly distancing themselves from undocumented immigrants. Of course, this argument elides the fact that more than half of undocumented immigrants in the United States also arrived in the United States legally on visas. And they are unable to enlist the military to prove their worth in this paradigm.

Finally, in an effort to demonstrate their deservingness, some MAVNIs drew boundaries between good and bad MAVNIs. They suggested that they were better than other, usually unspecified, MAVNIs who might very well pose a real security risk to the United States or dissemble in their motivations. This failure of solidarity among MAVNIs is another type of harm sustained in attempts to assimilate. Nikolai condemned fellow MAVNIs for faking injuries to get out after getting citizenship and for putting on an inauthentic performance of patriotism: "I mean, I understand why the army was upset, I would be honest with you. Because they were enlisting people, and people were using it to get a fast-track citizenship. And I don't know if anybody told me, but . . . what happens after they get citizenship, a lot of people claim fake medical cases." When I pointed out that faking medical cases to get out of military contracts was not unique to MAVNIs or even immigrants, Nikolai said that it was different because working in the military was a privilege for immigrants. Thus, it was not as bad for the US-born to fake medical conditions—because it was their military to quit. Jung-soo even expressed support for the way rules were changed on MAVNIs after they signed their contracts: "If I was a citizen, I would not want to endanger my country. Totally understand." In putting forth this argument, Jung-Soo appeared to support the rationale for the securitization of MAVNI, even as he insisted that his own unfavorable determination was an error. MAVNIs like Nikolai and Jung-Soo seemed to accept the system that harmed them but wanted an exception for themselves as not posing real security threats.

Narratives of deservingness are pervasive in US society, with claims to citizenship and belonging commonly constructed with arguments based on distinguishing the claimants as better and/or worthier than stated or unstated others. This is readily apparent in debates over the living wage, welfare, and criminal justice reform. Pointing to the nonviolent criminal, the hard-working single mother, and the immigrant farmworker being slowly poisoned for less than minimum wage, we say that these figures deserve remedy from the violence of the system. The violent criminals, "welfare queens," and immigrants unable to demonstrate uncomplaining hard work are left with few advocates because—implicitly or explicitly— they deserve their plight. In the immigrant rights movement, claims to relief are commonly based on noncriminality, heteronormative family, religiosity, and, of course, willingness to be exploited. "Legal" immigrants distinguish themselves from undocumented immigrants, asylees claim deservingness in comparison to economic migrants, and immigrants in the military talk about a more honorable path to citizenship compared to civilians. Lisa Marie Cacho demonstrates that deservingness requires that recognition of social value be premised on the devaluation of someone else, including members of one's own group or community. She shows that deservingness-based arguments undermine collective resistance: "We also expect less of struggle, especially political struggle, if a movement's legitimacy hinges on its constituents' deservingness as rights-bearing, law-abiding subjects because this focus pressures community leaders and committed activists to concentrate their efforts on lobbying the state to enforce its unfulfilled promises of privilege and protection."[74] Desiring security and belonging within systems that perpetuate injustice and inequity resulted in immigrants' negotiations of human value through the politics of deservingness, in a nested process of boundary making against US-born soldiers, non-MAVNI immigrant military workers, and even other, less deserving, MAVNIs.

Given the power of the deservingness narrative, it is not surprising that so many MAVNIs I spoke to drew on it and that deviations from it could be censored by the MAVNI community. Despite their shortcomings, deservingness narratives are difficult to resist as cultural material available in claims-making to vulnerable groups. Yet my interviews also revealed a complexity that belied easy categorization and exposed the task of fitting the realities of the temporary migrant lives into the straitjacket of the good immigrant soldier. For instance, Amy had said it was reasonable for the United States to suspect the foreigners it recruited into its military for their very foreignness. But she also accused the military of getting rid of MAVNIs to deal with their own errors: "They [the military] had tried to clean up those people who [are] already out of status because of the delay. They made the delay, and they kick out people because of their fault." Zhang Wei said it was right to shut down MAVNIs because too many people were just trying to use it to get citizenship. But although he refused to blame the government for MAVNI being "somehow broken," he argued that it treated MAVNIs unfairly. Jadhab both spoke proudly of the way MAVNIs were known to be patient and persevering in the face of unfair treatment and noted that this treatment would never be tolerated if it affected US-born recruits. This type of complexity was reflective of the potential of MAVNIs to move beyond deservingness claims to more systemic critiques of the military and immigration system, as well as a more inclusive basis of resistance.

The response of immigrants who became stuck in MAVNI limbo to their situation reveals the way individual narratives and coping strategies were embedded in the collective experience of this group. MAVNIs who were recruited for their foreignness and then punished for it, with promises broken, had to modulate their critique in the face of significant suspicion of their motives and loyalties, and the pressure to uphold the system with which they cast their lot in their desire to gain security and belonging. Deservingness politics threatened solidarity and disciplined dissent—telltale marks of injuries of assimilation as immigrants attempted to assume their place in the hierarchies. Yet MAVNIs did act collectively to seek redress, and they found ways to express their dignity and desires.

THE MAVNI EPILOGUE

In 2021, some MAVNI recruits still did not know what would happen to their military contracts or naturalization.[75] The election of President Joe Biden brought calls by some to reopen the MAVNI program, as well as to extend age eligibility to accommodate those who had now been waiting for as long as five years in limbo.[76] Individual and class-action lawsuits on behalf of MAVNIs continued to make their way through the court system. A few were able to win individual appeals and finally ship to basic training in 2020 and 2021.[77] A 2020 class-action lawsuit was adjudicated in favor of MAVNIs who were already in the military but prevented from naturalization by the background checks, yet this win did not apply to those who had never been allowed to begin basic training.[78]

The recruitment of temporary migrants into the US military through the MAVNI program took place at a time of personnel shortages for the military as well as an expanding temporary migration regime. MAVNI capitalized on the precarity built into the US system of temporary migration to offer a citizenship shortcut to highly skilled temporary migrants. In exchange, these migrants became military workers, laboring alongside a younger and less educated enlisted workforce, and being treated with suspicion for their foreignness. In MAVNI's earlier years, many did get citizenship quickly, even if naturalization did not open military career opportunities they were promised. In the later years of this short-lived program, the military placed these recruits in limbo: waiting interminably to begin their military jobs after signing contracts and undergoing extensive security checks, some MAVNIs lost legal status, were discharged from the military, and/or faced the prospect of becoming undocumented and being deported. The military packaged their foreignness as skills of vital national interest, placed them in occupations that for the most part did not require language or cultural skills, and, in the end, used the characteristics for which they had been recruited to break their contract.

An extraordinary story in many ways, the rise and demise of the MAVNI program is at the same time indicative of both the tightrope walked by immigrant military workers trying to prove their loyalty and the way immigration status feeds labor exploitation. MAVNIs embody the contradictions as deserving immigrants and suspicious foreigners more sharply than other immigrants not only because of their high levels of education and stronger and more recent ties to other countries, but also because so many of them are racialized as inherently foreign and suspicious, including Chinese and Muslim MAVNIs. As temporary migrants, they were channeled through a system structured to create temporal insecurity and uncertainty, and thus facilitate labor exploitation. The military was for a while a new option for these temporary migrants, but one that once again tied them to one employer and required proving one's deservingness to live and work in the United States. In this case, the employer was arguably the most powerful employer in the United States, if not the world.

6

DEPORTED VETERANS

In November 2019, I traveled south across the international border line that splits the metropolis of Ciudad Juarez–El Paso into Mexico and the United States. My purpose was to visit the Deported Veteran Support House and meet in person some of the veterans I had spoken with over the previous few years. Jose's chatty and light-hearted personality made him easy to recognize even though a year had passed since our Facebook video chat. Sporting a baggy white hoody and abundant tattoos, Jose stood out in the family restaurant where we ate a late breakfast.

Jose, then in his early forties, had been a deportee for a few years. He was born in Juarez to a single mother who crossed back from the United States to give birth and left him with his grandmother. Jose's mother knew that this would mean no birthright citizenship for her new baby but could not bear to give birth away from the support of her family in Mexico. When he was in elementary school, Jose's mother sponsored his green card, and he moved to the United States, where he met his younger, US-born siblings. Growing up in the Southwest, Jose remembers being called "wetback" and *mojado* for his accent and then being teased for being a gringo when he visited Juarez. College was not in the picture due to poverty and family expectations, and Jose's enlistment in the army after high school graduation fit the poverty draft narrative: "I was watching TV, and I was like, oh man, what am I going to do, you know? We didn't have much money, lower class, whatever. My mom was working two jobs to support five kids. And so I decided, you know what? I am going to join the service. You know? That's my way in." Presumably, the military would be Jose's way into productive American adulthood. He wanted the adventure, too. Jose spent seven years on active duty in the army. After an honorable discharge, he was pressured to plead guilty to a crime he says he did not commit, spent nine years in prison, and was then deported to Mexico, where he struggled to survive, cut off from his family and from veterans' benefits.

In this chapter, I draw on interviews with five deported Mexican American veterans, including Jose, plus a veteran from Trinidad who spent years in immigration detention but was not deported, and an undocumented self-deported Mexican American veteran who worked with deported veterans in Mexico.[1] I also employ analysis of media stories, nonprofit reports, and social media posts of deported veterans. Jose's story of enlistment as a teenager of color growing up in poverty is a common one among military workers, immigrant or not. The system of racial capitalism limited Jose's options and continues to circumscribe the lives of many others like him. Neither was Jose's experience with the criminal justice system particularly unique. The jails and prisons across the United States are full of people who did not have the resources to fight their case in court and pled guilty in exchange for a lighter sentence. The consequences of incarceration are lasting and profound, but what sets noncitizen veterans who have been incarcerated apart from citizen veterans is deportation.[2] The military may insist on having nothing to do with the immigration system, but Jose's life shows otherwise. Physically and mentally battered by poverty, military labor, and deportation, Jose came to embody the connections between the military, immigration, and prison systems. The existence of deported veterans triggers cognitive dissonance for many Americans. Yet, rather than being exceptional, deported veterans simply reveal the underlying fabric joining these institutions. The path from enlistment to deportation is easily forged. It is not that deported veterans fell through the cracks in the system, but that the system is set up to create deported veterans.

The recruiters were happy to see Jose. They asked to see his green card and told him enlistment would make him a US citizen. Jose was adamant that he did not join because of citizenship: "When I first decided to join the army, it was like citizenship never crossed my mind because I felt American." As I explain below, the insistence that they did not enlist for citizenship is common among deported veterans. The insistence itself is part of making a claim of moral worth—reclaiming their honor as veterans and establishing their belonging in the United States. It is a way of saying that even though they were foreign-born, the United States was their country and they wanted to serve it. Yet Jose never did get citizenship in the military or as a civilian, and veteran status did not trump his lack of citizenship in deportation proceedings.

Jose liked the military. He enjoyed traveling to different countries where the United States has military bases. His job was generator mechanic, but when deployed to the Middle East after 9/11, he was mostly on guard duty and patrols. By then, Jose was struggling. He mentioned "a couple of incidents over there that kind of made you think about life." His girlfriend gave birth to Jose's daughter and was trying to attend college. They had been a couple since high school but were not married, and Jose was repeatedly unable to secure the pay, housing, and educational benefits he needed to support his family because he was not married.

With the end of his contract in sight, Jose decided to check about his citizenship. Unfortunately, judge advocate general officers told him they didn't know anything about naturalization and did not refer him to anyone else. Then he got orders to deploy to Jordan and forgot about citizenship: "I was making my will, making sure everything was straight at home, and all that, you know? Who am I going to leave my car to? Who am I going to leave this to, [laughs] if something happens? And like I said, when you're gone, you're gone. You are not over there thinking about citizenship, you know?" The separation from the military was rough. Jose struggled with his mental health and could not find a job. He felt worthless and depressed. It did not cross his mind to apply for citizenship at that point: "I got three honorable discharges from the military.[3] And my recruiter told me that I was going to become a citizen, so, like, I'm good. I said, well, I am good. I'm a veteran, you know. From the United States Army, and that should mean something, you know. And in the end, it didn't mean anything [chuckles]."

Although Jose thought of his honorable service in the army as being worth something akin to formal citizenship, he would learn the vulnerability of noncitizen veterans upon his discharge from the military. Jose isolated himself and started to drink: "My escape was, you know, started drinking more, smoking marijuana, whatever, and basically that's what led to me having a fall out. Breaking down and stuff. And having run-ins with the law and stuff like that." One of these run-ins with the law landed Jose in prison. Jose said that he was falsely accused. As do the vast majority of people in the US criminal justice system, however, Jose pled guilty to the crime:[4] "I took the plea because at the trial, they were telling me that you're looking at thirty-five years and I said 'What? [*laughs*] For something I didn't do?' I said, 'No. I am not going to do thirty-five years.' So I pleaded out for like fifteen, you know? They ended up giving me ten years and I was like, 'All right. I'd rather do ten than thirty-five.'" It was not until he was sentenced that he learned about the immigration consequences. Changes in the immigration system passed in 1996 meant that a conviction of an aggravated felony—a broad category of crimes with a sentence of one year or more—led to mandatory deportation for noncitizens, including those who, like Jose, have lawful permanent residency.[5] After pronouncing the sentence, the judge wished Jose good luck in Mexico. Jose says he would not have pled guilty had he known that he would be deported after his sentence.

While in prison, Jose worked in a factory sewing pants for military uniforms. In a striking illustration of the military and prison industrial complexes, this former military worker was now an incarcerated worker fulfilling orders for the military. Jose said he started off getting paid about $3 per day and eventually got to $10–$15 per day. Occasionally, with overtime, he would make as much as $30–$50 per day. Jose was likely working for a company like UNICOR, which is a major supplier of military equipment and uses prison labor.[6] The military is required to source most of its vast supply of military uniforms from the United States. To save on costs, it contracts with companies that use the extremely cheap labor in federal prisons. In 2013, incarcerated workers sewed over $100 million worth of uniforms.[7]

The use of prison labor is nothing new for the military. Prison factories made a major contribution in World War II, producing weapons components, parachutes, and cargo nets. Incarcerated workers continued to produce for the military throughout the Cold War, as well for the Vietnam War. In addition to their shockingly low wages, these workers also labor without typical workplace protections. They are not considered real employees because they do not work voluntarily, and it is legal for the government to fix prison wages at zero, a rate persisting at some prisons.[8] As poignantly demonstrated in Ava DuVernay's 2016 documentary, *13th*, the Thirteenth Amendment to the US Constitution that abolished slavery does not cover people convicted of crimes.[9] Some young men of color move through the school-to-prison pipeline, becoming prison laborers. For others, like Jose, the military is a stop in this pipeline, and their labor serves the military even when they are imprisoned. For the first four years of his incarceration, much of Jose's earnings were deducted for court fees. Once those were paid off, Jose remembers making $400–$500 per month.

As Jose's incarceration neared its end, he did not think he would be deported. Unlike fellow immigrants in his prison, ICE did not contact him in his last year of incarceration. Other incarcerated veterans told him not to worry: "There was a lot of military veterans in the prison system, you know? And that's legal, legal ones. They were like, 'Nah, don't worry. You served your country. They are going to let you go.'" Jose asked prison officials whether ICE had a detainer on him, and they told him that he would be getting out. Yet on his day of release, the prison guard checking him out said that ICE was coming to pick him up. Instead of leaving the prison, Jose was transferred to immigration detention. Much of his adult life was spent in institutions: the military and two types of incarceration. As another deported veteran put it poignantly in a Facebook post accompanying pictures of himself in different uniforms: "From Greens in Uniform, to Prison blues . . . to Federal Immigration Grays."

The money that Jose saved working in the prison was not enough to either pay for a good immigration lawyer or bond himself out to better fight his deportation case. The lawyer he did hire filed for Jose's citizenship based on his work in the military, but Jose did not pass the good moral character criteria required for naturalization. Jose's argument was that he was a veteran being released early on good conduct, one who had "been working in the prison for the last six years doing military clothes . . . making the uniforms for the military." In our interview, Jose pointed out that when a US citizen veteran commits a crime, they can go to veterans' courts, where they can recuperate their "good standing with society," as he put it.[10] He felt deprived of that opportunity. Jose was also painfully aware of the improved naturalization processes for immigrant soldiers who enlisted after him.

The immigration judge advised Jose to keep appealing his case, but despite his family's pleas to keep fighting, Jose saw no way to overcome his criminal sentence: "I decided I was running out of money, the food was horrible, and I was locked up in a little room twenty-four hours a day. . . . I was ready to get out after doing nine years and then going to another cell for ten months and then not going out, getting no sun, being locked up, bad food. I was like, that's enough." Once Jose signed his deportation papers, he was driven to the border with other deportees. His shackles were removed and he was handed a small bag with one pair of sweats and one pair of shoes. He walked over the international bridge into Mexico, and was met by a Mexican organization, which provided him with temporary paperwork establishing him as a deportee. Jose used his remaining money on bus tickets to get to Juarez, where his grandmother still lived, along with uncles and cousins.

For a year, Jose lived with his grandmother, keeping to himself. He was depressed and thought about self-harm. His accent when he spoke Spanish and his limited Spanish vocabulary identified him as a deportee to his neighbors. Jose's mother and sister visited him regularly. Jose also found Hector Barajas, a deported veteran activist, on Facebook.[11] Hector told Jose that there was not a deported veteran support house in Juarez, and he would have to come to the one in Tijuana. About a year later, Jose learned that a support house opened up in Juarez: "I found out who the director was going to be, and I contacted him and I told him, you know, I'm a veteran. I'm here in Juarez. I've been deported for a year. I don't have money, but I got time. Any support you need, I'm here."

Jose became involved in the Juarez "bunker." He helped with social media and outreach, and provided fellowship and resources to struggling deported veterans in Juarez. Jose helped other deported veterans, many of them older, fill out paperwork to attempt to get their pensions and benefits. He connected to veteran organizations on the US side, which sent attorneys and medical professionals to the Juarez support house. He spoke with pride of his story being mentioned by a US politician at a public event. For money, Jose did handicrafts, although health problems stemming from his time in the military made it increasingly more difficult to perform this intricate physical labor.

When I saw him in 2019, Jose had finally had a medical exam to establish his disability with the Veterans Administration and was waiting for the results. He had traveled to Tijuana to be examined by a Spanish doctor contracted by the VA and flown to Mexico. There were plenty of doctors who could have certified his disability just miles away in El Paso, but deported veterans have no access to them. After years of fighting to even get this exam, Jose was cautiously hopeful. What preoccupied him was his physical pain and his distant relationship with his daughter. Three years of deported life made him feel heavy and unmotivated.

THE DEPORTATION REGIME AND GENDERED RACIAL REMOVAL

The story of deported veterans hinges on understanding a category of crimes termed "aggravated felony" because it is aggravated felony convictions that place noncitizen veterans in danger of deportation. The aggravated felony category was created in 1988 by the Anti-Drug Abuse Act and until 1990 was defined as murder, drug trafficking, or firearm trafficking. The Immigration Act of 1990 expanded aggravated felony as a category for adjudicating immigration cases to include money laundering, any violent crime with at least a five-year sentence, or any violation of foreign laws with a sentence of more than fifteen years.[12] In 1994, the category was again expanded, this time to include trafficking in destructive devices and explosives, theft and burglary offenses with at least five-year sentences, child pornography or running a prostitution business, offenses related to the Racketeer Influenced and Corrupt Organizations Act (RICO), income tax evasion in excess of $200,000, and offenses related to slavery and involuntary servitude, espionage, sabotage, and national security.[13] As the definition was expanded, there was still variable degrees of discretion available to immigration judges in applying deportation orders. This means that even immigrants convicted of these crimes were not necessarily deported.[14]

It was not until 1996 that two pieces of legislation profoundly changed the landscape of immigration policy in the United States regarding its criminal deportation capacity. The Antiterrorism and Effective Death Penalty Act (AEDPA) and the Illegal Immigration Reform and Immigrant Responsibility Act (IIRIRA) (1) drastically redefined the category of aggravated felony in immigration cases to include any crime punishable by a year or more, even if the immigrant was not actually sentenced to that and (2) made detention and deportation mandatory for noncitizens convicted of an aggravated felony.[15] It is important to keep in mind that these laws apply to all noncitizens, even those who are lawful permanent residents. In a 2014 report, the Immigrant Legal Resource Center listed examples of offenses that have been found to be aggravated felonies after 1996:

Misdemeanor theft of items of minimal value such as a $10 video game, $15 worth of baby clothes, or tire rims from an automobile.

Writing a bad check for $1500 worth of construction supplies.

The sale of $10 worth of marijuana or pointing out a suspected drug seller to a potential buyer.

Allowing friends to use a car to commit a burglary.

Pulling the hair of another during a fight over a boyfriend.[16]

The policies worked retroactively, meaning that a noncitizen who had been convicted before 1996 would also now be deportable. An additional danger to immigrants is posed by discrepancies between state laws and federal immigration laws. The former may classify a crime such as drug possession as a misdemeanor, but the federal immigration law classifies it as an aggravated felony and imposes harsh immigration penalties.[17] AEDPA and IIRIRA paved the way for mass deportation of lawful permanent residents, which was ramped up significantly after the influx of funding and reorganization of the Immigration and Naturalization Service into the Department of Homeland Security.[18]

Under the post-1996 deportation regime, there are no special legal provisions for veterans of the US military. If convicted of an aggravated felony, immigrant veterans face deportation. ICE policies issued in 2004 and 2015 that directed ICE officers to conduct additional evaluations and consult managers in cases involving deportable veterans were found to be virtually unimplemented, as reported by government investigators in 2019. In the summer of 2022, DHS issued yet another such directive that called on ICE officers to use veteran status as a mitigating factor, as well as to keep track of deported veterans, but it remained unclear why this iteration of the policy would become effective.[19] The Department of Homeland Security has not historically kept track of the number of deported veterans, and estimates vary, ranging from 3,000 to 30,000.[20] An aggravated felony forecloses the possibility of military naturalization because deported veterans are deemed to lack good moral character.[21]

The number of immigrants deported grew after 2003, peaking under the Obama administration at over 400,000 people each year.[22] Even with such high numbers, most deportable immigrants in the United States are not deported. Rather, the deportation regime serves to instill insecurity into the lives of immigrants. As sociologists Tanya Golash-Boza and Pierrette Hondagneu-Sotelo explain, deportation is selective and constitutes gendered racial removal: the primary target of US deportation policy are Latino and Caribbean men.[23] Over 90 percent are deported to Latin American or Caribbean countries and almost 90 percent are men.[24] Local law enforcement, such as police and sheriff's departments, contribute greatly to detention and deportation of immigrants through racialized policing practices.[25] The deportation regime exists within and alongside the criminal justice system, which also operates in a similarly gendered and racist fashion, and has its own ways of making the lives of Black and Latino men insecure.[26]

IMMIGRANT VETERANS AND THE CRIMINAL JUSTICE SYSTEM

There is a tight connection between the criminal justice system structured to criminalize Black and Latinx people and the immigration system structured to exclude some of the same people. The 1996 immigration laws took effect in the same era as the profoundly consequential 1994 crime bill, which helped shape mass incarceration, and welfare reform of 1996, which eviscerated the social safety net. Even as noncitizen immigrants face increased criminalization, the criminal justice system continues to disproportionately trap people of color, regardless of their place of birth and citizenship. Recall that a few enlistment stories in chapter 2 featured teenage boys of color seeing the military and jail as their only options.

With heavy military recruitment in underserved schools coupled with the veteran pathways into incarceration, the military becomes a stop in the school-to-prison pipeline for some. For others, the retroactive nature of 1996 immigration laws meant immigration detention and deportation years or even decades after a criminal conviction. In all, noncitizen veterans' lives are profoundly affected by living at the juncture of this system of incarceration and the immigration system set up to criminalize them.

Bureau of Justice Statistics data from 2011–2012 shows that veterans are incarcerated at the same rate as the general population in state and federal prisons, and at a lower rate than the general population in jails. This is in contrast to the 1970s and 1980s, when veterans were overrepresented behind bars, likely due to the aftereffects of the Vietnam War on drafted soldiers. In recent years, incarcerated veterans are more likely to be older and white than incarcerated nonveterans. Most were in the military before 9/11.[27] About 9 percent of post-9/11 veterans have been arrested.[28] More than half of incarcerated veterans have mental health problems or have substance abuse disorders, a higher rate than the general incarcerated population.[29] Three federal prisons and over seventy state prisons have separate housing for veterans.[30]

Popular police and courtroom TV dramas notwithstanding, fewer than 3 percent of defendants go to trial in the United States.[31] Whether or not they are guilty, people are pressured to plead guilty to avoid the risk of longer sentences were they to be found guilty in court, just as Jose did when faced with the possibility of thirty-five years in prison. Hector Barajas, of the Deported Veteran Support House, also faced tremendous pressure to plead guilty while in pretrial detention in a veterans' "dorm":

HECTOR: They were trying to get me for two attempted murders, even though nobody got hurt. You know, somebody was still put in harm's way, so they were trying to throw the book at me. So, yeah, I started learning about prison and politics. Prison ain't nice.

SOFYA: So, were you out on bail, or you were just in?

HECTOR: No, they put like a really lot of bail. They were like, "[You are] military, [from] Compton, Hispanic?" They throw the book at you.

Hector knew that the deck was stacked against him as a Latino man who grew up in the Southern California city of Compton, linked in the popular imagination with gang crime and violence, and given the suspicion of veterans as violent and unstable. Hector continually denied his guilt, until a judge told him that a trial would mean the risk of getting fifteen years to life. Terrified of spending the rest of his life in prison, Hector pled guilty to a lesser charge.

Many immigrants pleading guilty are not advised about the immigration consequences of doing so. Represented by public defenders or attorneys unfamiliar with the immigration system, immigrant veterans pled guilty not realizing that doing so paved the way for their deportation. This continued to occur despite a 2010 court decision requiring criminal defense attorneys to advise their clients of immigration consequences.[32] Ricardo pled guilty to an aggravated felony: "I was told that yes, I did plead guilty. That it would be an easier process. That they would have leniency [with me] being a first-time offender, being a military guy, and not having any, you know, background, any . . . any, any priors." No one told Ricardo about the immigration consequences of pleading guilty until he was already in prison serving an eighteen-month term. His veteran status did get Ricardo an opportunity to await his sentencing on bail. His mother urged Ricardo to escape to Mexico, but he knew that were he to do that, his many ties to the United States would mean that he would try to return, be caught, and face a longer sentence for running. At the sentencing, the fact that Ricardo was a Marine did not make a difference: "No special consideration, no special case, no second screening. Nothing like that. It felt very like, 'Next! Next! Next!' It was very, like a sequential [*sic*], I don't know. Very, I felt like a number in certain ways."

Ricardo and Hector were funneled into a massive US system of incarceration. This system is built on and helps reproduce white supremacy in the United States by disproportionately criminalizing people of color. Many immigrant communities—Black, Latinxs, Native Americans, Southeast Asians, and Muslims in particular—face disproportionate criminalization. Some of the veterans I interviewed grew up and lived in such criminalized communities, where aggressive and racist policing channeled immigrants into the hands of ICE for detention and deportation.

The families of the deported veterans who shared their stories with me were Mexicans displaced by poverty that stemmed in part from US infiltration of Mexican markets and extraction of its resources and labor. Thus, the pipeline from school to military to prison and deportation should really be extended backward to encompass the processes of migration and empire. In the case of Rudi Richardson, a veteran deported to Germany who shared his story in a 2010 radio interview, the role of the US military and imperial violence was even more readily apparent. Richardson was one of thousands of so-called brown babies, or children born to German women and African American GIs stationed in Germany after World War II. His mother had grown up in an orphanage after her half-Jewish father was murdered in a concentration camp. Richardson was born while his mother was in prison for sex work, placed in an orphanage, and eventually adopted by an African American GI family. Richardson grew up in the United States, served in the military, and was deported to Germany following his own prison term. His adoptive parents had not petitioned for his US citizenship, as was required before a new law on international adoption in 2000. It was the policy of the US military to not recognize the paternity of these mixed-race children and to actively break up interracial relationships of military workers. Richardson was unable to establish his claim to US citizenship through his biological father. He pointed out that the US military was happy to let him join the army, but that he was ultimately disposable to the United States as a child produced by US military occupation.[33]

Black and Latino men face additional danger from the criminal justice system because they can be criminalized as gang members, based on their associations, tattoos, social media posts, place of residence, or simply because of their race.[34] Immigrants from Mexico and Central America, in particular, face a presumption of gang membership.[35] Even after Hector was pardoned for his crime by the California governor, USCIS attempted to withhold US citizenship from him as a gang member, demonstrating the power and reach of this particular strand of racist criminalization:

They were trying to argue that I lacked moral character because of the friends I associated with. . . . And I told them, like, "If I hang out with gang members it's because these are friends that I went to school with or just [knew socially], you know. A guy comes in [to the Deported Veterans Support House] and he's a gang member. I'm not helping him or I'm not affiliated with him because he's a gang member; I'm just talking to him because he's a person, you know, it's more a social thing. But they were like, "Yeah, you're lacking moral character" because of the gang ties that I had.

The attempt to exclude a veteran from citizenship based on gang affiliation is ironic considering political scientist Benjamin Schrader's argument that there are multiple continuities between gangs and the military as warrior communities characterized by violence.[36] The good moral character provisions built into the naturalization process are used by immigration officials to deny citizenship for a wide range of reasons. Immigration officials have discretion to determine that the naturalization applicant lacks good moral character.[37] Even though Hector's criminal record was cleared by the governor's pardon, it took an intervention by the ACLU and a letter from a gang expert to get Hector's naturalization case through. Another irony is that Black and Latinx youth attempting to enlist in the US military are also scrutinized for gang membership, and there are concerns about military-trained gang members.[38] Thus, people like Hector spend their lives having to prove that they are not gang members.

For immigrant veterans of color living in nonwhite communities, criminalization is very difficult to avoid. As Tanya Golash-Boza argues, Black and Latinx immigrant youth get caught in the criminalization-to-deportation pipeline regardless of their attitudes, behavior, community ties, or any of the factors that sociologists of migration tend to focus on to predict how immigrant lives unfold.[39] This criminalization played out again and again in the lives of deported veterans whom I interviewed. Tadeo, a Marine Corps veteran born in Mexico, was stopped for a DUI. Police ran his name and brought up an outstanding warrant in another state. Under subsequent reform, the offense Tadeo was charged with would be reclassified as a misdemeanor, but in the 1990s, Tadeo became an aggravated felon and was sentenced to two years. Tadeo's path to prison is a common one. Being a veteran did not prevent him from being marked as a felon, nor did it keep him from being deported when his incarceration was over.

Recall that while in prison, Jose sewed military uniforms, continuing to labor for the US military and empire even after he was no longer a soldier. While in a California state prison, Tadeo was an imprisoned firefighter. He had wanted to be a firefighter before prison and even took college classes to prepare. But the spots for non-incarcerated firefighter jobs were so scarce in his county that there was a multi-year waiting list. In 2019, people in California's prisons were paid between $2.90 and $5.12 per day to work as firefighters next to non-incarcerated firefighters making over $90,000 per year before overtime.[40] The pay scale had not changed since the 1990s, when Tadeo was in prison.[41] Ricardo also spoke of his work in prison. He got paid $35 per month to teach English to other imprisoned people. Ricardo noted that his students were US citizens and not in danger of being deported themselves.[42] Ricardo's teaching job was in the middle of the prison job hierarchy, with cleaners making even less, and the best jobs going to those installing alarms and security for immigration detention: "Those were like the cream of the crop, the VIPs."

After noncitizen immigrants complete their incarceration, they are transferred to the custody of immigration authorities. While their incarceration had an end point, immigration detention can drag on, the only end point being eventual deportation.[43] Few detainees have the resources to get adequate representation from immigration lawyers or bond themselves out (an option not available to all). Unlike in the criminal justice system, there is no right to legal representation in the immigration system.

The conditions of immigration detention, where one has fewer rights than people in regular prisons, make it difficult to sustain lengthy fights against one's deportation. I interviewed one immigrant veteran who successfully fought his deportation. Jim's years-long ordeal demonstrates how difficult such a fight is. When Jim separated from the military, he struggled with unemployment. The VA gave him medications for his physical injuries but not for his PTSD, which he self-medicated through substance use. Jim was arrested and charged after a post-9/11 reclassification of an earlier charge as a more serious crime. He pled guilty but was sentenced only to probation. Still getting no assistance for his serious mental health struggles, Jim continued to live with substance use disorder and was hospitalized for attempted suicide. A failed drug test sent him to prison, followed by immigration detention: "I thought maybe something's wrong, and I wasn't too worried. And then I ended up spending three years and four months in immigration detention. Because the [immigration] judge said that by no means was he going to let me go, he was going to deport me. He was determined to deport me, and I was determined to stay because I really wanted to get medical treatment." What kept Jim going through years of immigration detention was support of his family and the organizers in Families for Freedom, a local organization that advocates for immigrants with criminal convictions. His story appeared on the local news. In detention, Jim faced harrowing conditions and retaliation for his persistence:

I was judged, I was condemned. The corrections officers used to laugh at me. I was put in this hole, which is a cell, which was—two weeks I was in the cell, thirty-two hours in, one hour out. Which is not supposed to happen in immigration, that's for criminals. . . . [The immigration judge] told me he was not going to let me go, he was going to deport me. They took my uniform, they threw it on the ground, they trashed me, the officers in the prison called me names, immigrant. They told me, "You left your country to come serve here, and look at that, they are deporting you now." They were just banging it. They were just . . . And this was all in order to get me to give up. They put me in the hole to try and get me to give up. And I had already made up my mind that I was not going to give up, I was going to fight 'til the end.

As Lisa Marie Cacho notes, immigrants like Jim are forced by the moral logics of immigrant disposability and deservingness to make claims to his humanity based on framing himself as a "good immigrant," not a "bad criminal."[44] In describing the torture (solitary confinement) that the US immigration system subjected him to in immigration detention, Jim says that such treatment is for criminals, not for immigrants in detention, appealing to a moral distinction that failed him for years, as his ordeal dragged on. His first immigration lawyer abandoned his case, taking tens of thousands of dollars in payment. Desperate to fight his deportation, Jim's family got help from a local veterans' organization, which helped him get a new attorney. When the money ran out to pay this new attorney, she continued to work on the case pro bono. The immigration judge intent on deporting Jim was a key obstacle, but he eventually caved under the pressure of the publicity generated by the case:

Even if it took me ten years, I was going to stay there, because I honestly believe, yes I did commit a crime, but I honestly believe that my commitment would have to be considered at some point in time, so long as we had the right people. And I didn't think the same judge was going to be there after that long, but he told me the first day he seen me that "I don't care what you do, I'm deporting you." And when I went the last time, he said, "You must have really wanted to stay" [*laughs*]. So I got the last laugh.

Jim was not able to claim innocence to make his case for citizenship. In immigration detention, his veteran status did not help either, as correction officers mocked him for it. Instead, Jim counted on his commitment to staying in the United States, filing endless appeals, and fighting deportation—all in the face of abuse and uncertain outcome—to help him build a successful case. Jim expressed pride that his case set a precedent for the release of other veterans in immigrant detention.

Just as the end of incarceration hardly marks the end of problems with the criminal justice system for many people trapped in that system, Jim's immigration troubles did not end after his release from immigration detention. Until he finally got his US citizenship, Jim worried about being picked up by ICE and detained again. At one point, ICE came to his home with "shields, and guns, and dogs": "So once you have a conviction, and you are not a citizen, they will make every effort to get you out. Every effort. They're going to do everything. Sit by your house if they have to. But that's what they have been doing." Fortunately, Jim was not home that day and was not apprehended. These SWAT team–like home-raid tactics by ICE are not an exaggeration and have been documented in New York City.[45] It was not until 2017 that Jim finally got his US citizenship and gained some measure of protection from deportation, twenty-four years after filing his first naturalization application.

Jim was able to stay in immigration detention as long as he did and to stave off deportation because of the support he had outside the prison and the media attention his case received. Jack, a deported veteran, also wanted to fight his deportation. Born in Mexico, Jack was adopted by a US citizen and did not speak Spanish. Just as in Rudi Richardson's case, Jack's adoption by a US citizen did not give him citizenship.[46] While in prison, Jack was terrified of being deported. He did not have money to hire both a criminal lawyer to fight his drug case and an immigration attorney to fight his immigration case, so he opted for the latter. At first, the immigration case seemed promising: "If I knew then what I know now, I mean, winning an immigration case, it's like hitting the lottery. It's really hard. Even though I had a bunch of stuff going for me, it would have been all lawyers [saying], 'Hey, they can't deport you. Don't worry. You are adopted by an American citizen. You were in the Marines with honorable discharge. Your [biological] mother naturalized before you were seventeen. So all the stuff is in your favor.'" Jack's public defender for the criminal case told him to plead guilty, and he did. Jack continued to fight what at first seemed like a promising naturalization case, willing to stay in immigration detention after his incarceration as long as it took:

And, again [a new lawyer] tells me the same thing, "You can't be deported, you've got all this going for you. This and that, but if we fight your case, you're going to have to do more time [in immigration detention]." I said, "That's fine, I'll do all the time that I have to do. I don't care, as long as I don't get deported." It was when Juarez was just insane with all the murders. I think it was the number one. It was the murder capital of the world. There was more people dying here than there were in Iraq and Afghanistan and stuff. So I was like, just incredibly scared, just terrified to come over here. People telling me, "Oh, they're cutting off people's heads." I was like, "That's not my choice. It's not like I want to go over there."

Jack thought he had at least another six months of immigration detention to fight his case, but one morning, he was told he would be deported that day. ICE agents forced Jack sign his deportation papers:

So we're getting all ready to get checked out, and the ICE agents said, "Okay, we need you to sign this paper." I said, "I'm not signing anything. I'm not signing the thing." He said, "Well, if you're not going to sign, we need your fingerprint." I said, "I'm not giving you anything, I'm not giving you any of that." So I'm in this staging setup where the people getting deported are in these cells, and they see what's going on outside the window, and I'm surrounded by four ICE agents, and I'm handcuffed. And these were, I apologize for using the bad words in the interview, but I'm surrounded by four big ICE agents, and they said, "Look, if you don't give us the fingerprint, we're going to break your fucking hand, and you're going to give it to us anyway." And I said, "Look, if you give me a phone call, then I'll give you a fingerprint." So I gave them my fingerprint, they let me call my sister. I said, "Look, I'm getting deported to this place, I don't have any money, nothing."

Regardless of his willingness to fight his deportation and his technical right to do so, Jack was forced by immigration officers to submit to deportation.

Hector, too, stayed in immigration detention at the infamously brutal Eloy Detention Center for a whole year to fight deportation. He eventually despaired of winning his case: "I pretty much got the idea that once you have an aggravated felony on your record, there's nothing that can be done." Hector was out of money and represented himself in front of the immigration judge. He got some advice from a nonprofit outreach program to try to use his history in the military to argue against deportation, but ultimately, he did not know how to effectively defend himself. The immigration judge thanked Hector for his service and told him he had no case. Although he could have lodged an appeal, Hector gave up: "I was tired, and said, you know what, I'm done. I think it's time for me to go home." He was deported to Mexico.

Tadeo did not even try to fight his deportation case. It was not until two weeks before his incarceration was slated to end that Tadeo learned that he would be deported. Fed up with being in prison, he just wanted out: "I didn't want to be locked up anymore. So I said I'll go back to Mexico. I didn't believe them that they'd deport me." He said he believed he was a US citizen. In 1997, soon after the passage of the new laws vastly expanding the grounds of deportation for lawful permanent residents, it was reasonable for an immigrant veteran to think deportation would not really happen to them. The big wave of deportations would not come until later. By the time Jim was in immigration detention ten years after Tadeo, he knew of other veterans getting deported, and knew it could happen to him. By then, the influx of funding to the newly formed Department of Homeland Security enabled the United States to deport hundreds of thousands of immigrants every year.

Also facing deportation well into the era of mass deportation, Ricardo did believe that he would be deported, but he did not try to appeal because it would place him in immigration detention. He says he did it to protect his family: "My mom [who was living in the United States] suffered very much when I was in prison, and I know my family did as well, and I didn't want to make them suffer anymore. And I said I'll fight it from the outside, you know what I mean? There's no use of me being held in immigration detention. Thank God I did that because of all the horror stories I've heard." To avoid the terrible conditions endemic to immigration detention and well known to this resident of a US-Mexico border community, Ricardo accepted deportation and focused on reintegration "even though it's in another country."

After years of life in Mexico as a deportee, Jack reflected on connections between military labor, criminalization, and deportation:

They [the military] were taking people, it didn't matter about your residency. The stories I heard, they recruited a homeless guy because he passed the ASVAB. So before ... when I had been recruited, and when I got deported, I was trying to be like, "Hey I'm a veteran. I've been deported, I need help." But it wasn't an issue. It wasn't like it is today where there's a spotlight on the issue. It just wasn't ... I was like, "Hey, I'm a veteran and I'm getting deported." They're like, "Well, you're a criminal, and you're also Mexican. You're a felon, and you're Mexican. You got to go. That's the bottom line." Kind of like the political climate when I was being deported was, you know, if you're Mexican, we don't want Mexicans here. Especially Mexican criminals. Get rid of all of them. Does that make sense?

Jack's analysis highlights the contrast between the role of his immigration status in recruitment and its role once he was enmeshed in the system of racialized incarceration. The Marine Corps was happy to use the labor of a noncitizen teenager. But being a Marine did nothing to forestall deportation or get him help as a deported veteran, particularly before deported veterans received any attention from the media or government officials. As Jack repeatedly underscores, being Mexican trumped every claim he had to citizenship, let alone as a "Mexican criminal." The racial character of the US immigration and criminal legal systems is made clear: racialized as Mexican, Jack does not belong in the United States, never mind his being a veteran.

Jack and all the other deported veterans were eligible to apply for naturalization based on their work in the military. Many had performed military labor during an official time of hostility, and thus were immediately eligible or quickly eligible for naturalization. Even those who were in the military at times of peace were eligible after a year. Had they indeed gotten US citizenship, they would all have been protected from deportation. Instead, being the targets of both the criminal justice and immigration systems, they moved along the immigration-school-military-prison pipeline to end up in immigration detention. Stripped of legal status in the United States, some veterans crossed back to live as undocumented immigrants, others attempted to build lives in Mexico, and all negotiated the increasingly militarized border and its symbolic weight (see figure 6.1).

NEGOTIATING THE BORDER AFTER DEPORTATION ORDERS

Before discussing the lives of immigrant veterans after deportation, I note that like other deportees, some deported veterans returned to the United States from Mexico after being deported. While the level of securitization and militarization of the US-Mexico border make unauthorized crossings increasingly risky and costly, this was less so in the not-so-distant past, particularly for deportees who were crossing a land border and could leverage their veteran identities to perform US citizenship. For example, Tadeo said that after he was deported, he would tell the Border Patrol at the international crossings that he was a US citizen, and they would wave him through on the merit of his successful performance of belonging. This relative porousness of the border was emblematic of life in the US-Mexico borderlands in the 1990s, before the major mobilization of technology and violence after 9/11.[47] As the border became more militarized, deportation made transnational lives more difficult.[48]

When after his deportation, Tadeo attempted to cross into the United States to visit his parents for Thanksgiving, he was taken to secondary inspection. After three years of crossing the border back and forth, Tadeo was flagged as a deportee and sent to a federal prison to serve a two-year term for entering the United States without authorization. However, given the presidential executive order granting expedited naturalization to immigrants who served in the Persian Gulf War, Tadeo was deemed by immigration officials to have a probable citizenship case. He was released

FIGURE 6.1

US-Mexico border wall painted with names
of deported veterans, Tijuana, Mexico. ©
Joseph Silva.

to Mexico. Subsequently, Tadeo had to cross to the United States for immigration court dates every few months: "I would go to the United States. I would present to them my court date, judge ordering me to be in court. So, I would be handcuffed. After I got a totally nude inspection, handcuffed, and then driven to the . . . immigration courthouse. I stayed in the cell until I was about to appear in front of the judge, go back to the cell, go back to your car handcuffed, taken to the border, and that was another deportation. . . . The same judge that deported me was the judge that handled my case for those eight years." In the end, Tadeo's naturalization case was denied, as was his application for a visitor's visa. He gave up hope of returning to the United States.

Like Tadeo, Hector did not stay in Mexico after his deportation. But while Tadeo crossed back and forth, Hector crossed back to the United States and lived an undocumented life. He moved in with his girlfriend, had a child, and worked in construction. In 2010, Hector got detained for an outstanding ticket for wearing headphones while driving.[49] After a couple of months in immigration detention, Hector was deported again, and this time he stayed in Mexico: "That was it. I was done. I just wanted to do the right thing. Because there was many times, man, how many times, man, I could literally just cross the border, but then I'd have to hide again. And I didn't want to have that, you know, that pressure or that anxiety of having to watch my back all the time. And I wanted to do things the right way, so, it took me a very long time." Ricardo did not cross back into the United States after being deported because he did not want to risk another incarceration. But he acknowledged the pain of deportation and the strong pull to return: "The magnetism of your loved ones is so strong."

While the border has become far less porous in the twenty-first century than it had been, it remains porous for US citizens. In fact, the scenic town of Rosarito, south of Tijuana, is home to communities of US citizens who are referred to not as migrants but as expatriates, with the presumption that they are wealthy individuals making a professional or a lifestyle choice to live in Mexico, particularly for retirement.[50] In reality, many of these expatriates are struggling economically in the United States, and they are part of a global pattern of movement of US citizens to Mexico, Central, and South America.[51] Some deported veterans, such as those who live in and around Tijuana, rebuild their lives in proximity to and even interact with these expatriate communities. For instance, Hector lived in Rosarito for several years, where he worked in an assisted living home catering to expatriates. There, he befriended the son of the elderly man he cared for; his new friend was also a veteran.[52] The borderlands bring into focus the complex flows of goods and people stemming from the intersection between US imperialism and immigration policies. The lives of veterans following their deportation disrupted linear narratives and solid lines demarcating national territories as some of them continued to cross the border after the state marked their presence in the US as illegal, resisting the terms of their exile.

ADJUSTMENT TO LIFE AS A DEPORTEE

The reentry of imprisoned people into their communities is a difficult process marked by stigma, strained family relations, criminalization, discrimination, and impoverishment.[53] For deported veterans, who tend to have grown up in the United States, these problems are exacerbated by deportation to a country most left as young children.[54] Deported veterans I spoke to share many experiences with deported Mexican immigrants more generally, but there are a number of experiences unique to them, including access to VA benefits, military-related mental health issues that can resurface with deportation, and targeted recruitment by drug cartels. Deported veterans who were in immigration detention close to the US-Mexico border were simply driven to the border and made to walk across. Not only was this a profoundly disorienting experience of ending years of imprisonment with release in another country, but it was also one fraught with danger. As geographer Jeremy Slack describes in his book, *Deported to Death*, deportees dumped across the US-Mexico border face intense surveillance, recruitment by drug cartels, violence, and death.[55] After Jack signed his deportation papers under the threat of having his fingers broken by ICE, he was put on a prison bus with other deportees and driven to the border: "And they just drop you off at the border and say, 'Good luck, don't come back.' Uh, so we walk across. It was, it was, it was bittersweet! You know, I'm out of prison, and, but I'm free but I'm in this place that I know nothing about. And my Spanish was really basic." Official-looking people in green vests met the group of deportees, asking them if they needed assistance. Jack's friend and fellow deportee steered him away: "Jack, don't even look at them, don't talk to them, don't say anything. . . . They say they're for assistance, but they're going to rob you." There are, in fact, organizations in Mexico that greet and truly help deportees. One such group helped Jose when he was deported. Yet there are others who pose as helpers and prey on deportees.[56] Next, Jack and his friend were approached by Mexican police officers, who also offered help. The two kept walking until they were picked up by the friend's brother.

Jack's sister and girlfriend traveled from the United States to the Mexican town where he was released to give him some clothes and money for a bus fare to Ciudad Juarez: "I picked Juarez because it was the closest place to my family that I could be." Repeating the names of transfer stations to himself, Jack made it to Juarez: "I'm homeless, I have no place to stay. I don't have a lot of money. I don't have really any clothes. I had nothing. Nothing. Not even Spanish to get by." From a room in an hourly motel, Jack moved to a rudimentary apartment a few blocks from the international bridge separating Juarez from El Paso:

I could see El Paso from my bedroom window. Which was the El Paso downtown skyline. Which was crazy. . . . And so once I got there, after my first week, I mean, I was scared to walk around. I had an air mattress that my girlfriend's friend's family had lent me. A little air mattress. I had two milk cartons: one to sit on, one to eat on, and somebody had given me this little TV. But it was when they did the digital switch, so I couldn't even get English channels on the digital TV. I was just watching Spanish stuff, and you know, doing my little workouts like I was in prison still. And every day, I would try to . . . because there was military at every corner. Like literally downtown, you couldn't walk outside without seeing military with like heavy, heavy artillery machine guns. Everything, it was crazy. So every day, I was trying to walk a little further in the town, but I was scared. I didn't want anyone to stop and ask me, you know, "Hey, what are you doing?" I mean it got really bad.

Like other veterans deported to Juarez, notorious for violent crime, Jack described the fear he experienced there. Jack recalled being attacked on the street due to his inability to speak Spanish fluently. Calling his adoptive mother on the phone, Jack told her he was going crazy from loneliness and isolation: "I'd never had to deal with depression, but it got so bad. I was contemplating suicide. It was just, it was bad. It got super dark." Jack's social isolation and fear lessened after his brother visited from the United States. Jack began to make friends and improve his Spanish.

When Ricardo was driven across the border in a police car and released in Juarez, a good friend drove there from the United States to pick him up. The experience of being deported at the end of a prison sentence put Ricardo in an introspective state: "And then, 'Welcome to Mexico.' That's all I heard from the immigration guys. Walking across the border [*pause*]. Thank God, I had some ties in El Paso, some good friends. My *compadre* he picked up me and took me out to eat. It felt weird eating. Felt weird looking at a menu. And then took me out to see a movie. I was just in, like, a meditative state. I didn't react. I wasn't like, 'Oh, I'm free!' No, it was very subtle." Ricardo was now free but cut off from his life and social ties in the United States.

Although they are Mexican citizens, deportees often have a difficult time accessing their full rights in Mexico because they lack the paperwork to prove it. This is exacerbated for deportees such as Jack, who did not have many ties to Mexico and did not speak Spanish:

I couldn't get an ID, and it's illegal here to walk around without an ID if the cops pull you over. Like, say you're walking from the gym and back, and they stop you and you don't have an ID. They can detain you. But I was trying to get an ID, and they were like, "Okay, bring two witnesses to get an ID, because we don't know that you're really from here." So I brought some friends to say, "Oh, no, he's just on the same street." So I went with one witness from the same street and one from another street and I said, "Is that close enough?" And they said, "Oh, but we're closed for the election, we can't give you an ID." It took me about six months to get an ID.

Aside from using public spaces, deportees need IDs to access employment and social benefits. Eventually, Jack got his ID by connecting to his extended biological family in Mexico.

Families were key in shaping the lives of deported veterans. Many of these veterans experienced multiple family separations: when their parents migrated to the United States and left them behind and again when they migrated themselves, again when they were incarcerated, and each time they were deported. Some US-based families supported their deported kin, such as Jack's adoptive mother who traveled multiple times to bring him furniture and clothes and paid for his medical expenses. However, fear of violence in places like Juarez kept some from visiting their deported family members. A few deported veterans started new families in Mexico. Others rebuilt or deepened connections to extended families. Deportation often caused painful rifts between deported parents and their children living in the United States, as well as estrangement and agonizing separation from aging parents.

As parents aged, visits became more difficult. Jack described his adoptive mother as a saint in his life and an angel. Chronically ill and requiring an oxygen tank, she was no longer able to travel to visit Jack. He dreamed of getting US citizenship just so he could visit her. When Ricardo's father fell ill, he rushed to the border, attempting to see him one last time:

And the one that completely knocked me down, completely emotionally, physically, everything was my dad passing on. . . . He had bad circulation, he had diabetes. He went to the hospital and didn't come out. The lack of humanity in the inspection, border stations, from the officials, treating you like you are literally less of a human being than they are. I have never experienced that again. I mean I never experienced it to that magnitude. And I was like, "Wait a minute, you're speaking to a veteran, honorably discharged from the United States Army. What's going on? Why are you doing this?" "Oh, really?" You know, they were kind of shocked, but most of them knew that that's going on, and um, "Sorry buddy, we can't help you." It broke my heart.

Ricardo fell into a deep depression for months after his father's death. When I spoke to him, Ricardo's mother was ill with a litany of acute chronic conditions, and Ricardo ached to take care of her: "So my mom right now is bouncing around from nursing home to nursing home. You could get her in the best state-of-the-art nursing home, but the fact that she's still not with family, she feels like she's in prison. Just to take her out to have breakfast. To take her to Walmart to do some shopping, she wants some socks or a new sweater, basic stuff that we take for granted. For her it's like a blessing. My aunt used to take care of her, she passed away.

So she feels more lonely." In addition to the painful separation from his parents, Ricardo lived with constant distress of separation from his son. When he was first deported, Ricardo's ex-wife would walk his son over the border to spend time with Ricardo. Ricardo described the wrenching experience of letting go of his young son every week:

I remember my ex-wife and my son visited me once a week. And it was exciting to see them, the pre-excitement of knowing that they're coming and then walking them to the bridge, for safety. And once you hit mid-bridge when you see the flags, Mexican flag and the American flag, having all these mixed emotions inside, battling each other. And my son, "Why can't you come over?" You know, heartbreak. . . . What broke my heart . . . was the day, one of these visits where he asked me to walk him to his first day of class. When I said goodbye, I just broke down on the bridge. And those emotional outbreaks [are] where you feel that impotence. When you feel that I don't deserve this, I'm a good human being. I'm, like, how could you do this to me? Some guy somewhere wrote down this law. Some judge without even taking into consideration your background.

Every time he had to let go of his son, Ricardo took several days to recover emotionally. This painful experience is akin to family visits for incarcerated people, many of whom at least have an end date in sight.[57]

Tadeo was deported a decade before Ricardo. He had been separated from his young adult children since they were babies, seeing them only a few times when they came to visit from the United States. His oldest son also joined the military. Tadeo's children were angry and did not have much of a relationship with their father. When Tadeo asked them for letters of recommendation to bolster his case for pardon, they refused:

"You're not getting anything from us. Where have you been?" They don't understand. My oldest son that was in the Marine Corps. He kind of is leaning towards trying to understand. But no, they won't accept it. That I wasn't there for them. That really hurt. During all those years. My first son's mother died about ten years. And that must have hurt even worse; where is his dad? So [they] have that kind of . . . you know, grudge. And resentment. Towards me. "No, I'm not giving you my address, not giving you a letter of recommendation. Not giving you anything." And so, I'm the bad guy. But I really am not.

Tadeo said his children blamed him for not being there during their childhood. Ricardo shared that separation from children is a common topic of discussion among the deported veteran community. For older deported veterans, there was the additional pain of not knowing their grandchildren.

Most of the deported veterans whom I interviewed had family members in Mexico. Deportation pushed some of them to get closer to these kin. Jose, whose story opened this chapter, lived with his grandmother in Juarez when he was first deported, and saw his Mexico-based uncles and cousins. Tadeo also lived with his grandmother at first. Jack had not known his father but was able to reconnect to his father's family and grew close to them. They embraced him as one of their own and provided him with material support and a sense that someone always had his back.

As with deportees more generally, there was variety in how deported veterans found ways to survive financially. Some deported veterans were indigent, especially after first being deported, while others were able to tap into the local economy, often relying on their English. They worked as translators, help desk personnel, English teachers, and employees of data processing centers. A few turned their talents and hobbies into money-making enterprises.

Veterans living in the United States receive comprehensive health care services, disability compensation, and pensions. Veterans living abroad are not eligible for comprehensive health care, but they can get reimbursed for treatment of "service connected disabilities," which are injuries or illness "incurred or aggravated during active military service."[58] In order to get the reimbursements, a VA-designated physician has to determine that they have a service-connected disability. Even those who have official determinations of disability face a reimbursement process that is plagued with lengthy delays.[59] The process is made more difficult by the obstacles in communicating with the VA as a deported veteran. For instance, deported veterans cannot use the VA online portal for their military benefits because it requires identity verification through a valid US-government issued ID and proof of a financial account. Veterans who cannot come up with those are required to come to the VA in person, which, of course, deported veterans are unable to do. In 2021, a newly launched collaboration between DHS and the VA, the Immigrant

Military Members and Veterans Initiative, established an online portal for deported veterans to facilitate their access to VA benefits and humanitarian parole, but its reach remained narrow, and it did not significantly address obstacles to accessing VA benefits commonly faced by deported veterans.[60]

Veterans living outside the United States are eligible for disability compensation, but they need to get an exam by a designated physician to determine the extent of the disability and to connect this disability to their military labor. Despite a vast network of US military installations across the globe, there are few physicians contracted by the VA to conduct these exams. Deported veterans are also technically eligible for pension benefits, but once again, they need to go through a verification exam. In the case of disability and pension benefits, deported veterans cannot appeal the decisions of VA contractors—if they are even able to access them—because they cannot come to the United States for the appeal process.[61] Health care, disability benefits, and pensions would be a tremendous help to deported veterans, who often live in poverty, yet all three benefits have been difficult to obtain without the ability to cross the border.[62]

With the help of advocacy organized through the Deported Veterans Support House, deported veterans are increasingly able to get evaluated for service-connected disabilities and receive monthly disability payments, which can be helpful in providing financial security. After he left the military, Jack was determined to be partially disabled due to his multiple knee injuries. His disability payments were drastically reduced when he was in prison. When he was deported, the VA required him to come to their office in the United States in person to get his full payments set up, which of course he could not do. It took over a year and a half to get that sorted out. Jack compared the $100 per month he was earning working in data processing to the $400 per month he was eventually getting in disability pay. Ricardo was able to get his disability pay after over a decade in Mexico and referred to it as "a beacon of light . . . [I'm] able to take a deep breath for the first time . . . kind of like a safety net." He felt fortunate to have regular payments that exceeded the incomes of most people around him.

Access to health care continued to be limited even for those deported veterans who were able to secure disability payments. As inadequate as medical care can be for veterans who are in the United States, deportation cuts off health care benefits and opportunities to treat physical and mental illness. While some deported veterans have recently been able to get disability determinations and receive disability pay from the military, health care remains inaccessible because they would have to travel to the United States to receive it. Ricardo used his disability payments to cover some of his medical expenses, like basic blood tests and dental work. He had to abruptly pause treatment when his disability checks got delayed for a few months. Jack's hernia surgery was paid for by US family members. Had they been in the United States, health care for these veterans would have been provided by the VA at no cost.

It is not known how many deported veterans have died because they were deprived of medical treatment, but the Deported Veteran Support House has regularly held memorials for deported veterans. In one case, the ACLU helped an ill deported veteran to obtain a humanitarian visa to go to the VA in person and apply for his veteran benefits. José Solorio was in advanced stages of pulmonary fibrosis and was admitted to a San Diego VA hospital. Solorio needed a lung transplant, but his visa did not give him enough time for the recovery he would need. By the time the Customs and Border Protection extended his humanitarian visa, it was too late. Solorio died without receiving lifesaving treatment.[63] A year after the Immigrant Military Members and Veterans Initiative was launched in 2021, sixteen veterans were approved for temporary humanitarian parole to receive treatment at the VA in the United States.[64]

As is clear from their accounts of separation from the military, many deported veterans were already struggling with mental health issues and substance use disorders before they were incarcerated and deported. The social isolation that many experienced upon deportation could exacerbate these problems. Those who had developed PTSD from military labor were likely to have particular difficulties living in places like Juarez, which experience spells of extreme violence. For instance, Ricardo recalled "a wave of violence, brutal violence, from 2008 to 2012. Four thousand and something murders happened during that period. It was declared most dangerous city at one time. So it comes to the point where you have to find ways to keep your sanity, to keep your mental health . . . if we have PTSD or we had the beginnings of it from war or from being in Iraq or Saudi

Arabia or wherever. Believe it or not, it would flourish here completely." Deportees who grew up in the United States stand out in Mexico. They struggle with Spanish and fitting in culturally. Veterans are vulnerable to recruitment by the drug cartels.[65] Tattoos, which many of the deported veterans sport in profusion in visible places like hands and neck, may lead to being singled out by cartels, as well as by the police.[66] Jeremy Stock argues that easy categorizations and narratives about good and bad guys fail to capture the complexity of the drug trade on the border and the deportees' role in it: participation can be coerced and a matter of survival, and ground-level employees of the cartels are routinely slaughtered themselves. More than other deportees, deported military veterans are sought by the cartels: "military service . . . places deportees and migrants at risk of forced recruitment, as the skills associated with such service are highly valuable to drug cartels."[67]

While the violence perpetrated by the drug cartels in Mexico is real, it is important to complicate the story that blames Mexico for drug trade brutality and recognize the role of the United States, which provides the enormous market for drug consumption, forces neoliberal reforms on Mexico that impoverish working people, and whips up cycles of violence through its War on Drugs and anti-narcotics operations in Mexico.[68] In fact, the militarization of the Mexican drug cartels can be traced to their recruitment of military personnel from the Mexican and Guatemalan armed forces, which were, in turn, trained by the United States, Israel, and France to fight in the War on Drugs.[69] Deported veterans are in danger of becoming minor and disposable cogs in this massive system. Another fact further blurring moral boundaries is that US military personnel participate in what the US government construes as human smuggling across the US-Mexico border. For instance, in 2019, the Naval Criminal Investigative Service charged a group of eighteen Marines and one sailor at Camp Pendleton in California with migrant smuggling. Border Patrol officials framed this as a pattern in which drug cartels "lure" military personnel, police officers, and Border Patrol agents to participate in trafficking.[70] As the US military personnel and equipment are increasingly used to create a highly militarized and violent border between Mexico and the United States, military workers are helping construct this border both as enforcers and as hired smugglers.

Deported veterans I spoke with were aware of the danger of being recognized as a veteran. For instance, when Ricardo recounted just how bad his Spanish was when he was first deported, he also noted the danger of being recruited by cartels: "They recruit ex-military background in our situation, they offer them a lot of money to keep doing bad things. Because it's easier to train. They're dependable. They know how to use arms. They know how to follow orders." In fact, Ricardo tried to hide not only that he had been deported but also that he was a veteran, because he felt both were stigmatizing and would disadvantage him in getting jobs. He did not begin to assume an identity of a deported veteran until much later, when he became involved in collective organizing with other deported veterans.

Adjustment to life as deportees posed multiple challenges for deported veterans, including cultural dislocation, difficulties establishing a formal identity in Mexico and finding work, severed and strained family relationships, lack of access to VA benefits and adequate health care, vulnerability to recruitment by organized crime, and struggling with mental health issues exacerbated by deportation. Community building and collective organizing cast a lifeline to some deported veterans facing numerous interrelated risks.

BANISHED VETERANS AND THE DEPORTED VETERANS SUPPORT HOUSE

The work of Banished Veterans and of the Deported Veterans Support House has been crucial in raising awareness about the plight of deported veterans and improving their access to veteran benefits and even, in some cases, US citizenship. A key organizer in both organizations is Hector Barajas, who served as the face of deported veterans for most of the 2010s. Recall that Hector was deported in 2004 but came back to live in the United States as an undocumented immigrant until his second deportation in 2010. While he was living as an undocumented immigrant, Hector found news articles about deported veterans online. Reading through the comments, he found deported veterans from Ecuador and Chile and connected with them. Hector also met and connected with advocates in San Diego. At that point, he did not divulge his own situation, but worked to organize families of deported veterans.

Once deported the second time, Hector continued his organizing work—all while experiencing a lack of stable housing and mental health struggles.[71] Hector and other deported veterans put on regular protests at the border wall in Tijuana. Hector spent long days at the border crossing between San Ysidro, California, and Tijuana, weaving through the traffic waiting to cross into the United States. Wearing his army uniform, Hector carried handwritten signs advocating for deported veterans and handed out pamphlets to raise awareness. In 2013, political scientist and veteran Benjamin Schrader joined Hector on the border as part of his research on veteran activism, noting that the armed Homeland Security officers carried the same assault rifles as he did in Iraq. Schrader stressed the fact that Hector—a striking sight in his dress uniform alongside vendors selling toys and gum to waiting border crossers—was "being kept out of the United States by the very militarization that is his claim to citizenship."[72]

Due to their own tireless organizing, deported veterans garnered increasing media and public attention, received legal and material assistance from individual supporters and organizations such as Swords to Plowshares and the ACLU, were visited by US politicians, and starred in several documentaries. Meanwhile, Hector managed the Deported Veteran Support House, or the "bunker," in Tijuana, which provided assistance to deported veterans. Other such support houses opened in Ciudad Juarez and in other countries, including the Dominican Republic and Jamaica. Hector fielded messages from deported veterans from across the world and compiled a database. Congressional bills to give deported veterans citizenship went nowhere, but some deported veterans got individual remedies. Hector and two other veterans were pardoned by the California governor in 2017, opening up the path to naturalization by vacating their aggravated felonies. In 2019, I shadowed Hector in New York City, while he worked on connecting with local immigrant veterans and immigrant advocates with the goal of building a node for deported veterans and their families there. The COVID-19 pandemic underscored the lack of access to adequate health care for deported veterans. In 2022, Hector continued to advocate for deported veterans even as he suffered from life-threatening medical crises.

The deported veterans that I spoke to were connected to Banished Veterans and Hector by friends and relatives who saw pamphlets or news stories or found the organization's Facebook page. More than ten years after deportation, Tadeo found the Support House online and traveled to Tijuana, getting pro bono legal assistance. Tadeo pointed out that the collective work of deported veterans is not only about obtaining justice for them but also about publicizing their plight so that other veterans do not get deported in the future. The countless interviews and intense social media presence of deported veterans in Mexico generated outrage and support but met with negative and dismissive reactions by those for whom their criminality trumped any claim to veteran status or who questioned why they had not become naturalized.

For some deported veterans, the Deported Veterans Support House was a place of community. In the Juarez "bunker," Ricardo described a place for deported veterans to find a sympathetic ear and get recognition:

We don't lope around, we try to be upbeat, happy, but sometimes some of these guys they need to let this stuff out, you know what I mean. Sometimes they just need somebody to listen to them. . . . You know there's a guy from Arizona . . . a US citizen. He bought us some jackets, bought us some uniforms. And I'm, like, man, that was so cool. It was not the physical gift itself, just the fact that they took their time. . . . Those things give us hope. Just to have that contact, just to have somebody hear your story. Because even though we try to blend in, even though we try to live our life, we need to tell the world that we are consistently suffering. Because our minds are over there. Our loved ones are over there.

Ricardo, too, wanted to raise awareness of deported veterans in the United States. He saw the collective goal as regaining the dignity of deported veterans. Ricardo and many other deported veterans saw the fruits of advocacy in the improved access to disability payments once the VA hired contractors to administer the disability evaluations in Mexico. In 2019 and 2020, they traveled to Tijuana or Mexico City to be seen by a contracted doctor. Access to veterans' benefits was a tremendous boon to deported veterans, yet at least one worried that access to these benefits would blunt the fight for justice by making deported veterans more complacent and less willing to criticize the system that deported them. The Immigrant Military Member and Veteran Initiative opened a slim crack in the door in 2021, leading to the return and naturalization of four deported veterans, including a longtime active member of the "bunker" in Juarez.[73]

One of the veterans who became involved in the Deported Veteran Support House was Roberto, who actually was not technically deported. Roberto was in the United States on a dependent visa that expired when he turned eighteen. He had used fraudulent documents to enlist, was found out, and after a frustrating spell of living as undocumented immigrant, moved to Tijuana, essentially self-deporting. Roberto's uncle showed him one of the pamphlets Hector had been passing out at the border. Despite being an undocumented immigrant with no criminal record, Roberto saw himself as akin to the deported veterans, who had had legal status in the United States: "I was amazed. I thought I was the only one but there turned out to be others." Roberto knew he qualified for naturalization through the military route but had not been able to afford the attorney fees before connecting to pro bono legal help himself through his advocacy work with the deported veterans.

In 2019, after many snags in the process, including an attempt by USCIS to paint him as a gang member, which I described earlier, Hector became a US citizen. He began to split his time between Tijuana and California, where he tried to rebuild his relationship with his teenage daughter. He traveled around the United States and to other countries, attending film festivals and meeting with advocates, allies, deported veterans, and their families (see figure 6.2). In June 2020, Hector posted a picture he took from inside his car as he waited to cross into the United States from Tijuana. It had this caption: "For many years I walked these lines in my uniform, at one point I ended up homeless and I still wore my uniform while at a homeless camp with 700 other people, struggling with addiction, missing my family . . . it has been a long road of 14 years of deportation and many other things I don't talk about. I'm reminded today as I'm about to cross that God gave me strength to carry on." The image of Hector in a military uniform in a homeless encampment in Tijuana might strike the reader as shocking and incongruous. Yet most will be able to picture homeless veterans in the United States panhandling on city streets or highway ramps, with clothing and signs

FIGURE 6.2

Steven Pierre, deported US Navy veteran,
and Hector Barajas share a moment on a
balcony in Port-au-Prince, Haiti, June 2018.
© Joseph Silva

identifying their connection to the military. It is estimated that 9 percent
of homeless people in the United States are military veterans.[74] Hector
was simply on the wrong side of the border to fit into this social imaginary
of veterans.

Hector's work and the work of other deported veterans and their allies
in building advocacy and service organizations provided much needed
material, social, and legal assistance to deported veterans while raising
their visibility as a group seeking redress. In their advocacy work connecting with the US media and with politicians, nonprofit organizations, and
US-based veterans, deported veterans operated amid dominant narratives
that rejected them as inherently criminal and naturalized their expulsion

from the United States. They had to construct stories that would have the best chance of effectively refuting their stigmatized status.

MAKING CLAIMS TO CITIZENSHIP

The work of deported veteran activists cannot be done without the construction of narratives that help them make their case for US citizenship and belonging. Part of organizing collectively is sharing and spreading these narratives, which are not without tensions and contradictions. While deported veterans try to convey an image of deserving and patriotic Americans willing to die for their country, they also grapple with anger at the country that discarded and exiled them. By constructing their claims of belonging around deservingness, deported veterans create internal hierarchies of moral worth among themselves and police each other. Of course, the anti-immigrant climate, white supremacy, and entrenched militarism strongly shape the narratives that resonate with the public and policy makers. The dependent and precarious position of deported veterans further constrains their capacity for systemic critique. Yet in the work and words of deported veterans, we can glimpse alternative framings and solidarities.

Recall that Jose, whose story opened this chapter, insisted that he did not enlist in the army because he wanted US citizenship. Although US citizenship is what they need now to be able to travel to or live in the United States, deported veterans underscored that their enlistment had nothing to do with it. They do so even though their detractors sometimes question why they did not become naturalized. Yet this criticism is less harmful to the case deported veterans are building than the suspicion that they had enlisted instrumentally—in order to get citizenship—rather than out of patriotism. This is clear in Ricardo's comment that is about both citizenship and the idea of enlistment for the money:

I never really thought about the money, never really thought about becoming a US citizen because I thought that that would be more like . . . crossing your T's, dotting your I's. It was more like a political thing because I felt American. And I felt like I was needed, and I welcomed it, you know. I didn't sign up like, "Oh, oh, can

I become a citizen if I join the army?" "Yeah, definitely." It's not like that. No, no. I wanted to serve. I wanted to serve the country. And I was willing to give my life for it because in return, it was a risk that I was willing to take.

The purity of their commitment and intent and their claim of moral deservingness would be tainted by admitting that they enlisted in any part to get citizenship.[75] My interviews with immigrants in the military who grew up in the United States and who were not deported show that few of them were particularly aware of the citizenship benefits when they enlisted. Their interest in enlistment was driven, rather, by the poverty draft, a search for exciting experiences, and/or an expression of masculinity. Nor was citizenship an important benefit for them the way it was for those who came to the United States at older ages. So, it is not likely that deported veterans are minimizing the role of citizenship in their accounts of why they enlisted. In contrast, the military itself uses citizenship openly and instrumentally to recruit and retain immigrant workers.

Deported veterans denied that they enlisted to get citizenship.[76] At the same time, some of their advocates foreground the lack of information or support for naturalization that these immigrants faced in the military. For instance, the Texas Civil Rights Project, which assists deported veterans who call Texas their home, outlines multiple ways the military falls short in facilitating naturalization, including immigrants being told that naturalization was automatic with the enlistment oath. They argue that deportation of veterans "fails to respect individuals' rights to make a fully informed and voluntary decision to enlist and serve in the military."[77]

The Texas Civil Rights Project criticizes the military for not facilitating naturalization for its immigrant workers, but deported veterans themselves have to circumscribe their criticism. Building a veteran identity and upholding the US military and militarism are additional tools among immigrant veterans seeking to reverse their deportations. As Tadeo put it, "I had no doubts when I was sent out to do what they asked me to do," and therefore he earned citizenship. One of Tadeo's drill instructors wrote him a letter of recommendation that spelled out that he deserved citizenship because of his work in the military. According to Tadeo, the letter stated: "I truly believe in this Marine, and he deserves to be a US citizen because not only has he walked the walk, that's one of them, for this country. I don't see no other reason why he should not be able to be US citizen." Jim painted a picture of courageous immigrants joining the military to protect the United States:

I believe that the government has given us a slap in our face. I believe that our commitment and our sacrifice to serve and to protect this country that we love—I know I love it and I know they love it because to put your life on the line is a sacrifice. Some people prefer to stay at home and just enjoy their life. I believe that the government has turned their back against the very people who [have] willingly offered up themselves to make sure that Americans can enjoy and sleep at peace. And I believe the government owes them the right to be American. I mean what benefit is it that a veteran that's deported can only come back to this country when they die? There's no benefit, it makes no sense.

Since their claim to US citizenship is based on their military labor, deported veterans have to emphasize their military identities and accept the premise that the work of the military is keeping Americans safe. Vibrant, dissenting veteran movements notwithstanding, the image of a patriotic veteran does not leave much room for doubt of US foreign policies or the military itself. They also have to downplay the violence they experienced from the military, from injuries and lack of treatment to being exposed to harmful chemicals and drugs. Deported veterans validate military labor, insisting that they would enlist again if given a do-over.

For some deported veterans, building an identity as a veteran is a process. Not all people who have worked in the US military identify strongly as veterans or emphasize their veteran identities, including those who are immigrants. For deported veterans in Mexico, divulging military experience can be dangerous. But to make a case of moral worth to the US public and policy makers, a veteran identity is needed to differentiate yourself from other deportees. The emphasis on veteran identity and honorable military service is, in part, to counterbalance being marked as criminals (see figure 6.3). Thus, when Ricardo hid his veteran identity when he was first deported, it was for safety and to obtain employment, but when he began emphasize it, it was on social media and in organizing with other deported veterans, oriented toward the United States: "And in my sense, a lot of people on Facebook didn't know I was a veteran, and now I . . .

FIGURE 6.3

A display of medals and the US flag in the home of a deported veteran, Ciudad Juarez, Mexico. © Joseph Silva.

post things, Happy Veterans Day to me and to all my veterans and especially my deported veterans. And I'm not afraid because I'm kind of like at peace with it. I try to be careful with it as much as I can, but if you go to my profile, you'll see a bunch of deported veterans articles and stuff." Ricardo recalled that his high school teacher thanked him for his service after one of these posts, and he felt honored. Thus, building a veteran identity can also be a way to gain honor for people who have been deemed disposable nonpersons by the US government.[78] Notably, Ricardo specified that the high school teacher was a "white guy"; recognition by a white US man is worth more because white men embody the idea of Americanness the way Mexican Americans like Ricardo could never do under

US white supremacy. An endorsement of a deported immigrant by such a man is also perhaps less expected, and thus worth more in the moral marketplace.

When Tadeo connected with other deported veterans, he began to build his own veteran identity as well. Being a veteran was not that important to him when he left the military. He did not go to the VA and did not use any of his benefits. Tadeo said he had forgotten and given up on being a veteran after being deported. But years after his deportation, alongside other deported veterans, Tadeo reclaimed his veteran identity and felt proud of it. He became a member of an American Legion chapter in California, listing his parents' address. When we were talking over Skype, he showed me his dog tags and an issue of a veterans' magazine: "I order stuff, whatever I can afford. Pictures. I mean, actually, I want to be a Marine again. Once a Marine, always a Marine. So, okay, I'm with it. I want to sport my dress blues one more time." Tadeo had lost his dress blues—the formal uniform of the Marines—and wanted to get another set. As with Hector walking through border traffic in his dress uniform, the uniform is key to projecting a veteran identity. The uniform speaks for itself and is an essential ingredient in collective actions put on by deported veterans, alongside ceremonial treatment of the US flag.[79]

Hector, who has been the face of deported veterans for many years, acknowledged the utility of that identity and the way it obscured other facets of his life:

The one [identity] that I focus [on] because of the work that I do is just veteran, veteran, veteran [*laughs*]. You know, you have to use certain things to your advantage and you know how to reach people. I think I kind of, it's kind of been my role, not my character, no. But I have yet to find an identity. Especially this endeavor that I am going on [as a US citizen]. A new man . . . Before, it was like this big Mexican and I got tattoos on my arms that say Mexico. And I guess I have these different identities over the years, from being a smart kid to being a lost kid [*laughs*], deported, soldier, addict, homeless, lots of different things. American. That's one of the identities that are there, that I can relate to, that I think about.[80]

Adjusting to life as a US citizen had Hector reevaluating who he was beyond a veteran. Being a veteran was a well-trodden path not only to claims to belonging and moral worth but to membership within the larger community of US veterans. Recognition as a member of this wider veteran community positioned what happened to deported veterans in the criminal justice system as unjust.

The veteran identity is a powerful tool for deported veterans. One consequence of premising deservingness of remedy as a deported person on military labor is that deported veterans police each other over the validity of veteran identities. With the rising visibility of deported veterans, and the availability of uniforms and other military paraphernalia for purchase online, they worry that other deportees would impersonate being veterans. They also worry that those who were dishonorably discharged or dropped out of boot camp would attempt to stake their place under the deported veteran mantle. This would compromise deported veterans' framing of themselves as good soldiers. For instance, Hector recounted how a new visitor at the Deported Veterans Support House was outed as an impostor when he pronounced the Marine Corps motto, Semper Fi, incorrectly. Deported veterans are not unique in this policing of veteran authenticity, as veterans in general engage in this as well, suspecting "stolen valor," which can carry criminal charges.[81]

Sniffing out stolen valor is part of a larger politics of deservingness within the deported veterans movement. To a certain extent, working within the existing system necessitates playing the deservingness game, picking immigrants who are closest to conforming to a model of the good immigrant: a member of a heteronormative family, working hard, with no handouts from the government.[82] Although many deported veterans fall short of this portrait, it does not preclude a process of stratification and hierarchy within the group. When the ACLU worked with deported veterans, they picked a small number as candidates for pardons. As Hector put it, "they were just looking for good candidates that didn't have a long criminal history and first-time offense." Other advocates of deported veterans likewise focus their efforts on those who committed nonviolent and drug- or alcohol-related offenses.[83] The failed bipartisan 2017 Repatriate Our Patriots Act that would have given a path to citizenship for deported veterans contained a long list of crimes to be excluded, as well as limiting its remedies to those honorably discharged.[84] It followed the other similar, and also failed, Veterans Visa and Protection Acts of 2016 and 2019.[85]

In arguing for individual deservingness, Ricardo emphasized that he had no driving while intoxicated or domestic violence charges and had never even used drugs. Had he been a US citizen, he would have been given probation or been sent to a halfway house. Of course, many of Ricardo's fellow deported veterans had all these things on their record—and more—and drawing the line of deservingness there would have left them out. In describing deported veterans, Ricardo noted that "most of us are not violent. Most of us are first-time offenders. Most of us are not career criminals. So, to be treated like that, it's a slap in the face." Moral distinctions made between offenders—violent and nonviolent; first-time, repeat offender, or "career criminal"—are a common part of arguments made by some criminal justice reformers.[86] There are notable overlaps with the way some immigrant advocates construct narratives about deserving immigrants[87] and the criminal justice reformers' deserving offenders.[88] Deported veterans sit at the intersection of the two. By distancing himself from violent "career criminals," Ricardo implies that there are people who deserve the double jeopardy of deportation. While Latino men like Ricardo and his fellow Mexican American deportees fit prevailing racialized stereotypes of dangerous criminality—exacerbated by the imagery of violent and mentally unstable veterans—Ricardo's arguments also imply an attempt at distancing from Black men, whose racialization is tied even more tightly to violent criminality.[89]

In making claims to citizenship, deported veterans carefully construct and foreground a patriotic veteran identity, emphasizing their military identities and reproducing narratives of empire and militarism. They insist on the purity of their commitment to the US military, starting with enlistment for patriotic reasons, rather than the poverty draft or US citizenship. There is little room to criticize the US government or to dwell on the harm they experienced at its hands as military workers and incarcerated people. In constructing their collective narratives, deported veterans grapple with multiple tensions that arise from deservingness politics, internal stratification, and the overwhelming focus on veteran identity.

Publicly and collectively, deported veterans maintained their image as patriotic veterans. Yet in interviews, they revealed internal tensions in the arguments they were constructing to claim moral worth, as well as critiques of the United States. And while the public narrative was that they were exiled and were fighting to return home, some actually did not want to return to the United States. Rather than the right to live in the United States, citizenship, rather, meant mobility and recognition. For example, Jack said that although he did not fully fit in in Mexico, he valued the life he built there, the strong connections to his large extended Mexican family, and his sense of belonging: "It's something that I couldn't get in the States. The city really took me in here. If you hear the way I speak Spanish, I'm clearly not from here, but . . . the whole city just kind of took me in." Jack wanted citizenship so he could travel back and forth across the border. Jack's world view came to include a rejection of nationalism: "You're expendable to whatever country you're at. . . . I understand about having pride for your country and all that, but I'm not doing that. It's not in me."

Like Jack, Tadeo wanted to get US citizenship so he could cross the border to visit family, take his daughter to Disneyland, and watch a 49ers game. In addition, after two decades as a deportee, Tadeo wanted US citizenship to validate his own feeling of belonging in the United States: "I love that I lived there [in the United States] for [many years]. That's what I know . . . and I think that's why I belong. I really believe I am a US citizen. I've earned it. But I don't want to say that. I want somebody else to tell me that." Although Tadeo had recently embraced his identity as a Marine, note that his claim to belonging above is also based on living in the United States, akin to the #HomeIsHere campaign by undocumented youth organizers.[90] When first deported, Tadeo went to college to try to understand what happened to him. He said that for the first time, he learned that "the United States, half of it was Mexico's before." This new understanding of the imperial relationship between the United States and Mexico and his own place in it as a Mexican migrant gave Tadeo pride.

In making sense of their lives, deported veterans embraced veteran identities while critiquing the system that made them disposable. But because the military is part of this violent system, this task could be complicated. One way to manage this tension was by emphasizing the brotherhood of veterans and deemphasizing the military itself, which is common in the military more generally.[91] We can see this in Tadeo's focus on solidarity and sense of responsibility to other (immigrant) veterans:

From now on, every Marine is your brother. That's a nice part. And I forgot all about the Marines for a while, all about the United States. I was, figured Mexico was my life. If I wanted to go anywhere I was going Canada. Not the United States; I'd just erase it off the map. But I can't. Anyways, the Deported Veterans helped me along with this. I'm there. I'm back with my military friends. I'm back with them. Yes, I started wearing my dog tags again. And I proudly sport my T-shirts that say "Deported Veterans." And if we don't go across—which is a possibility, that we might never go back to the US—at least I would love to know that we helped our brothers behind us, that this won't happen to them. That they need to be taught what can happen if you don't do this, if you don't that. How the system works, which we didn't know.

Tadeo is a veteran who wants to make sure that his brothers, his fellow immigrant veterans, do not get deported and that they are better at understanding and navigating the system that is rigged against them. For Tadeo and others, the fellowship of veterans transcends borders and moves away from nationalism, coexisting with a critique of the United States. These veterans' adversary is the government that they served. As Jack put it: "The same system that I vowed to protect and die for is the same system that I got screwed in." Or Ricardo: "I'm angry at the government for not protecting us."

The grievances directed at the United States clash with the warrior masculinity emblematic of veteran identity. Military identity makes victimhood difficult. It is difficult to talk about the need to be protected and having been wronged when the ideal of militarist masculinity is a stoic who unquestioningly accepts the chain of command. This difficulty is illustrated by Ricardo: "I was angry at the country for not protecting us better. Because at the time I didn't realize but now I realize that I was willing to give my life for the cause, for patriotism, for our country, to serve, and they basically gave you a boot and you're gone. But I didn't want to be a victim. I used my skills that I had acquired in schools and military to be a clean-cut guy, to be on time, to be formal." Ricardo tries to resolve the difficulty of being a victim by pointing to what he, as an individual, did with his military background. This allows him to retain a measure of agency unavailable to victims.

A poignant example of reclaiming agency as a victim was provided by the family of Hector Barrios, a Vietnam War draftee and deported veteran who died in 2014, in poverty and never having gained access to his veteran benefits. Barrios had been deported for possession of marijuana in 1999.[92] Deported veterans and their advocates often talk about how the only way they are allowed to enter the United States is after their death, to be buried in a military cemetery.[93] Yet Hector Barrios's family refused to have his body buried with military honors in the United States.[94] Barrios's story is a reminder that the deported veteran activists—as traumatic as their lives have been—are the success stories. They have figured out a way to survive, constructing a sense of belonging and a collective identity.

The narratives of deservingness that deported veterans aim at the US public obscure the systemic critiques they also make. While they lobby for US citizenship that they argue is owed to them, deported veterans disrupt and expand definitions of citizenship to encompass mobility across borders and symbolic recognition even when they reject the assumption that they would want to return to the United States to live. Their desire for connection with the community of veterans trumps blind loyalty to the US government, allowing critiques to surface. Deported veterans attempt to embody their military identities while claiming victimhood, all while finding ways to express their agency.

ALLIANCES AND ALTERNATIVES

Deported veterans foreground their work in the military to make a case for deserving veteran benefits, reversal of deportations, and US citizenship. Not surprisingly, this means that they try to build connections with other veterans and veteran organizations. Many individual veterans have responded with support and assistance for their deported counterparts, while others dismiss them because of the stain of criminality. Some progressive veteran organizations, such as Vets for American Ideals, advocate for deported veterans. In 2018, the American Legion, the largest veteran nonprofit organization in the United States, issued a resolution urging Congress to let deported veterans apply for citizenship if they had an honorable discharge and no felony convictions.[95] Since most were deported because they pled guilty or were convicted of offenses classified as aggravated felonies, such a policy would not make much of a difference. The 2018–2019 legislative agenda of another major veteran organization, AMVETS, called for noncitizen veterans convicted of crimes to be treated the same way as US citizens.[96]

As with most collective organizing efforts, deported veterans are not always a cohesive group, free of conflict. The United Deported Veterans Resource Center is an organization in Tijuana that is distinct from Banished Veterans and the Deported Veterans Support House. While the latter tries to work with traditional veteran organizations, the Resource Center is actually a chapter of Veterans for Peace, a national antiwar organization.[97] Vets for Peace serves as this group's fiscal sponsor and runs a Deported Veterans Advocacy Project.[98] The chapter is named after Hector Barrios, the deported veteran whose family did not want his body to be repatriated. It is fair to say that the United Deported Veterans Resource Center has received a fraction of the media attention received by Banished Veterans and the Deported Veterans Support House. Even though antiwar veteran organizations are more likely to advocate for deported veterans than mainstream veteran organizations, working with them threatens the image of patriotism that many deported veterans try to cultivate. Publicly embracing an antiwar veteran critique of the US military negates the social status afforded to veterans who are in the United States, let alone to criminalized and deported veterans. But it remains an intriguing possibility for a more radical movement, one that is being explored by the less visible deported veteran organizations. And while some shy away from such connections, others already do work with both dissenting veterans and Banished Veterans.

While antiwar veterans contribute to immigrant rights movements, judging from my interviews and analysis of organizational social media and public statements, deported veterans are less intent on building alliances with immigrant rights groups. Neither do they appear to try to build alliances with incarcerated or formerly incarcerated organizers.

This makes sense if we understand their claim to belonging as being built on their exceptionality, with their status as military workers trumping their status as noncitizen immigrants and formerly incarcerated people. When deported veterans garner support from US veterans and the public, it often takes the shape of shock that veterans could be deported. This is easy to observe in social media comments, comments on news stories, and even during presentations of this research project. It is shocking that veterans can be deported only because it is not shocking that immigrants are deported. The normalization of deportation of undocumented immigrants and lawful permanent residents who have been criminalized serves as the background against which deported veterans build their case of exceptionality. Thus, seeking the support of large veteran organizations makes strategic sense, while alliances with migrant justice groups would undermine their claims. Some deported veterans emphasize that they were not undocumented. For instance, Ricardo said: "In the twenty-first century, this literally is an injustice due to the fact that I was legally there. I had obtained legal status, I was paying taxes, didn't have any criminal record whatsoever, so we're perfect candidates—if somebody deserves a second chance, it would be somebody like me." The implication is that Ricardo is a better candidate for a second chance than undocumented immigrants. But Ricardo obtained his legal status through the 1986 Immigration Reform and Control Act (IRCA) amnesty. Had there been such an amnesty since, many of the undocumented immigrants he distances himself from would have been "legal" as well.

There are some ways in which deported veterans work with other immigrant constituencies affected by the US immigration system. In 2019, when Hector came to New York, he met with the New Sanctuary Coalition, a major local player in the immigrant rights movement, to discuss building an organizational space for deported veterans. In Tijuana, Banished Veterans work with DREAMer Moms, an organization supporting deported women separated from their US children—and have faced criticism from supporters who see these women as "illegals" deserving deportation.[99] Hector also connected with Yea Ji Sea, a MAVNI soldier facing deportation from her military base, establishing a precedent of solidarity between these two groups of immigrant military workers.[100] Some deported veterans and veterans in immigration detention receive assistance from immigrant rights organizations. Yet the way deported veterans shape their claims and strategize does not center working together with fellow immigrants.

In the complicated advocacy work of deported veterans explored in this chapter, we see the limitations of moral claims making. By employing a discourse of deservingness, deported veterans limit critiques of the system that discarded them, upholding it while seeking an exception. Given that this strategy has yielded limited dividends thus far, either for individuals or for deported veterans as a group, perhaps the movement is poised to embrace new strategies that disrupt the status quo. It brings to mind the movement of undocumented youth, who banked on exceptionality and deservingness at first, then embraced a broader and more radical platform that included all undocumented immigrants.[101]

There are some signs that this reorientation could be in the works, such as connections with immigrant rights groups and antiwar veterans. An alternative strategy of resistance by deported veterans might at the very least embrace veteran deportees with other-than-honorable discharges from the military. More broadly, it might include solidarity with all deportees—even helping deportees fake veteran identities rather than police for stolen valor (although that would still reinforce moral hierarchies of deservingness). Such a strategy would borrow from the struggles of Chinese migrants in the early twentieth century, who, faced with extreme immigration crackdowns, created a system of "paper sons" to get their compatriots into the United States.[102] Deported veterans can draw on their history of military labor and immigrant roots to critique the militarization of the US-Mexico borderlands. With their firsthand experience as foot soldiers of the US empire while also being targets of its punishment, deported veterans are uniquely positioned to use their social position to lead a challenge to the US immigration regime, the system of racialized incarceration and surveillance, and the military industrial complex. In fact, they can lead a challenge to these systems because they embody and make visible the interconnections between them.

SPEAK TRUTH TO THE POWER OF THE WAR MACHINE

This whiteness and the power remains unchallenged by the kind of minority identity politics that does not call out the identity politics of whites or speak truth to the power of the war machine. Minorities must dissent from the terms that a regime of whiteness offers. They must call forth anger and rage, demand solidarity and revolution, critique whiteness, domination, power, and all the faces of the war machine.
—Viet Thanh Nguyen[1]

Green card soldiers are the tools and the victims of the US empire. They can be empire's beneficiaries, its resisters, or both. Above all, they labor under powerful constraints to seek safety and belonging, pursue evolving desires, and make sense of their lives. These immigrants' predicament cannot be understood in isolation from the workings of imperialism inside and outside the borders of the country currently known as the United States. A focus on enlisted immigrant military workers disrupts hegemonic parables about the US military keeping Americans safe or protecting democracy across the world, even as it disrupts facile explanations of immigrant participation in the military. Rather, we see how often the US military creates migrants in the first place, then uses them as labor across the world in protecting imperial resource extraction, enforcing political regimes benefiting US capital, and expanding and conquering new territory for further exploitation. Inside the United States, the military and militarized law and immigration enforcement agencies crush popular resistance to resource extraction and white supremacy and maintain the violence of the border with Mexico. With dwindling prospects for good jobs and looming debt, youth are drawn into the military labor force through the poverty draft aided by a culture of militarism and extensive marketing campaigns. Arguing for inclusion of immigrants in and through the military, advocating for immigration reform by holding up immigrant veterans, or demonstrating how well the US military assimilates immigrants all feed the war machine and entrench imperial violence. In the context of pervasive and normalized militarism, this means thinking and organizing against the grain in order, as Viet Thanh Nguyen implores, to speak truth to the power of the war machine.

Given the exploitation and harm inflicted on migrants by US militarism before, during, and after migration, there are policies that would improve the lives of current and former green card soldiers. Ending deportations of veterans and offering naturalization to deported veterans who want US citizenship, as well as full access to veteran benefits, would begin to compensate for some of the injustices they have suffered. Making citizenship acquisition easier for enlisted military workers and veterans who want to naturalize would give them access to the protections of US citizenship, albeit variably accessible for different groups based on racialization, gender, and other stratifying processes. For MAVNI enlistees who were stranded in a legal limbo by the securitization of the program, a direct path to permanent status is a basic demand of remediation. The military should no longer be allowed to engage in predatory recruitment of children and youth regardless of immigrant background. Immigration reform—not least any version of the DREAM Act—must be purged of any connections to military labor to begin to demilitarize the US immigration system.

However, I do not want to dwell on the details of these policy recommendations. Instead, I want to note how easily they can get conflated with attempts to make the military more immigrant-friendly. While I recognize the utility of some reform efforts, I leave their elaboration to others because disproportionate focus on policy recommendations that amount to making the military more immigrant-friendly ultimately helps reproduce borders and empire. It seems inadequate and disingenuous to call for the end of deportations of veterans without calling for an end of all deportations, to call for facilitation of naturalization for one group without demanding an end to the oppressive system of citizenship as an exclusionary marker of belonging, to ask for legal remedies for MAVNIs and not for all immigrants, to make work in the military more bearable for the workers without calling to defund the US military until it has no workers, to protect vulnerable youth in the US from predatory recruitment into military labor without protecting youth across the globe whose flourishing is limited by the US empire. Instead, I end this book by holding up some examples and possibilities of resistance that reach beyond improving the plight of a subgroup of military workers to provide glimpses into a just future for the billions of human and countless nonhuman lives affected by the US military's presence on earth.

Some examples and possibilities come from the green card soldiers themselves. Even as they are produced by the US empire and serve as its foot soldiers, they also resist it in ways big and small, collective and individual, alongside other workers, military and otherwise. Among the first US military casualties of the War on Terror were immigrants. But immigrant military workers were also among the first resisters to the US invasion of Afghanistan and Iraq. The first soldier to refuse deployment to Iraq was a green card soldier, Camilo Mejía. In 2004, Mejía, an immigrant from Nicaragua and already an Iraq veteran, refused to be deployed there again. In the course of his eight years in the military, and after witnessing the bloody work of imperialism firsthand, Mejía came to see "the absolute clarity of the wrongfulness not only of the war against Iraq, but of war in general."[2] As he wrote in his memoir, *Road from ar Ramadi*, Mejía fought his own war: "war against the system I had come from, a battle against the military machine, the imperial dragon that devours its own soldiers and Iraqi civilians alike for the sake of profits."[3]

Mejía's experience with US citizenship underscores the way the US military uses citizenship as a labor technology. When after eight years in the military, Mejía argued that the army's own regulations prohibited a noncitizen like him from remaining in the military beyond the eight-year contract, his supervisors developed a sudden and acute interest in trying to get him naturalized. In other words, naturalizing this noncitizen worker would have allowed them to press him into military labor in a time of labor shortages, against his will. Meanwhile, Mejía pinned his hopes of getting out of the military on not becoming a US citizen.[4] In the end, this strategy did not bear fruit. He was court-martialed, charged with desertion, spent a year in military prison, and was dishonorably discharged. Mejía's act of moral courage carried the risk of losing his lawful permanent residency and foreclosed the path to US citizenship. Mejía went on to become an outspoken critic and organizer against US imperialism while living with uncertainty about his future in the United States. Mejía publicly decried the way US soldiers were treated as disposable tools of empire, and the torture, mass murder, and racism directed at Iraqis. He spoke against the DREAM Act, condemning the militarization and exploitation of vulnerable immigrant youth and predicting their pathway to deportation rather than citizenship. Mejía's public stance against the war encouraged other acts of dissent by military workers and contributed to the organizing work of Iraq Veterans against the War and, later, About Face.[5]

Like many of the people interviewed for this project, Camilo Mejía was a working-class immigrant who enlisted in the military in search of financial stability and in hopes of finding a place for himself in US society.[6] Counterrecruitment activists organize to disrupt the funneling of youth into the military workforce. They speak out against schools sharing student information with recruiters, and they try to educate youth and families about the realities of military work. For understandable pragmatic reasons, counterrecruitment activism has tended to deemphasize critiques of US imperialism in favor of a neoliberal emphasis on freedom from state interference. Yet US imperialism has a direct impact on counterrecruitment organizing against militarism.[7] My focus in this book specifically on immigrants in the military provides some insights and strategies for the counterrecruitment movement. The US military understands immigrants as a distinct pool of labor with special skills beneficial to the imperial project—a population to reach through specialized marketing. An effective counterrecruitment movement must respond in kind, with strategies around the use of US citizenship for recruitment and special vulnerabilities of noncitizen youth. Counterrecruitment organizers should inform immigrants about the limitations that their lack of citizenship poses within the military occupational structure, the reality of how difficult it can be to acquire citizenship through the military route, the racist and xenophobic treatment they may encounter as immigrant military workers and the severe constraints on redress for these in the military workplace, the discriminatory workings of the military justice system that could jeopardize their immigration cases, and the existence and plight of deported veterans. They should also initiate and encourage difficult conversations with youth about the harm of military labor not only on the military worker but on people, places, communities, and environments that suffer from US military presence.

A promising example of ongoing resistance to military recruitment that encompasses immigrants is the opposition to the militarization of the City University of New York. CUNY organizers—including faculty, staff, and their union, as well as CUNY students—situate recruitment of immigrant youth of color in the larger context of neoliberal gutting of public higher education.[8] The US military views CUNY and New York City in general as a venue to diversify its labor force with workers who can, in the words of Cheryl Miller, writing for the American Economic Institute, "supply the cultural competency and language skills the military needs to fulfill its many and varied global responsibilities."[9] CUNY's School for Civic and Global Leadership is named after Colin Powell, City College graduate and a child of immigrants, who played a key role in orchestrating false evidence justifying the US invasion of Iraq.[10] Powell helped bring ROTC programs back to CUNY campuses forty years after antiwar campus movements shut them down.[11] Antimilitarism and counterrecruitment struggles at CUNY are grounded in a long and robust history of anti-militarist organizing at the university and intertwined with the #CopsOffCampus movement.[12]

In calling for a focus on immigrants in counterrecruitment organizing, I argue that organizers not only should be concerned with disrupting military recruitment of immigrant youth but should connect counter-recruitment more integrally to global anti-imperialist and antimilitarist movements, denaturalize national borders, and rejuvenate possibilities for international solidarity work. Paul Foos notes that during the US invasion of Mexico in the mid-nineteenth century, US soldiers—many of whom were recent immigrants—"realized that their part in conquest would be as wage-earning guardians of the propertied classes, Mexican and Anglo, with their 'glory' collected in the form of atrocities against the poor and dispossessed."[13] The Irish immigrants' Saint Patrick/San Patricio battalion actually deserted the US Army as a unit to join the Mexican side. This act stemmed from a complex combination of factors, not simply class solidarity, but it nevertheless opens a way of thinking and being beyond fruitless arguments proving that immigrants are not security threats.[14] For perhaps they are, and they should be, a threat to the security of the US empire. But so are all youth recruited into the US military potentially a threat to it. Thinking through the path of immigrant youth into the US military labor force helps us see how much all recruitment is a product of empire rather than a more or less desirable career opportunity. And how all recruits are potential disruptors of empire.[15]

Through the centuries of US imperialism across the world, people living in the US—some of them immigrants—took concrete actions of international solidarity, finding common ground with the targets of the US empire as members of the working class, as socialists, and as internally colonized and marginalized people.[16] In the words of Muhammed Ali upon being sent to fight in Vietnam: "No, I am not going ten thousand miles from home to help murder and burn another poor nation simply to continue the domination of white slave masters of the darker people the world over."[17] Understanding youth being recruited by the military as products of the US empire allows us to build more powerful resistance to militarization across the US border and to work with anti-imperialist movements, from environmental advocates opposing ongoing bombing in Vieques, Puerto Rico, to indigenous resistance of Ryukyuans to military occupation of Okinawa, Japan.[18]

US military veterans already do the work that makes these connections. Veterans were important participants in the mobilization against US wars on Vietnam, protests against US imperialism in Central America, and the opposition to Iraq and Afghanistan invasions.[19] The organization Veterans for Peace has sent delegations to Palestine, Okinawa, and other sites of resistance to occupation.[20] In 2021, members of the antiwar veteran group About Face protested the Line 3 pipeline alongside indigenous activists. In a 2021 Indigenous Peoples Day email blast, they wrote, "The history of settler colonialism is directly linked to the global militarism and white supremacy that endures today. We cannot separate the violence of global militarism from the violence toward Indigenous Peoples."[21] (Of course, some members of About Face are themselves indigenous, just as others are immigrants.) Veterans participated in the Standing Rock occupation against Dakota Access oil pipeline in the thousands in 2015 and 2016. The post-9/11 generation of veteran resisters engages in intersectional organizing and analysis, connecting their antiwar work to struggles against white supremacy, border militarization, and the climate crisis. They march in Black Lives Matter protests and use their medical and tactical skills in confronting white nationalist groups like Proud Boys in the streets.[22] In 2019, veterans protested the use of the Fort Sill army base as a detention center for migrant children, alongside Japanese Americans whose families had been interned there during World War II.[23] About Face activists work with migrant justice organizations to push back against the militarization of undocumented youth through political education and to publicize the connections between technologies used at the US-Mexico border, in suppressing Black Lives Matter uprisings, and in Afghanistan.[24] Their emphasis on confronting militarization and colonialism in migrant justice work is an invaluable adjustment to dominant human rights–based and liberal frameworks.

The vibrant movements of dissident veterans and international worker solidarity not only provide a ray of hope but disrupt and destabilize the edifice of militarism and empire. They help us see the lies in the facile veneration of the military and the normalization of imperial aggression because they do what we do not expect in a hegemonic nationalist system. We do not expect veterans—idolized for defending "American freedoms" and embodying patriotism—to speak out against and fight the very project they were meant to guard with their lives. We do not expect ordinary Americans to feel that their fate is connected to that of people in countries under attack by the US government when such sense of linked fate is undermined by the powerful propaganda and racist dehumanization that accompany the violence of war. We do not expect working-class college students of color to push back against military career opportunities presented to them as an avenue for social mobility and integration. These movements break out of the inherent futility of liberal arguments of deservingness and incorporation into systems of oppression.

Not formally of the nation but recruited into its military workforce, green card soldiers expose the articulations between the military and immigration systems. Framed as a benefit to individual immigrants, citizenship is instead a technology of labor, used to manage and discipline the military labor force, even as immigrant inclusion legitimates the imperial project. The experience of immigrants laboring in the military raises questions beyond their specific plight. Their position as both model immigrants and potential security threats is an accentuated version of constrained options facing all immigrants trying to make claims on belonging in the United States. The use of citizenship by the state as a labor management tool highlights the inextricable connection between citizenship and colonialism. Citizenship, in the words of writer Indi Samarajiva, is "barbed wire around an indigenous graveyard. It's a moat around a colonial crime scene."[25] If it is to do more than lighten the suffering of select people deemed most deserving of inclusion into an unjust system, the struggle for migrant justice must see the ways in which migration fits into the entrenchment and extension of the US empire, making it imperative to build connections to anticolonial, antiracist, anticapitalist, and abolitionist struggles across borders.

ACKNOWLEDGMENTS

I could not have written the book without the generosity of immigrants who agreed to speak with me about their experiences. This book is grounded in these conversations. There is a special place in these acknowledgments for the deported veterans who welcomed me to the "bunker" in Ciudad Juarez in 2019. No words can adequately express my indebtedness to Hector Barajas. I never met Camilo Mejía, but his words and work shaped how I think about war and empire. I imagine a future without borders for all of us.

I am lucky to be able to include Joseph Silva's evocative photographs in this text. A talented artist and a tireless ally to deported veterans across the world, Joseph's work is an inspiration. I am thrilled that the book cover was created by radical artist Josh MacPhee. I am grateful for these collaborations.

Many individuals facilitated this research project by sharing information and making connections, including Jeremy Slack, Diane Vega, David Brotherton, Juan Jose Bustamante, Alfredo Gonzalez, Matt Howard, Claude Copeland, Louis Deli, and Cecilia Menjívar. In the time of academic labor casualization and defunding of public higher education in the United States, it is increasingly rare to receive material support for research and writing as part of a faculty position. University management teams and state governments are replacing tenure track lines with short-term teaching-intensive appointments, not to mention the exponential growth in exploitation of part-time adjunct instructors who lack job security and fair wages. As an author in the MIT Press Labor and Technology series, it behooves me to acknowledge that my regular full-time faculty salaries at the University of Massachusetts Boston and City University of New York School of Labor and Urban Studies were intended to provide material support for writing and research, as well as teaching and service. My rights as an academic worker at these institutions were upheld by the Faculty Staff Union and Professional Staff Congress. I am keenly aware of the advantages of being a union member for the morale and community needed to research and write. A UMass Boston College of Liberal Arts Dean's Research Fund grant covered some of the costs of research. The William Joiner Institute at UMass Boston helped me understand the history and current state of veteran dissent and the political landscape of veteran activism. I am especially thankful to Mitch Manning. Several graduate students provided invaluable assistance in outreach, interview transcription, and media analysis. I thank Katsyris Rivera Kientz, Nicole Young, Rebecca Hooper, Theresa Knapp, Jennifer Skinnon, Miranda MacKinnon, Keitaro Okura, and Doug Pariseau. Aaron Eaton generously drew on personal networks to help with recruitment at the very beginning of the project. Nagita Sykes connected me to her military coworkers, let me accompany her on base, and otherwise has helped me understand military labor.

I wrote much of the book in the company of two outstanding critical scholars, Lisa Sun-Hee Park and Miriam Ticktin, whose brilliance and generous spirits I can only aspire to. Drs. Park and Ticktin saw what I was trying to do with this book, and helped the vision emerge through words, paragraphs, and chapters in a way I could never have done on my own. Throughout, they provided invaluable professional support and advice. Thank you for the gift of your time and friendship.

I am deeply grateful to the three anonymous reviewers of the manuscript. The time and attention to detail they gave are a gift I hope to pay forward. Thank yous are owed to Katie Helke and the editorial team at MIT Press, who made book publishing seem easy.

Ideas are best nurtured in relation. Several colleagues provided indispensable feedback on written work and pointed me to existing literature on specific topics. I thank Amy Hsin, Karen Suyemoto, Meghan Kallman, Sarah Mayorga-Gallo, Saher Selod, and Leslie Wang. Andrea Leverentz was especially helpful as an expert on the US criminal justice system and the intricacies of qualitative research. Rakhshanda Saleem shared essential comments on the book's conclusion and drew my attention to the importance of terminology. The research group at the CUNY School of Labor and Urban Studies generously grappled with the chapter on deported veterans. Shannon Gleeson helped me conceptualize military service as labor. Conversations with Sonia Sanchez developed my critical analysis of migration processes and systems. James Rodriguez and Adam Wilson jumped in to provide essential help at the end.

I could not have written this book without the daily morning boost of the Grittycize team. Thanks for humoring me and sticking with it for so long, Shannon Gleeson, Amada Armenta, Amy Hsin, and Pam Sertzen.

For years, I listened to two leftist military podcasts. I learned a lot about military labor from Francis Horton and Nate Bethea of *What a Hell of a Way to Die*, and Spenser Rapone and Mike Prysner of *Eyes Left*.

I am grateful for my community at the City University of New York, home to determined resistance to militarism and empire. Rank and File Action, the Cross CUNY Working Group against Racism and Colonialism, FreeCUNY!, and CUNY for Palestine epitomize the beauty of solidarity and collective action. I am humbled to work alongside these comrades.

Especially in the time of the COVID-19 pandemic, when our work was literally done in our homes, I am thankful for being able to make my home in the Aptekar-Finn-Gutierrez-Wilson household.

APPENDIX

The genesis of this book reaches back to an earlier research project, in which I observed naturalization ceremonies, watching as immigrants became US citizens. At some of these ceremonies, immigration officials would single out immigrants in military uniforms among the crowd. I started to learn about the special naturalization provisions that apply to US military workers. While in the end it warranted only a note in my first book, the story of immigrants in the military continued to intrigue me. As an immigrant, I had firsthand experience of taking the citizenship oath and the immigration steps that come before for those, like myself, who are deemed deserving of legal inclusion. I was not, however, a veteran. As a teenager growing up in New York City, I did not feel drawn to the military, nor did I need to join the military to pay for college or support myself and my family.

My interest in the subject of immigrants in the US military was shaped by my opposition to the US invasion of Iraq and Afghanistan and to my growing discomfort with immigrant military workers being used to legitimize the War on Terror. I struggled with my complicity as a US citizen in the violence and destruction perpetrated by the US military, as well as the way my own immigrant story contributed to the harmful ideology of exceptionalism propping up the US empire. I thought and talked about this project well before I conducted the first interview, gathering background knowledge and momentum. Interviewing proceeded in spurts and starts over five long years, fit into the interstices of my academic labor, with many breaks to process, analyze, and doubt.

INTERVIEWS

This book is based largely on interviews with immigrants who enlisted in the US military and did not have US citizenship when they enlisted.

I interviewed seventy-two people between 2015 and 2019. These semi-structured interviews were organized diachronically, starting with questions about immigration trajectories, moving to enlistment, military labor, and separation, if applicable. I asked participants to tell me their stories "starting from the beginning," and I used short prompts to keep the stories going, reacting empathetically. I asked vaguely worded questions about experiences in the military, such as, "What happened after you completed your training?," rather than more focused questions about violence or deployments. Several participants early on in the research expressed concern before speaking with me about discussing these topics and referenced psychology studies on PTSD that they felt were invasive. I adjusted to these concerns by being especially careful in constructing questions in a way that would minimize any pressure participants might feel to speak about their experiences of violence and combat if they were not inclined to share these. I also adjusted my explanation of the study to potential participants by differentiating it from psychology studies. As a result, work-related parts of the interview were especially interviewee-driven. I paid close attention to markers dropped by participants and referred to them to encourage extension and deeper detail.[1] For instance, when one participant said, "there were things here and there" in the course of describing his work in the military, I followed by asking him to tell me more about these "things." In cases when the participants did not bring it up on their own and where it was applicable, I asked them about identifying as a veteran and what US citizenship meant to them. (See table A.1.)

I recruited participants by contacting veteran-serving agencies and organizations such as community college veteran offices and legal clinics, referrals through personal networks, and posts on social media. Some of the people I interviewed referred their friends and colleagues to me. The process of recruiting interview participants provided additional data, as many of the entities I contacted insisted that there were no immigrant veterans on their campus or in their clinic or organization. This was likely the case for many organizations, but it is also true that many people in the United States are not aware that noncitizens are able to enlist in the US military, nor do they understand the way military labor intersects with the naturalization process. This became apparent as multiple people I

TABLE A.1

Interview guide

1. Immigration history of participant and family

2. Decision to enlist in armed forces (timing, incentives, drawbacks, doubts, key people, decision-making process, role of immigration status, role of citizenship as incentive)

3. If the participant is a US citizen: decision to seek naturalization, key people (e.g., recruiters, commanding officers), institutional incentives and barriers, details of the process, meanings attached to the experience, meanings attached to citizenship, counterfactuals (how things may be different if participant were not a citizen); if the participant naturalized after leaving the military, reasons for not doing it while in the military

4. If the participant is not a US citizen: reasons for not having citizenship (obstacles, disincentives), meanings attached to citizenship, plans for future regarding citizenship acquisition, counterfactuals (how things may be different if participant were a citizen)

5. Experience in the military as an immigrant

6. Experience as an immigrant veteran, reintegration into community, difficulties, positive experiences, goals, role of family, role of the VA, role of veteran organizations

7. Identity as veteran, identity as immigrant, other identities, transnational practices, social networks with veterans, immigrants, co-ethnics

reached out to at veteran services and clinics commented that they did not think noncitizens served in the military. It took many fruitless hours of outreach to track down a single interview.

When interviewing military workers and veterans, I presented myself as a college professor interested in immigrants in the military, and one who was not intimately familiar with the institution. I shared that I was a first-generation immigrant. My whiteness and cis-gendered femininity likely helped me to successfully convey my desired presentation of self in interviews. Interviewees kindly explained the workings of the US military to me as an outsider, although I gradually became more fluent in the terminology and the vast body of military acronyms. It helped that my personal experiences and extensive research on the US immigration system and the naturalization process gave me a nuanced understanding of the legal and practical concerns of immigrants navigating both the military and immigration systems at once.

Most interviews lasted forty-five minutes to an hour and a half. I spoke to people over meals or coffee, over various video-conferencing platforms, and sometimes simply over the phone. When I conducted interviews before the pandemic, remote interviewing was less common among researchers. Some of the participants were more versed in video conferencing than I was due to their experience in communicating with loved ones while deployed or deported, or communicating with family in their country of origin while in the United States. Although remote interviewing can make it difficult to observe body language and contextual factors and to establish rapport, I found ways to compensate for and minimize these challenges. I expanded pre-interview communications when possible, and used remote video interviewing as an opportunity for participants to show me artifacts or contextualize their surroundings when they wanted to do so. For instance, some deported veterans brought certificates, medals, photographs, and other material to show me during the video interview.[2] Some participants shared photos of themselves in uniform or at their naturalization ceremonies using Facebook Messenger.

Remote interviewing allowed me to have a geographical reach across the United States and Northern Mexico that I would not otherwise be able to have as an assistant professor at a defunded public university with scant support for research travel. This enabled access to a diverse collection of interviews from multiple immigrant groups. Since the beginning of the COVID-19 pandemic in 2020, many qualitative researchers have been conducting interviews using online video-conferencing platforms, recognizing the potential and challenges that remote interviewing modalities present.[3] I offered a modest $20 in cash or money order to thank people for participating in my study. Some participants asked me to donate the incentive to a veteran cause, and I donated to the Deported Veteran Support House, with their permission.

The immigrant military workers and veterans whose stories I share in this book were an extremely diverse group, born in twenty-eight countries across the world: Brazil, Canada, Cape Verde, Dominican Republic, Ecuador, Germany, Haiti, India, Indonesia, Ireland, Jamaica, Kenya, Korea, Malaysia, Mexico, Nepal, Netherlands, Pakistan, People's Republic of China, Peru, Philippines, Poland, Russia, Slovakia, Sri Lanka, Taiwan, Trinidad, and Ukraine. In table A.1, I show the distribution of my study participants by region of origin. It is important to consider how my group of participants compares to the characteristics of all noncitizen immigrants in the US military. Such comparison is complicated by lack of accurate data on

TABLE A.2

Study participant characteristics and characteristics of US armed forces personnel

	Study participants	Foreign-born recruits in the US armed forces*
Region of origin		
Latin America and the Caribbean	18 (25%)	39%
Asia	41 (57%)	36%
Africa	3 (4%)	5%
Europe	9 (13%)	6%
Canada	1 (1%)	1%
Woman-identified	11 (15%)	17%
Army	57 (79%)	22%
Navy	6 (8%)	40%
Marines	8 (11%)	16%
Enlisted before 9/11	15 (21%)	
Enlisted after 9/11	57 (79%)	
Enlisted as undocumented	3 (4%)	
Enlisted into the MAVNI program	39 (54%)	
Total	72 (100%)	65,000

* Data reported by the Migration Policy Institute in 2008, including 13 percent with unknown country of origin. Percentages reflect all foreign-born citizens and noncitizens. https://www.migrationpolicy.org/article/immigrants-us-armed-forces-2008.

the country of birth for foreign-born military workers, and lack of tracking of citizenship status by country of birth.[4] Taking 2008 data of all foreign-born enlisted military workers, including citizens—approximately the midpoint of my participants' military service—it seems that my study might include disproportionately more Asians. Slightly over half of people I interviewed were noncitizen enlistees born in Asia. A quarter were born in Latin America and the Caribbean. The rest were born in Africa, Europe, and Canada. The high number of Asian participants is due to my special interest in MAVNI recruits, who are a relatively small and mostly Asian group (10,000 total ever recruited).

Most of the noncitizen immigrants I interviewed enlisted in the army, with a smaller number in the navy and the Marine Corps. The army is the largest branch of the US military, with over a third of all military personnel, followed by the navy and air force.[5] The navy has the largest proportion of the foreign-born. The larger proportion of my participants who joined the army is due to the inclusion of MAVNIs, who were recruited primarily into the army. Reflecting the low number of women in the US military, only 15 percent of the interviews were with women-identified immigrants. The majority of those I spoke to enlisted after the attacks of September 11, 2001, during the War on Terror that was still ongoing twenty years later as I wrote this book.

To protect the confidentiality of my study participants, I used pseudonyms throughout the book. In some cases, such as when criminalized activity was mentioned, I further changed participant characteristics, altering information that was not essential to understanding the examples or using less specific descriptions. For example, I may have changed the geographic regions involved in a participant's life trajectory, or substituted a region for a more specific city or state. I chose to omit some resonant stories when I felt they might lead to deductive disclosure or identification by a member of the group or community despite the use of pseudonyms.[6] I did not create new composite characters. I use the real name of Hector Barajas, a deported veteran, because he insisted on it and has shared his story widely elsewhere. All but one interview was conducted in English. One participant responded to my questions in Russian. I simultaneously transcribed and translated his responses into English. Another respondent spoke English, interspersing Russian phrases and idioms to convey his meaning more clearly to a fellow Russian speaker.

MAVNI RECRUITS

There were three main subgroups of participants: regular recruits, MAVNI recruits, and deported veterans. Of the seventy-two interviews, thirty-nine were with MAVNI recruits, mostly international students who enlisted as part of the short-lived program aimed at migrants who are in the United States on temporary visas designated for "highly-skilled" workers. Among these thirty-nine participants, fourteen enlisted without serious problems, eight enlisted and experienced long waits and uncertain legal status that was in the end resolved favorably, and another fourteen were still waiting for their situations to be resolved or had had an unfavorable outcome. Of the last group, some approached the interview as a way to publicize the plight of MAVNI recruits who enlisted but were not able to access the benefits promised in their contracts. This was different from the regular immigrant enlistees I interviewed, who did not have a sense of being part of a group like those who enlisted through MAVNI and who framed their tribulations either in a more individualized manner or by relying on other shared characteristics such as race and gender. In contrast, the distinct experience of MAVNIs shaped by the military itself led others to identify them as a discrete group and for MAVNIs to experience themselves as a group, approaching interviews as an opportunity to present an individual *and* a collective story.

The recruitment process for interviews with MAVNI recruits was somewhat different from recruitment for the other two subgroups of participants. I obtained permission from the administrator of a closed MAVNI Facebook page with thousands of members to invite MAVNI recruits to participate in my study. I also asked those who responded to share the invitation with other MAVNIs they knew. MAVNIs are predominantly college-educated and many are heavy users of social media, which became essential as a source of information for them in navigating the vagaries of the legal system. The resulting large Facebook community proved to be a productive source for recruitment, and many of my participants responded when they saw my post or when it was shared with them by friends who were active in the Facebook group. I interviewed thirty-eight MAVNIs: eleven participants were born in the People's Republic of China, nine were from India, five from Korea, three each from Nepal and Pakistan, and one each from Brazil, Taiwan, Indonesia, Kenya, Malaysia, Russia, and Ukraine. The predominance of Asian participants reflects their relative numbers among international students, the primary target of MAVNI recruitment.

DEPORTED VETERANS

The deported veterans interviewed for this book are part of the deported veteran community that engages in collective memory making through storytelling within the group and facing the public, in hopes of getting a reprieve from their expulsion from the United States.[7] As such, these participants are used to sharing their stories with outsiders such as journalists, advocates, and politicians. Talking to me was part of the work of spreading awareness of deported veterans' plight. Yet these interviews, leisurely paced, confidential, and largely open-ended, revealed details, tensions, and framings that differed from the more stylized public stories I saw in my examination of media produced by and about deported veterans. I take the relative complexity of stories revealed in my interviews to be a reflection of lower pressure these participants experienced to construct a particular veteran story when talking to me, who was not connected to levers of power nor had a large audience. Were I a reporter, a political staffer, an Ivy League professor, or an immigration attorney, I suspect I would have heard something closer to the public-facing stories produced by this group. Of course, media production necessarily involves some streamlining of complexity as well.

In interviewing deported veterans, the section of the interview focused on life after separation from the military expanded to encompass stories of imprisonment, detention, deportation, and life as a deportee. My trip to Ciudad Juarez in the fall of 2019 allowed me to visit the support house there and spend social time with some deported veterans and their families—an invaluable, if brief, ethnographic opportunity that shaped my analysis. At the support house, I met a participant whom I had previously interviewed on video, and subsequently interviewed another participant on video whom I first met in Juarez. I spoke informally with other deported veterans without formally interviewing them. The trip was a sobering experience of the border, which I crossed with a flash of my US passport while the people I came to visit could legally cross only after their deaths, since even deported veterans have a right to be buried in a military cemetery.

This book reflects my social position as a tenured academic located in the imperial core. The labor of immigrants in the US military can be understood differently from other angles. Veneration of the military pervades US society across the political spectrum. Many readers and even the participants in my research will disagree with the political principles that shape my work. On the other hand, the people across the world bearing the brunt of US military occupations might object to the humanization of imperial military workers. In sharing my account in this book, I hope to pry open the platitudes around immigrant military labor and pull the rug out from under hegemonic militarism that normalizes plunder and death.

ACRONYMS

ACLU	American Civil Liberties Union
AEDPA	Antiterrorism and Effective Death Penalty Act
ASVAB	Armed Services Vocational Aptitude Battery
CBP	US Customs and Border Protection
CIA	Central Intelligence Agency
DACA	Deferred Action for Childhood Arrivals
DADT	"Don't Ask, Don't Tell"
DHS	US Department of Homeland Security
DOD	US Department of Defense
DREAM Act	Development, Relief, and Education for Alien Minors Act
DUI/DWI	driving under the influence/driving while intoxicated
FBI	Federal Bureau of Investigation
FOIA	Freedom of Information Act
ICE	US Immigration and Customs Enforcement
IIRIRA	Illegal Immigration Reform and Immigrant Responsibility Act
IRCA	Immigration Reform and Control Act
ISIS	Islamic State of Iraq and Syria
JAG	judge advocate general
JROTC	Junior Reserve Officers' Training Corps
MAVNI	Military Accessions Vital to the National Interest
MOS	military occupational specialty
OCS	officer candidate school
OPT	Optional Practical Training

PTSD	post-traumatic stress disorder
RICO	Racketeer Influenced and Corrupt Organizations Act
ROTC	Reserve Officers' Training Corps
SEVIS	Student and Exchange Visitor Information System
SWAT	Special Weapons and Tactics
TPS	temporary protected status
USCIS	US Citizenship and Immigration Services
VA	US Department of Veterans Affairs

NOTES

CHAPTER 1

1. Following the example set by antiwar veterans, I seek to disrupt hegemonic language by using the term *military worker* rather than *service member* throughout the book, and generally use *work* and *labor* instead of *service*. At the cost of sounding awkward, my intent is to foreground military work as labor, while rejecting the conceptualizing of military labor as service. The caveat is that I do not write about people working for private military and security companies contracted by the US military—a topic deserving its own volume.

2. Guillermina Jasso, Douglas Massey, Mark Rosenzweig, and James Smith, "From Illegal to Legal: Estimating Previous Illegal Experience among New Legal Immigrants to the United States," *International Migration Review* 42, no. 4 (2008): 803–843.

3. Niels Eichhorn, "Mexican-American War (1846–1848)," in *Imperialism and Expansionism in American History: A Social, Political, and Cultural Encyclopedia and Document Collection*, ed. Chris Magoc and David Bernstein (Santa Barbara, CA: ABC-CLIO, 2015), 161–164; James Jacobs and Leslie Anne Hayes, "Aliens in the U.S. Armed Forces: A Historico-Legal Analysis," *Armed Forces and Society* 7, no. 2 (1981): 187–208; Amy Lutz, "Race-Ethnicity and Immigration Status in the U.S. Military," in *Life Course Perspectives on Military Service*, ed. Janet Wilmoth and Andrew London (New York: Routledge, 2012), 69–96; Catherine Lutz, "Making War at Home in the United States: Militarization and the Current Crisis," *American Anthropologist* 104, no. 3 (2002): 723–735; John Whiteclay Chambers, *To Raise an Army: The Draft Comes to Modern America* (New York: Free Press, 1987).

4. Robert Draper, "Soldiers of Misfortune," *Texas Monthly*, August 1997, https://www.texasmonthly.com/articles/soldiers-of-misfortune-2/; Manny Fernandez, "U.S. Troops Went to the Border in 1997. They Killed an American Boy," *New York Times*, November 27, 2018, https://www.nytimes.com/2018/11/27/us/esequiel-hernandez-death-border-mexico.html.

5. Eve Tuck, "Suspending Damage: A Letter to Communities," *Harvard Educational Review* 79, no. 3 (October 6, 2009): 409–428.

6. Chambers, *To Raise an Army*. Immigrants who are US citizens or permanent legal residents can enlist in the military. However, only US citizens are able to be commissioned as officers. Commissioned officers are the managerial rank of the military, who are commissioned by completing ROTC and graduating from college, attending officer candidate school, or graduating from West Point.

Enlisted soldiers can advance to become noncommissioned officers (NCOs) who supervise lower ranks.

7. Chambers, *To Raise an Army*; Eichhorn "Mexican-American War (1846–1848)," 161–164; Jacobs and Hayes, "Aliens in the U.S. Armed Forces: A Historico-Legal Analysis"; Lutz, "Race-Ethnicity and Immigration Status in the U.S. Military," 69–96; Lutz, "Making War at Home in the United States," 723–735.

8. Cara Wong and Grace Cho, "Jus Meritum Citizenship for Service," in *Transforming Politics, Transforming America: The Political and Civic Incorporation of Immigrants in the United States*, ed. Taeku Lee, S. Karthick Ramakrishnan, and Ricardo Ramírez (Charlottesville: University of Virginia Press, 2012).

9. Michael LeMay and Elliott Barkan, *U.S. Immigration and Naturalization Laws and Issues: A Documentary History* (Westport, CT: Greenwood, 1999); Cara Wong, "Who Fights: Substitution, Commutation, and 'Green Card Troops,'" *Du Bois Review: Social Science Research on Race* 4, no. 1 (2007): 167–188.

10. Dimitry Kochenov, "Ending the Passport Apartheid. The Alternative to Citizenship Is No Citizenship—A Reply," *International Journal of Constitutional Law* 18, no. 4 (December 1, 2020): 1525–1530.

11. Patrick Weil, *The Sovereign Citizen: Denaturalization and the Origins of the American Republic* (Philadelphia: University of Pennsylvania Press, 2012).

12. Catherine Barry, *New Americans in Our Nation's Military: A Proud Tradition and Hopeful Future* (Washington, DC: Center for American Progress, 2013), https://www.americanprogress.org/issues/immigration/reports/2013/11/08/79116/new-americans-in-our-nations-military/; Mae Ngai, *Impossible Subjects: Illegal Aliens and the Making of Modern America* (Princeton, NJ: Princeton University Press, 2014); Daneesh Sohoni and Amin Vafa, "The Fight to Be American: Military Naturalization and Asian Citizenship," *Asian American Law Journal* 17 (2010): 119–151; Lutz, "Race-Ethnicity and Immigration Status in the U.S. Military," 69–96; Jie Zong and Jeanne Batalova, *Immigrant Veterans in the United States* (Migration Policy Institute, May 16, 2019), https://www.migrationpolicy.org/article/immigrant-veterans-united-states-2018.

13. Lutz, "Race-Ethnicity and Immigration Status in the U.S. Military," 69–96; Henry A. J. Ramos Henry, *The American GI Forum: In Pursuit of the Dream, 1948–1983* (Houston: Arte Publico Press, 1998).

14. The United States is not alone in employing noncitizens in its military forces. Although some of the other settler colonial nations, like Canada and Australia, limit military positions to immigrants who are citizens or in the process of applying for citizenship, the United States is more similar to former colonial superpowers like the UK and France. The French Foreign Legion was formed largely out of recent immigrants to police French colonies in the early nineteenth century. Today, it continues to comprise a nontrivial portion of the French military, recruiting soldiers from all over the world. Even after the formal independence of its colonies, the UK employs troops from its former possessions, such as Nepal. The actual British armed forces remained white, however, until the push

to diversify in the twenty-first century led to the recruitment of Commonwealth citizens. These Commonwealth troops, from countries like Jamaica, are not eligible for any special citizenship considerations. French Legionnaires, however, are eligible for citizenship after five years of service. Vron Ware, "Whiteness in the Glare of War: Soldiers, Migrants and Citizenship," *Ethnicities* 10, no. 3 (2012): 313–330; Vron Ware, *Military Migrants: Fighting for YOUR Country* (Basingstoke: Palgrave Macmillan, 2012); Martin Windrow, *French Foreign Legion: Infantry and Cavalry since 1945* (London: Bloomsbury Publishing, 2013).

15. Gay Becker, Yewoubdar Beyene, and Leilani Cuizon Canalita, "Immigrating for Status in Late Life: Effects of Globalization on Filipino American Veterans," *Journal of Aging Studies* 14, no. 3 (2000): 273–291; David Nakamura, "Filipinos Who Fought to Aid U.S. in World War II Still Await Green Cards for Grown Children," *Washington Post*, January 3, 2015, https://www.washingtonpost.com/politics/filipinos-who-fought-to-aid-us-in-world-war-ii-still-await-green-cards-for-grown-children/2015/01/03/a370e704-913d-11e4-ba53-a477d66580ed_story.html.

16. Nick Estes, *Our History Is the Future: Standing Rock versus the Dakota Access Pipeline, and the Long Tradition of Indigenous Resistance* (New York: Verso, 2019); Julian Go, *Patterns of Empire: The British and American Empires, 1688 to the Present* (New York: Cambridge University Press, 2011); Eve Tuck and K. Wayne Yang, "Decolonization Is Not a Metaphor," *Decolonization: Indigeneity, Education & Society* 1, no. 1 (September 8, 2012).

17. Ray Burdeos, *Filipinos in the U.S. Navy and Coast Guard during the Vietnam War* (Bloomington, IN: Author House, 2008).

18. James Proceso Paligutan, "American Dream Deferred: Filipino Nationals in the US Navy and Coast Guard, 1947–1970," PhD diss., University of California, Irvine, 2012; Yen Le Espiritu, "Colonial Oppression, Labour and Importation and Group Formation: Filipinos in the United States," *Ethnic and Racial Studies* 19, no. 1, (1996): 29.

19. Go, *Patterns of Empire*, 58.

20. Estes, *Our History Is the Future; American Indian Veterans Have Highest Record of Military Service* (NICOA—National Indian Council on Aging, November 8, 2019); Winona LaDuke and Sean Aaron Cruz, *The Militarization of Indian Country* (East Lansing: Michigan State University Press, 2013), 34.

21. Go, *Patterns of Empire*.

22. Tanya Maria Golash-Boza, *Immigration Nation: Raids, Detentions, and Deportations in Post-9/11 America* (London: Routledge, 2015).

23. Irene Garza, "Advertising Patriotism: The 'Yo Soy El Army' Campaign and the Politics of Visibility for Latina/o Youth," *Latino Studies* 13, no. 2 (2015): 245–268.

24. Jason K Dempsey and Robert Y. Shapiro, "The Army's Hispanic Future." *Armed Forces & Society* 35, no. 3 (2009): 526–561; Garza, "Advertising Patriotism," 245–268; Jorge Mariscal, "No Where Else to Go: Latino Youth and the Poverty Draft," *Public Affairs Magazine*, September 23, 2004, http://www.politicalaffairs.net/no-where-else-to-go-latino-youth-and-the-poverty-draft-print-edition/.

25. Tarak Barkawi, *Globalization and War* (Lanham, MD: Rowman & Littlefield, 2005); Usha Zacharias, "Legitimizing Empire: Racial and Gender Politics of the War on Terrorism," *Social Justice* 30, no. 2 (2003): 123–132.

26. Roxanne Dunbar-Ortiz, *Not a Nation of Immigrants: Settler Colonialism, White Supremacy, and a History of Erasure and Exclusion* (New York: Beacon Press, 2021); Estes, *Our History Is the Future.*

27. Craig Whitlock, Leslie Shapiro, and Armand Emamdjomeh, "The Afghanistan Papers: Read the Confidential Documents That Reveal a Secret History of the War in Afghanistan," *Washington Post*, December 9, 2019, https://www.washingtonpost.com/graphics/2019/investigations/afghanistan-papers/documents-database/.

28. Robert Draper, *To Start a War: How the Bush Administration Took America into Iraq* (New York: Penguin, 2021). However, US military attacks on Iraq predate the War on Terror. The United States first invaded Iraq in 1991, and its involvement there goes back many decades. In the 1960s, the CIA actively facilitated two bloody coups, which would maintain US dominance in the region and protect its interest in Middle Eastern oil. The United States supported and aided its client, Saddam Hussein, through the Iran-Iraq War in the 1980s, but turned on Hussein when he invaded Kuwait in 1991. The terrorist attacks of 9/11 provided an opportunity to eliminate Hussein. William Blum, *Killing Hope: US Military and CIA Interventions since World War II* (London: Bloomsbury Academic, 2014); Daniel Immerwahr, *How to Hide an Empire: A History of the Greater United States* (New York: Farrar, Straus and Giroux, 2019).

29. *Casualty Status* (US Department of Defense, 2022), https://www.defense.gov/casualty.pdf, accessed October 27, 2022.

30. *An Unheralded Contribution: Honoring America's Fallen Foreign-Born Service Members Post 9/11* (Partnership for a New American Economy, New American Economy Research Fund, 2015), http://www.newamericaneconomy.org/wp-content/uploads/2015/11/Miltary-Casualties.pdf; Luis Plascencia, "Citizenship through Veteranship: Latino Migrants Defend the US 'Homeland,'" *Anthropology News* 50 (May 7, 2009): 8–9.

31. Neta Crawford, *Human Cost of the Post-9/11 Wars: Lethality and the Need for Transparency* (Watson Institute for International and Public Affairs, Brown University, November 2018), https://watson.brown.edu/costsofwar/files/cow/imce/papers/2018/Human%20Costs%2C%20Nov%208%202018%20CoW.pdf.

32. Jane Arraf, "U.S. Announces End to Combat Mission in Iraq, but Troops Will Not Leave," *New York Times*, December 9. 2021, https://www.nytimes.com/2021/12/09/world/middleeast/us-iraq-combat-mission.html; Thomas Gibbons-Neff and Eric Schmitt, "Despite Vow to End 'Endless Wars,' Here's Where about 200,000 Troops Remain," *New York Times*, October 21, 2019, https://www.nytimes.com/2019/10/21/world/middleeast/us-troops-deployments.html; Go, *Patterns of Empire*; Roger Morris, "Opinion: A Tyrant 40 Years in the Making," *New York Times*, March 14, 2003, https://www.nytimes.com/2003/03/14/opinion/a-tyrant-40-years

-in-the-making.html. Hussein was a client of the United States in the direct sense of being on the CIA payroll, according to Roger Morris.

33. "Economic Costs," Watson Institute for International and Public Affairs, Brown University, September 2021, https://watson.brown.edu/costsofwar/costs /economic.

34. William Hartung, *Profits of War: Corporate Beneficiaries of the Post-9/11 Pentagon Spending Surge* (Watson Institute for International and Public Affairs, Brown University, September 13, 2021), https://watson.brown.edu/costsofwar/files/cow /imce/papers/2021/Profits%20of%20War_Hartung_Costs%20of%20War _Sept%2013%2C%202021.pdf; Christian Sorensen, *Understanding the War Industry* (Atlanta, GA: Clarity Press, 2020).

35. Reece Jones and Corey Johnson, "Border Militarisation and the Re-articulation of Sovereignty," *Transactions of the Institute of British Geographers* 41, no. 2 (2016): 187–200; Stuart Schrader, *Badges without Borders: How Global Counterinsurgency Transformed American Policing* (Berkeley: University of California Press, 2019).

36. Emily Brissette, "Waging a War of Position on Neoliberal Terrain: Critical Reflections on the Counter-Recruitment Movement," *Interface: A Journal for an about Social Movements* 5, no. 2 (2013): 377–398; Cynthia Enloe, *Globalization and Militarism*, 2nd ed. (Lanham, MD: Rl, 2016); Robert J. González, *Militarizing Culture: Essays on the Warfare State* (Walnut Creek, CA: Left Coast Press, 2010).

37. *Active Duty Military Strength Summary* (Defense Manpower Data Center, 2020), https://dwp.dmdc.osd.mil/dwp/app/dod-data-reports/workforce-reports; Gibbons-Neff and Schmitt, "Despite Vow to End 'Endless Wars'"; David Vine, *Base Nation: How U.S. Military Bases Abroad Harm America and the World* (New York: Metropolitan Books, 2015).

38. Lizette Alvarez, "Army Effort to Enlist Hispanics Draws Recruits, and Criticism," *New York Times*, February 9, 2006, https://www.nytimes.com/2006/02/09/us /army-effort-to-enlist-hispanics-draws-recruits-and-criticism.html; Garza, "Advertising Patriotism," 245–268; Na Ma and Ninuo Zhang, "More Chinese Immigrants Pick US Military Career Path," *Global Times*, December 12, 2017, http:// www.globaltimes.cn/content/1079356.shtml.

39. Jorge Mariscal, "The Poverty Draft," *Sojourners*, June 2007, https://sojo.net /magazine/june-2007/poverty-draft.

40. Brissette, "Waging a War of Position on Neoliberal Terrain," 377–398; Jorge Mariscal, "Fighting the Poverty Draft," *CounterPunch.Org*, January 28, 2005, https:// www.counterpunch.org/2005/01/28/fighting-the-poverty-draft/; Kyle Rempfer, "Student Loan Crisis, Not Mideast Wars, Helped Army Leaders Exceed Recruiting Goals This Year," *Army Times*, September 18, 2019, https://www.armytimes .com/news/your-army/2019/09/17/student-loan-crisis-not-mideast-wars-helped -army-leaders-exceed-recruiting-goals-this-year/.

41. Jennifer Mittelstadt, *The Rise of the Military Welfare State* (Cambridge, MA: Harvard University Press, 2015); Deborah Cowen, "Fighting for 'Freedom': The End of Conscription in the United States and the Neoliberal Project of Citizenship,"

Citizenship Studies 10, no. 2 (2006): 167–183; Deborah Cowen, *Military Workfare: The Soldier and Social Citizenship in Canada* (Toronto: University of Toronto Press, 2008).

42. "Immigrant Children," Child Trends, https://www.childtrends.org/indicators /immigrant-children, accessed October 27, 2022.

43. Tanya Golash-Boza and Pierrette Hondagneu-Sotelo, "Latino Immigrant Men and the Deportation Crisis: A Gendered Racial Removal Program," *Latino Studies* 11, no. 3 (2013): 271–292; Tanya Golash-Boza, "Structural Racism, Criminalization, and Pathways to Deportation for Dominican and Jamaican Men in the United States," *Social Justice* 44, nos. 2–3 (2017): 137–162.

44. Saher Selod, *Forever Suspect: Racialized Surveillance of Muslim Americans in the War on Terror* (New Brunswick, NJ: Rutgers University Press, 2018).

45. Michael Ewers and Joseph Lewis, "Risk and the Securitisation of Student Migration to the United States," *Journal of Economic and Social Geography* 99, no. 4 (2008): 470–482.

46. Sofya Aptekar, *The Road to Citizenship: What Naturalization Means for Immigrants and the United States* (New Brunswick, NJ: Rutgers University Press, 2015).

47. *Muslims Need Not Apply* (ACLU Southern California, August 21, 2013), https://www .aclusocal.org/sites/default/files/field_documents/161849063-muslims-need-not -apply-aclu-socal-report.pdf.

48. Priscilla Alvarez, "Justice Department Creates Section Dedicated to Denaturalization Cases," *CNN*, February 26, 2020, https://www.cnn.com/2020/02/26 /politics/justice-department-denaturalization-cases/index.html; Weil, *The Sovereign Citizen*.

49. *Trends in the Timing and Size of DHS Appropriations: In Brief* (Congressional Research Service, December 6, 2019), https://fas.org/sgp/crs/homesec/R44604.pdf.

50. Meghann Myers, "More Troops Are Heading to the US-Mexico Border," *Military Times*, July 17, 2019, https://www.militarytimes.com/news/your-military/2019/07 /17/more-troops-are-heading-to-the-us-mexico-border/; Jeremy Slack, *Deported to Death: How Drug Violence Is Changing Migration on the US-Mexico Border* (Oakland: University of California Press, 2019).

51. David FitzGerald, *Refuge beyond Reach: How Rich Democracies Repel Asylum Seekers* (New York: Oxford University Press, 2019).

52. Estes, *Our History Is the Future*; Schrader, *Badges without Borders*.

53. Victoria Hattam, "Imperial Designs: Remembering Vietnam at the US–Mexico Border Wall," *Memory Studies* 9, no. 1 (January 1, 2016): 27–47; Schrader, *Badges without Borders*.

54. *Population Representation in the Military Services: Fiscal Year 2010 Summary Report* (Center for Naval Analysis, 2011), https://www.cna.org/pop-rep/.

55. George Reynolds and Amanda Shendruk, *Demographics of the US Military* (Washington, DC: Council on Foreign Relations, 2018), https://www.cfr.org/article /demographics-us-military; Zong and Batalova, *Immigrant Veterans in the United States*.

56. Alejandra Martinez, "Veterans Banished: The Fight to Bring Them Home," *Scholar: St. Mary's Law Review on Race and Social Justice* 19, no. 3 (2016): 321–360.

57. Muzaffar Chishti, Austin Rose, and Stephen Yale-Loehr, *Noncitizens in the U.S. Military: Navigating National Security Concerns and Recruitment Needs* (Migration Policy Institute, May 2019), https://www.migrationpolicy.org/research/noncitizens-us-military-national-security-concerns-recruitment-needs.

58. Alex Horton, "The Pentagon Promised Citizenship to Immigrants Who Served. Now It Might Help Deport Them," *Washington Post*, June 26, 2017, https://www.washingtonpost.com/news/checkpoint/wp/2017/06/26/the-pentagon-promised-citizenship-to-immigrants-who-served-now-it-might-help-deport-them/.

59. Philip Kretsedemas, "The Limits of Control: Neo-Liberal Policy Priorities and the US Non-Immigrant Flow," *International Migration* 50, no. s1 (2012): e1–e18; Denise Obinna, "The Challenges of American Legal Permanent Residency for Family- and Employment-Based Petitioners," *Migration and Development* 3, no. 2 (2014): 272–284.

60. Chishti, Rose, and Yale-Loehr, *Noncitizens in the U.S. Military*; Horton, "The Pentagon Promised Citizenship to Immigrants Who Served"; Richard Sisk, "These Recruits Were Promised Citizenship in Exchange for Military Service. Now They Fear the US Has Forgotten Them," Military.com, March 16, 2021, https://www.military.com/daily-news/2021/03/13/these-recruits-were-promised-citizenship-exchange-military-service-now-they-fear-us-has-forgotten.html.

61. Hector Amaya, "Dying American or the Violence of Citizenship: Latinos in Iraq," *Latino Studies* 5, no. 1 (2007): 3–24; Lisa Marie Cacho, *Social Death: Racialized Rightlessness and the Criminalization of the Unprotected* (New York: NYU Press, 2012).

62. Sofya Aptekar, "Citizenship in the Green Card Army," in *Migration Policy in the Age of Punishment: Detention, Deportation and Border Control*, ed. David Brotherton and Philip Kretsedemas (New York: Columbia University Press, 2018); Margaret Lee and Ruth Wasem, *Expedited Citizenship through Military Service: Current Law, Policy and Issues* (Congressional Research Service, 2008); Jocelyn Pacleb, "Soldiering Green Card Immigrants: Containing United States Citizenship," in *A New Kind of Containment: The "War on Terror," Race, and Sexuality*, ed. C. R. Lugo-Lugo and M. K. Bloodsworth-Lugo (New York: Rudopi Press, 2009), 135–148; Kurt Rowland, "Realizing a Dream: Expedited Paths to Citizenship for Servicemembers," *The Army Lawyer* (June 2016): 37–46; *Naturalization through Military Service: Fact Sheet* (US Citizenship and Immigration Services, 2016), https://www.hsdl.org/?view&did=807376.

63. Aptekar, *The Road to Citizenship*.

64. Kochenov, "Ending the Passport Apartheid"; Aristide Zolberg, *A Nation by Design: Immigration Policy in the Fashioning of America* (Cambridge, MA: Harvard University Press, 2009).

65. *2017 Yearbook of Immigration Statistics* (US Department of Homeland Security, Office of Immigration Statistics, 2019), https://www.dhs.gov/sites/default/files/publications/yearbook_immigration_statistics_2017_0.pdf, accessed October 27, 2022.

66. Margaret Stock, *Essential to the Fight: Immigrants in the Military Eight Years after 9/11* (Immigration Policy Center, American Immigration Council, 2009), https://www.americanimmigrationcouncil.org/research/essential-fight-immigrants-military-eight-years-after-911.

67. Lucy Salyer, "Baptism by Fire: Race, Military Service, and U.S. Citizenship Policy, 1918–1935," *Journal of American History* 91, no. 3 (December 1, 2004): 847–876; Sohoni and Vafa, "The Fight to Be American," 119–151.

68. Brittany Blizzard and Jeanne Batalova, *Naturalization Trends in the United States* (Migration Policy Institute, 2019), https://www.migrationpolicy.org/article/naturalization-trends-united-states.

69. Amaya, "Dying American or the Violence of Citizenship," 3–24.

70. Irene Garza, "'Army Strong': Mexican American Youth and Military Recruitment in All She Can," in *The War of My Generation: Youth Culture and the War on Terror*, ed. David Kieran (New Brunswick, NJ: Rutgers University Press. 2015), 189–208.

71. Cacho, *Social Death.*

72. Pacleb, "Soldiering Green Card Immigrants."

73. Victor Ray, "Militarism as a Racial Project," in *Handbook of the Sociology of Racial and Ethnic Relations*, 2nd ed., ed. Pinar Batur and Joe Feagin (Cham: Springer, 2007), 163.

74. Elizabeth Beaumont, "Rights of Military Personnel," in *The First Amendment Encyclopedia* (Free Speech Center, Middle Tennessee State University, 2009), https://www.mtsu.edu/first-amendment/article/1131/rights-of-military-personnel.

75. Quoted in *On the Front Line: The Impact of Immigrants Military Force Readiness* (Veterans for Immigration Reform, June 12, 2014).

76. Caitlin Patler and Roberto G. Gonzales, "Framing Citizenship: Media Coverage of Anti-deportation Cases Led by Undocumented Immigrant Youth Organisations," *Journal of Ethnic and Migration Studies* 41, no. 9 (2015): 1453–1474; Grace Yukich, "Constructing the Model Immigrant: Movement Strategy and Immigrant Deservingness in the New Sanctuary Movement," *Social Problems* 60, no. 3 (2013): 302–320.

77. Wong, "Who Fights," 167–188.

78. Wong, "Who Fights," 179.

79. Zolberg, *A Nation by Design.*

80. Christopher Parker, *Fighting for Democracy* (Princeton, NJ: Princeton University Press, 2009).

81. *Lynching in America: Targeting Black Veterans* (Equal Justice Initiative, 2017), https://eji.org/reports/targeting-black-veterans/.

82. Charles Moskos and John Sibley Butler, *All That We Can Be: Black Leadership and Racial Integration the Army Way* (New York: Basic Books, 1997).

83. Ray, "Militarism as a Racial Project," 167.

84. Ray, "Militarism as a Racial Project."

85. Cowen, "Fighting for 'Freedom'"; Cowen, *Military Workfare*.

86. Lesley Bartlett and Catherine Lutz, "Disciplining Social Difference: Some Cultural Politics of Military Training in Public High Schools," *The Urban Review* 30, no. 2 (1998): 119–136; Charles Goldman, Jonathan Schweig, Maya Buenaventura, and Cameron Wright, *Geographic and Demographic Representativeness of the Junior Research Officers' Training Corps* (Santa Monica, CA: RAND Corporation, 2017).

87. Lisa Sun-Hee Park, *Entitled to Nothing: The Struggle for Immigrant Health Care in the Age of Welfare Reform* (New York: NYU Press, 2011).

88. Juana Summers, "GOP Split over Bill to Let Immigrants in U.S. Illegally Serve in Military," *It's All Politics*, NPR, May 13, 2015, https://www.npr.org/sections/itsall politics/2015/05/13/406309565/bill-endorsing-illegal-immigrants-to-serve-in -military-splits-gop.

89. Cowen, *Military Workfare*.

90. Jorge Mariscal, "Immigration and Military Enlistment: The Pentagon's Push for the Dream Act Heats Up," *Latino Studies* 5, no. 3 (September 1, 2007): 358–363.

91. Margaret Stock, "The DREAM Act: Tapping an Overlooked Pool of Home-Grown Talent to Meet Military Enlistment Needs," *Engage* 6, no. 2 (2005): 100.

92. Stock, "The DREAM Act," 101.

93. Cacho, *Social Death*.

94. Molly McIntosh, Seema Sayala, and David Gregory, *Non-Citizens in the Enlisted U.S. Military* (Alexandria, VA: CNA Analysis and Solutions, 2011), https://www .cna.org/CNA_files/PDF/D0026449.A1.pdf.

95. Roberto J. González, *Militarizing Culture: Essays on the Warfare State* (Walnut Creek, CA: Left Coast Press, 2010).

96. E.g., General George W. Casey Jr.'s remarks to the Military Leadership Diversity Committee. *From Representation to Inclusion: Diversity Leadership for the 21st Century Military* (Military Leadership Diversity Committee, 2011), 16, https:// diversity.defense.gov/Portals/51/Documents/Special%20Feature/MLDC_Final _Report.pdf. A combat multiplier is a factor that enhances the combat power of a fighting force while expending no additional resources or fewer than anticipated resources. For example, an element of surprise in a battle or exemplary unit morale could provide a combat multiplier. Krewasky Salter, *Combat Multipliers: African-American Soldiers in Four Wars* (Fort Leavenworth, KS: Combat Studies Institute Press, 2003), https://apps.dtic.mil/sti/pdfs/ADA631467.pdf.

97. Brief of Lt. Gen. Julius W. Becton Jr., Gen. John P. Abizaid, Adm. Dennis C. Blair, Gen. Bryan Doug Brown, Lt. Gen. Daniel W. Christman, Gen. Wesley K. Clark, Adm. Archie Clemins, Gen, Ronald R. Fogleman, et al., As *Amici Curiae* in Support of Respondents, Abigail Noel Fisher v University of Texas at Austin, No. 11-345, https://www.scotusblog.com/wp-content/uploads/2016/08/11-345-respon dent-amicus-becton.pdf.

98. Robert Knowles, "The Intertwined Fates of Affirmative Action and the Military," *Loyola University of Chicago Law Journal* 45, no. 4 (2014): 1027–1084; Hugh Mc-Clean, "The Diversity Rationale for Affirmative Action in Military Contracting," *Catholic University Law Review* 66, no. 4 (2017): 745–794.

99. Ruth Igielnik and Kim Parker, *Majorities of U.S. Veterans, Public Say the Wars in Iraq and Afghanistan Were Not Worth Fighting,* Pew Research Center, July 10, 2019, https://www.pewresearch.org/fact-tank/2019/07/10/majorities-of-u-s-veterans-public-say-the-wars-in-iraq-and-afghanistan-were-not-worth-fighting/; Dorothy Manevich and Hanyu Chwe, *U.S. Power Increasingly Seen as Threat to Countries,* Pew Research Center, August 1, 2017, https://www.pewresearch.org/fact-tank/2017/08/01/u-s-power-and-influence-increasingly-seen-as-threat-in-other-countries/.

100. Congressional Record, 108th Congress, 1st Session, Vol. 149, No. 8 (June 4, 2003).

101. Monica Kim, *The Interrogation Rooms of the Korean War* (Princeton, NJ: Princeton University Press, 2019). I use the term *concentration camp* rather than *internment camp* to refer to the imprisonment of Japanese Americans during World War II because *internment* is associated with detention of enemy aliens, which misrepresents the fact that many of the prisoners were US citizens.

102. Pawan Dhingra and Robyn Rodriguez, *Asian America: Sociological and Interdisciplinary Perspectives* (Malden, MA: Polity Press, 2014); Sohoni and Vafa, "The Fight to Be American."

103. Danny Hakim, "Vindman's Lawyer Asks Fox News to Retract Espionage Allegation," *New York Times,* November 20, 2019, https://www.nytimes.com/2019/11/20/us/alexander-vindman-fox-news-espionage.html; Sheryl Gay Stolberg, "Meet Alexander Vindman, the Colonel Who Testified on Trump's Phone Call," *New York Times,* October 29, 2019, https://www.nytimes.com/2019/10/29/us/politics/who-is-alexander-vindman.html.

104. Wong and Cho, "Jus Meritum Citizenship for Service."

105. Bruce Finley, "Military Eyeing 'Unknowns': Thousands in Ranks May Not Be Citizens," *Denver Post,* February 24, 2004.

106. James Rosen, "Pentagon Investigators Find 'Security Risks' in Government's Immigrant Recruitment Program, 'Infiltration' Feared," *Fox News,* August 1, 2017, https://www.foxnews.com/politics/pentagon-investigators-find-security-risks-in-governments-immigrant-recruitment-program-infiltration-feared.

107. Second Declaration of Stephanie P. Miller in Response to July 19, 2017 Order of the Court, No.: 1:17~cv~0098 (ESH), *Kusuma Nio v. United States Department of Homeland Security,* US District Court for the District of Columbia.

108. The US Air Force continues to call its workers "airmen," regardless of gender.

CHAPTER 2

1. Beth Bailey, "The Army in the Marketplace: Recruiting an All-Volunteer Force," *Journal of American History* 94, no. 1 (2007): 47–74.

2. Emily Brissette, "From Complicit Citizens to Potential Prey: State Imaginaries and Subjectivities in US War Resistance," *Critical Sociology* 42, nos. 7–8 (2016): 1163–1177; Brissette, "Waging a War of Position on Neoliberal Terrain," 377–398; Charles Moskos, John Allen Williams, and David Segal, *The Postmodern Military: Armed Forces after the Cold War* (New York: Oxford University Press, 2000).

3. Bailey, "The Army in the Marketplace," 47–74; Scott Harding and Seth Kershner, "Just Say No: Organizing against Militarism in Public Schools," *Journal of Sociology & Social Welfare* 38 (2011): 79.

4. Brissette, "From Complicit Citizens to Potential Prey," 1163–1177; Moskos, Williams, and Segal, *The Postmodern Military*.

5. Mittelstadt, *The Rise of the Military Welfare State*.

6. Jacob Siegal, "Troops of the Uniform Unite! The Military Is a Socialist Paradise!" *The Daily Beast*, July 12, 2017, https://www.thedailybeast.com/troops-of-the-uniform-unite-the-military-is-a-socialist-paradise.

7. *2016 Demographics: Profile of the Military Community* (US Department of Defense, 2016), https://download.militaryonesource.mil/12038/MOS/Reports/2016-Demographics-Report.pdf.

8. Brissette, "Waging a War of Position on Neoliberal Terrain," 391; another, less common term is "backdoor draft" (Amy Hagopian and Kathy Barker, "Should We End Military Recruiting in High Schools as a Matter of Child Protection and Public Health?," *American Journal of Public Health* 101, no. 1 [2011]: 19–23).

9. Meredith Kleykamp, "College, Jobs, or the Military? Enlistment during a Time of War," *Social Science Quarterly* 87, no. 2 (2016): 272–290; Amy Lutz, "Who Joins the Military?: A Look at Race, Class and Immigration Status," *Journal of Political and Military Sociology* 36, no. 2 (2008): 167–188.

10. Dave Philipps, "The Army, in Need of Recruits, Turns Focus to Liberal-Leaning Cities," *New York Times*, January 2, 2019, https://www.nytimes.com/2019/01/02/us/army-recruiting-tech-industry-seattle.html.

11. US Department of Defense, Office of People Analytics, "Spring 2017 Propensity Update," January 2018, https://jamrs.defense.gov/Portals/20/Futures-Survey-Spring-2017.pdf.

12. Benjamin Luxenberg, "Does Free College Threaten Our All-Volunteer Military?," *Texas National Security Review*, September 8, 2016, https://warontherocks.com/2016/09/does-free-college-threaten-our-all-volunteer-military/.

13. Beth Asch, Christopher Buck, Jacob Alex Klerman, Meredith Kleykamp, and David Loughran, *What Factors Affect the Military Enlistment of Hispanic Youth? A Look at Enlistment Qualifications* (Santa Monica, CA: RAND Corporation, 2005), https://www.rand.org/pubs/documented_briefings/DB484.html. Amid a recruitment crisis in the summer of 2022, the US Army suspended the requirement for a high school diploma or GED for enlistees, only to reverse the policy a week later following an outcry about quality (Steve Baynon, "Army Swiftly Backpedals on Policy Dropping High School Diploma Requirement," Military.com, June 30,

2022, https://www.military.com/daily-news/2022/06/30/army-swiftly-backpedals-policy-dropping-high-school-diploma-requirement.html).

14. National Academies of Sciences, Engineering, and Medicine, *The Economic and Fiscal Consequences of Immigration*, ed. Francine D. Blau and Christopher Mackie (Washington, DC: National Academies Press, 2017).

15. "High School Dropout Rates," ChildTrends.org.

16. Abby Budiman, Christine Tamir, Lauren Mora, and Luis Noe-Bustamante, *Facts on U.S. Immigrants, 2018: Statistical Portrait of the Foreign-Born Population in the United States*, Pew Research Center, 2020, https://www.pewresearch.org/hispanic/2020/08/20/facts-on-u-s-immigrants-current-data.

17. Brissette, "Waging a War of Position on Neoliberal Terrain," 392.

18. Lolita Baldor, "Army Lowers 2017 Recruiting Goal; More Soldiers Staying On," *Associated Press*, April 20, 2018, https://www.boston.com/news/politics/2018/04/20/army-wont-meet-recruiting-mission-lowers-2017-goal/; Lawrence Korb and Sean Duggan, "An All-Volunteer Army? Recruitment and Its Problems," *PS: Political Science & Politics* 40, no. 3 (July 2007): 467–471.

19. González, *Militarizing Culture*. See, for example, the National Guard in the violent repression of Standing Rock protestors or during the Ferguson uprisings. Estes, *Our History Is the Future*; Keeanga-Yamahtta Taylor, *From #BlackLivesMatter to Black Liberation* (New York: Haymarket Books, 2016).

20. Adalberto Aguirre and Brooke Johnson, "Militarizing Youth in Public Education: Observations from a Military-Style Charter School," *Social Justice* 32, no. 3 (2005): 148–162.

21. Aptekar, "Citizenship in the Green Card Army"; Tanya Golash-Boza, *Deported: Immigrant Policing, Disposable Labor and Global Capitalism* (New York: NYU Press, 2015).

22. Joseph, "Still Left Out," 2089–2107.

23. Douglas Massey, Jorge Durand, and Nolan Malone, *Beyond Smoke and Mirrors: Mexican Immigration in an Era of Economic Integration* (New York: Russell Sage Foundation, 2002). The Immigration Control and Reform Act of 1986 authorized amnesty for over 2 million undocumented immigrants who could prove continuous residency for the prior four years or were farmworkers.

24. Golash-Boza and Hondagneu-Sotelo, "Latino Immigrant Men and the Deportation Crisis," 271–292.

25. See, for example, Josmar Trujillo and Alex Vitale, *Gang Takedowns in the De Blasio Era: The Dangers of "Precision Policing"* (Policing and Social Justice Project, Brooklyn College, CUNY, 2019), https://policingandjustice.squarespace.com/gang-policing-report.

26. Jim Absher, "Post-9/11 GI Bill Rates," Military.com, May 18, 2021, https://www.military.com/education/gi-bill/gi-bill-tuition-rates.html.

27. *Digest of Education Statistics, 2017* (National Center for Educational Statistics, Department of Education, January 2018), https://nces.ed.gov/programs/digest/d17.

28. Rempfer, "Student Loan Crisis, Not Mideast Wars."

29. Commissioned officers work as managers of the enlisted soldiers. US Army Officer Program, "Become an Officer: Frequently Asked Questions," https://www.goarmy.com/careers-and-jobs/become-an-officer/army-officer-faqs.html#.

30. Mittelstadt, *The Rise of the Military Welfare State*.

31. Brissette, "Waging a War of Position on Neoliberal Terrain," 377–398.

32. Brissette, "Waging a War of Position on Neoliberal Terrain," 377.

33. Bartlett and Lutz, "Disciplining Social Difference," 119–136; Michael Geyer, "The Militarization of Europe, 1914–1945," in *The Militarization of the Western World*, ed. John Hillis (New Brunswick, NJ: Rutgers University Press, 1989), 79; Enloe, *Globalization and Militarism*; Lutz, "Making War at Home in the United States," 723–735.

34. Aguirre and Johnson, "Militarizing Youth in Public Education," 148–162; Gary Anderson, "The Politics of Another Side: Truth-in-Military-Recruiting Advocacy in an Urban School District," *Educational Policy* 23 (2009): 267.

35. Anderson, "The Politics of Another Side."

36. Bartlett and Lutz, "Disciplining Social Difference," 119–136.

37. Tamara Nopper, "Military Service as Liberal Policing: A Brief Racial History of Project 100,000," *The Abusable Past* (blog), September 2, 2020, https://www.radicalhistoryreview.org/abusablepast/military-service-as-liberal-policing-a-brief-racial-history-of-project-100000/.

38. Brian Lagotte, "Gunning for School Space: Student Activists, the Military, and Education Policy," in *Be the Change*, ed. R. Verma (New York: Peter Lang, 2010).

39. Alexandra Pannoni and Josh Moody, "What to Know about High School JROTC Programs," *US News and World Report*, May 7, 2021, https://www.usnews.com/education/blogs/high-school-notes/2014/11/10/3-things-to-know-about-high-school-jrotc-programs.

40. Anderson, "The Politics of Another Side"; Brissette, "Waging a War of Position on Neoliberal Terrain."

41. Robertson Allen, *America's Digital Army: Games at Work and War* (Lincoln: University of Nebraska Press, 2017); Chad Garland, "Uncle Sam Wants You—To Play Video Games for the US Army," Military.com, November 9, 2018, https://www.military.com/daily-news/2018/11/09/uncle-sam-wants-you-play-video-games-us-army.htmlhttps://taskandpurpose.com/army-esports-team; George Morris, "Yes, the Army Encourages This Sergeant to Play Video Games All Day (for Recruiting Purposes)," *Task & Purpose*, August 7, 2019. As Harding and Kershner point out, video game development itself is connected to Pentagon-funded research on war simulation. Harding and Kershner, "Just Say No," 79.

42. Stuart Allan and Kari Andén-Papadopoulos, "'Come on, Let Us Shoot!': WikiLeaks and the Cultures of Militarization," *TOPIA: Canadian Journal of Cultural Studies* 23–24 (2018): 244–253; Erin Steuter and Deborah Wills, *At War with*

Metaphor: Media, Propaganda, and Racism in the War on Terror (Lanham, MD: Lexington Books, 2009).

43. Anderson, "The Politics of Another Side"; Francine D'Amico, "Policing the Military's Race and Gender Lines," in *Wives and Warriors: Women and the Military in the United States and Canada*, ed. Christie White and Laura Weinstein (Westport, CT: Greenwood, 1997).

44. *2016 Demographics.*

45. Cacho, *Social Death.*

46. Enloe, "Globalization and Militarism."

47. David Vine, *Base Nation: How U.S. Military Bases Abroad Harm America and the World* (New York: Metropolitan Books, 2015).

48. Catherine Lutz, *The Bases of Empire: The Global Struggle against U.S. Military Posts* (New York: NYU Press, 2009).

49. Victoria Reyes, *Global Borderlands: Fantasy, Violence, and Empire in Subic Bay, Philippines* (Stanford, CA: Stanford University Press, 2019).

50. Kleykamp, "College, Jobs, or the Military?"

51. Counterintuitively, some immigrants join the US military to avoid conscription in their home country. This happens because they see service in the military in their home country as having more dangers and fewer rewards. For instance, I interviewed Aslan, who migrated from Azerbaijan and was trying to join the US military so that he would get US citizenship and finally return to Azerbaijan to see his family. He could not return otherwise because he had skipped out on conscription.

52. McIntosh, Sayala, and Gregory, *Non-Citizens in the Enlisted U.S. Military*; Veterans for Immigration Reform, *On the Front Line.*

53. Eric Lutz, "Army Reserve Green Card Ban 'Sends Chilling Message' to Immigrants, Veterans Group Says," *Mic*, October 19, 2017, https://www.mic.com/articles/185400/army-reserve-green-card-ban-sends-chilling-message-to-immigrants-veterans-group-says.

54. Kretsedemas, "The Limits of Control," e1–e18; Obinna, "The Challenges of American Legal Permanent Residency," 272–284.

55. *Green Card for Immigrant Investors* (US Citizenship and Immigration Services, July 6, 2022), https://www.uscis.gov/green-card/green-card-eligibility/green-card-for-immigrant-investors.

56. *Enlistment/Reenlistment Document—Armed Forces of the United States* (US Department of Defense, 2020), https://www.esd.whs.mil/Portals/54/Documents/DD/forms/dd/dd0004.pdf.

57. David Bier, *Immigration Wait Times from Quotas Have Doubled: Green Card Backlogs Are Long, Growing, and Inequitable* (Cato Institute, June 18, 2019); Obinna, "The Challenges of American Legal Permanent Residency," 272–284; *Facts on Foreign Students in the U.S.*, Pew Research Center, 2017, https://www.pewresearch.org/global/fact-sheet/foreign-students-in-the-u-s; *H1-B Petitions by Gender and Country of Birth. Fiscal Year 2018* (US Citizenship and Immigration Services,

2018), https://www.uscis.gov/sites/default/files/USCIS/Resources/Reports%20and%20Studies/H-1B/h-1b-petitions-by-gender-country-of-birth-fy2018.pdf.

58. Jesse Barton, "Home Free: Combatting Veteran Prosecution and Incarceration," *Justice Policy Journal* 11, no. 2 (2014): 1–25; Hagopian and Barker, "Should We End Military Recruiting?," 19–23; Casey MacGregor and MarySue Heilemann, "Deserving Veterans' Disability Compensation: A Qualitative Study of Veterans' Perceptions," *Health & Social Work* 42, no. 2 (2017): e86–e93; Karen Seal, Greg Cohen, Angela Waldrop, Beth Cohen, Shira Maguen, and Li Ren, "Substance Use Disorders in Iraq and Afghanistan Veterans in VA Healthcare, 2001–2010: Implications for Screening, Diagnosis and Treatment," *Drug and Alcohol Dependence* 116, no. 1 (2011): 93–101.

59. Cacho, *Social Death*; Plascencia "Citizenship through Veteranship," 8–9.

60. This might be surprising if one imagines that adult immigrants are more tied to their home countries than immigrants who grew up in the United States. However, formal citizenship status and naturalization, on the one hand, and sense of belonging or ties to home countries, on the other, are not necessarily connected. Many immigrants naturalize defensively, to protect their eroding rights in an anti-immigrant context. Many also feel a connection to the United States or to other countries that is distinct from formal citizenship status. Further complicating this issue is the existence of dual citizenship. See Aptekar, *The Road to Citizenship*.

61. Irene Bloemraad, Anna Korteweg, and Gökce Yurdakul, "Citizenship and Immigration: Multiculturalism, Assimilation, and Challenges to the Nation-State," *Annual Review of Sociology* 34 (2008): 153–179.

62. Moskos and Butler, *All That We Can Be*; Ray, "Critical Diversity in the US Military."

63. Bartlett and Lutz, "Disciplining Social Difference."

64. Cowen, *Military Workfare*, 19.

65. Sergei spoke Russian during the interview. I simultaneously translated and transcribed that interview.

66. For example, Barry, "New Americans in Our Nation's Military"; Eiko Strader, Jennifer Lundquist, and Rodrigo Dominguez-Villegas, "Warriors Wanted: The Performance of Immigrants in the US Army," *International Migration Review* 55, no. 2 (2021): 382–401; Walter Schumm, "Willingness to Have One's Children Serve in the Military: An Indicator of Acculturation among Arab Immigrants to the United States: A Brief Report," *Journal of Political & Military Sociology* 24, no. 1 (1996): 105–115.

67. Cacho, *Social Death*.

68. Cacho, *Social Death*, 108.

69. Lymari Morales, "Nearly All Americans Consider Military Service 'Patriotic': Symbolic Gestures Valued More Highly by Older Americans and the Less Educated," Gallup poll, July 3, 2008, https://news.gallup.com/poll/108646/nearly-all-americans-consider-military-service-patriotic.aspx.

70. Adam McGlynn and Jessica Lavariega Monforti, *Proving Patriotismo: Latino Military Recruitment, Service, and Belonging in the US* (Lanham, MD: Lexington Books, 2021)

71. Cacho, *Social Death*; George Mariscal, *Aztlan and Viet Nam: Chicano and Chicana Experiences of the War* (Berkeley: University of California Press, 1999); Pacleb, "Soldiering Green Card Immigrants."

72. Pacleb, "Soldiering Green Card Immigrants," 147.

73. Saher, *Forever Suspect*.

74. Garza, "'Army Strong.'"

75. Meanwhile, Lee's parents and grandparents in Korea supported his decision to enlist as a way to give back to the United States, which "helped Korea during the Korean War."

76. Gendered expectations from parents and other family members have been shown to be a factor in the enlistment of Latinx male youth. Eligio Martinez and Adrian H. Huerta, "Deferred Enrollment: Chicano/Latino Males, Social Mobility and Military Enlistment," *Education and Urban Society* 52, no. 1 (January 1, 2020): 117–142.

77. Patrick Coffee, "Esports, Comic-Con, and Momfluencers: How the US Army Is Revamping Its Multi-Billion-Dollar Marketing Plan," *Business Insider*, October 12, 2019, https://www.businessinsider.com/us-army-marketing-esports-comiccon-momfluencers-2019-10.

78. Garza, "'Army Strong.'"

79. McGlynn and Monforti, *Proving Patriotismo*.

80. Deborah Davis, "Illegal Immigrants: Uncle Sam Wants You," *In These Times*, July 25, 2007, http://inthesetimes.com/article/3271/illegal_immigrants_uncle_sam_wants_you.

81. Lizette Alvarez, "Army Effort to Enlist Hispanics Draws Recruits, and Criticism," *New York Times*, February 9, 2006, https://www.nytimes.com/2006/02/09/us/army-effort-to-enlist-hispanics-draws-recruits-and-criticism.htmlhttp://www.globaltimes.cn/content/1079356.shtml; Ma and Zhang, "More Chinese Immigrants Pick US Military Career Path."

82. Aguirre and Johnson, "Militarizing Youth in Public Education," 148–162; Anderson, "The Politics of Another Side"; Bartlett and Lutz, "Disciplining Social Difference," 119–136; Cowen, "Fighting for 'Freedom,'" 167–183; Garza, "Advertising Patriotism," 245–268.

83. Harding and Kershner, "Just Say No."

84. Aguirre and Johnson, "Militarizing Youth in Public Education," 148–162; Gina Perez, "JROTC and Latino/a Youth in Neoliberal Cities," in *Rethinking America: The Imperial Homeland in the 21st Century*, ed. Jeff Maskovsky and Ida Susser (Boulder, CO: Paradigm Publishers, 2009). Colleges that receive federal funding are also obligated to permit military recruiters on campus and to share student

directories, which is especially relevant for recruitment of international students into the MAVNI program.

85. González, *Militarizing Culture*, 49.

CHAPTER 3

1. Ana Gonzalez-Barrera and Jens Manuel Krogstad, *Naturalization Rate among U.S. Immigrants Up since 2005, with India among the Biggest Gainers*, Pew Research Center, 2008, https://www.pewresearch.org/fact-tank/2018/01/18/naturalization-rate-among-u-s-immigrants-up-since-2005-with-india-among-the-biggest-gainers/.

2. Aptekar, *The Road to Citizenship*; Amada Armenta, *Protect, Serve, and Deport: The Rise of Policing as Immigration Enforcement* (Oakland: University of California Press, 2017); Juliet Stumpf, "The Crimmigration Crisis: Immigrants, Crime, and Sovereign Power," *American University Law Review* 56 (2006): 367.

3. Anne Parsons, "A Fraudulent Sense of Belonging: The Case for Removing the 'False Claim to Citizenship,'" *The Modern American* 6, no. 2 (Spring 2011): 1–19, https://digitalcommons.wcl.american.edu/cgi/viewcontent.cgi?article=1130&context=tma.

4. Immigration and Naturalization Act Sections 328 and 328; Susan Timmons and Margaret Stock, "Immigration Issues Faced by US Servicemembers: Challenges and Solutions," *Clearinghouse Review* 43, no. 3 (2009): 270–276.

5. *Changes to the Expedited Naturalization Process for Military Service Members* (Immigrant Legal Resource Center, March 2018), https://www.ilrc.org/sites/default/files/resources/changes_expedited_natz_process_military-20180329.pdf; Plascencia, "Citizenship through Veteranship," 8–9.

6. Timmons and Stock, "Immigration Issues Faced by US Servicemembers," 271.

7. Barry, *New Americans in Our Nation's Military*.

8. Blizzard and Batalova, *Naturalization Trends in the United States*.

9. Jeanne Batalova, *Immigrants in the U.S. Armed Forces* (Washington, DC: Migration Policy Institute, 2008), http://www.migrationpolicy.org/article/immigrants-us-armed-forces; Zong and Batalova, *Immigrant Veterans in the United States*.

10. Barry, *New Americans in Our Nation's Military*; Chambers, *To Raise an Army*; Michael LeMay and Elliott Barkan, *U.S. Immigration and Naturalization Laws and Issues: A Documentary History* (Westport, CT: Greenwood, 1999); Wong, "Who Fights."

11. Barry, *New Americans in Our Nation's Military*; Sohoni and Vafa. "The Fight to Be American," 119–151.

12. Ngai, *Impossible Subjects*; Sohoni and Vafa, "The Fight to Be American."

13. Gay Becker, Yewoubdar Beyene, and Leilani Cuizon Canalita, "Immigrating for Status in Late Life: Effects of Globalization on Filipino American Veterans," *Journal of Aging Studies* 14, no. 3 (2000): 273–291.

14. Ngai, *Impossible Subjects*.

15. Zong and Batalova, *Immigrant Veterans in the United States*.

16. Blizzard and Batalova, *Naturalization Trends in the United States*.

17. Associated Press, "Mother Uses Son's Iraq Death to Change Law, Help Soldiers Get Citizenship," *New York Daily News*, June 27, 2008, http://www.nydailynews.com /latino/mother-son-iraq-death-change-law-soldiers-citizenship-article-1.295840.

18. Camilo Montoya-Galvez, "Soldier's Immigrant Mother Could Be among the Last to Benefit from Program," *CBS News*, August 22, 2019, https://www.cbsnews .com/news/parole-in-place-soldiers-immigrant-mother-could-be-among-the -last-to-benefit-from-program/; US Citizenship and Immigration Services, Policy Memorandum, Parole of Spouses, Children and Parents of Active Duty Members of the U.S. Armed Forces, the Selected Reserve of the Ready Reserve, and Former Members of the U.S. Armed Forces or Selected Reserve of the Ready Reserve and the Effect of Parole on Inadmissibility under Immigration and Nationality Act §212(a)(6)(A)(i) PM-602-0091, 2013, https://www.uscis.gov/sites /default/files/document/memos/2013-111_Parole_in_Place_Memo_.pdf.

19. Ruth Tam, "MacArthur Fellow Margaret Stock: The Public 'Doesn't Understand' Illegal Immigration," *Washington Post*, September 27, 2013, https://www.wash ingtonpost.com/blogs/she-the-people/wp/2013/09/27/macarthur-fellow-marga ret-stock-the-public-doesnt-understand-illegal-immigration/.

20. *Naturalization through Military Service: Fact Sheet* (US Citizenship and Immigration Services, December 22, 2016); Erin Statel, "Basic Combat Training Now Includes Naturalization," *Military Times*, April 27, 2011, https://www.army.mil /article/55590/basic_combat_training_now_includes_naturalization.

21. Amaya, "Dying American or the Violence of Citizenship," 3–24.

22. Vera Bergengruen, "The US Army Promised Immigrants a Fast Track for Citizenship. That Fast Track Is Gone," *BuzzFeed News*, March 5, 2018; Margaret Stock, "A Beginner's Guide to Earning Your Citizenship through Military Service," *Task & Purpose* (blog), April 13, 2021, https://taskandpurpose.com /immigration-rundown/how-to-earn-citizenship-through-military-service/.

23. Jason Buch, "Immigrants Aiming to Serve Stymied," *San Antonio Express-News*, December 26, 2017; Alex Horton, "US Army Kills Contracts for Hundreds of Immigrant Recruits. Some Face Deportation," *Washington Post*, September 15, 2017, https://www.washingtonpost.com/news/checkpoint/wp/2017/09/15/army-kills -contracts-for-hundreds-of-immigrant-recruits-sources-say-some-face-depor tation/; Eric Lutz, "Army Reserve Green Card Ban 'Sends Chilling Message' to Immigrants, Veteran Group Says," *Mic*, October 19, 2017, https://www.mic.com /articles/185400/army-reserve-green-card-ban-sends-chilling-message-to-immi grants-veterans-group-says.

24. Blizzard and Batalova, *Naturalization Trends in the United States*.

25. Richard Sisk, "The Naturalization Process Just Got Harder for Noncitizen Troops Stationed Overseas," Military.com, September 30, 2019, https://www

.military.com/daily-news/2019/09/30/naturalization-process-just-got-harder
-noncitizen-troops-stationed-overseas.html.

26. Sig Christenson, "Immigrant GI Booted Out of Army at Fort Sam," *San Antonio
    Express-News,* August 3, 2018, https://www.expressnews.com/news/local/article
    /Immigrant-GI-booted-out-of-Army-at-Fort-Sam-13130805.php.

27. "Medal-Earning Soldier Faced Deportation after Honorable Discharge," ACLU
    Southern California, press release, August 17, 2008, https://www.aclusocal.org
    /en/press-releases/aclu-army-specialist-yea-ji-sea-has-been-granted-citizenship.

28. Aptekar, *The Road to Citizenship;* Irene Bloemraad, *Becoming a Citizen: Incor-
    poration of Immigrants and Refugees in the United States and Canada* (Berkeley:
    University of California Press, 2006); Linda Bosniak, *The Citizen and the Alien: Di-
    lemmas of Contemporary Membership* (Princeton, NJ: Princeton University Press,
    2006).

29. Stock, "A Beginner's Guide to Earning Your Citizenship through Military Ser-
    vice"; US Citizenship and Immigration Services, Policy Manual, Volume 12,
    "Citizenship and Naturalization. Part I Military Members and Their Families.
    Chapter 7 Revocation of Naturalization," 2019, https://www.uscis.gov/policy
    -manual/volume-12-part-i-chapter-7.

30. Golash-Boza, *Deported.*

31. *2016 PIT Estimate of Homeless Veterans by State* (US Department of Housing and
    Urban Development, 2016).

32. Cathy Ho Hartsfield, "Deportation of Veterans: The Silent Battle for Natural-
    ization," *Rutgers Law Review* 3 (2011): 835–862; Craig Shagin, "Deporting Private
    Ryan: The Less than Honorable Condition of the Noncitizen in the United States
    Armed Forces," *Widener Law Journal* 17, no. 1 (2007): 245–316.

33. ABC, "Veteran Fighting Deportation after 2 Tours in Afghanistan," *ABC 7 Eyewit-
    ness News,* Chicago, February 5, 2017, http://abc7chicago.com/news/veteran
    -fighting-deportation-after-2-tours-in-afghanistan/1739129/; *Discharged, Then
    Discarded: How US Veterans Are Banished by the Country They Swore to Protect*
    (ACLU of California, July 2016), https://www.aclusocal.org/sites/default/files
    /dischargedthendiscarded-acluofca.pdf; Julia Alsop, "War Veteran Smokes Pot,
    Faces Deportation," *NPR, Latino Voices,* November 13, 2015, http://latinousa
    .org/2015/11/13/war-veteran-smokes-pot-faces-deportation/.

34. Ming Hsu Chen, *Pursuing Citizenship in the Enforcement Era* (Stanford, CA: Stan-
    ford University Press, 2020), 65.

35. Golash-Boza, *Deported.*

36. Cecilia Menjívar and Leisy J. Abrego, "Legal Violence: Immigration Law and the
    Lives of Central American Immigrants," *American Journal of Sociology* 117, no. 5
    (2012): 1380–1421.

37. Aptekar, *The Road to Citizenship.*

38. See also Amaya, "Dying American or the Violence of Citizenship."

39. See also Chen, *Pursuing Citizenship,* 54.

40. Suzanne Schafer, "Army, Navy Add Citizenship Option to Boot Camp," *Associated Press*, April 21, 2011, http://www.boston.com/news/nation/articles/2011/04/21/army_navy_add_citizenship_option_to_boot_camp/.

41. Plascencia, "Citizenship through Veteranship."

42. Chen, *Pursuing Citizenship*, 49.

43. *Discharged, Then Discarded*.

44. Blizzard and Batalova, *Naturalization Trends in the United States*.

45. *Immigration Enforcement: Actions Needed to Better Handle, Identify, and Track Cases Involving Veterans* (US Government Accountability Office, June 2019), https://www.gao.gov/assets/gao-19-416.pdf.

46. *2020 Yearbook of Immigration Statistics* (US Department of Homeland Security, Office of Immigration Statistics, 2022), https://www.dhs.gov/immigration-statistics/yearbook/2020.

47. ACLU, "Letter to President Biden on DOD Obstacles to Expedited Naturalization of Service Members in the U.S. Military," June 28, 2022, https://www.aclu.org/letter/letter-president-biden-dod-obstacles-expedited-naturalization-service-members-us-military.

48. Joanna Kao, "Good Enough to Fight for the US but Missing the Mark for Citizenship," *Al Jazeera America*, May 8, 2015, http://america.aljazeera.com/multimedia/2015/5/good-enough-to-be-soldier-but-not-citizen.html.

49. Kao, "Good Enough to Fight for the US."

50. Blizzard and Batalova, *Naturalization Trends in the United States*.

51. Beth Caldwell, *Deported Americans: Life after Deportation to Mexico* (Durham, NC: Duke University Press, 2019).

52. *Casualty Status* (US Department of Defense, 2022), https://www.defense.gov/casualty.pdf accessed October 27, 2022.

53. Sohoni and Vafa, "The Fight to Be American"; US Citizenship and Immigration Services, "N-644, Application for Posthumous Citizenship," https://www.uscis.gov/n-644.

54. Batalova, *Immigrants in the US Armed Forces*.

55. Margaret Stock, *Essential to the Fight: Immigrants in the Military Eight Years after 9/11* (Washington, DC: American Immigration Council, 2009).

56. Tracy Buenavista, "Citizenship at a Cost: Undocumented Asian Youth Perceptions and the Militarization of Immigration," *AAPI Nexus* 10, no. 1 (2012): 101–124.

57. Section 1703 of Public Law 108-136, National Defense Authorization Act for Fiscal Year 2004, https://www.congress.gov/108/plaws/publ136/PLAW-108publ136.htm.

58. Amaya, "Dying American or the Violence of Citizenship."

59. Aptekar, *The Road to Citizenship*.

60. Kim, *The Interrogation Rooms of the Korean War*.

61. Clyde Haberman, "Becoming an American Citizen, the Hardest Way," *New York Times*, September 18, 2007.

62. LaDuke and Cruz, *The Militarization of Indian Country*; Stephen W. Silliman, "The 'Old West' in the Middle East: U.S. Military Metaphors in Real and Imagined Indian Country," *American Anthropologist* 110, no. 2 (2008): 237–247; Tuck and Yang, "Decolonization Is Not a Metaphor," 31–32.

63. Estes, *Our History Is the Future*.

64. Haberman, "Becoming an American Citizen."

65. Amaya, "Dying American or the Violence of Citizenship," 4.

66. Lorgia García Peña, "One Hundred Years after the Occupation," *NACLA*, May 25, 2016, https://nacla.org/news/2016/05/25/one-hundred-years-after-occupation.

67. Amaya, "Dying American or the Violence of Citizenship"; Estes, *Our History Is the Future*.

CHAPTER 4

1. Barry, *New Americans in Our Nation's Military*; Chen, *Pursuing Citizenship in the Enforcement Era*; Strader, Lundquist, and Dominguez-Villegas, "Warriors Wanted," 382–401.

2. Moon-Kie Jung, "The Racial Unconscious of Assimilation Theory," *Du Bois Review: Social Science Research on Race* 6, no. 2 (2009): 375–395; Vilna Bashi Treitler, "Social Agency and White Supremacy in Immigration Studies," *Sociology of Race and Ethnicity* 1, no. 1 (2015): 153–165; Lihn T. Nguyễn, "'Loving Couples and Families': Assimilation as Honorary Whiteness and the Making of the Vietnamese Refugee Family," *Social Sciences* 10, no. 6 (2021): 209.

3. Catherine Ramirez, *Assimilation: An Alternative History* (Oakland: University of California Press, 2020).

4. Cacho, *Social Death*, 27.

5. Jung, "The Racial Unconscious of Assimilation Theory"; Treitler, "Social Agency and White Supremacy in Immigration Studies"; Regine Jackson, "Black Immigrants and the Rhetoric of Social Distancing," *Sociology Compass* 4, no. 3 (2010): 193–206.

6. Karen D. Pyke, "What Is Internalized Racial Oppression and Why Don't We Study It? Acknowledging Racism's Hidden Injuries," *Sociological Perspectives* 53, no. 4 (2010): 551–572; Monica M. Trieu, "Understanding the Use of 'Twinkie,' 'Banana,' and 'FOB': Identifying the Origin, Role, and Consequences of Internalized Racism within Asian America," *Sociology Compass* 13, no. 5 (2019), https://doi.org/10.1111/soc4.12679.

7. Dunbar-Ortiz, *Not a Nation of Immigrants*.

8. James Burk and Evelyn Espinoza, "Race Relations within the US Military," *Annual Review of Sociology* 38, no. 1 (2012): 401–422; Victor Erik Ray, "Collateral Damage: Race, Gender, and the Post-Combat Transition," PhD thesis, Duke University, 2014.

9. Matt Kennard, *Irregular Army: How the US Military Recruited Neo-Nazis, Gang Members, and Criminals to Fight the War on Terror* (London: Verso, 2012); Dave Philipps, "White Supremacism in the U.S. Military, Explained," *New York Times*, February 27, 2019, https://www.nytimes.com/2019/02/27/us/military-white-nationalists-extremists.html.

10. Burk and Espinoza, "Race Relations within the US Military," 401–422.

11. Ryan Van Slyke and Nicholas Armstrong, "Communities Serve: A Systematic Review of Need Assessments on U.S. Veteran and Military-Connected Populations," *Armed Forces & Society* 46, no. 4 (2020): 564–594.

12. Victor Erik Ray, "Critical Diversity in the U.S. Military: From Diversity to Racialized Organization," in *Challenging the Status Quo: Diversity, Democracy, and Equality in the 21st Century*, ed. David G. Embrick, Sharon M. Collins, and Michelle S. Dodson (Leiden: Brill, 2018), 289.

13. Ray, "Collateral Damage"; Ray, "Critical Diversity in the US Military."

14. Naturalization is one of the frames of color-blind racism according to Eduardo Bonilla-Silva in *Racism without Racists: Color-Blind Racism and the Persistence of Racial Inequality in America* (Lanham, MD: Rowman & Littlefield, 2013).

15. Eric Milzarski, "This Is How the Army Teaches You to 'See Green'—Not Brown, Black or White," *We Are the Mighty*, August 27, 2020, https://www.wearethemighty.com/articles/this-is-how-the-army-teaches-you-to-see-green-not-brown-black-or-white.

16. Sandra Whitworth, *Men, Militarism, and UN Peacekeeping: A Gendered Analysis* (Boulder, CO: Lynne Rienner, 2004), 242–243.

17. Ray, "Critical Diversity in the US Military."

18. Philip Kretsedemas, *Migrants and Race in the US: Territorial Racism and the Alien/Outside* (New York: Routledge, 2013).

19. Kretsedemas, *Migrants and Race in the US*, 5.

20. Lisa Lowe, *Immigrant Acts: On Asian American Cultural Politics* (Durham, NC: Duke University Press, 1996); Ngai, *Impossible Subjects*.

21. Frantz Fanon, *Black Skin, White Masks* (London: Pluto Press, 2017); Pyke, "What Is Internalized Racial Oppression and Why Don't We Study It?"; Trieu "Understanding the Use of 'Twinkie,' 'Banana,' and 'FOB.'" Jienian Zhang refers to "the hidden injuries of assimilation" in demonstrating that subjective assimilation is positively correlated with poor mental health outcomes among children of immigrants. Jienian Zhang, "The Hidden Injuries of Assimilation: Exploring the Relationship between Subjective Assimilation and Mental Health," pre-print published on *SocArXiv*, July 19, 2022, https://osf.io/preprints/socarxiv/a6j9b/.

22. Deepti Hajela, "Asian American Soldier's Suicide Called a 'Wake-Up Call' for the Military," *Washington Post*, February 21, 2012, https://www.washingtonpost.com/politics/asian-american-soldiers-suicide-called-a-wake-up-call-for-the-military/2012/02/19/gIQA7Ke4QR_story.html.

23. See Selod, *Forever Suspect*.

24. Chalsa Loo, "Race-Related PTSD: The Asian American Vietnam Veteran," *Journal of Traumatic Stress* 7, no. 4 (December 1, 1994): 637–656; Chalsa Loo and Peter Kiang, "Race-Related Stressors and Psychological Trauma: Contributions of Asian American Vietnam Veterans," in *Asian Americans: Vulnerable Populations, Model Interventions, and Clarifying Agendas*, ed. L. Zhau (Sudbury, MA: Jones and Bartlett, 2003), 19–42; Chalsa Loo, John Fairbank, and Claude Chemtob, "Adverse Race-Related Events as a Risk Factor for Posttraumatic Stress Disorder in Asian American Vietnam Veterans," *Journal of Nervous and Mental Disease* 193 (July 1, 2005): 455–463.

25. Andrei Tsygankov, *Russophobia: Anti-Russian Lobby and American Foreign Policy* (Basingstoke: Palgrave Macmillan, 2009).

26. As described in chapter 3, despite being mistaken for a US citizen, Filip did feel that he needed to formally become a US citizen in order to advance in his military career.

27. *Demographics of the US Military* (Council on Foreign Relations, 2010), https://www.cfr.org/backgrounder/demographics-us-military.

28. Kat Stafford, James Laporta, Aaron Morrison, and Helen Wieffering, "Deep-Rooted Racism, Discrimination Permeate US Military," *AP*, May 27, 2021, https://apnews.com/article/us-military-racism-discrimination-4e840e0acc7ef07fd635a312d9375413; *Demographics: Profile of the Military Community* (US Department of Defense, 2018), https://download.militaryonesource.mil/12038/MOS/Reports/2018-demographics-report.pdf.

29. Khalil Saucier, *Necessarily Black: Cape Verdean Youth, Hip-Hop Culture, and a Critique of Identity* (East Lansing: Michigan State University Press, 2015).

30. Rachel Woodward and Claire Duncanson, eds., *The Palgrave International Handbook of Gender and the Military* (London: Palgrave Macmillan, 2017); Melissa Herbert, *Camouflage Isn't Only for Combat: Gender, Sexuality, and Women in the Military* (New York: NYU Press, 1998); Ray, "Collateral Damage."

31. Aline Quester, Anita Hattiangadi, Gary Lee, Cathy Hiatt, and Robert Shuford, *Black and Hispanic Marines; Their Accession, Representation, Success, and Retention in the Corps* (Alexandria, VA: CNA Analysis and Solutions, 2007).

32. Yen Ling Shek, "Asian American Masculinity: A Review of the Literature," *Journal of Men's Studies* 14, no. 3 (2006): 379–391.

33. Cynthia Enloe, *Globalization and Militarism: Feminists Make the Link* (Lanham, MD: Rowman and Littlefield, 2007).

34. Amanda Barroso, *The Changing Profile of the U.S. Military: Smaller in Size, More Diverse, More Women in Leadership*, Pew Research Center, 2019, https://www.pewresearch.org/fact-tank/2019/09/10/the-changing-profile-of-the-u-s-military/; Julia Melin, "Desperate Choices: Why Black Women Join the US Military at Higher Rates Than Men and All Other Racial and Ethnic Groups," *New England Journal of Public Policy* 28, no. 2 (2016): 8.

35. Shannon Barth, Rachel Kimerling, Joanne Pavao, Susan McCutcheon, Sonja Batten, Erin Dursa, Michael Peterson, and Aaron Schneiderman, "Military Sexual

Trauma among Recent Veterans: Correlates of Sexual Assault and Sexual Harassment," *American Journal of Preventive Medicine* 50, no. 1 (2016): 77–86. See also Laura C. Wilson, "The Prevalence of Military Sexual Trauma: A Meta-Analysis," *Trauma, Violence, & Abuse* 19, no. 5 (December 2018): 584–597.

36. *Annual Report on Sexual Assault in the Military, Fiscal Year 2018* (US Department of Defense, 2018), https://int.nyt.com/data/documenthelper/800-dod-annual-report -on-sexual-as/d659d6d0126ad2b19c18/optimized/full.pdf#page=1.

37. Ray, "Collateral Damage."

38. For example, *Invisible War*, directed by Kirby Dick (2012); Heather Osbourne and Jessica Priest, "Vanessa Guillen's Killing at Fort Hood Leaves Family Grieving, Grasping for Clues," *USA Today*, July 21, 2020; https://www.usatoday.com/story /news/investigations/2020/07/17/vanessa-guillens-family-struggles-answers-after -soldiers-slaying/5451246002/.

39. Joane Nagel, "Gender, Violence and the Military," in *Handbook on Gender and Violence*, ed. Laura Shepherd (Cheltenham: Edward Elgar, 2019).

40. Tessa Wright, "Women's Experience of Workplace Interactions in Male-Dominated Work: The Intersections of Gender, Sexuality and Occupational Group," *Gender, Work and Organization* 23 (2016): 348–362; Roberta Hunte, "Black Women and Race and Gender Tensions in the Trades," *Peace Review* 28, no. 4 (2016): 436–443.

41. Michelle Mengeling, Brenda Booth, James Torner, and Anne Sadler, "Reporting Sexual Assault in the Military: Who Reports and Why Most Servicewomen Don't," *American Journal of Preventive Medicine* 47, no. 1 (2014): 17–25.

42. Woodward and Duncanson, *Handbook of Gender and the Military.*

43. Woodward and Duncanson, *Handbook of Gender and the Military.*

44. Notably, the exclusion of and persecution of queer people was imbricated with eugenic and anticommunist immigration and border policies of the early twentieth century. Liz Montegary, "Militarizing US Homonormativities: The Making of 'Ready, Willing, and Able' Gay Citizens," *Signs: Journal of Women in Culture and Society* 40, no. 4 (June 1, 2015): 891–915.

45. Women were expelled at a rate almost three times at which they served. Forty-five percent of discharges under DADT were of people of color, even though they made up only 29 percent of all personnel. Anurandha Bhagwati, "Sexism and Racism Lurk in Don't Ask, Don't Tell Enforcement," *WNYC, It's a Free Blog*, November 30, 2010, https://www.wnyc.org/story/102488-sexist-and-racist-lurk-dont -ask-dont-tell-enforcement/.

46. J. P. Lawrence, "Free to Be a Better Soldier: Transgender Service Members Cheer Reversal of Ban," Military.com, April 30, 2021, https://www.military.com/daily -news/2021/04/30/free-be-better-soldier-transgender-service-members-cheer -reversal-of-ban.html.

47. Jody Herman and Jack Harrison-Quintana, "Still Serving in Silence: Transgender Service Members and Veterans in the National Transgender Discrimination Survey," *LGBTQ Policy Journal at the Harvard Kennedy School*, October 21, 2013,

https://lgbtq.hkspublications.org/2013/10/21/still-serving-in-silence-transgender
-service-members-and-veterans-in-the-national-transgender-discrimination
-survey/.

48. Cynthia Enloe, *Maneuvers: The International Politics of Militarizing Women's Lives* (Berkeley: University of California Press, 2000); Montegary, "Militarizing US Homonormativities."

49. Dean Spade and Aaron Belkin, "Queer Militarism?!: The Politics of Military Inclusion Advocacy in Authoritarian Times," *GLQ* 27, no. 2 (2021): 281–307; Catherine Connell, "Now That We Can Ask and Tell: The Social Movement Legacy of the DADT Repeal," *Sociology Compass* 11, no. 9 (2017). See also Jasbir Puar, *Terrorist Assemblages: Homonationalism in Queer Times* (Durham, NC: Duke University Press, [2007] 2017) on the fusing of homosexuality to US pro-war, pro-imperialist agendas.

50. Tamara Nopper, "Why I Oppose Repealing DADT and Passage of the DREAM Act," *War Resisters' International* (blog), August 28, 2012, https://wri-irg.org/en /story/2012/why-i-oppose-repealing-dadt-passage-dream-act.

51. Nopper, "Why I Oppose Repealing DADT and Passage of the DREAM Act."

52. Catherine Lutz and Andrea Mazzarino, eds., *War and Health: The Medical Consequences of the Wars in Iraq and Afghanistan* (New York: NYU Press, 2019); David Kieran, *Signature Wounds: The Untold Story of the Military's Mental Health Crisis* (New York: NYU Press, 2019).

53. Rachel Hoopsick, D. Lynn Homish, Gregory Homish, Jennifer Fillo, and Bonnie Vest, "Substance Use and Dependence among Current Reserve and Former Military Members: Cross-Sectional Findings from the National Survey on Drug Use and Health, 2010–2014," *Journal of Addictive Diseases* 36, no. 4 (2017): 243–251; Sonya Norman, Emily Schmied, and Gerald Larson, "Predictors of Continued Problem Drinking and Substance Use Following Military Discharge," *Journal of Studies on Alcohol & Drugs* 75, no. 4 (2014): 557–566; Brian Smith, Emily Taverna, Annie Fox, Paula Schnurr, Rebecca Matteo, and Dawne Vogt, "The Role of PTSD, Depression, and Alcohol Misuse Symptom Severity in Linking Deployment Stressor Exposure and Post-Military Work and Family Outcomes in Male and Female Veterans," *Clinical Psychological Science: A Journal of the Association for Psychological Science* 5, no. 4 (July 2017): 664–682.

54. In the *Washington Post*'s 2014 survey of veterans across the United States, almost a third of respondents noted that the state of their emotional and mental health was worse post-service than it was pre-service. *Survey of Iraq and Afghanistan Active Duty Soldiers and Veterans* (*Washington Post*/Kaiser Family Foundation, March 2014), https://www.kff.org/wp-content/uploads/2014/03/8563-t1.pdf.

55. *National Veteran Suicide Prevention Annual Report, Office of Mental Health and Suicide Prevention* (US Department of Veterans Affairs, 2020), https://www.men talhealth.va.gov/docs/data-sheets/2020/2020-National-Veteran-Suicide-Prevention -Annual-Report-11-2020-508.pdf.

56. "Employment Situation of Veterans—2020," US Department of Labor, Bureau of Labor Statistics, news release, https://www.bls.gov/news.release/pdf/vet.pdf.

57. Ray, "Collateral Damage"; Van Slyke and Armstrong, "Communities Serve."

58. The remainder of the seventy-two interviewed enlisted through MAVNI and got stuck in legal limbo, going to regular drills but not being able to start basic training.

59. Institute of Medicine, *Interactions of Drugs, Biologics, and Chemicals in U.S. Military Forces* (Washington, DC: National Academies Press, 1996).

60. *Exposure to Hazardous Chemicals and Materials* (US Department of Veterans Affairs, April 30, 2020), https://www.va.gov/disability/eligibility/hazardous -materials-exposure/.

61. John Hamilton, "Contamination at U.S. Military Bases: Profiles and Responses," *Stanford Environmental Law Journal* 35 (2016): 223.

62. Carrie Farmer, Lisa Jaycox, Grant Marshall, Terry Schell, Terri Tanielian, Christine Anne Vaughan, and Glenda Wrenn, *A Needs Assessment of New York State Veterans: Final Report to the New York State Health Foundation* (Santa Monica, CA: RAND Corporation, 2011), https://www.rand.org/pubs/technical_reports/TR920 .html.

63. Van Slyke and Armstrong, "Communities Serve."

64. *Long-Term Implications of the 2021 Future Years Defense Program* (Congressional Budget Office, September 2020), https://www.cbo.gov/publication/56554.

65. Ken MacLeish, "Churn: Mobilization–Demobilization and the Fungibility of American Military Life," *Security Dialogue* 51, nos. 2–3 (2020): 194–210.

66. MacLeish, "Churn," 195.

67. For more on mental health and military labor, see Paul Taylor and Andrew Reeves, "United States: 'Combatting' Self-Harm and Suicide in the US Military and After: Culture, Military Labour and No-Harm Contracts," in *Military Past, Civilian Present: International Perspectives on Veterans' Transition from the Armed Forces*, ed. Paul Taylor, Emma Murray, and Katherine Albertson (Cham: Springer International Publishing, 2019), 107–120.

68. Michael White, Philip Mulvey, Andrew Fox, and David Choate, "A Hero's Welcome? Exploring the Prevalence and Problems of Military Veterans in the Arrestee Population," *Justice Quarterly* 29, no. 2 (2012): 258–286.

69. Zoë H. Wool, *After War: The Weight of Life at Walter Reed* (Durham, NC: Duke University Press, 2015), 151.

70. Luis Martinez and Karen Travers, "President Trump Minimizes Concussion-Like Injuries in Iraq Attack as Merely 'Headaches,'" *ABC News*, January 22, 2020, https://abcnews.go.com/Politics/president-trump-minimizes-concussion-inju ries-iraq-attack-headaches/story?id=68448853.

71. Daniel Huang, "VA Disability Claims Soar," *Wall Street Journal*, October 27, 2014, https://www.wsj.com/articles/va-disability-claims-soar-1414454034.

72. "Motrin and water" is a joke among veterans, referring to military health care. A popular meme on the subject shows a picture of a bottle of water and ibuprofen,

with a caption that reads "You might be a veteran if you were told these two cure everything" (https://www.pinterest.com.mx/pin/140033869639668818).

73. Harold Braswell and Howard Kushner, "Suicide, Social Integration, and Masculinity in the U.S. Military," *Social Science & Medicine* 74, no. 4 (2012): 530–536.

74. "Med boarded" refers to the process by which the Medical Evaluation Board determines whether the service member's medical condition makes them unfit to carry out their duties.

75. Alair MacLean, "The Things They Carry: Combat, Disability, and Unemployment among US Men," *American Sociological Review* 75, no. 4 (2010): 563–585.

76. MacLean and Kleykamp, "Generations of Veterans."

77. Reservists serve part-time, living a civilian life when not deployed. They do, however, experience some difficulties in employment that stem from their military service. Research shows that some employers are reluctant to hire them because they worry that the National Guard or Reserve member would be deployed, and then would have to be replaced. Carrie Farmer, Terri Tanielian, Shira Fischer, Erin Duffy, Stephanie Dellva, Emily Butcher, Kristine M. Brown, and Emily Hoch, *Supporting Veterans in Massachusetts: An Assessment of Needs, Well-Being, and Available Resources* (Santa Monica, CA: RAND Corporation, 2017), https://www.rand.org/content/dam/rand/pubs/research_reports /RR1600/RR1698/RAND_RR1698.pdf; Carol Morris, *Coming Home: Support for Returning Veterans in Mecklenburg* (Charlotte Bridge Home, May 2012), https:// www.fftc.org/sites/default/files/2017-07/Coming%20Home%20Assessment%20 Report%20for%20Charlotte-Mecklenburg%20FINAL%205-26.pdf.

78. *The Military-Civilian Gap: War and Sacrifice in the Post-9/11 Era*, Pew Research Center, October 5, 2011, https://www.pewresearch.org/social-trends/2011/10/05 /chapter-6-a-profile-of-the-modern-military.

79. Armed Forces of the United States, Enlistment/Reenlistment Document, May 2020, https://www.esd.whs.mil/Portals/54/Documents/DD/forms/dd/dd0004.pdf.

80. US Army, Soldier for Life website, https://soldierforlife.army.mil.

81. MacLeish, "Churn."

82. Laura Reiley, "The Rising Cost of Being in the National Guard: Reservists and Guardsmen Are Twice as Likely to Be Hungry as Other American Groups," *Washington Post*, June 22, 2021, https://www.washingtonpost.com/business/2021/06/22 /hunger-national-guard-reserves/. Some members of the military prioritize paying bills over buying food because their credit reports are connected to security clearances, and a missed bill can jeopardize their jobs.

83. For example, Chen, *Pursuing Citizenship in the Enforcement Era*; McGlynn and Monforti, *Proving Patriotismo*; Strader, Lundquist, and Dominguez-Villegas, "Warriors Wanted."

84. Van Slyke and Armstrong, "Communities Serve."

85. Lisa Sturtevant, Maya Brennan, Janet Viveiros, and Ethan Handelman, *Housing and Services Needs of Our Changing Veteran Population* (National Housing

Conference, Center for Housing Policy, June 2015), https://nhc.org/wp-content /uploads/2017/10/Housing-and-Services-Needs-of-Our-Changing-Veteran-Popu lation.pdf.

86. Gregory Lewis and Rahul Pathak, "The Employment of Veterans in State and Local Government Service," *State & Local Government Review* 46, no. 2 (2014): 91–105.

87. Gerald R. Ford, Executive Order 11935—Citizenship Requirements for Federal Employment, https://www.presidency.ucsb.edu/node/268643.

88. Van Slyke and Armstrong, "Communities Serve."

89. Keith Aronson, Daniel Perkins, Nicole Morgan, Julia Bleser, Katie Davenport, Dawne Vogt, Laurel Copeland, Erin Finley, and Cynthia Gilman, "Going It Alone: Post-9/11 Veteran Nonuse of Healthcare and Social Service Programs during Their Early Transition to Civilian Life," *Journal of Social Service Research* 45, no. 5 (2019): 634–647.

90. Erving Goffman, *Asylums: Essays on the Social Situation of Mental Patients and Other Inmates* (New York: Routledge, 2007).

91. Tyson Smith and Gala True, "Warring Identities: Identity Conflict and the Mental Distress of American Veterans of the Wars in Iraq and Afghanistan," *Society and Mental Health* 4, no. 2 (July 1, 2014): 147–161; Van Slyke and Armstrong, "Communities Serve."

92. Thomas Crosbie and Meredith Kleykamp, "Fault Lines of the American Military Profession," *Armed Forces & Society* 44, no. 3 (July 2018): 521–543; John Hammill, David Segal, and Mady Wechsler Segal, "Self-Selection and Parental Socioeconomic Status as Determinants of the Values of West Point Cadets," *Armed Forces & Society* 22, no. 1 (October 1995): 103–115.

93. Smith et al., "The Role of PTSD, Depression, and Alcohol Misuse"; Amiram Vinokur, Penny Pierce, Lisa Lewandowski-Romps, Stevan Hobfoll, and Sandro Galea, "Effects of War Exposure on Air Force Personnel's Mental Health, Job Burnout and Other Organizational Related Outcomes," *Journal of Occupational Health Psychology* 16, no. 1 (2011): 3–17.

CHAPTER 5

1. Beth J. Asch, Jennie W. Wenger, and Troy D. Smith, *The Military Accessions Vital to the National Interest (MAVNI) Program: Army Performance, Cost, Security Risk, and Potential Pool for Recruiting* (RAND Corporation, 2017), https://www.document cloud.org/documents/4578092-MAVNI-RAND-Report.html.; Chishti, Rose, and Yale-Loehr, *Noncitizens in the U.S. Military.*

2. Ewers and Lewis, "Risk and the Securitisation of Student Migration to the United States"; Obinna, "The Challenges of American Legal Permanent Residency."

3. Asch, Wenger, and Smith, *The Military Accessions Vital to the National Interest (MAVNI) Program*; Horton, "The Pentagon Promised Citizenship to Immigrants Who Served."

4. Languages considered critical to the Department of Defense in 2015 included Albanian, Amharic, Arabic, Azerbaijani, Bengali, Bulgarian, Burmese, Cambodian-Khmer, Cebuano, Chinese, Czech, Dhivehi (language of Maldives), French (limited to individuals possessing citizenship from an African country), Georgian, Haitian-Creole, Hausa, Hindi, Hungarian, Igbo, Indonesian, Kashmiri, Korean, Kurdish, Lao, Malay, Malayalam, Moro, Nepalese, Pahari, Persian (Dari & Farsi), Polish, Portuguese, Punjabi, Pushtu (aka Pashto), Russian, Serbo-Croatian, Sindhi, Sinhalese, Somali, Swahili, Tagalog, Tajik, Tamil, Thai, Turkish, Turkmen, Ukrainian, Urdu, Uzbek, and Yoruba. "Military Accessions Vital to National Interest [MAVNI] Recruitment Pilot Program," US Department of Defense Fact Sheet, 2016, https://dod.defense.gov/news/mavni-fact-sheet.pdf.

5. Applicants had to have valid immigration status for at least two years before enlistment, with no trips out of the country for longer than ninety days. They could not be green card holders or in the process of applying for legal permanent residency. "Military Accessions Vital to National Interest [MAVNI] Recruitment Pilot Program."

6. When the program began, language recruits had to enlist for a minimum of four years of active duty. Health care professionals could choose between three years of active duty or six years in the Selected Reserve. Like all enlistees, MAVNIs were obligated to eight years total of military service and could be reactivated. Margaret Stock, "Ten Things That Immigration Lawyers Should Know about the Army's New Non-citizen Recruiting Program," Shusterman.com (website of Carl Shusterman, immigration lawyer), https://www.shusterman.com/pdf/mavni armyimmigrationfornonimmigrants209.pdf.

7. Asch, Wenger, and Smith, *The Military Accessions Vital to the National Interest (MAVNI) Program*.

8. Tam, "MacArthur Fellow Margaret Stock."

9. Sig Christenson, "GI Who Joined the Army and Dreamed of Citizenship Could Be Deported," *San Antonio Express-News*, July 15, 2018, https://www.express news.com/news/local/article/GI-who-joined-the-Army-and-dreamed-of-citizen ship-13077064.php.

10. Alex Horton, "Pentagon Program in Doubt, Foreign Recruits Flee U.S. to Avoid Deportation," *Washington Post*, July 18, 2017.

11. Julia Preston, *The Double Limbo of Dreamer-Soldiers* (The Marshall Project, September 20, 2017), https://www.themarshallproject.org/2017/09/19/the-double -limbo-of-dreamer-soldiers.

12. Julia Preston, "Pentagon Reopens Program Allowing Immigrants with Special Skills to Enlist," *New York Times*, October 27, 2012, https://www.nytimes.com /2012/10/28/us/pentagon-reopens-program-allowing-immigrants-with-special -skills-to-enlist.html.

13. The cutoff for ASVAB scores for MAVNI recruits was higher than for the general population. Stock, "Ten Things That Immigration Lawyers Should Know."

14. Preston, "Pentagon Reopens Program Allowing Immigrants with Special Skills to Enlist."

15. Fonda Bock, "Recruiting Summit Considers More Foreign Nationals," *US Army*, June 10, 2015, https://www.army.mil/article/150185/recruiting_summit_considers _more_foreign_nationals.

16. Horton, "Pentagon Program in Doubt, Foreign Recruits Flee U.S. to Avoid Deportation."

17. Asch, Wenger, and Smith, *The Military Accessions Vital to the National Interest (MAVNI) Program.*

18. Asch, Wenger, and Smith, *The Military Accessions Vital to the National Interest (MAVNI) Program.*

19. Asch, Wenger, and Smith, *The Military Accessions Vital to the National Interest (MAVNI) Program.*

20. MacLeish, "Churn."

21. Alex Horton, "The Military Looked to 'Dreamers' to Use Their Vital Skills. Now the U.S. Might Deport Them," *Washington Post*, September 7, 2017.

22. Asch, Wenger, and Smith, *The Military Accessions Vital to the National Interest (MAVNI) Program.*

23. Asch, Wenger, and Smith, *The Military Accessions Vital to the National Interest (MAVNI) Program.*

24. Horton, "The Pentagon Promised Citizenship to Immigrants Who Served."

25. Alex Horton, "Lawmakers Press Trump Not to Deport Foreign-Born Military Recruits," *Washington Post*, July 28, 2017.

26. US District Court, Western District of Washington at Seattle, *Tiwari v. Mattis*, 2019.

27. Alex Horton, "U.S. Army Kills Contracts for Hundreds of Immigrant Recruits. Some Face Deportation," *Washington Post*, September 15, 2017.

28. Monsey Alvarado, "New Jersey Immigrant Soldiers' Path to Citizenship Stalled," *NorthJersey.com*, June 11, 2017, https://www.northjersey.com/story/news/2017 /06/11/new-jersey-immigrant-soldiers-path-citizenship-stalled/350266001/.

29. Dave Philipps, "Army Suspends Its Purge of Immigrant Recruits," *New York Times*, August 9, 2018, https://www.nytimes.com/2018/08/09/us/mavni-program -army-discharge-immigrants.html.

30. US District Court for the District of Columbia, *Nio v. DHS*, 2017.

31. Garance Burke and Martha Mendoza, "Army Reinstates at Least 36 Discharged Immigrants," *Associated Press*, August 20, 2018.

32. Horton, "Pentagon Program in Doubt, Foreign Recruits Flee U.S. to Avoid Deportation."

33. Catherine Lutz, *Homefront: A Military City and the American Twentieth Century* (Boston: Beacon Press, 2002).

34. US District Court for the District of Columbia, *Nio v. DHS*, 2017.

35. Vanessa Romo, "U.S. Army Is Discharging Immigrant Recruits Who Were Promised Citizenship," *NPR*, July 9, 2018, https://www.npr.org/2018/07/09/626773440/u -s-army-is-discharging-immigrant-recruits-who-were-promised-citizenship.

36. Massoud Hayoun, "The U.S. Is Denying Citizenship to Service Members at an Unprecedented Rate," *Pacific Standard*, 2019, https://psmag.com/social-justice/the-u-s-is-denying-citizenship-to-service-members-at-an-unprecedented-rate.

37. Kretsedemas, "The Limits of Control."

38. Payal Banerjee, "Transnational Subcontracting, Indian IT Workers, and the U.S. Visa System," *Women's Studies Quarterly* 38, nos. 1–2 (2010): 93.

39. Catherine Dauvergne and Sarah Marsden, "The Ideology of Temporary Labour Migration in the Post-Global Era," *Citizenship Studies* 18, no. 2 (2014): 224–242; Cecilia Menjívar, "Liminal Legality: Salvadoran and Guatemalan Immigrants' Lives in the United States," *American Journal of Sociology* 111, no. 4 (2006): 999–1037.

40. Ewers and Lewis, "Risk and the Securitisation of Student Migration to the United States."

41. Niall Hegarty, "Where We Are Now: The Presence and Importance of International Students to Universities in the United States," *Journal of International Students* 4 (2014): 223–235.

42. Emma Israel and Jeanne Batalova, *International Students in the United States* (Migration Policy Institute, January 14, 2021), https://www.migrationpolicy.org/article/international-students-united-states-2020.

43. Farcy and Smit, "Status (Im)Mobility and the Legal Production of Irregularity: A Sociolegal Analysis of Temporary Migrants' Lived Experiences," *Social & Legal Studies* 29, no. 5: 629–649.

44. Sarah Pierce and Julia Gelatt, *Evolution of the H-1B: Latest Trends in a Program on the Brink of Reform* (Migration Policy Institute, March 2018), https://www.migrationpolicy.org/sites/default/files/publications/H-1B-BrinkofReform-Brief_Final.pdf.

45. Neil Ruiz, *The Geography of Foreign Students in U.S. Higher Education: Origins and Destinations* (Global Cities Initiative, Brookings and JPMorgan Chase, 2014), https://www.brookings.edu/wp-content/uploads/2014/08/Foreign_Students_Final.pdf.

46. Catalina Amuedo-Dorantes and Delia Furtado, "Settling for Academia? H-1B Visas and the Career Choices of International Students in the United States," *Journal of Human Resources* 54, no. 2 (2019): 401–429.

47. Daniel Costa and Don Hira, *H-1B Visas and Prevailing Wage Levels: A Majority of H-1B Employers—Including Major U.S. Tech Firms—Use the Program to Pay Migrant Workers Well below Market Wages* (Economic Policy Institute, May 4, 2020), https://www.epi.org/publication/h-1b-visas-and-prevailing-wage-levels/; Kevin Thomas and Christopher Inkpen, "Foreign Student Emigration to the United States: Pathways of Entry, Demographic Antecedents, and Origin-Country Contexts," *International Migration Review* 51, no. 3 (2017): 789–820.

48. Mark Rosenzweig, Douglas Irwin, and Jaffrey Williamson, "Global Wage Differences and International Student Flows [with Comments and Discussion]," *Brookings Trade Forum* (2006): 57–96.

49. Stock, "Ten Things That Immigration Lawyers Should Know about the Army's New Non-citizen Recruiting Program."

50. US District Court of Minnesota, *Jakiul Alam v. USCIS, Leslie Tritten, and Ur M. Jaddou*, 2022.

51. Tara Copp, "Immigrant Soldier Dies Waiting for US Military to Clear Him for Duty," *Military Times*, April 19, 2018, https://www.militarytimes.com/news/your-military/2018/04/19/immigrant-soldier-dies-waiting-for-us-military-to-clear-him-to-serve/.

52. While 80 percent of enlisted people only have a high school diploma, 44 percent of officers have bachelor's degrees, and 41 percent have advanced degrees. MAVNI recruits were on average twenty-six years old, five years older than the average non-MAVNI recruit. *2016 Demographics*.

53. Asch, Wenger, and Smith, *The Military Accessions Vital to the National Interest (MAVNI) Program*

54. US Army, "92A Automated Logistical Specialist," https://www.goarmy.com/careers-and-jobs/career-match/support-logistics/transportation-inventory/92a-automated-logistical-specialist.html.

55. Interview with Minzhe, international student from China.

56. Alex Marquardt, "US Army, Citing Security Concerns with Recruiting Program, Discharging Immigrants," *CNN*, July 9, 2018, https://www.cnn.com/2018/07/09/politics/us-army-immigrants-denials/index.html.

57. Miriam Jordan, "Fast Track to Citizenship Is Cut Off for Some Military Recruits," *New York Times*, September 15, 2017.

58. Asch, Wenger, and Smith, *The Military Accessions Vital to the National Interest (MAVNI) Program*.

59. Marisa Schultz, "Immigrant Recruits Booted by the Army Left Facing Deportation, Death," *New York Post*, August 9, 2018.

60. Jeff Schogol, "No, President Trump Is Not Purging the Military of Immigrants," *Task & Purpose*, July 7, 2018, https://taskandpurpose.com/analysis/trump-purging-military-immigrants-mavni/.

61. Horton, "U.S. Army Kills Contracts for Hundreds of Immigrant Recruits."

62. Saulo Cwerner, "The Times of Migration," *Journal of Ethnic and Migration Studies* 27, no. 1 (2001): 7–36; Farcy and Smit, "Status (Im)Mobility and the Legal Production of Irregularity."

63. Farcy and Smit, "Status (Im)Mobility and the Legal Production of Irregularity."

64. Alvarado, "New Jersey Immigrant Soldiers' Path to Citizenship Stalled."

65. Schultz, "Immigrant Recruits Booted by the Army Left Facing Deportation, Death."

66. Schultz, "Immigrant Recruits Booted by the Army Left Facing Deportation, Death."

67. Dave Philipps, "Red Flags for Immigrant Recruits: Calling Parents, Not Laughing at Jokes," *New York Times*, August 22, 2018, https://www.nytimes.com/2018/08/21/us/immigrant-recruits-mavni.html.

68. Horton, "The Pentagon Promised Citizenship to Immigrants Who Served."

69. Christenson, "GI Who Joined the Army and Dreamed of Citizenship Could Be Deported."

70. Christenson, "Immigrant GI Booted Out of Army at Fort Sam."

71. Marquardt, "US Army, Citing Security Concerns with Recruiting Program, Discharging Immigrants."

72. Lolita Baldor, "Problems for Pentagon's Immigrant Recruit Program," *AP*, October 1, 2018, https://apnews.com/article/e39121259b5848788647f1667ed10eea.

73. Katie Benner, "U.S. Army Reservist Is Accused of Spying for China," *New York Times*, September 26, 2018, https://www.nytimes.com/2018/09/25/us/politics/ji-chaoqun-china-spy.html.

74. Cacho, *Social Death*, 143.

75. Richard Sisk, "These Recruits Were Promised Citizenship in Exchange for Military Service. Now They Fear the US Has Forgotten Them," Military.com, March 16, 2021, https://www.military.com/daily-news/2021/03/13/these-recruits-were-promised-citizenship-exchange-military-service-now-they-fear-us-has-forgotten.html.

76. Joey Antohi, "I Dream of Serving in the Military, but Can't until US Policy Changes," *Inquirer*, March 31, 2021, https://www.inquirer.com/opinion/commentary/mavni-program-non-citizen-immigrant-military-recruits-20210331.html.

77. Sean Bigley, "What's New in the World of MAVNI?," *ClearanceJobs*, January 31, 2021, https://news.clearancejobs.com/2021/01/31/whats-new-in-the-world-of-mavni/.

78. *Samma v. U.S. Department of Defense—Lawsuit Challenging Policy Denying U.S. Military Service Members Expedited Path to Citizenship* (ACLU, January 27, 2021), https://www.aclu.org/cases/samma-v-us-department-defense-lawsuit-challenging-policy-denying-us-military-service-members; Karen Jowers, "Federal Judge Rules DoD's Policy Unlawfully Slows Immigrant Troops' Path to Citizenship," *Military Times*, August 26, 2020, https://www.militarytimes.com/pay-benefits/2020/08/25/federal-judge-rules-dods-policy-unlawfully-slows-immigrant-troops-path-to-citizenship/; Sisk, "These Recruits Were Promised Citizenship in Exchange for Military Service."

CHAPTER 6

1. In 2018, 65 percent of all deportees were sent to Mexico, and 61 percent of criminal deportees were sent to Mexico. *2018 Yearbook of Immigration Statistics* (US Department of Homeland Security, Office of Immigration Statistics, 2019),

https://www.dhs.gov/immigration-statistics/yearbook/2018, accessed October 27, 2022; "self-deported" is a politically laden term that refers to immigrants choosing to return to their countries of birth or leave the United States because of policies that have made their lives in the United States difficult. K.-Sue Park, "Self-Deportation Nation," *Harvard Law Review* 132, no. 7 (2019): 1878–1942.

2. Devah Pager, *Marked: Race, Crime, and Finding Work in an Era of Mass Incarceration* (Chicago: University of Chicago Press, 2008); Bruce Western, *Punishment and Inequality in America* (New York: Russell Sage Foundation, 2006).

3. Jose got multiple honorable discharges because he re-upped his contract twice, getting discharge paperwork in the process during those times, as well as when he separated from the military one final time in 2004.

4. *The Trial Penalty: The Sixth Amendment Right to Trial on the Verge of Extinction and How to Save It* (National Association of Criminal Defense Lawyers, 2018), https://www.nacdl.org/Document/TrialPenaltySixthAmendmentRighttoTrialNearExtinct.

5. Golash-Boza, *Deported*; Emma Hilbert, *Land of the Free, No Home to the Brave: A Report on the Social, Economic, and Moral Cost of Deporting Veterans* (Texas Civil Rights Project, 2018), https://texascivilrightsproject.org/wp-content/uploads/2018/02/2018-VeteransReport-FINAL.pdf.

6. Marie Gottschalk, *Caught: The Prison State and the Lockdown of American Politics* (Princeton, NJ: Princeton University Press, 2016).

7. Chris Gentilviso, "Military Turns to Prison Labor for $100 Million In Uniforms—At $2-per-Hour Wages," *Huffington Post*, December 24, 2013, https://www.huffpost.com/entry/military-prison-uniforms_n_4498867.

8. Gottschalk, *Caught*. Some uprisings by incarcerated workers have focused specifically on their lack of pay and working conditions, e.g., Michelle Chen, "Georgia Prison Strike: A Hidden Labor Force Resists," *In These Times*, December 17, 2010, http://inthesetimes.com/working/entry/6784/georgia_prison_strike_a_hidden_labor_force_resists.

9. The Thirteenth Amendment states: "Neither slavery nor involuntary servitude, *except as a punishment for crime whereof the party shall have been duly convicted*, shall exist within the United States, or any place subject to their jurisdiction"; emphasis added.

10. Some states have veterans' courts, a type of diversionary program in which certain offenders who are veterans are provided with "monitoring, training, and occupational and psychological counseling in lieu of imprisonment." Claudia Arno, "Proportional Response: The Need for More-and More Standardized-Veterans' Court," *University of Michigan Law Review Reform* 48 (2014): 1039.

11. Hector insisted that I use his real name.

12. Alejandra Martinez, "Veterans Banished: The Fight to Bring Them Home," *Scholar: St. Mary's Law Review on Race and Social Justice* 19, no. 3 (2016): 321–360.

13. RICO has been used to criminalize young men of color as gang members. This includes mass militarized raids and arrests carried out by ICE and other federal

agencies in cooperation with local police. Trujillo and Vitale, *Gang Takedowns in the De Blasio Era.*

14. Martinez, "Veterans Banished."

15. Tanya Golash-Boza, "Structural Racism, Criminalization, and Pathways to Deportation for Dominican and Jamaican Men in the United States," *Social Justice* 44, nos. 2–3 (2017): 137–162.

16. Immigrant Legal Resource Center, "Aggravated Felony Factsheet," May 21, 2013, https://www.ilrc.org/sites/default/files/resources/ijn-aggravated-felony-fact sheet.pdf.

17. Hilbert, *Land of the Free, No Home to the Brave.*

18. Golash-Boza, *Deported.*

19. *Immigration Enforcement: Actions Needed to Better Handle, Identify, and Track Cases Involving Veterans* (US Government Accountability Office, June 2019), https://www.gao.gov/assets/gao-19-416.pdf; ICE Directive 10039.2, "Consideration of U.S. Military Service When Making Discretionary Determinations with Regard to Enforcement Actions against Noncitizens," May 23, 2022, https://www.ice.gov/doclib/news/releases/2022/10039.2.pdf.

20. Pilar Marrero, "The US Has Deported Thousands of Veterans. A New Policy Change Offers New Hope for 'Soldiers Left Behind,'" *PBS SoCal*, November 17, 2021, https://www.pbssocal.org/shows/voces/the-u-s-has-deported-thousands-of-veterans-a-new-policy-change-offers-new-hope-for-soldiers-left-behind; Jorge Rivas, "It's Veterans Day and U.S. Veterans Are Getting Deported," *Splinter*, November 11, 2013, https://splinternews.com/it-s-veterans-day-and-u-s-veterans-are-getting-deporte-1793840071.

21. Martinez, "Veterans Banished."

22. John Gramlich, *How Border Apprehensions, ICE Arrests and Deportations Have Changed under Trump*, Pew Research Center, March 2, 2020, https://www.pewre search.org/fact-tank/2020/03/02/how-border-apprehensions-ice-arrests-and-de portations-have-changed-under-trump/.

23. Golash-Boza, *Deported*; Golash-Boza and Hondagneu-Sotelo, "Latino Immigrant Men and the Deportation Crisis."

24. Golash-Boza, *Deported*. By comparison, women comprise about half of all immigrants, and about half of immigrants are from Latin American and Caribbean countries. *Gender and Migration*, Pew Research Center, July 5, 2006, https://www.pewresearch.org/hispanic/2006/07/05/ii-migration-and-gender/; Budiman et al., *Facts on U.S. Immigrants. 2018. Statistical Portrait of the Foreign-Born Population in the United States.*

25. Golash-Boza, *Deported*; Armenta, *Protect, Serve, and Deport.*

26. Sarah Brayne, "Surveillance and System Avoidance: Criminal Justice Contact and Institutional Attachment," *American Sociological Review* 79, no. 3 (2014): 367–391; Andrea Leverentz, "Churning through the System: How People Engage with

the Criminal Justice System When Faced with Short Sentences," *After Imprisonment (Studies in Law, Politics, and Society)* 77 (2018): 123–143.

27. Bureau of Justice Statistics, "Veterans in Prison and Jail, 2011–12," December 2015, https://www.bjs.gov/content/pub/pdf/vpj1112_sum.pdf.

28. Eric Elbogen et al., "Criminal Justice Involvement, Trauma, and Negative Affect in Iraq and Afghanistan War Era Veterans," *Journal of Consulting and Clinical Psychology* 80, no. 6 (2013): 1097–1102.

29. Andrea Finlay et al., "Sex Differences in Mental Health and Substance Use Disorders and Treatment Entry among Justice-Involved Veterans in the Veterans Health Administration." *Medical Care* 53, no. 4, suppl. 1 (2015): S105–S111; Bureau of Justice Statistics, "Veterans in Prison and Jail, 2011–12."

30. National Institute of Corrections, "Prisons and Jails with Dorms for Veterans," Justice Involved Veterans, 2020, https://info.nicic.gov/jiv/node/27.

31. National Association of Criminal Defense Lawyers, "The Trial Penalty."

32. Martinez, "Veterans Banished."

33. "p1Rudi Richardson 08 Nov 2010," radio interview with Rudi Richardson, YouTube, https://www.youtube.com/watch?v=_ZmuRk5RQUA; "Brown Babies' Long Search for Family, Identity," *CNN*, November 20, 2011, https://www.cnn.com/2011/11/20/us/germanys-brown-babies-still-searching-for-their-american-fathers/index.html. Until 2000, adoptive parents had to petition for US citizenship for their adopted children. Many did not do so, and their children were subsequently deported, as happened to Richardson. See DeLeith Duke Gossett, "[Take from Us Our] Wretched Refuse: The Deportation of America's Adoptees," *University of Cincinnati Law Review* 85 (2017): 33.

34. Trujillo and Vitale, *Gang Takedowns in the De Blasio Era.*

35. Golash-Boza and Hondagneu-Sotelo, "Latino Immigrant Men and the Deportation Crisis."

36. Benjamin Schrader, *Fight to Live, Live to Fight: Veteran Activism after War* (Albany: SUNY Press, 2019).

37. Aptekar, "Citizenship in the Green Card Army."

38. Robert Johnson, "The FBI Announces Gangs Have Infiltrated Every Branch of the Military," *Business Insider*, October 22, 2011, https://www.businessinsider.com/fbi-gang-assessment-us-military-2011-10; Carter Smith, "Gangs and the Military Note 4: The Role of the East Coast in the Development of Military-Trained Gang Members," *Small Wars Journal*, February 15, 2020, https://smallwarsjournal.com/jrnl/art/gangs-and-military-note-4-role-east-coast-development-military-trained-gang-members.

39. Golash-Boza, "Structural Racism, Criminalization, and Pathways to Deportation."

40. Nicole Goodkind, "Prisoners Are Fighting California's Wildfires on the Front Lines, but Getting Little in Return," *Fortune*, November 1, 2019, https://fortune.com/2019/11/01/california-prisoners-fighting-wildfires/.

41. California Senate Concurrent Resolution No. 69—Relative to Prisoner Compensation, https://leginfo.legislature.ca.gov/faces/billTextClient.xhtml?bill_id=201920 200SCR69.

42. They were likely naturalized US citizens who were convicted of crimes after acquiring US citizenship, which protects from deportation, or US-born US citizens who grew up outside the United States.

43. Except in the case of countries that do not accept deportees from the United States.

44. Cacho, *Social Death*.

45. *ICE Raids Toolkit: Defend against ICE Raids and Community Arrests* (Immigrant Defense Project and Center for Constitutional Rights, July 2019), https://www.immigrantdefenseproject.org/raids-toolkit/.

46. Gossett, "[Take from Us Our] Wretched Refuse."

47. Lawrence Herzog, "Border Commuter Workers and Transfrontier Metropolitan Structure along the United States–Mexico Border," *Journal of Borderlands Studies* 5, no. 2 (1990): 1–20; Oscar Martínez, *Border People: Life and Society in the US-Mexico Borderlands* (Tucson: University of Arizona Press, 1994).

48. This binational life and intimate connections that exist across the Southwest borderlands are lost in arguments that emphasize that deported veterans are returned to countries they do not know. This is true of some but not all.

49. Hector's experience parallels that of citizens with outstanding warrants, whose lives are suddenly interrupted during routine encounters with law enforcement and who live with constant stressful anticipation of being caught. Leverentz, "Churning through the System."

50. Alex Schafran and Paavo Monkkonen, "Beyond Chapala and Cancún: Grappling with the Impact of American Migration to Mexico," *Migraciones Internacionales* 6, no. 2 (2011): 223–258.

51. Raúl Lardiés-Bosque, Jennifer Guillén, and Verónica Montes-de-Oca, "Retirement Migration and Transnationalism in Northern Mexico," *Journal of Ethnic and Migration Studies* 42, no. 5 (2016): 816–833; Matthew Hayes, *Gringolandia: Lifestyle Migration under Late Capitalism* (Minneapolis: University of Minnesota Press, 2018).

52. As reported in Garcia, *Without a Country: The Untold Story of America's Deported Veterans* (New York: Hot Books, 2017).

53. Andrea Leverentz, *The Ex-Prisoner's Dilemma: How Women Negotiate Competing Narratives of Reentry and Desistance* (New Brunswick, NJ: Rutgers University Press, 2014); Leverentz, "Churning through the System."

54. Although there are no statistics available, deported veterans in my small sample and the deported veterans whose stories I came across in the media and advocates' reports were almost all immigrants who grew up in the United States.

55. Slack, *Deported to Death*.

56. Slack, *Deported to Death*.

57. Melinda Tasca, Philip Mulvey, and Nancy Rodriguez, "Families Coming To-gether in Prison: An Examination of Visitation Encounters," *Punishment & Society* 18, no. 4 (2016): 459–478; Jillian Turanovic and Melinda Tasca, "Inmates' Experiences with Prison Visitation," *Justice Quarterly* 36, no. 2 (2019): 287–322.

58. US Department of Veteran Affairs, Office of Public and Intergovernmental Affairs, *Federal Benefits for Veterans, Dependents and Survivors*, chapter 2, Service Connected Disabilities, https://www.va.gov/opa/publications/benefits_book/benefits_chap02.asp.

59. *Immigration Enforcement.*

60. Rebecca Kheel, "16 Deported Vets, Family Members Temporarily Allowed Back into US in the Last Year, DHS Says," Military.com, June 30, 2022, https://www.military.com/daily-news/2022/06/30/16-deported-vets-family-members-temporarily-allowed-back-us-last-year-dhs-says.html.

61. *Immigration Enforcement.*

62. *Discharged, Then Discarded.*

63. *Discharged, Then Discarded*; Nelson Goodson, "Deported Former Marine José Solorio Passed Away after Receiving Humanitarian Visa to Return for Treatment," *Hispanic News Network*, June 19, 2015, https://hngwiusa.wordpress.com/2015/06/19/deported-former-marine-jose-solorio-passed-away-aft-er-receiving-humanitarian-visa-to-return-for-treatment/.

64. Kheel, "16 Deported Vets." The program also ran a one-day COVID immunization clinic that allowed deported veterans and family members to briefly cross the border into San Ysidro, California. Alexandra Mendoza, "Group of Deported Veterans Allowed Back Into the U.S. Just to Get Their COVID Vaccine," *San Diego Union-Tribune*, September 19, 2021, https://www.sandiegouniontribune.com/news/border-baja-california/story/2021-09-19/deported-vets-allowed-back-briefly-into-the-u-s-to-get-their-covid-shot.

65. *Discharged, Then Discarded.*

66. *Land of the Free, No Home to the Brave.* In the United States, tattoos on Latinx bodies are equated with violent gang membership in both the criminal justice and immigration enforcement systems. Victor Rios, *Human Targets: Schools, Police, and the Criminalization of Latino Youth* (Chicago: University of Chicago Press, 2017).

67. Slack, *Deported to Death*, 108.

68. Guadalupe Correa-Cabrera and Laura Weiss, "El Chapo and Mexico's Drug War Spectacle," *NACLA*, March 3, 2019, https://nacla.org/news/2019/03/04/el-chapo-and-mexico%E2%80%99s-drug-war-spectacle; Markus-Michael Müller, "The Rise of the Penal State in Latin America," *Contemporary Justice Review* 15, no. 1 (2012): 57–76; Marylee Reynolds, "The War on Drugs, Prison Building, and Globalization: Catalysts for the Global Incarceration of Women," *NWSA Journal* 20, no. 2 (2008): 72–95.

69. Guadalupe Correa-Cabrera, *Los Zetas Inc.: Criminal Corporations, Energy, and Civil War in Mexico* (Austin: University of Texas Press, 2017).

70. Julie Watson, "Smugglers Offer Cash to Troops, Others to Drive Migrants," *AP*, July 26, 2019, https://apnews.com/article/47c9799c15e64e64848cff1a7dca92be.

71. See K. C. Brouwer et al, "Deportation along the U.S.-Mexico Border: Its Relation to Drug Use Patterns and Accessing Care," *Journal of Immigrant and Minority Health* 11, no. 1 (2019): 1–6.

72. Schrader, *Fight to Live, Live to Fight*, 123.

73. Algernon D'Ammassa, "Welcome Home: Deported Veteran from Las Cruces Takes Citizenship Oath," *Las Cruces Sun News*, July 15, 2022, https://www.lcsun-news.com/story/news/local/2022/07/15/deported-veteran-from-las-cruces-new-mexico-gets-citizenship-immigration/65372259007/.

74. *Homelessness in America: Focus on Veterans* (US Interagency Council on Homelessness, June 2018), https://www.usich.gov/resources/uploads/asset_library/Homelessness_in_America._Focus_on_Veterans.pdf.

75. At the same time, deported veterans have to reconcile their claims of deservingness with their criminal convictions. They tend to do so by referring to the sentences they served as the debt they already paid to society.

76. Some deported veterans were drafted to serve in the Vietnam War. I was not able to interview any of these older veterans, but their case presents a different scenario for claims making because they did not enlist voluntarily, as well as the stigma attached to Vietnam War veterans in particular.

77. *Land of the Free, No Home to the Brave*. These veterans' right to make informed decisions is also violated when they are not told of immigration consequences of taking a guilty plea.

78. Cacho, *Social Death*.

79. For example, Kristine Phillips, "The Story behind This Powerful Photo of Deported Military Veterans Saluting the U.S. Flag," *Washington Post*, November 16, 2017, https://www.washingtonpost.com/news/checkpoint/wp/2017/11/16/the-story-behind-this-powerful-photo-of-deported-military-veterans-saluting-the-american-flag/.

80. Hector's experience is reminiscent of what Wool describes among injured veterans who are primarily perceived as wounded soldiers: "being overdetermined, a certain weakening of the always contingent ability to feel self-contained and private, to pass or to pass unnoticed." Wool, *After War*, 140.

81. Todd South, "Army Veteran Faces Federal Prison Time, Fines for Stolen Valor and Lying about PTSD," *Army Times*, January 14, 2020, https://www.armytimes.com/news/your-army/2020/01/14/army-veteran-faces-federal-prison-time-fines-for-stolen-valor-and-lying-about-ptsd/.

82. See Cacho, *Social Death*.

83. *Land of the Free, No Home to the Brave*.

84. H.R.3429—Repatriate Our Patriots Act, https://www.congress.gov/bill/115th-congress/house-bill/3429. ICE uses the term "repatriate" to refer to deportations.

85. H.R.5695—Veterans Visa and Protection Act of 2016, https://www.congress.gov /bill/114th-congress/house-bill/5695; H.R.2098—Veterans Visa and Protection Act of 2019, https://www.congress.gov/bill/116th-congress/house-bill/2098.

86. Alexi Jones, *Reforms without Results: Why States Should Stop Excluding Violent Offenses from Criminal Justice Reforms* (Prison Policy Initiative, April 2020), https:// www.prisonpolicy.org/reports/violence.html.

87. Katie Dingeman-Cerda, Edelina Muñoz Burciaga, and Lisa M. Martinez, "Neither Sinners nor Saints: Complicating the Discourse of Noncitizen Deservingness," *Association of Mexican American Educators Journal* 9, no. 3 (2015: 62–73.

88. Dingeman-Cerda, Burciaga, and Martinez, "Neither Sinners nor Saints."

89. Some advocates of deported veterans take the deservingness argument further. The Texas Civil Rights Project argues that deporting veterans wastes taxpayers' money and detracts from the work of apprehending those posing a real threat to national security and public safety. *Land of the Free, No Home to the Brave.*

90. Jose Munoz, "The Home Is Here Coalition Commemorates Eight Years of DACA," *United We Dream*, June 2020, https://unitedwedream.org/2020/06/the -home-is-here-coalition-commemorates-eight-years-of-daca/.

91. See Dave Grossman, *On Killing: The Psychological Cost of Learning to Kill in War and Society* (New York: Open Road Media, 2014).

92. Garcia, *Without a Country.*

93. *Chapter 8 Burial and Memorial Benefits. Federal Benefits for Veterans, Dependents and Survivors* (US Department of Veteran's Affairs, 2017), https://perma.cc /W2MC-Z9HD.

94. Slack, *Deported to Death*; Garcia, *Without a Country.*

95. National Executive Committee of the American Legion, "Resolution No. 10: Expedited Citizenship Applications for Deported Veterans," 2017, https://archive .legion.org/bitstream/handle/20.500.12203/9277/2018S010.pdf?sequence=1&is Allowed=y.

96. American Veterans, "National Legislative Agenda 2018–2019," https://amvets .org/wp-content/uploads/2019/01/resources-legislative-agenda-2019.pdf.

97. Unified US Deported Veterans website, https://www.uusdepvets.org/?page_id=52.

98. Veterans for Peace, Deported Veterans Advocacy Project, https://www.veteransfor peace.org/our-work/vfp-national-projects/deported-veterans-advocacy-project.

99. Rebekah Sager, "'DREAMers Moms' Help Deported Mothers in Tijuana, Mexico Reunite with Their U.S. Kids," *Fox News*, August 26, 2016, https://www.foxnews .com/lifestyle/dreamers-moms-help-deported-mothers-in-tijuana-mexico -reunite-with-their-u-s-kids.

100. Hector Barajas, Facebook page, August 24, 2018, https://www.facebook.com /hector.barajas2/posts/10204876527470890.

101. Walter Nicholls, *The Immigrant Rights Movement: The Battle over National Citizenship* (Stanford, CA: Stanford University Press, 2019).

102. Kitty Calavita, "The Paradoxes of Race, Class, Identity, and 'Passing': Enforcing the Chinese Exclusion Acts, 1882–1910," *Law & Social Inquiry* 25, no. 1 (2000): 1–40.

CHAPTER 7

1. Viet Thanh Nguyen, *Nothing Ever Dies: Vietnam and the Memory of War* (Cambridge, MA: Harvard University Press, 2016), 221.

2. Camilo Mejía, *Road from ar Ramadi: The Private Rebellion of Staff Sergeant Camilo Mejía* (Chicago: Haymarket Books, 2008), 233.

3. Mejía, *Road from ar Ramadi*, 23.

4. Mejía, *Road from ar Ramadi*, 189–193.

5. "Racism and War the Dehumanization of the Enemy (4 of 18)—Camilo Mejía," YouTube, September 15, 2011, https://www.youtube.com/watch?v=a3kHoii3sxY; Sarah Lazare, Buff Whitman-Bradley, and Cynthia Whitman-Bradley, *About Face: Military Resisters Turn against War* (Oakland, CA: PM Press, 2011); Mejía, *Road from ar Ramadi*; Ariana E. Vigil, *War Echoes: Gender and Militarization in U.S. Latina/o Cultural Production* (New Brunswick, NJ: Rutgers University Press, 2014).

6. Mejía, *Road from ar Ramadi*.

7. Brissette, "Waging a War of Position on Neoliberal Terrain"; Brissette, "From Complicit Citizens to Potential Prey."

8. Zoltán Glück, Manissa McCleave Maharawal, Isabel Nastasia, and Conor Tomas Reed, "Organizing against Empire: Struggles over the Militarization of CUNY," *Berkeley Journal of Sociology* 58 (October 20, 2014), http://berkeleyjournal.org/2014/10/organizing-against-empire-struggles-over-the-militarization-of-cuny/.

9. Cheryl Miller, *Underserved: A Case Study of ROTC in New York City* (Washington, DC: American Enterprise Institute, 2011), https://www.aei.org/wp-content/uploads/2011/10/ROTC-Final-May-2011.pdf?x91208.

10. Robert Draper, *To Start a War: How the Bush Administration Took America into Iraq* (New York: Penguin, 2021).

11. Jeff Mays, "Colin Powell Helps City College Re-Launch ROTC Program," *DNA Info*, May 21, 2013, https://www.dnainfo.com/new-york/20130521/hamilton-heights/colin-powell-helps-city-college-re-launch-rotc-program/#slide-1.

12. Sofya Aptekar, Corinna Mullin, and Karanja Keita Carroll, "Abolition vs. the Myth of 'Public Safety': Past and Present Struggles for a Liberated CUNY," *CUNY Struggle*, January 29, 2021, https://cunystruggle.org/2021/01/29/abolition-vs-the-myth-of-public-safety-past-and-present-struggles-for-a-liberated-cuny/; Glück et al., "Organizing against Empire."

13. Paul Foos, *A Short, Offhand, Killing Affair: Soldiers and Conflicts during the Mexican-American War* (Chapel Hill: University of North Carolina Press, 2000), 8.

14. James E. Sanders, *The Vanguard of the Atlantic World: Creating Modernity, Nation, and Democracy in Nineteenth-Century Latin America* (Durham, NC: Duke University Press, 2014).

15. Relatedly, there are examples of colonial subjects working in imperial militaries who had cooperated with underground revolutionary forces to resist imperial power. In the case of Indian independence, the military uprisings were critical to the success of the independence movement. Rakesh Krishnan Simha, "The Forgotten Mutiny That Shook the British Empire," *Indian Defense Review*, June 6, 2016, http://www.indiandefencereview.com/spotlights/the-forgotten-mutiny-that-shook-the-british-empire/.

16. Steve Striffler, *Solidarity: Latin America and the US Left in the Era of Human Rights* (London: Pluto Press, 2019).

17. Lewis A. Erenberg, *The Rumble in the Jungle: Muhammad Ali and George Foreman on the Global Stage* (Chicago: University of Chicago Press, 2019), 35.

18. Lutz, *The Bases of Empire*.

19. Lisa Leitz, *Fighting for Peace: Veterans and Military Families in the Anti–Iraq War Movement* (Minneapolis: University of Minnesota Press, 2014).

20. Michael A. Messner, *Unconventional Combat: Intersectional Action in the Veterans' Peace Movement* (New York: Oxford University Press, 2021).

21. About Face, "Three Indigenous Peoples' Day Actions You Can Take," email, October 11, 2021.

22. Messner, *Unconventional Combat*.

23. About Face: Veterans against the War (@VetsAboutFace), Twitter post, July 20, 2019, https://twitter.com/vetsaboutface/status/1152607980065607680; Michael Edison Hayden, Catherine Thorbecke, and Evan Simon, "At Least 2,000 Veterans Arrive at Standing Rock to Protest Dakota Pipeline," *ABC News*, December 4, 2016, https://abcnews.go.com/US/2000-veterans-arrive-standing-rock-protest-dakota-pipeline/story?id=43964136.

24. Interview with About Face members Matt Howard and Claude Copeland.

25. Indi Samarajiva, "Abolish Citizenship: The Only Way to Be a Good Global Citizen," *Medium*, December 30, 2020, https://indica.medium.com/abolish-citizenship-the-only-way-to-be-a-good-global-citizen-dc530cf13b7a.

APPENDIX

1. Robert Weiss, *Learning from Strangers: The Art and Method of Qualitative Interview Studies* (New York: Free Press, 1995).

2. Valeria Lo Iacono, Paul Symonds, and David H. K. Brown, "Skype as a Tool for Qualitative Research Interviews," *Sociological Research Online* 21, no. 2 (May 2016): 103–117, https://doi.org/10.5153/sro.3952.

3. Marnie Howlett, "Looking at the 'Field' through a Zoom Lens: Methodological Reflections on Conducting Online Research during a Global Pandemic," *Qualitative Research* (January 2021), https://doi.org/10.1177/1468794120985691.

4. McIntosh, Sayala, and Gregory, *Non-Citizens in the Enlisted U.S. Military*.

5. Jim Parker, Anthony Cilluffo, and Renee Stepler, *6 Facts about the U.S. Military and Its Changing Demographics*, Pew Research Center, 2017, https://www.pewresearch.org/fact-tank/2017/04/13/6-facts-about-the-u-s-military-and-its-changing-demographics/.

6. Martin Tolich, "Internal Confidentiality: When Confidentiality Assurances Fail Relational Informants," *Qualitative Sociology* 27, no. 1 (March 1, 2004): 101–106.

7. I write in more detail about studying deported veterans' memory work in Sofya Aptekar, "Building a Case for Citizenship: Countermemory Work among Deported Veterans," in *Interpreting Contentious Memory: Countermemories and Conflicts over the Past*, ed. Janet L. Jacobs and Thomas DeGloma (Bristol University Press, forthcoming).

INDEX

Page numbers followed by t refer to tables.

Military Accessions Vital to the National Interest (MAVNI) (cont.)

Patriotism (cont.)
Military Accessions Vital to the National Interest (MAVNI) and, 184–186
nationalism and, 234
poverty draft and, 29, 38, 48, 55–59, 67
proving, 2, 16, 57, 67
recruitment and, 9, 15–16, 20, 23
serving country and, 55–57
veterans and, 48, 57, 100, 103, 227, 229, 233–237, 247
People of color
assimilation and, 105–109, 112, 116, 126, 129, 137–138, 143, 286n14
citizenship and, 101–102
criminalization of, 298n13
deportation and, 192, 195, 199–203
"Don't Ask, Don't Tell" and, 288n45
DREAM Act and, 19
education and, 4, 17, 19, 32, 62, 101–102, 245
inclusion and, 18
military overrepresentation of, 17
poverty draft and, 32, 34, 62, 67
sense of belonging and, 4
Permanent residents
assimilation and, 117, 139
border issues and, 2–3
citizenship and, 2–3, 12–13, 18, 22, 44, 47, 66, 69–72, 76–82, 149–150, 157, 160–163, 178, 244
deportation and, 194, 198, 208, 238
enlistment and, 2–3, 12, 18, 22, 32, 38, 44, 47, 82, 117, 139, 149, 157, 160, 265n6, 293n5
green cards and, 2 (see also Green cards)
India and, 46
Military Accessions Vital to the National Interest (MAVNI) and, 149–150, 152, 157, 159–163, 178, 293n5
poverty draft and, 32, 38, 44–47, 66
Persian Gulf War, 9, 131–132, 210
PhD programs, 159–160, 167, 178
Philippines, 7, 35, 41–42, 71, 139, 256

Physical health
assimilation and, 129–138
basic training and, 131
chemicals and, 11, 131, 229
drug exposure and, 131–132
fractures, 131, 137–138
Physicians, 150, 218–219
Poland, 40, 47, 79, 256
Post-traumatic stress disorder (PTSD)
assimilation and, 106, 113, 129, 132–134
deportation and, 204, 220
homelessness and, 77
invasive psychological studies and, 254
mental health and, 77, 106, 113, 129, 132–134, 204, 220, 254, 264
psychology studies on, 254
race and, 106
research methodology and, 254
self-medication and, 204
US Department of Veteran Affairs (VA) and, 204
violence and, 220
Poverty draft
9/11 attacks and, 32, 34, 44, 55
active duty personnel and, 28, 34, 45
Armed Services Vocational Aptitude Battery (ASVAB) and, 28, 31, 37, 65
Asians and, 31–32, 46, 52, 57, 60
austerity policies and, 36
belonging and, 29, 44, 49–56, 67, 279n60
Black people and, 31–32, 34, 50
border issues and, 41, 43, 49, 55, 59, 67
children and, 32–33, 39, 52, 54, 57, 59
Chinese and, 59–62
citizenship and, 43–54
civilians and, 23, 29, 36, 43–49, 59, 63
coining of term, 10
college and, 4, 10, 27, 30–36, 40, 43, 61–67, 253
criminalization and, 32, 49
Deferred Action for Childhood Arrivals (DACA) and, 44–45, 47
education and, 9–10, 28–37, 46, 53, 61–62, 66

veterans and, 17, 67, 101, 146, 227, 242, 246–247

violence and, 17, 146, 242, 246

Whitworth, Sandra, 109

Women

assimilation and, 103, 105, 109, 115, 122–129, 137, 143, 145

citizenship and, 11, 79

deportation and, 202, 238

expulsion rates of, 126, 288n45

inclusion and, 4, 122, 128, 258

misogyny and, 124, 126, 128, 146–147

poverty draft and, 31, 39–40, 51

rape of, 103, 123–124

research methodology and, 58

security issues and, 18, 20

violence and, 4, 105, 123, 125, 129, 202

Wong, Cara, 16

Working class, 53, 60, 62, 244–247

World War I, 6, 16–17, 73

World War II, 6, 9, 17, 73, 194, 202, 247, 274n101

Xenophobia, 15–16, 50–51, 180, 245

Yo Soy El Army, 63

Youth

assimilation and, 103, 121, 126, 128–129, 135

border issues and, 1–2, 5, 10

Deferred Action for Childhood Arrivals (DACA) and, 44–45, 47, 79, 153, 155t, 181, 263

deportation and, 203, 234, 239, 244

DREAM Act and, 18–19, 128, 238, 242, 244, 263

economic issues and, 10, 31, 126, 245

education and, 10, 31–34, 103, 244–245, 247

exploitation of, 68

gendered expectations and, 280n76

glorification of war and, 36–43

Junior Reserve Officers Training Corps (JROTC), 17, 27, 32, 50, 178, 263

Latinx, 280n76

nationalism and, 9–10, 247

poverty draft and, 31–34, 37–38, 41–43, 61, 63, 67–68, 242–247, 280n76

Reserve Officers Training Corps (ROTC) and, 40, 245, 264, 265n6

security issues and, 17–18

undocumented, 1–2, 18, 128, 234, 239, 247